HOMELAND

HOMELAND

INTO A WORLD OF HATE

nick ryan

MAINSTREAM
PUBLISHING

EDINBURGH AND LONDON

First published in Great Britain in 2003 by
MAINSTREAM PUBLISHING COMPANY (EDINBURGH) LTD
7 Albany Street
Edinburgh EH1 3UG

ISBN 1 84018 465 5

A catalogue record for this book is available from the British Library

Typeset in Stone
Printed and bound in Great Britain by
Creative Print Design Wales

CONTENTS

ACKNOWLEDGEMENTS

My special thanks to Nick Lowles, author of *White Riot* and *Mr Evil*, and to my editor Ethan Casey of the global journalism community BlueEar.com (www.blueear.com), without whom this book would not have been possible.

Also to Graeme Atkinson and the rest of the staff at *Searchlight* (www.searchlightmagazine.com), and to the network of 'friends': Rolf, Rasmus, Wim, Tammy, Erik Jensen of *Demos* (www.demos.dk), Stieg Larsson of *Expo* (www.expo.se), Karl Pfeifer, Heribert Schiedel and the Documentary Archive of the Austrian Resistance (www.doew.at), Jimmy and APABIZ (www.apabiz.de), Marc Spruyt, Dr Cas Mudde, Thomas Grumke of the Center for Democratic Culture, Lenny Zeskind, Devin Burghart and Justin Massa of the Center for New Community (www.newcomm.org), Heidi Beirich and Mark Potok of the Southern Poverty Law Center (www.splcenter.org), David Goldman of Hatewatch (www.hatewatch.org), my agent Robert Kirby at PFD and anyone else I may have forgotten to mention.

I'm grateful to everyone who was interviewed, whether we agreed or not, and I hope they can understand my motives and aspirations.

And finally to my partner, whose support has seen me through some dark days.

PROLOGUE

NOVEMBER 2001

Julie (not her real name) is British, through and through. Her father came here decades ago, from Jamaica. Her mother is English. So she's British. Not in the Midlands, though. There, she's a half-caste. Mixed race. Mulatto.

'Nigger' to her neighbours, and those who thrust National Front (NF) hate mail through her door. 'Black cunt' to the kids pushing lighted paper and matches into the window of her two-year-old daughter's bedroom.

She won't crack in front of me. And I don't tell her that the current NF leadership have offered to meet with me. But she does care, when it comes to her kids. 'No one's going to 'urt my kids. No one.' She's had bricks through the windows, eggs thrown against the walls. Been called a 'black bastard' by mothers of other kids when she collects her boy from school, and then seen her boy and girl called 'little black bastards' by those same women. 'I'll put 'em six feet under if that little black fucker comes near me!' screams one mum. A mother, not a tattooed neo-nazi.

I'm reminded of the scenes at the Holy Cross Primary school in Northern Ireland, when Catholic children have to endure a wall of hatred and need police protection to walk through a Protestant estate. The sheer hate and fear rippling through the faces truly terrify me, because I've been and seen places where this can lead.

'I even had a bloke come up to me on a bus,' Julie says, 'who said he was going to rape me. That was after they'd already tried to run me down on a motorbike.'

'I just hate those people now,' she says, not even looking me in the eye. 'What else can you say about them? About a whole place – my entire estate – when this goes on? With me kids crying all the time, getting beaten up. When even a little white girl can come up to me, at me own door, and call me a 'black bastard'. Where do you think she learns that, eh?'

ONE

HOMELAND

WINTER 1996, HOLBORN, CENTRAL LONDON

The rain cracks hard on the cold London tarmac. The drumming rhythm vibrates through bone, into my head. I rub my jaw, yawning to relieve the tension.

Ahead, past the worrying commuters, a grim face regards me through the gloom. Broad shoulders, baseball cap, partly shadowed face. He shifts against the railings, impatient. I approach, terrified and fascinated. A cigarette glows fitfully for a moment, beneath the hood of his sodden sweatshirt.

'Aw'right mate, follow me,' he orders. His features flash, lean and intense. I recognise the rough south London accent from our mobile phone conversations. It's blunt, uncompromising, simple. His eyes narrow. Then he turns, without another word. I stand there, water streaming down from my fingertips.

'Fuck.'

By the time I catch up, he's almost at The Princess Louise, a grand Victorian pub nestled close to the haven of Holborn Tube station.

Past the frosted glass and familiar chatter, staring across the broad expanse of tables, they wait. Their gear is casual, but the faces are hard, sullen, full of mistrust. Angry-looking tattoos poke out from under smart shirt sleeves. Mobile phones lie in a neat row, next to bottles of Bud and pints of Guinness. The talk, in a melting pot of accents from across London's council estates, is of football 'firms' (gangs), lads, and 'jobs' (robberies). I swallow hard and walk over.

'We don't want to live with Africans and Pakis, we want to live with our own people – don't we?' quips a Humpty-Dumpty figure with a receding hairline and a dull leer. He grabs a beer from my outstretched hand. Covered in a heavy lace of tattoos and carrying a bulky bag of CDs, Paul David 'Charlie' Sargent is a leader not so much by charisma as by force and fear. He has a habit of putting rhetorical questions at the ends of his

11

sentences, leaving little room for discussion. His three companions drag on cigarettes and pull baseball caps down over their tight-cropped hair as they talk of revolution – White Revolution.

'Our kids are learning *their* way of life before their own,' laments Scott, a gruff-faced former squaddie. A clamour of guttural 'yeahs' supports him. 'They're taking us over,' adds Charlie in his animated, nasal voice. 'The whole of London is just becoming a cesspit.'

'The solution?'

'National Socialism.'

'Which is?'

'Racism,' he says, with a characteristically challenging look. 'The easiest politics in the world.'

To Charlie and the others, 'they' – meaning either the State, which they call ZOG (Zionist Occupation Government), or the immigrant communities – are the Enemy. So now they want no part of the system. 'I don't vote. What's the point? I'm not gonna play their fucking silly little games,' spits Charlie.

These men are members of a paramilitary struggle, based on punishment beatings, control, and fear. 'I know perfectly well we're gonna win. I'm under no disillusions about it. Sooner or later we're gonna win.'

'But win what?'

'The War.'

'What war?'

'The war against the government and the people invading this fucking land.'

* * *

It was Charlie who introduced me to this tribal world of maleness, identity, and violence. To networks and ideologies of hate and extremism operating across frontiers.

It was a place where the boundaries with my own understanding and beliefs sometimes blurred. Where respectable folk could be race haters. Where I swapped gossip about beer prices and TV programmes with men who could squirt acid into the face of an Asian woman, then laugh it off. Charlie was at the raw, elemental end of this world. Most of the time, though, I discovered that hate wears a different face altogether.

It had all begun so simply. Or so it seemed to me at the time.

I was what both the right and the left would call a classic 'liberal'. Wishy-washy, left-of-centre, worthy of their contempt – but perhaps useful in helping spread their propaganda. Another 'lazy journalist' from the Establishment, who could unwittingly draw attention to the cause.

And perhaps, at the beginning, they were right.

Living in Kuwait during 1990, I had narrowly missed being caught in the

Iraqi invasion. I lost my job and was spun into 18 months of travel through Asia and the Middle East, which forced me to reappraise my life and embark on a decade of writing and exploration. I visited countries such as Algeria, Bosnia, Albania, China, and Turkey, gaining an ever greater appreciation for the power of community in adversity. Despite this, I found myself ignorant of my own country and the forces that were shaping it. I knew more about the Kurds in Turkey and Iraq than about my fellow Britons in our northern cities.

In the autumn of 1996, I was putting the finishing touches to a project looking at the growth of subculturalism in Britain. I'd been meeting 'weekend rebels', people who lived otherwise normal lives, but devoted themselves passionately to forms of escapism. From club culture, to neo-pagans, to roleplayers and extreme sports fanatics, I began to move outwards, encountering evangelical Christians, then the environmental protest network. I was fascinated by these new communities taking shape before my very eyes. I spent more and more time with the environmentalists in particular, getting to understand their beliefs and cause, forming friendships and sharing parts of their lives.

But it was the people I termed the 'outsiders' who soon interested me most: those who didn't want to be subject to the same conventions as the rest of us, who lived by Belief, who 'knew' they were right. Weekend rebellion was not for them. They included cults and new religious movements, as well as violent extremists who believed in some notion of racial purity. Those who were not simply 'proud' of their ethnic heritage, but sought to elevate it above others.

I wondered who these people really were. What did they say for themselves, and would I ever be able to approach them? I had no contacts in this world, no political or state affiliations, and no commission. That was when I discovered *Searchlight*.

In the travels that followed, I found zealots of all shades mixing together: fascists with vegans, animal liberation extremists with anti-abortionists, and a mêlée of tiny left, right, anarchist, and environmental groups on the fringes of the anti-capitalist crusades.

During this six-year journey, millions of my fellow Europeans, people who loved their children, worked 9 to 5, and thought of themselves as respectable citizens, voted for neo-nazi and ultra-nationalist parties. Which was my world and which theirs? I often couldn't tell.

Was it fear that drove us all? Of the mythical 'Other': the stranger, the foreigner? Why was it that Brits often distrusted the French or Germans, yet the white Americans I met thought all 'white men' had some common brotherhood? And if we all hated each other – naturally, as the racists would contend – why were there deeply ingrained hospitality codes in many of the countries I visited? Educated folk could be ignorant too, assuming the multicultural melting pot worked just one way.

In the wings, lurking behind the smiles and smooth talk of the racial politicians, I discovered the pale faces of the boy-next-door killers, barely men, burning with frustration, needing belief, prepared to act. Loners and zealots like London nailbomber David Copeland, or Oklahoma bomber Timothy McVeigh.

I was driven by one question: Why?

* * *

A few months after our first meeting, I watched Charlie being sent down for murder, hearing the screams of rage and anguish from his victim's girlfriend.

A sardonic smile slid across his face, as the pale, slight woman charged at the dock. 'You bastard, you fucking bastard!' she shrieked. Someone grabbed her. Her streaked, blonde hair was plastered to a sweat-beaded forehead, as thin arms strained to free herself. To my right, away from the press gallery, there was an instant, almost animal shift in tension amongst part of the audience. I looked back at the woman, hands clawing at the air. I should have felt sorry for her. I do now. At the time, though, I was more embarrassed and frightened at the sudden, shattering noise inside the austere courtroom. I didn't truly understand her loss.

The judge called for order. One of the barristers found himself preoccupied with the hem of his gown. 'C'mon love, c'mon,' said a detective, encircling the sobbing woman with a bulky arm, guiding her away. She resisted, then buried her face in his shoulder, suddenly frail and child-like. I could hear her sobs echo off the corridor walls outside.

Charlie had helped butcher her partner, 'Catford Chris' Castle, with a 20 cm knife during a double-cross deal with a rival. He and his henchman, Martin Cross, had ambushed Castle just before nine o'clock one morning, on the doorstep of Charlie's trailer. Charlie's stepchildren had been forced to watch. It was supposed to be a simple swap of the group's mailing lists and one thousand pounds in cash, in return for Charlie's plastering tools. A peaceful recognition that he had lost control of the gang to his chief lieutenant.

Cross was an expressionless psychopath who already had a conviction for attacking a man with an axe. He rammed the knife through Castle's leather jacket and into his back, pushing it hard as far as it would go. Later, he would call Castle a 'casualty of war'. Charlie had then punched the mortally wounded man as he stumbled back down the path and collapsed into his friend's arms, choking on his own blood. Now, that man – Charlie's rival and the new leader of the British neo-nazi gang Combat 18 (C18) – sat opposite me.

Will 'The Beast' Browning was a man I heard described throughout my journeys. I met him only once, but I sensed his pall-like presence constantly. His reputation suggested he was a fearsome, psychopathic individual, relentless in pursuit of an enemy or goal. He'd earned respect for an ability to mete out extreme violence. Others who were there told me he'd been part of an attack that destroyed a Chelsea pub, meant as a lesson for anti-racist fans. Throats had been slashed, bottles thrust into faces, pool balls smashed against heads. I could describe the scene, but I couldn't understand it. 'You may be the world's best kickboxer, but would you go into someone's house at the dead of night and kill them in their sleep? Just think on that,' one of his friends tried to explain.

Steve Sargent, Charlie's softer-spoken younger brother, would recall how he had been 'unfairly' picked up that day, for being nearby after the attack. He once claimed, only half-jokingly, that Browning spent every day 'training for the war' in a specially constructed gym in his house. Soon, Browning would vow to kill Steve. The Beast was not without intelligence, however, and had helped build the gang's white-power music empire. And he later embarked on the first international neo-nazi bombing campaign.

I didn't know all that then. I was simply shoved aside as his mob of supporters waded past me and towards the armed police. The Beast turned and briefly stared at me with a dark, fixed expression. His lieutenant hissed, 'Don't speak to him, he's that cunt, the journalist!' Hostile eyes turned towards me. Crowded by his supporters, with their shaven heads and fanatical glares, The Beast seemed more a warlord surrounded by his bloody henchmen than a modern-day Englishman.

Of course, he wasn't bothered by anyone as insignificant as me. He turned back to stare at Charlie, the man who'd once been a father figure in this angry underworld. Thick blunt hands held him down as he seethed under his breath, 'He's fucking smiling at me!' He struggled to stand, then turned swiftly and stomped out. Charlie simply sat slumped where he was in the dock, a pair of old glasses sliding down his short, chubby nose. Then he was led away. It was the last I would see of him.

* * *

In the end, all it had taken was a letter. In September 1996, I found myself sitting in a tiny Soho pub opposite Nick Lowles, an accomplished TV producer and reporter for *Searchlight*, part of Europe's premier anti-racist and anti-fascist network. Blessed with pleasant yet instantly forgettable features, Lowles has an uncanny ability to blend into a crowd. It's certainly helped him in his work penetrating far-right gangs and football hooligan groups across Europe.

As we talked over our pints, he agreed to give me a list of names and addresses of key C18 members. We discussed the gang's motives and whether they would want to meet an outsider like me. Lowles said he'd often briefed other journalists with tip-offs for good stories, but this would be unique. He'd been tracking the gang for years and knew that a power struggle was developing between Charlie and The Beast. He also suspected that Charlie's mob were keen to talk about their 'Aryan Homeland' project, a desire to build a new community in the hinterlands of Essex, a predominantly white area east of London. No one had yet been able to question them about their beliefs.

'Don't take anything with your address on it,' warned Lowles' boss, Gerry Gable. A small, balding man, he seemed an unlikely figure for a former left-wing street fighter, let alone a hate figure for the extreme right. His face was framed by what his enemies would call classic 'Jewish' features. He had a pronounced nose, a soft, nasal voice, and a strong London accent. In the past he'd been strongly linked with the Communist movement and would probably describe himself as from the old school of the left. He'd also survived several attempts on his life. According to Nick Lowles, Browning once tried to throw a petrol bomb at his house.

He settled opposite me, at a secret family address. His young son played on the floor around us as we spoke. The gang had written back to my letters (forwarded via private mailboxes), and I'd spoken with an anonymous member on a variety of mobile phone numbers. Now I needed Gable's advice.

With his wife – a woman I later learned had infiltrated the National Front – watching, Gable said the gang could well try to follow me home. They viewed journalists as 'scum', having been doorstepped many times and subjected to various tabloid and TV exposés. 'Look, I don't want to bullshit you here,' he said. 'It could be dangerous. But you're not one of us, and they've got no reason to suspect you.'

Listening to Gable talk, though, the terror gripped me. What if it all went wrong? What if the gang lynched me? I needed to assure them that I wasn't part of the *Searchlight* network. Paranoia runs high among the extremists, who often view all 'liberals' and, worse still, 'liberal journalists' as the Enemy.

* * *

C18 had garnered a fearsome reputation as vicious football hooligans and for their links to Loyalist (Protestant) paramilitaries in Northern Ireland, as well as to criminal gangs and a violent white-power music scene. Yet now they wanted to talk.

They carved their name in history in the early 1990s. Theirs was the first right-wing group in the UK to confront the State head-on, entirely rejecting conventional politics. They originally promised a violent race war against 'invading' immigrants and a system they believed had abandoned working-class white people. It was an attractive cocktail to disillusioned young men, particularly on the council estates of the south-east, because it brooked no compromise and promised direct action against the 'oppressors'.

The gang had originated as a group providing security for the British National Party (BNP), the UK's principal far-right organisation. It took its name from the numerical position of Adolf Hitler's initials in the alphabet. In a departure from previous right-wing ventures, the gang didn't try to convert ordinary people to its cause, or to win elections – it just acted. As Charlie Sargent told me: 'It would be a lie to think we are attractive to most people, because we're not. We are what we are. We don't pretend we're something we're not.'

It looked for support among ultra-violent football hooligan firms, and around the white-power skinhead music scene. However, few of its supporters were actually skinheads; most preferred the designer-casual image of the hooligans. 'Skinheads are basically wankers,' laughed Steve. 'The only skinheads are Reds and queers.'

A number of members also worked as cocaine dealers and illegal debt collectors in the criminal underworld. They were happy to show me how to 'bosh' someone in the stomach with a knife, punishment for failure to pay up on a loan. They mocked the British government's law and order strategy, claiming it was ineffectual and that the prisons were C18's natural recruiting ground. With their jailbird tattoos, they casually referred to the police as 'scum'. By their own admission they were violent people. 'We're thugs who follow an ideology,' boasted Charlie.

C18 quickly attracted the street-hooligan elements of the right, mainly from around London and the Home Counties area. Initially numbering just a few dozen members, the group grew rapidly as it went on the offensive, attacking left-wing bookshops, gay pubs and anti-apartheid activists. It began to produce its own bulletin, *Redwatch*, a tatty photocopied sheet listing the names of its opponents. C18 members recall battles against left-wing activists with a sense of tribal pride.

'The Reds were going around, beating the living daylights out of the right wing,' Charlie reminisced as we sat, smoking and drinking together. 'They were kicking in doors, petrol-bombing people and beating old men black and blue with hammers.' This was a reference to an attack by anti-fascists on a right-wing meeting in Kensington Library in 1992. 'Red Action [an extreme left-wing group] were absolutely battering the right. We decided we weren't having that, and we thought we'd do something about it.'

'Which meant?'

'We fuckin' battered 'em wherever we met, until there was no fucker left standing,' he laughed, puffing out his chest. 'Now we don't see 'em no more.'

The relationship between C18 and the larger BNP began to deteriorate during 1993, as the BNP became increasingly embarrassed by C18's violent behaviour. The September 1993 election of Derek Beackon as the BNP's first-ever local councillor, in east London's Isle of Dogs, sealed the split. From then on, the BNP proscribed joint membership (sometimes to little effect, because C18 didn't have any 'official' members as such). As C18 developed a more extreme National Socialist position, it attracted a hard core of 200 or so followers nationwide. Although its numbers would sometimes swell with occasional support from football hooligans and skinheads from the white-power music scene, this core remained constant.

'Race not nation,' Charlie told me, rolling a piece of gum between his blunt teeth. 'We're not British nationalists, we're racialists.' C18 believed in the white European/Aryan 'race', as opposed to the BNP's belief in the British 'nation'. This is a common difference between neo-nazis and white supremacists, particularly from the USA, and the ultra-nationalists of far-right movements, which tend to be in Europe.

'The BNP's view is just bullshit,' said Steve Sargent, 'but we're not under no illusions. The BNP say they're gonna sweep the country in ten years' time, but that's bullshit, 'coz it's never gonna happen.' Where the BNP had the idea of repatriating black and other communities to their 'native' countries, C18 believed in building white-power bases from which to attack minority communities.

In another departure from previous extremist thinking, C18 drew ideological inspiration from the USA, particularly from theories espousing 'race war'. Thus, in a French Nazi publication, *Terror Elite*, Charlie Sargent explained that the race war desired by neo-nazis would not happen of its own accord: 'We have to incite the niggers and Arabs. I and others are personally dedicated to declaring war on the system over the coming years. I know that could mean death or life imprisonment, but I hope to light a touchpaper to a fire so powerful that ZOG will never put it out.'

One of their key ideologues is a strange, reclusive figure in America, an ageing former physics professor named William Pierce, who lives on a compound in West Virginia. He holds almost mythical status among white supremacists, running an international empire, which is particularly strong in northern Europe and Scandinavia. Almost everyone I encountered on my travels knew of Pierce, had met him, or had read his works, even senior ex-Republicans in the States.

Once a member of the American Nazi Party, Pierce left his teaching position to pursue a National Socialist career, creating the now-infamous National Alliance. This is an exclusive white-power organisation with an almost cult-like structure. It controls book publications, cadres, and a sprawling neo-nazi music business – the largest such network in the world.

Pierce's best-known works are his novels, *The Turner Diaries*, about a mythical white uprising that ends with the nuclear destruction of Tel Aviv, and *Hunter*, about a man who slays 'race mixers'. These works continue to prove extremely popular with discontented youth in both the US and Europe. They were found in the possession of Timothy McVeigh and the London nailbomber, David Copeland. McVeigh's bomb bore a startling similarity in design and target to that featured in *The Turner Diaries*.

Other developments in the States also inspired Charlie and his pals. C18 claimed to adopt a strategy called 'leaderless resistance', wherein small cells of activists operate autonomously, theoretically making the organisation more resistant to infiltration. Mark 'Ackie' Atkinson, the gang's 'chief of security', and his friends from the hooligan scene in west

London formed one such cell, which I would visit early in 1997.

This system was devised following the collapse of America's most notorious white-power gang, The Order, which murdered prominent Jewish radio host Alan Berg in Denver in 1984, as well as one of its own members. It also ran counterfeiting operations and carried out robberies, including America's largest bullion heist, netting millions of dollars. The group's leader, Robert Matthews, was a favourite of William Pierce. It's alleged that Matthews laundered hundreds of thousands of dollars into the white supremacist movement across the US. Although he was eventually killed in a shootout with the FBI, Matthews and The Order inspired neo-nazis worldwide. The concept of leaderless resistance was suggested by Vietnam veteran and prominent white separatist Louis Beam, who saw that the more obvious hierarchy of The Order was prone to discovery and destruction.

C18 thugs regularly targeted figures on both the left and the right. Indeed many on the right, including BNP members, grew to fear C18 more than the left did, as it viciously attacked members of what it saw as rival organisations.

The gang also had strong links with Loyalist paramilitaries. While other right-wing groups paid lip service to this cause, C18 actively took up their struggle. In 1993, one follower was caught with six handguns in his car; the following year, veteran neo-nazi Terry Blackham was arrested with sub-machine guns and grenades whilst travelling to Northern Ireland with a member of the paramilitary Ulster Defence Association (UDA). This close relationship with the Loyalists led some to suggest that C18 was an MI5 honeytrap, created to infiltrate the Loyalist terror world. The security services dispute this, of course. Furthermore, C18 controlled a lucrative and illegal music business, making it the first such organisation with access to a significant amount of capital. White-power bands were promoted at secret gigs, and CDs and other merchandise were sold illegally throughout the world. Nazi bands which didn't join, or that criticised C18 control, suffered punishment beatings and regular intimidation from the hardliners.

The theme of intimidation and violence could be seen on Europe's largest housing estate, Harold Hill, in Romford, Essex. The local C18 cell subjected an Asian family to several months of attacks and racial harassment. A boulder was thrown through the family's front door, graffiti was sprayed on the outside of their house, wheel nuts were loosened, and a corrosive liquid was thrown into the wife's face. When I asked him about this incident, Steve Sargent was coy but eventually said with a guttural laugh: 'I only heard that the family dog was thrown through the front window – dead.'

Another victim of C18's violence was Ross Fraser, a former editor of the *Chelsea Independent* soccer fanzine. Following remarks he made that racism had no place in football, Fraser was left needing seven stitches to his face and with his sight permanently damaged, after he was struck with a broken bottle during a C18-led attack on a London pub, The Finborough Arms. Three others required hospital treatment, one with a slashed jugular vein. The attack was led by Will Browning and Mark Atkinson, screaming 'Sieg Heil!' from atop the pool table. Two months after the Finborough incident, Fraser narrowly missed further injury after Browning tried to stab him in the face, following a Chelsea game in Prague.

Despite the rhetoric, this was where C18 was most dangerous, attacking individuals and small, isolated groups rather than large 'enemies' such as the State. C18's reputation grew beyond its rather small core following; for example, Charlie Sargent falsely claimed that the gang had initiated a huge riot at an England v. Ireland soccer match in Dublin in 1995. In fact, there was only one C18 supporter present. The press went wild for the story, though. T-shirts were printed and distributed across Europe, with young skinheads proud to wear Combat 18 insignia. Thus the C18 name and legend grew.

* * *

WINTER 1996

The Railway Tavern is a small, grotty pub with peeling green paint, squatting inconspicuously opposite Chelmsford railway station. Inside, Charlie and Steve Sargent sit silently, awaiting my arrival. Charlie is in a dark, tetchy mood, answering questions with a brief 'eah' or 'naa'. A baseball cap is perched precariously on his large head. As the Big Man of C18, he has already warned me 'not to stitch us up, or we'll fuck you over badly'.

I've come to see the brothers on home territory, to try to understand something about them as people, their motivations and aims. Unknown to me, the battle between Charlie and Will is already building in the background.

This bustling Essex commuter town, with its territorial pubs and large, white council estates, will be the centre of a paramilitary struggle, C18 argues. The group will slowly and surely take over the estates, populated as they see it by white East End émigrés, and become the dominant political force in the area.

Like other such areas, Chelmsford has a schizophrenic character. On one hand, there are tidy suburban parks and greenbelt areas. Marconi has its headquarters there. Bright Christmas lights hang over the old market area, and a single tiny mosque nestles modestly behind a curry house. From this angle it seems a standard commuter town. However, the street with the longest row of pubs is known locally as 'The Road of Death', due to the number of fights that take place there. At weekends, lads from the surrounding towns and villages pile into nightclubs – looking, as Steve Sargent says, for 'booze, a shag, and a fight'. And the predominantly white, working-class estates are a breeding ground for the insularity and youthful discontent on which C18 thrives.

'You go to any Essex town, and they've trebled in size, yeah?' says Charlie, chubby fist gripping a pint of lager. 'They're building, building, building in every Essex town, and the reason is that the whites are leaving London.'

'It's always been a bit stronger for racist support, always,' says Steve, waiting deferentially for Charlie to finish. He speaks slowly, in a more measured tone than his elder brother. 'The East End's always had its racist support, 'asn't it? Now them racists,' he emphasises, 'that voted for the BNP and National Front in the 1970s, most of them now live in Essex.'

'If we stand for election, we'll get eliminated,' Charlie butts in. 'The Loyalist paramilitaries or Sinn Fein, when they stand for elections, they're humiliated basically, but as a paramilitary group they get respect. That's how we've got to go.' He adopts his challenging look. 'We're targeting certain estates, because we need more local support. I mean, we're not going to be able to go into the middle-class areas of Chelmsford and win support – we know that.'

It's a working-class movement, full of dull anger and resentment at the bias of 'The System'.

'Our community has been smashed,' complains Charlie. 'When I grew up, right, you knew everyone and everyone knew you. Now you have the blacks come in. Most of the blacks and whites, whether people like it or not, don't mix. Then you have the Asians coming in. Then you have people who have mixed-race kids. It splits everyone up. You ain't got any real community left, and that fucks everything up. That's how it is on any estate, on any street in London now.'

Charlie argues that most white working-class people aren't interested in politics, but in race. 'They're either for it or against it,' he states, with a chopping gesture. 'And the ones that don't agree with us, well . . . we've got to make them respect us, fear us, or however you want to say it.'

In this scenario, Chelmsford would be part of an Aryan Homeland, with the paramilitary struggle taking place on the working-class estates, while a kibbutz-style smallholding or commune is set up in the countryside. The Homeland would also contain a school and doctors, and would operate a barter system instead of using money. It would function as a simpler form of community from which to attack the State and its organs.

Again, stemming from an American concept, and inspired by the belief that 'The System' is fixed against them, the plan is to withdraw as much as possible from society. One of C18's myriad (and illegal) publications states:

> The inner cities are lost. We must realise this and take our only real option – converge as many of our people as we can in the Homeland area and gradually take control of it and run it on strict Aryan-only lines. One has only to look at the religious divides in Belfast to see that we can achieve our aim, the only difference being ours will be on racial not religious divides.

Five years later, some northern English cities already have a de facto racial divide between poor white and Asian communities.

C18 has even created a National Socialist Alliance (NSA) of various extreme right-wing groups, which would function as a cross-party forum. One of its aims is to support the Homeland. It has gathered funds for the project (ten pounds per share, with 1,000 shares giving you the right to work permanently and reside on the site) and helped arrange accommodation for prospective recruits. C18's profits from its music business also support the venture.

Charlie is keen to extol the virtues of the Homeland and the success he and Steve have had in attracting supporters. 'The more powerful you become in that area, the more chance you've got,' explains Steve. 'You gotta do it bit by bit, you can't do it in the whole country straight away.' In this way, drug dealers would be forced from estates ('He'll be told to leave and if he don't, his house is gonna go up and that's the end of it, like the IRA and UDA,' says Charlie) and local building and contract work would be controlled directly by C18 (both Charlie and Steve are plasterers by trade).

Any opposition would get 'seriously fucking hurt' in a paramilitary-style struggle.

'Would racial intimidation be used, as at Harold Hill?'

'Of course. They've got the whole fucking country to live in, in't they? If they come here, they're just trying to provoke us, in't they? Well, if they come here, that's what they can expect. Simple as that. I don't eat curries and I don't eat chapatis,' he adds, laughing. 'They're not the same as us, are they? You're English, you understand, don't you?'

So speaks Charlie, a man of simple answers. Challenging any of them too openly provokes an aggressive 'What do you mean by that?', his mouth set in a small, intimidating 'o'. He's known for his fearsome temper. He's survived an axe attack and always carries a knife, by his own admission. Steve later tells me he once saw Charlie bite off an opponent's nose during a fight. I don't remind him of my Irish ancestry.

Steve is quieter, but when he looks down into his pint, his close-cropped head displays a rough set of scars, sustained during a confrontation in which C18 attacked Asian shops in east London. He was slashed by machetes across his head and back and needed more than 100 stitches. He laughs when recounting this story, how he discharged himself from hospital when the police came to question him. But his laugh is nervous.

When he does look up, his eyes are clear and honest, and his hands and mouth expressive. It's sometimes hard to believe both are family men, well travelled (Steve lived in eastern Europe for a year, Charlie claims to have backpacked for three years) and can at times be warm and expressive. Both have a regular, if slightly rough, sense of humour. Charlie has four kids and a partner in Harlow for whom he professes 'undying' love. He's upset when they're targeted by the local press or are sent 'jiffy bags full of excrement by anti-fascists'. He wants to protect them, he says.

Why then such fanaticism, such hate? What terrible event set them on this course? The brothers both claim they had happy, uneventful childhoods, raised in a family of three brothers and two sisters on an estate in Barnet, north London. Their father was a Loyalist supporter from Clacton, a seaside town in Essex, who brought up his children to be 'proud racists'.

'He was hard but fair, our old man, I'll give him that,' says Steve.

'He brought us up to believe in certain things, just like if your dad was a communist, you'd grow up believing communist things,' adds Charlie.

'What does that mean, exactly?' I ask.

'We were brought up as fascists and nationalists.'

I spoke once on the phone to the father, and then to the mother, but never met them in person. They sounded pretty normal.

Football and music were the gathering points for the young Sargents. Their older brother Billy had already become a heavy for various groups on the right. To Charlie, fighting with 200 other fans at an Arsenal away game became 'a way of proving your manhood'. The talk turns to football firms and how trust and loyalty to your mates are incredibly important, and how one must never 'grass' to the police. This later proves highly ironic in Charlie's case, when it's revealed he's almost certainly an informer.

'We were both involved in the hooligan thing and started out fighting,' says Charlie, munching with gusto on the lunch I've just bought him. Between mouthfuls, he adds: 'It's always been that way, 'asn't it? There's nothing wrong with that.' From there it was a natural progression to shaving his head, joining National Front marches and becoming a heavy for the British Movement, a violent neo-nazi group active in the late 1970s.

When that group split in the early 1980s, 'about 30 of us left, and that's when we got involved in robberies and all that,' says Charlie matter-of-factly. The aim was to put away money for 'projects' to do with the right, but he's vague about specifics. He was just 20 at the time. Since then he's been imprisoned four times, including for possession of guns and drugs. They tell me 'some things went down this summer which were worth five to ten [years]'.

Both brothers reminisce about life 'back then'. For Steve it meant having only 'one Paki' in his school. To Charlie, the 1950s and the era of Ealing TV comedies were 'a good time for this country. Everyone had work. London was probably one of the cleanest and crime-free cities in the world. Now look at it. It's a fucking cesspit.'

In their view, cultures should not mix – except white Europeans, of course: 'We're all the fucking same, ain't we? What the fucking 'ell's the difference between a Norman and a Saxon in 1066?' Yet they admit admiration for 'the Jews and Asians' for maintaining strong communities. Charlie also laments the lack of moral guidance in today's society. 'The Church of England now is so full of poofs and every sort of scum, what can you expect?'

Respect, trust, loyalty, and honour are the main virtues in this tribal society. Football battles with your mates are described in glowing terms. Steve in particular gets carried away, showing me how he bounces up and down before a fight between two sets of fans. His face flushes with excitement as he mimics these motions, while his mouth screams imaginary abuse. 'You respect the geezer who can beat everyone up,' says Charlie. 'Everyone wants to know who's the best fighter on the estate. It's always been the way. People arse lick 'em.' His is a highly territorial world. But it also revolves around control and Charlie's view of who should have it – usually him. He dominates conversations both physically and verbally, often cutting others off. Steve stays unusually silent in his elder brother's company.

It's also a male world. 'Our women are our partners, but not our equals and betters,' says Charlie. 'The flags, the drums, the nationalist spirit – it's not really a thing for women. Their place is at home with the kids. They should be doing that, not out fighting.'

* * *

On a dark, freezing November night I meet Liz, one of these women. We've chosen an elaborate route from the station of the Middlesex town. It's taken three attempts to choose this particular pub, in order to avoid the police and other prying eyes.

On the stool next to Liz sits – occupies – a tanned, heavy-browed figure, her partner, Mark 'Ackie' Atkinson. The blunt, grimy ends of his fingers rest on remarkably smooth, Guinness-flushed skin. Occasionally Mark's face creases into a smile, an unnatural pose for his serious features. It makes him seem more human. I have to remind myself of his vicious reputation.

For several weeks we've swapped letters and talked. We seemed to strike up a passable relationship over the phone, although his laugh still cut too short. Sometimes I'd hear people chatting or kids playing in the background. He told me he was going to get me 'checked out' before anyone would speak with me. There was constant suspicion that I was working for *Searchlight*, the State, or both.

''Ere, where'd you get my address?' he growled.

Mutual friends passed me his details, I told him, and I read his name in one of their magazines. Surprisingly, this seemed to work.

'Awright, 'ey've said yes,' he said, calling late one evening as I was relaxing with my girlfriend.

'Who's that?' she asked.

'No one.' I didn't want to drag her into this.

'Holborn, 2 o'clock, next Thursday,' Ackie's voice said in my other ear.

Liz's voice brings me back to the present. She's slim (although now pregnant), attractive, with hair styled in a slight 'post-skin' style. She met

Mark a year ago at a white-power music concert. Raised in Deptford, east London, she has four kids and works as a hairdresser. They got in a babysitter, special, so they could come out and see me tonight, she adds with a smile. 'You should be honoured.'

I hide my feelings as I frequently, nervously, gulp at my drink, which sends me repeatedly to the toilet. That sense of unreality creeps in again. Even when the feeling becomes familiar, after I've met with the extremists many times, it still unnerves me. Their world and mine are crossing.

I talk at some length to Liz about her background, as the office workers around us enjoy their pre-Christmas drinks. How her parents and Mark's were working-class Tories, how his folks owned a mushroom farm in Northamptonshire, and just how BIG! she remembers her family house being. 'The whole area's too dangerous now,' she says with a flick of her slim hand, emphasising 'right?' at the end of her sentence. It's a curious East End turn of phrase. She needs 'somewhere clean and hassle-free' to bring her kids up. Looking at her in the flickering light, watching her lean on his arm as they gaze into each other's eyes, I slowly relax. Just for a moment, the illusion holds, and I could be talking to any young couple.

Fixing me with an earnest, attractive gaze, Liz tells me: 'The problem is really bad around there [where she was born]. You wouldn't have a chance in hell of walking around on your own.' She's seen the population 'become 90 per cent black' in her lifetime. I've been there many times myself. I'm not sure I agree with her, but I don't tell her that. She says there are constant attacks reported in the local papers every week. 'Always black, black, black, all the time.' This reminds me of the Irish competing with the new immigrants arriving in New York a century ago. It always seems to be people at the bottom of the pile who end up struggling against each other.

Starting to relax and chatting more easily, Liz complains that, even as a kid, most of her school was black, and she couldn't say 'nigger' or 'Paki' without being suspended.

'What's the problem?'

''Coz they're a different colour to us – I don't know how to explain it really.' She says she was pissed off because they 'were always getting their own way'.

She claims she has her own computer, which is used secretly to produce much of the C18 material. I don't know why she would want to tell this to me, someone she has known only for a few minutes: 'They're trying to say it's him, but it's me, the other girls, everyone in fact. Everyone gets involved.'

She can't stop, it seems. 'I'm good with my words.' A smile, perhaps smug, plays and flickers above the slender jaw line. 'I'd love to sit down with Gerry Gable and tell him what really goes on. He doesn't know absolutely anything. I wouldn't worry about people like Mark, I'd tell him, I'd worry about people like me, working around the edges.'

Women, she tells me, have been involved in 'some of the physical stuff.

No, no, but I can't go into it.' She shakes her head, swapping a look with Mark, and her jaws suddenly clamp shut again. 'Put it this way,' she suddenly continues, glaring back at Mark. 'Sod the feminism and all that, but that doesn't mean you're not scared to have a row. If someone punches you on the nose, you don't say thanks very much! There's no point me sitting at home having my beliefs and no action, when all our comrades are actually out somewhere doing it.'

'We believe in the same thing and go to gigs together, like,' Mark says. I can see he's been struggling to speak for a while now, edging between her tumbling words. Compared to her fast rhythm, his speech is slow and difficult. Liz interrupts again and tells me she's got just as much right to her opinions and place as the men have, because 'after all, we're the ones giving birth to the future race. We want to bring them up with our values, in our area, in our own way. We should have a say as much as men have.'

Mark then changes the subject, talking wistfully of their Homeland project, a place with its own shops, schools, teachers, businesses and church. To me it seems like pie in the sky, but I daren't challenge the violent young lovers and their dreams. Even though, as we drink and chat about mundane matters later on, Liz admits she's doubtful about the future.

Something else strikes me. It's their use of Americanised, white supremacy phrases such as 'ZOG'. There's a common belief, particularly in the US extreme right, that a Jewish block of some kind is seeking to impose a world government. As ever with such conspiracies, it infiltrated the US first. Sometimes the UN is blamed, other times the media, sometimes the Holocaust – or 'Holohoax', as they misname it – or other bodies like the Bilderberg Group (the secretive network that hosts conferences of leading financiers and foreign policy strategists). Or just about anyone associated with the forces of globalisation. But although Mark and Liz pepper their phrases with these terms, neither really seems to understand what they mean. 'That's what we all call it,' says Liz, referring to ZOG, with a little hesitant laugh.

Mark adds: 'S'pose it's from the Jews, I 'spose. I'm not too sure about that at all.'

'You know what we talk about, if you know what I mean,' adds Liz.

I nod. There's silence for a second, then Mark pipes up: 'We're National Socialists with a mission.' He smirks, downing the last dregs of his pint, leaving a thin foam moustache on his hard, smooth face. 'Watch this space.' With that he grins, and leaves. The words haunt me as I step out into the cold night air.

* * *

The ideological heavyweight behind much of this is a man named David Myatt. An eccentric and widely travelled former monk, Satanist, and martial arts expert, Myatt has previously attempted to establish a Nazi-occultist commune in Shropshire. He's been producing a regular bulletin, *The National Socialist*, which espouses race war, the supremacy of the Aryan nation, and a fanatical devotion to 'warrior values' of Loyalty, Duty and Honour.

A typical theme in his writings runs thus: 'So-called racial hatred and racism itself are Nature's way of protecting her creations and protecting herself – it is race mixing which is the ultimate evil. Race mixing is a crime against life itself.' Elsewhere, he calls for a 'holy war against our enemies, for these enemies are threatening our very racial existence'.

Myatt provides much of the intellectual legitimacy groups like C18 lack, mainly composed as they are of self-educated, working-class young men. His writings go into often tortuous detail about National Socialist values, but he has the ear of people like the Sargents, in particular Steve.

Unlike C18, Myatt draws inspiration from a fanatical devotion to Germany in the 1930s. 'National Socialist Germany is the closest thing to there being a cultural expression of something which is natural and healthy for Aryan peoples,' he says in a polite, soft-spoken accent when we meet at the tea shop in Malvern railway station. We're surrounded by oblivious old-age pensioners, deep in the rolling hills of rural England.

Steve has told me that Myatt might 'want to slap you round the face wiv the white gloves, like. He-he.' When Myatt later falls out with Will Browning, he insists on a duel to right his 'slighted' honour. I'm told he backs down only when The Beast claims the right to use a baseball bat as his weapon.

Listening to him is a surreal experience. A diminutive figure in bright cycling gear and a huge beard, he has a passion for toasted teacakes and translating Greek literature. We talk for exactly an hour about race war, Aryan supremacy, and warrior values. He sees his role as educating and guiding young neo-nazis. In particular he believes in the supremacy of Aryan warriors, represented by today's skinheads, whose raw violence can be harnessed for the National Socialist cause. 'I'm trying to raise these people up, to harness their own instincts in a productively useful way,' he tells me, sipping delicately at his tea. He holds his thin fingers perfectly steady. He expresses great admiration for Spartan and ancient Japanese societies. In his ideal world, we would all be warrior-farmers – or enslaved to those who were.

Unlike C18's members, Myatt is well educated and, in his own words, 'of independent means'. His father worked 'for the British Empire' and, as a child, he lived in East Africa and Asia. He read widely about National Socialism and Hitler, becoming a convert in his teens. Yet by his own admission he's a loner and a fanatic, who hates cities and motor cars, and who became disillusioned with groups such as the National Front. He even spent 18 months as a monk – but 'I had a great struggle between my political beliefs and religious dogma. I finally decided they were incompatible.'

We share several awkward silences. He's a shy man, and I'm the first outsider to interview him. He seems uncomfortable in the company of others, and it's difficult really to find out why or how he was so drawn to

Nazism. All he'll admit is that he's been in prison twice for his beliefs and that he was profoundly affected by the death of a loved one. He's since decided that revolution and a great leader are needed to bring about the resurgence of the Aryan peoples. He admits to a similarity between himself and extremist religious figures. 'I know I'm right,' he states simply.

We meet several times after this, including one memorable occasion when rival C18 mobs turn up at London's annual Bloody Sunday remembrance march in 1998. He's always polite to me, excessively so even. I can't help but wonder how the brutal toughs I'm hanging out with suffer his company. This is, after all, a man who's produced reams of fanatical material that Nick Lowles and I download from the Internet. I even have a copy of a letter from him to another extremist, claiming one of his aims is to 'infiltrate various Occult groups and societies'. Some of this material is laughable, some quite chilling, particularly concerning the 'culling' of opponents. Even other Satanic groups are wary of Myatt's Order of Nine Angles.

To me, Myatt's conversation and writings show little understanding of or empathy with human nature. He stresses again and again the need for fanatical values in bringing about his new society, attacking other cultures and 'traitors' to the Aryan cause. Yet he admits to being continually disappointed by 'real life'. His vision of a Homeland – organic farming, horse-drawn equipment, no contact with the outside world – also differs sharply from the reality of the Sargent brothers.

One day soon, he will threaten to challenge me, too, to a duel to the death. I'll be one of those who reveal his Satanic connections – connections he has always denied. Steve Sargent tells me I've been followed, and that Myatt knows my address. He recites a listing that's close to my girlfriend's house. It's unnerving. We never do work out if he actually has someone follow me, or if a contact is procuring details for him. When Nick Lowles finally goes to meet him, he takes a former SAS man for protection.

I watch Myatt's bright, yellow-clad back turn and mount the cycle, steadily climbing the hills in the near distance. Waiting a safe time, I run to the nearest phone box and, breathless, call my contacts to tell them of my latest encounter. Did I know he usually carries a dagger or sword cane with him? No, I didn't. Perhaps I was naive. But I survived.

Back in London, things are beginning to fall apart.

* * *

The reality on the ground for Combat 18 was football violence and the far-right music scene. When I first met Charlie, for example, he was holding a large bag of illegal white-power CDs, which he willingly displayed. These discs helped fund the group's activities. With the formation of ISD Records – the name taken from the late lead singer of skinhead band Skrewdriver, neo-nazi hero Ian Stuart Donaldson – C18 launched into the world of commerce. It was the first time a right-wing group had controlled such a large money-making venture. ISD produced scores of albums and made hundreds of thousands of pounds for the gang.

These profits, though, were one of the main causes of the feud within C18 and the murder of Chris Castle. Browning controlled the music business and differed with Charlie over how to spend the funds. During the autumn of 1996 the two men began to argue over this, and over the group's future direction. Sargent wanted to dominate the far-right scene as a territorial, tribal gang – an extension of a football hooligan firm, really – while Browning preferred to create a smaller, terrorist-style organisation. This disagreement eventually resulted in Castle's murder and a series of Danish letter bombings, with each side accusing the other of working for the State and acting as police informants. The surviving C18 faction became committed to existing as a smaller, more hard-line group.

On the day of the verdict, the atmosphere spilled outside the courtroom. The two factions squared up in the street, promising vengeance against one another. The cameras perched atop the shoulders of surrounding newsmen and women seemed like a flock of strange, taunting gulls. I watched as the two sides drew closer, ebbing and flowing, throwing their mocking challenges. A scarf wrapped about a scarred face flashed close by. The face disappeared back into the throng, as gang members hurled abuse at one another and at the thin line of police.

Suddenly I was hauled sideways, across the road and into a nearby pub. The man holding my arm was one of Steve's Harold Hill mates. A face leered into mine. 'You fucking journalists are all the same!' I couldn't make out the features at first. Dark hair, acne, a pallid complexion that jarred with dull, expressionless eyes. Blunt fingers grabbed my jacket and hauled me close. Inadvertently, I swallowed and tasted his hot, sour breath. It made me want to retch.

'Come to look, have you? Look at 'er,' the figure said, his bulky body pressing into mine. He pointed to a plump, wild-haired woman with streaks of mascara-etched tears printed over her face. It was Charlie's common law wife, Maxine. Her dyed red hair chimed with her dark brows. 'People like you don't know what we've gone through,' she clamoured, pointing a crudely painted set of nails at me. 'My kids had to watch their dad fight for his life. Me oldest was covered in blood. Covered. And that bastard Wilf [Will Browning] says 'im and Martin attacked 'im!'

'Wanna write that, eh?' exclaimed the face in front of me. Something was going to happen. The police were nowhere to be seen. The squat, untidy bar was full of C18 and only a few locals. The barman busied himself polishing empty pint glasses. 'We're gonna fucking kill 'em,' said a squat guy I recognised from the court. Standing next to him was a guy who claimed from the stand to have a mixed-race partner.

'Hey, leave 'im, he's all right,' said Steve Sargent, coming back into the main bar from the toilet. A muscular forearm was pressed towards my throat then suddenly released again. 'Thanks, Steve,' I muttered nervously. 'I only wanted to ask some questions.'

'Well, people 'ere don't feel too good about journalists at the moment.' His eyes lifted to the press pack outside, down the road. One of them had already been haranguing me for my story. Another hack trying to lift a piece.

Steve explained that they were anxious. His Homeland partner, a French neo-nazi called Hervé, had been dragged off his bicycle that week and dealt a beating by Browning's supporters. I didn't know what to say, so remained silent as the gang members came forward to speak with me in turns.

A plump hand suddenly dropped onto my shoulder. I turned, seeing Maxine's face push back close to mine. I smelt booze on her breath. 'Yeah, I'm bloody upset. My nerves are a wreck. The kids are even worse. Who's gonna take care of them now?' she asked. Perhaps it was rhetorical. Wobbling slightly on her feet, she kept talking about the kids and how Charlie was such a good partner to her. Every now and then she seemed to calm down. Then one of the gang members would chime in, speaking over her, and the anger would flare up again.

I couldn't take any more. I told them I had to get back to meet the photographer from my paper. As they say, I made my excuses and left.

* * *

For Steve Sargent, recreating a community was simply 'the only realistic option we have'. Like Charlie, he believed 'their' community had been smashed. Wandering with him around the pubs of Chelmsford, he was less confident, less absolute, than Charlie. He was uncomfortable with the label 'Nazi', saying the right already attracted too many 'bedsit weirdos'. He seemed much happier describing old football days and street battles than any notion of the future.

He yearned for a simpler life. 'I've spent half my life punching and fighting my way through different people, and I just don't want it no more, you know. I'm too fucking old for it all. You get some 20-year-old come along and he's gonna knock the fucking shit out of ya.' I asked him what he really wanted. He paused for a while. 'I don't know really. It's whether you talk fantasy or reality. In fantasy, I want lovely clean streets and blue-eyed blonde birds. In reality,' he pauses again, 'pretty much like what it's like now.'

The reality was that the Homeland never took off. The Sargents attracted only one outsider, the French neo-nazi Hervé, to the area. Although they had support from individuals, such as Martin Cross, already based in Essex, the dream remained just that. Despite its propaganda, the group was rarely a national danger, other than to individuals or small groups. It was never really a committed terrorist organisation, with a few notable exceptions. C18's long-promised race war and attacks on the State never ignited. Was this, finally, the reality of 'Aryan man'?

TWO

HUNTING THE BEAST

The first few months of 1997 were a strange time. I was trapped inside a violent subculture, whilst around me the very nature of the country seemed on the verge of change. After 18 years of Thatcherism, a new era was approaching. My friends were excited at the chance to overthrow Conservative rule. It was all we'd ever really known, and we had high hopes.

Meanwhile, a civil war of some sort was taking place within the movement. People were threatening retribution, whilst Browning was busy cajoling different white-power bands to join his cause. It was a vicious, cruel time. Not so different, though on a smaller scale, to behaviour I witnessed in the Balkans. Prejudice, fear, frustrated identity, violence: all were at play. In the former Yugoslavia, I'd gazed at the snow-covered fields and woods as I travelled in convoy through Slovenia, down into Croatia, and across into Bosnia. Now you could sense a similar atmosphere building around you. Yet the people I met claimed they were also loving men, with kids, wives, girlfriends, responsibilities. I still couldn't understand why they couldn't see what they were doing to their lives and to those around them.

Charlie had spent those months fighting a losing battle with The Beast. There were rumours he'd been dragged out of one of the gang's East End pubs and threatened with a gun. I didn't really understand what was going on or how close I'd come to getting hurt. Just before Charlie and Martin Cross had murdered Chris Castle, I'd been trying to get invited to a C18 music concert. What a coup that would have been, I thought, naively. Charlie had prevaricated for weeks. 'We gotta take precautions, like, y'know?' he'd told me, fixing me with his trademark look. He'd already told me I was 'all right' by his standard of journalists, that I 'wasn't like the rest'.

'But some of the blokes, 'ey're still a bit wary of people like you,' he said. 'We've got a bloke, a photographer or somefink, already coming from the *News of the World*, doing some photos for the 'undreffh anniversary of

Mosley. I dunno if we can get annuver in.' He cropped his words, ending the sentence abruptly. I sat silently, waiting for him to make his mind up. I thought his cap looked faintly ridiculous perched on his fat, balding head. For once, I kept my mouth shut.

'Okay, let me 'ave a word wiv Will,' he said, standing up and heading quickly out of the pub, leaving me to collect the tab. It was the last I was to see of him before the trial. Unknown to me, Will would storm the stage at the gig, taking the mike from the band and claiming C18 was now firmly under his control. His guys had moved into the audience, too. Charlie smiled weakly from the side of the stage, as though agreeing to the whole thing, rubbing his nervous hands down the sides of stale-smelling jeans. My invite had never arrived, anyway. Neither did one turn up for the *News of the World* photographer. In a way, I was glad. I was doing everything for the story at the time. Hanging out with these guys wasn't always a great laugh. Turns out I'd actually had a lucky escape. There'd been a plan from The Beast's supporters to attack all journalists present. The new C18 wasn't about talking to scum like me.

Most of these struggles took place in and around my visits, as Steve introduced me to the various gang members who'd remained loyal. I didn't know much about the war during that odd period, only that it culminated in the stabbing of Catford Chris.

As this tiny, tribal world turned in on itself, the Conservatives, several of whom I later discovered had connections to far-right groups such as the British National Party, were losing their hold on power. The day after the elections, I forgot the neo-nazis and white supremacists. Now there was Change. All the papers referred to it. People walked around with idiotic, dreamy smiles. It wasn't to last, but for a short time it really did feel magical. I guess it was hope.

The irony was that the extremists welcomed the change too. When they started taking areas of the deprived northern cities, it was initially in traditional Labour strongholds that they were successful. I suppose it made sense. A right-wing government had stolen much of their natural support, particularly on issues such as immigration. The far right had cowered, it seemed, beneath a large stone. Now that was going to change.

Few around me seemed to see this. There was little hint of comprehension from my friends or acquaintances that safe lives in leafy suburbs were built on something darker.

* * *

'This fucking country, eh?' I half-muttered, glancing up into the soft, liquid eyes again. I imagined them gummy, rheumy, as they would be when he was an old man. It made him more human, less intimidating.

Steve lowered his scar-cropped pate towards the pint. The glass seemed ready to glide across the tiny table, which was printed with dark circles of spilled booze. 'Eh, too fuckin' right,' he slurped, dribbling a thin film of cider onto his stubble. I'd never seen him unshaven before. He seemed eager to chat. Perhaps he realised the fantasy he'd created for himself was finally collapsing.

'How's Charlie?' I asked. 'Any more news of his transfer?'

'Naah. Dunno what's gonna happen yet. We're still waitin' ta hear from the judge what the sentence will be. Probably 15 years, innit, for life?'

I didn't know. No one I knew had ever murdered anybody.

'That bloody Wilf though,' he continued. 'I bin thinking about it. I'm sure, sure of it – he's a fucking grass, got to be. 'Ow else could it have come down so soon?'

His gaze lost its focus. He seemed to ruminate on the point for a moment. Then he snapped up again with a start, eyes widening. 'It'll come out sooner or later. That and MI5, I tell ya . . . 'At cunt Gable, too.'

I was feeling a little woozy, still not used to these daytime drinking sessions. It was an odd time indeed. Few of my friends or family knew what I was doing. Neither did I, perhaps. Until now I had counted Kurds, Arabs and others among my friends. I'd only recently returned from a trip to the region called Kurdistan, part of which is located in south-eastern Turkey. Before that, I'd been in northern Syria, sitting in the border town of Qamishle eating watermelon and discussing politics with refugees in tea houses.

Kurdistan was a terrible, war-torn place. Dirty grey buildings, freezing weather, beautiful, alien mountainscapes, shepherds fleeing burned-out villages. I remember the smoke of the Newroz (New Year) fires in south-eastern Turkey stinging my eyes, and the secret police following us at every turn. A villager who spoke to me about forcible rationing was dragged off into the back of a jeep and never seen again. Just a small stain of dark blood marked the spot where he was taken. Stone-faced men in jeans and dark glasses casually hoisted their M16s as they smiled at us with rictus grins. Another story, as they say, but it makes me laugh when I hear people complain about life in the West.

It was a world about which few of my liberal mates or newfound neo-nazi pals had any comprehension. Disappearances, rape, torture, civil war, all inside a NATO country seeking EU membership. In a few years, there'd even be a neo-fascist party, the MHP (National Action) – nicknamed the 'Grey Wolves' – in coalition government in Turkey. Volunteers had fought in other conflicts in the region. Here in London, its supporters beat up a photographer friend of mine with bicycle chains.

Back in England, I was still nervous. My first article would be coming out soon, in *GQ* magazine. For the first time, I'd be showing the gang what I thought of them – or at least making clear the conclusions that could be drawn from our encounters. How would they react? I didn't contemplate dropping the story and moving on to something new. I too had changed in the 15 months since The Princess Louise.

These thoughts and others drifted into my mind as I gazed out onto a cramped, cobbled backstreet. It was visible in a small crescent of light, peeking through the faded curtains which shrouded the pub from casual view. Very old-fashioned. We were just down the road from the private mailbox company where Steve went to collect his central London mail. I'd been there with him several times already.

'What'chew fink, then, Nick? You reckon Charlie dun it, dontcha? I can tell.'

What? I'd obviously drifted off. Not too difficult after all this drinking. But why are you asking me, I thought? Should I tell him, 'No, he's a wonderful man and father, treats his kids great'? Or perhaps that he was a forgotten and misguided guy, who hadn't grabbed the chances life had offered? More likely a failure, a fraud to his own cause, who thought no more of his girlfriend or stepkids that day of the murder than he ever did, and a grass and a coward to boot.

'I dunno, Steve, it's difficult. Obviously, he's your brother. I dunno, mate,' I said, somewhat falsely. 'He did seem to, well, dominate things – you – quite a lot. Hope you don't mind me saying that.' He just stared at me. 'Look, why don't you get on with things, get on with your life? Do the plastering, go off travelling, enjoy yourself with your mates. Or find a girl. Thought you said you had a kid or something in Czechoslovakia?'

He guffawed and brought his glass up for another gulp. That had probably been bullshit for my benefit, the talk of girls. 'I can't get rid of Martin's bird, that Kelly. She keeps followin' me arand. Bloody 'ell,' he said, rolling his eyes heavenwards. I laughed too. He recounted some one-night stand with 'a dreadful fat bird', and we went back to the drinking and talking.

Steve must have thought differently to me, those times we talked. Not just about women, but about life. You could see it cut into his face, around the crow's feet creeping from his eyes, and in the way he carried himself. Now, I thought, I could reach through to him. Perhaps now he would accept defeat and see reason. I spent many afternoons trying to persuade him to change his ideas and see what else life offered. Maybe I could rescue him from this path of destruction. How foolish, how naive.

It was, in many ways, the end of the road. The end of his dream and fantasy. He was just too stupid or foolish to see it. I think I saw it then too, but I didn't realise what I was dealing with. When someone has been trapped in this role – of *being* someone (so they think) – for so long, they can't give it up overnight. I've seen it since with other members of extremist groups. People who know they're right, even when 99 per cent of us might think otherwise. In some ways, such hostility from the mainstream even reinforces their belief.

Steve had thrown his entire identity and life into this movement. A guy in his mid-3os who even other C18 members had joked (perhaps unfairly) still wet his bed as an adult. He'd gone from being a nobody plasterer, who couldn't get a girl, to being the top of the country's hardest 'firm'. Where he came from, that earned respect. I couldn't help but feel sad that he was trapped in this role. But at the end of the day, it was his choice. I had to lead my life, not his.

I still followed his path with interest, though. For years afterwards, Steve would join other little grouplets and retreat to his older brother's place in Norfolk. Plastering and fascism, drink and sad lust. One day he would repay me by calling me a wanker and claiming I was working for *Searchlight*. That was the only way he could fit me into his squalid little worldview.

It seemed funny, almost. Only a short time after the murder verdict against his brother, Steve was printing his little leaflets and articles again – Albion Wolf, as he liked to style himself – and had accused 'Wilf', The Beast, and his followers of treachery and compliance with the State. I for one wouldn't have baited The Beast. The rumours were starting to go around that he was looking for Steve. We all knew what would happen if he found him.

'I'm not fucking scared of 'im,' he blustered, throwing back his shoulders. He rocked back and forth in front of me, on a small bar stool. We were talking of the past and future, sitting in a sprawling Victorian pub, next to Barnet railway station. A tired, sagging lady with dyed black hair chatted to an older scrawny woman behind the bar. I thought she looked bored. Smoke wafted around us in thick wreaths, the clack of pool balls rattling in the background. A jukebox played hits at least ten years out of date.

This semi-commutersville on the end of the Northern Line was where the Sargents had been raised. It was also, I later discovered, where BNP leader Nick Griffin had been born. Once a pretty little village, it was now a sprawling collection of estates and tidy houses and shops. The night had dropped early, leaving kitchen lights and the glow from passing buses the only signatures in the still air. The usual background noise of central London was absent. Only the sound of the Tube trains, reversing in the depot, reminded me I was still in the capital. In Civilisation, I joked to myself.

'He's the one 'oo should watch aat,' Steve's voice piped up suddenly.

'Why?' I asked. 'Have you got something planned then?'

He snorted. 'Well, them Romford lot ain't too 'appy for one. You don't wanna cross someone like Phil or Eddie. Get seriously fuckin' 'urt.' He took another sip from his glass.

I remember when he'd introduced me to them. It was after Charlie had been arrested, but before the trial. They'd sat in a row, five or six of them from Romford, watching me approach from the other end of the long bar. We were in one of the 'Road of Death' pubs in Chelmsford. Despite what Steve had told me, it was quite a nice old place, with roaring fire and stone floor. They'd got their backs to the wall. In any other situation, I might have said they looked a bit like an old-fashioned interview board, lined up and ready to ask their questions.

It was an odd, intimidating few moments. The walk seemed interminably slow. My voice croaked as I tried to speak, making a tiny, pathetic sound. One of the younger guys, dark-haired with pasty skin stretched tight over pumped muscles, gave me an ugly stare. It clearly wasn't his idea to be here. By contrast Eddie Stanton, the unofficial leader, reached over and shook my hand. His manner was chatty, almost cheeky. 'Awright mate, so are you gonna get a whole wodge [of money] for writing this thing then?' Obviously, they thought I was some kind of tabloid hack, being paid thousands. Still, the grin on Stanton's face was only half joking. It was a predator's smile. 'Don't bullshit us, we know you're getting loads for this!' He pulled back his slicked ponytail to reveal handsome features, drawing on a cigarette as he did so. I caught a flash of nicotine-stained ivory. 'So what you wanna know then, Nick? Some juicy quotes, eh?'

We spent most of the night talking about their lives. How they were going to become the 'real' C18. Threats had been bandied about. Revenge would be taken against Browning's supporters. Again, as I glanced nervously to my side, I could see life going on as normal in the rest of the pub.

'Oi,' said Stanton, thrusting his cigarette in my direction, ''ow would you feel if your kids, like Charlie's, 'ad blood splattered all over 'em, eh?' There was an aggressive growl to his voice. ''is ten year old 'ad to see it all, the whole fucking thing,' he pointed again. 'That cunt Browning, I don't care 'ow tough anyone says 'e is, 'e's got it coming.' Like Steve, Eddie also believed that Browning must have been a grass.

I did like Eddie, in a way. I still couldn't fathom the attraction of the movement, though. Booze (or something stronger) and 'birds', I suppose. Perhaps it was just loyalty to his mates from the estate.

Back in Barnet again, and Steve introduced me to a heavily tattooed guy in his 40s, a former heavy in the British Movement (BM). The BM had been born from a group created in the 1960s by Colin Jordan, another long-time figure on the British far-right fringe. Jordan had been photographed with former BNP and National Front leader John Tyndall, sitting with the leader of the American Nazi Party, George Lincoln Rockwell (who was later assassinated). This was just one of many cross-Atlantic attempts at cooperation between extreme-right groups. The BM itself was, in a way, a precursor to C18, providing the muscle for National Front marches – and for those fed up with the Front's electoral road.

Steve and I spent the rest of the night touring pubs and cheap, flaking wine bars, getting drunk (again) and talking about days gone by. Of C18 and football hooliganism. Of Highbury and Arsenal football ground. It reminded me that Islington held a darker side than most of its yuppie denizens cared to know. Steve's eyes came alive talking about the time he and others were fighting rival football supporters in Tunisia. Back then he clearly thought he'd been somebody.

He also took great delight in telling me what had happened during the C18 heyday of the early 1990s. An American white supremacist had come over, and they'd taken him down to one of their Bethnal Green pubs. Inside, it was packed with the crew. Beer and noise, coke snorting, and a black stripper dancing on one of the tables in the back. 'You shoulda seen 'is fucking face,' Steve said, almost crying even now with laughter. The American was so shocked by the behaviour that he never returned.

Despite the humour though, Steve still seemed preoccupied with proving Charlie's innocence. He talked about it all the time in a grim, pensive mood. I didn't tell him about the conversation I'd had with Special Branch a few weeks before. They were clearly interested in the gang – whether because Charlie had been informing for them, or because of the links to Loyalist paramilitaries in Northern Ireland. Perhaps Steve was reducing this to his level of understanding – a turf war. I still found it hard to understand him, let alone Charlie. I clearly hadn't grasped the man Charlie really was, or what he'd been capable of doing. Stupid, I know. At first, I'd even shown up back in Chelmsford, thinking to visit Charlie in prison. Perhaps it'd provide a good coda to my story. Steve had been there waiting, breath frosting as a weak sun struggled to poke through the blanket of cloud overhead.

It was shortly after the trial. The town felt the same as always. The Christmas lights were gone, but shoppers rushed by, kids tugged at their mums' hands, and the little mosque still nestled in the same place. It looked and felt like an English market town; starting to change fast, but still recognisable. A nice place to live. I stood on a bridge and looked down at the river flowing beneath. I thought how this place, like so many others I was starting to visit, held its secrets.

Later that day, Nick Lowles of *Searchlight* joined us. Ostensibly, he and Steve were clear enemies. In reality, I was surprised at how easily they got on. I'd already introduced them at the end of the trial.

'You work for the other side, dontcha?' said Steve, as we tucked into a curry, nestled in a small restaurant near the courthouse. *'Searchlight.'* A faint smile played around Nick's lips and his eyes glittered. 'I know them, that's all, I'm just a journalist like Nick here,' he said, nodding at me. 'Yeah!' muttered Steve, cradling his fork in his right hand, the way a child would shovel up peas. I watched it dip, then dive into the pinkish Tandoori sauce. 'Well, I don't care if you are,' he said again, and with that, we proceeded to chat the night away.

He seemed happy to recount how his former friend, Mark Atkinson, was now languishing in jail and getting beaten up by black inmates. Unknown to me, Steve – as he later claimed, with some glee – was also taping our conversation. Not that it would have made any difference. Perhaps he thought he was an agent or would be able to reveal some amazing secret. Later, he took great pleasure in trying to reveal his subterfuge to any of the comrades in his little movement, or to the bedsit conspiracy nuts who hang around the scene.

Not long after, he invited us round to his flat. I was surprised at his candour. It was a fair walk from the town. We wandered down through the crowded high street and towards the outskirts. As we paced over the old cobblestones and onto the tarmac, the estates began creeping up around us. Our path took us through featureless stretches of grassland. Rows of squat, box-like houses appeared on the slope of the hill before us. Very mundane. Very British.

''Ere we are,' Steve cawed, from our side. 'It's not much, but it's home.' He led us to a nondescript glass door in a cheap, whitewashed frame. His key entered the lock with a soft clunk, then the wood seemed to give a quick shudder before opening. We followed him up the narrow staircase.

'Tea?' Steve turned, creasing his neck into thick folds. We thumped up the stairs onto a small landing, then turned sharply into the front room. Stale smoke lingered above the overflowing ashtrays. 'I've only got this cheap shit, Happy Shopper,' he said, gesturing with a sideways nod. 'That cunt Hervé never goes shopping. Sometimes I don't know why I put up with 'im.' He clacked his tongue against the back of his teeth. 'Fucking dirty bastard.' He crossed the few feet into the cramped kitchen. His fingers sought, then found a clutch of tea bags. One slowly fell from his hand, fluttering to the floor.

I glanced to my right at the stack of unwashed plates and crockery, leaning dangerously either side of the sink. 'Er, ain't had much time to do the washing recently. Court case and all that, y'know?' I half-laughed. Nick stood in the centre of the small room, glancing at the shit-brown wallpaper, his face expressionless.

'So, what've you been up to, Steve? Got any thoughts about life after all this?'

'Nah, not really,' he replied, munching on a biscuit. A crumb settled on his chest, as the kettle began to bubble at his side. 'Might do some more plastering. Maybe go and see Bill [his brother]. I could resurrect Albion Wolf, of course,' he added, referring to his fictional alter ego, writing in the C18 newsletters. He walked back into the main room with us. ''Ere, seen these?' he grinned, grabbing a handful of well-thumbed magazines sitting on top of a hi-fi stack. 'Got 'em for 40p each down the market. Second 'and. Not bad, eh?' He offered one forwards, in my direction. A pair of blondes cavorted in an unlikely pose on one cover. Nick and I swapped smiles. Sad smiles.

I took a chipped mug from Steve's hands, burning myself in the process. He kicked a bundle of Hervé's clothes out of his way. 'Fucking dirty French bastard,' he tutted to himself. I got the feeling life on the Homeland hadn't been too great. When Nick and I later reminisced on this scene, we used the phrase 'bedsit weirdo'. It seemed to suit many of the people we met in these movements, at the subcultural end of neo-nazism. The irony was that Steve himself had suggested the phrase.

'. . . spends all his time doin' weights. Doesn't pay too much attention to personal hygiene,' Steve continued, still talking about Hervé. 'Don't fink he knows what a bar of soap is.' The guttural laughter was back. It coughed out of him with a wheeze. It reminded me that, for all the tabloid headlines, Steve was still a human being. Perhaps I wasn't what he expected from a journalist either.

'. . . still, we've 'ad some good times. When we go away, we always send Gable something. Last time, Hervé stuffed one of them jiffy bags with shit and sent it to Gable's address. Bet that caused a stink at "Searchlies",' he said, with a wink at Nick. Nick laughed back. It was sad; sadder still that I laughed at the time. He seemed to have no way of understanding why others might want to oppose him.

I sat down slowly and sucked the tea through clenched teeth. It tasted foul and watery, metallic. I looked into the cup and saw the sides caked with tannin and other stains. Steve seemed oblivious to me for the moment, chatting away to Nick. It was clear they knew, or knew of, many of the same people. I was amazed by Nick's level of knowledge, and at Steve's acceptance of him. Soon after, Nick would be talking face to face with Will Browning's men, seeking to turn them from their path too.

As we sat long into the darkening afternoon, we told Steve what we knew of his companions. Of people like David Myatt, who we already suspected had tried to have me followed. Of suspected paedophiles and other assorted weirdos associating with C18 and Steve's nascent National Socialist Movement (NSM). He nodded sagely, agreeing – it seemed – with much of what we'd said. 'Can't you see, Steve, it doesn't look good for you, mate?' I said, sincerely. I hoped he would leave the whole, sorry scene. 'Hanging out with these types? What about Browning and his pals? They don't sound like they're going to give up, either.'

'Fuck 'im,' he said again, with false bravado. 'Look, I know it ain't what it was. But it ain't all bad. Not yet. We're still gonna win.' He paused, pondering what we'd said. 'Look, I'm gonna be a bit busy the next fortnight. Then give me a bell and we'll hook up again.' He scratched at the entrance of a nostril, then sank into the felt-brown settee.

I never saw him again, except years later on a BBC TV documentary. He was being door-stepped by journalists after London was hit by a series of nailbombs. It turned out the bomber had belonged to the NSM. His name was David Copeland, and he was targeting blacks, Asians and gays in their supposed 'heartlands'. His bombs affected people that I personally knew. Nearly me, too. Now he's in Broadmoor Psychiatric Hospital. Afterwards, I thought back to Steve and his promises. Maybe he'd never intended to leave. Maybe he couldn't.

I spent that night getting drunk, elated and depressed at the end – so I thought – of the whole strange C18 affair. It was time to move on to other things. I tried to consider my thoughts in my drunken haze. I placed one hand on the tiled wall as I swayed in front of a pub urinal, late, just after last orders, trying not to piss on my shoes. The bar had already emptied. I followed the hoary air steaming from my mouth. Outside, Chelmsford was night-silent. Where would it all end, I wondered? Where would I end up, for that matter? Why was I still chasing after nazis? When I finally staggered out, I'd missed the last train. Collapsing into a telephone box, I dialled the number for a cab. The journey seemed to take forever, my head lolling as I made forced conversation with the driver. I arrived home at 3 a.m., exhausted.

* * *

His voice catches my attention: gruff, with the ends of the words sliced off. But there's a hint, too, of education, of softer beginnings.

'What gets me is that I counted him as a friend. A good friend,' he's saying. I look up. His face is blunt. Dark, puffy circles creep under his eyes. Beneath the hurt of life lies humour, an understated, higher pitch that lilts in between the 'fucks' and 'punch-ups' as he speaks rapidly.

'Me and 'im, we 'ad some really good times. The best. He was my best friend, I suppose . . .' he catches his breath for a moment, '. . . until Wilf and me. Now I ain't got no words for it. Scum, that's just what they are.'

Darren Wells is in full flow, stopping only to wet his full lips with the contents of his glass, wiping a surprisingly fragile-looking hand across his mouth. The mottled purple behind his knuckles speaks of drink. His words fall in a quick tumble of vitriol, as he describes his former friendship with Steve. 'We did everyfing together, hung out, got pissed, 'e 'ad a real good sense of humour, like. Ah. Oh well. I see he's scum now, but I still feel let down, y'know?'

'Why?' I ask.

The world seems to have shrunk around us. Despite the pub chatter, it feels like the three of us are alone: 'It was just that we did loads together. Everyfing. S'pose I didn't have so many other friends, the ones from school and the like.'

'Was it like a new family?' I feel like spitting to clear my throat.

'No. Well, yeah, a bit. I never thought of it like that, but I s'pose some of that were there. Steve was always good for a laugh, a joke, y'know.'

'Yeah, right,' Nick Lowles mutters as he leans back, moulding himself into the cushioned upholstery. Darren then tells several stories of the C18 'away' missions, laughing as he recounts the casual sex, drink, and violence.

Darren is a C18 insider, chief lieutenant to The Beast. He rose through the ranks of the gang from its earliest days. By day an insurance broker, he became part of the C18 Chelsea mob. Charlie Sargent was at first 'a kind of father figure'. It was an unwise choice. Under Charlie's tutelage, he went on to glass, even stab, various opponents, many of them from rival right-wing or football groups, and earned himself prison time.

Sitting beside me, he is an unassuming figure. Moderately tall, slightly heavy-set, with a dusting of short brown hair framing a drab face. Looking closely, I think I can spot hints of sensitivity scarred beneath the blunt features. But that could be wishful thinking. You wouldn't really pick him out from a crowd (although he did once take his shirt off to reveal scars and a swastika tattoo on his chest). As if to confirm this, he goes on to explain how he was raised in well-to-do surroundings. His mother took holidays to India, and Darren went to a grammar school in an affluent suburb. But he remembers best the beatings he got from his stepfather. The rage built in Darren and led him away from a life of study and settled existence into C18.

During our meetings, we talk for a long time about the different girlfriends he's had. It's clear he finds it difficult to hold down relationships. Nick Lowles jokes with him about it. 'Another one bites the dust, eh, Darren?' he chuckles, as Darren tells me about his latest break-up, swearing as he does so. He seems genuinely offended that we're laughing. He also tells me about the time he attacked his stepfather with a broken beer glass at a drinks party, claiming he had insulted his mother. 'And that was the end of that,' he says.

Even so, he managed to hold down a good job for a while, until the football riots got the better of him. He travelled away with the gang to England and Chelsea games, meting out violence to those he encountered on his journeys. Sometimes it was just from other parts of London. It was a laugh, he says. He quickly became Steve's friend. Steve seemed to shrug it off when I asked him about it.

Over time, Darren gradually became Will's best friend, too. Then, when things began to get strained with Charlie, he became Will's number-two man. It was him who threatened me in the courtroom. Now, he's talking to us, he feels betrayed.

'Wilf will tell you what 'e's doing and why. If you say that to Steve, 'e's got no answer. Coz 'e's got no other mates anywhere else. 'E'll just probably show you some porn.' He's speaking fast, hardly pausing for breath. 'And that's it. 'Ow fucking sad, eh?'

About us, inside The Finborough Arms, the decor is a deep, pleasant, inviting green. Not lime, nor harsh. Fake classical music is being piped into the pub, near the bright lights of the King's Road. The clink of glasses is punctured now and then by a mobile phone. It is the heart of Chelsea. A far cry from the sounds of 1994.

In August of that year, on a sweltering summer's day, Darren was in a group that attacked the pub. He talks about it casually now, even joking how the women and children had carefully left before they arrived, leaving only 'legitimate targets'. Even after all this time, and because Darren seems such a nice guy, it's shocking to hear him speak like this.

'We drifted in, in small numbers. It was horrific, I suppose. Frenzied.' He falls silent and ruminates for a moment, as though far away. 'Yeah, it was frenzied.' They were a mix of Chelsea and C18. Charlie didn't turn up. 'He came up with some excuse; a medical condition called cowardice.'

They drank as normal, so as not to attract attention. He tells me about the feelings. 'You get that nervous adrenaline, excitement, buzz, a mixture of all those. It's like . . .' he pauses, 'like there was no way we were gonna lose.'

'So who were the enemy?' I ask, careful to remain expressionless.

'We didn't know them specifically as such, just that they were the Reds.' He claims not to have seen it kick off. 'Everyone started Sieg Heiling. Then a few things got thrown. Then it was pandemonium.'

The other Nick asks if there were any punches, his keen eyes focused on Darren's face. 'No. It wasn't like a football fight. It was just . . . obliteration, like.'

The noise and shouting made it incredibly intimidating. He calls it a 'cross between panic and a buzz'. What did he do then, I wonder. He pauses for quite a while. 'Finished my beer!' he exclaims, his voice rising in a jokey manner. Nick laughs too.

I ask again: 'Did you glass someone?'

'That's what they say, yeah,' he replies. 'Although who it was I can't tell ya.'

'Perhaps we should change your name in my book, to protect the guilty?' It's a joke.

He goes 'um' and, by his sudden dour expression, obviously doesn't find it funny.

C18's main target that day was Ross Fraser, head of the Chelsea FC fan club, who'd been spearheading an anti-racist campaign at the football ground. Chelsea had long been known for its infamous fans. During the attack Fraser was glassed in one eye, someone tried to slash his throat, and a pool ball had smashed off his head – though not before he'd grabbed hold of a C18 hooligan and, half-blinded, repeatedly smashed his head against a table. Darren sounds oddly respectful when he mentions this.

'How is someone glassed?' I'm morbidly curious.

He casually demonstrates with my beer bottle, mimicking a motion to crack it down on the table, then stabbing it towards my face. Instinctively, I draw back. Matter-of-factly he talks about the problems of breaking it too far down the neck and cutting your own hand. 'I got hit round the 'ead with one and it didn't break,' he muses. 'But it bloody 'urt.' He remembers hitting a champagne bottle into someone's face in Germany. He stabbed a rival there, too. In a few years' time, Darren will be working for *Searchlight* as a mole inside C18 and the racist gangs.

The talk turns to Will Browning: his terrifying rages, and what he's really like as a person. Not The Beast. I say that I want to see him. Darren replies, 'That'll happen, don't worry, no problem. Just give it some time.'

Nick Lowles laughs evilly in the background and jokes, 'Then you'll see what happens when someone doesn't behave!' He chuckles, holding his pint.

'It's down to you now, Slippery,' Darren jokes back, using the nickname The Beast has somewhat bizarrely given Nick.

Inside, though, it seems Browning's beginning to question things too, losing heart for a movement which led to his friend dying in his arms.

* * *

SUMMER 1998

'That's how it was. Bloody weird.'

The way Nick now tells it, as we walk the long, nervous minutes from the station, I feel as if I already know him. I'm fascinated. Why is he the way he is? What set him on this road? How will he react to me – if we can meet?

Nick's recalling their encounters, including the surreal moments at Charlie's trial and the berserk rage he'd seen during filming for a documentary about the gang. Now, as we talked, I wondered if this man Browning would lose his thirst for the cause? Would Chris Castle's death finally shake The Beast?

I scratch absentmindedly, mulling over these thoughts and my fears for a moment. The skin peels away beneath my fingers. I look down. The deep, dark tan has yet to fade. It's been only a few days since I got off the plane from Paris, and before that Algeria, one of the most frightening places I've ever visited. Civil war, Islamic fundamentalism, death squads, a furious, boiling desert. As I talked with my contacts, in the one hotel in Algiers which permits foreigners, a bomb ripped through a nearby market. We heard the loud 'crump', then sirens, as we sipped sweet mint tea. My Ministry of Interior bodyguards barely gave it a glance, before turning back to our conversation.

I held the hand of a friend, a photographer, as he told me of the people he'd seen blown apart. Of the death threats and pressure. The work had brought him fame, but at a terrible price. Tears had washed thin lines of sorrow onto his fine features. It became a period burned onto my brain. And still, I think, I understood it better than the world I was walking through now.

* * *

That world turns red, as I close my eyes and look up towards the sun. Basking in the warm summer's light, I try to calm my fears.

Surrey Quays is a mecca of consumer life burning bright behind me, Canary Wharf a looming presence, jutting needle-like into the skyscape around us. Down, past the playing fields and brown-brick estates we now walk, past the Union Jacks and St Georges hanging from the tower blocks, next to neat little window boxes. Down past the car lots and small patches of green, towards the end of this long, narrow road lies The Beast's lair.

We pass old, forgotten pubs, moving away with each minute from the land of bright, monickered bars, away from the Wetherspoons and Harvesters. We soon catch sight of The New Den, Millwall's ground, looming over the backs of the houses. I see the signs – 'No football colours please' – sigil-like over the doorways. Strange, that, I think. What self-respecting football firm wears colours anyway? It's all casual these days.

As I glance around, a small gang of kids moves towards us on the narrow pavement, pacing their territory, playing the ritual. They saunter to their own rhythm, pack animal and hunter rolled into one. Four white, one black, all designer labels. Conflict? Our eyes lock for a second – my heartbeat quickens – then break as the challenge is passed. There's laughter. The shirt sticks uncomfortably to my back.

We finally stroll past *his* office, full of blacks and Chinese, all windows, open plan, '50s style. It's a McDonald's. His office: a joke. He holds his meetings there, makes calls from the phone box outside.

Eventually we come to rest in a small, modern estate. It's a first-time buyer's kind of place: compact, tidy, thin walls. The sort of place where you hear every argument. Every scream of a baby, every cry of passion. The start of the Edge City.

A small patch of green is rolled, carpet-like, in front of each box-shaped house. A deflated football rests gently on a little bird table, leaning crookedly against a porch. A wind chime tinkles softly above a doorway somewhere. There's his big brown Ford outside the two-up, two-down, the sun half-blinding me as it winks off the net-covered windows.

An odd sensation grips me. Nick reckons we could ring the bell – if I wanted. The Beast could well be out at work. But he might be in there, too. Rumour has it he's gone back to his business as a carpenter. He makes good money, apparently. I'm reluctant to move, standing here on the other side of the road, dressed down in my roughest gear and desperate to be invisible.

I'm recalling Darren's words from The Finborough, his high voice talking of the time Will threatened Charlie. Bending towards the shorter, fatter man, looming crag-like over him, as he screamed, shrinking Charlie back into his chair. Where had all the money gone? Will wanted to know. Who was it who'd helped build up the music business in the first place, who'd seen off the opposition and held true to their revolutionary principles?

'And all the time Wilf's just looking right through him, like, 'freatening to kill 'im,' says Darren. He seems excited, poised to laugh. 'It was a terrifying moment.' A pause. He scratches at the high collar of his Stone Island sweater. 'Even for me.'

Darren talks of some pub fight or other, Will lifting an iron table and smashing it down on a guy on the floor, as well as on one of their own people who happened to be in the way. 'Then he charged three people with it.' He's speaking fast again, animated. 'I couldn't even pick the fucking thing up. Fucking thing was way too 'eavy. But that's Wilf for ya,' he half snorts, with what seems a resigned tone.

'Will's got a problem,' pipes in Nick. It's the first time I've heard him use The Beast's name. 'His obsessive behaviour will continue to get him in problems.' Again, he sounds resigned. And concerned. Almost.

'Oh yeah,' Darren replies swiftly. 'He confronts things head on. He couldn't be sneaky if he tried.' He's leaning forwards, talking into my face. 'His first action is that violence is the only option. But he is changing now. Slowly.'

'How?'

'Being more sneaky, like.'

'Sneaky?' Nick laughs.

Darren looks momentarily annoyed at the interruption, as though imparting some great secret. He turns back to me, after a quick glance at Nick. 'So he called up Sargent's people and then told 'em he's doing this – getting all sneaky like them, not playing the usual game. Huh! Jackie [Browning's fiancée] just shakes her head and tells him he's got no idea.'

* * *

'I've often said that to 'er. I've said, "Eh Jacks, you've got a degree an all that. Why dontcha do something with yerself?"' Darren's words are echoing in my head. I think I see some movement behind the curtains. We move, quickly, past the bend in the road, and on back to the main street. His words return, unbidden as I walk.

'For the first couple of years with Wilf, she was really wanting to get out, do her own thing. They used to have all these internal battles about it, y'know? But then he would win all the time, so there you go . . .'

'Did he hit her?' After all, a man with a name like The Beast didn't sound exactly the sensitive type.

'It's not like that!' says Darren, almost shocked. 'Having said that,' he adds, 'he's quite scared of her. She's not physically scared of him, though. Not at all.'

'She talks to him like no one else can,' Nick now says, puffing to keep up with me as I motor away from Browning's house. 'At least, that's what Darren says.' I've bottled it. I don't want to risk dropping in unannounced. Others might, but not me. Not this time.

'Does she know what he's doing?' I'd asked Darren. She must be mad not to, I think. What was it, this bond between them?

'Initially, not that much,' he replies. 'Partly it was to protect her. He didn't tell her, basically.' We both look out of the pub, to the pedestrians clogging the pavement outside. 'But since the split with Charlie, they share everything together.' Turns out she hasn't told her parents anything about this mystery man either, her Will. 'When she's round there, if there's anything about the right on the telly, she quickly turns it over before they see!' He sounds fond of her. Like she's a surrogate mother or sister figure.

'She often says she wishes it was like the old days, like a football firm, when you went off to have a punch-up, then came back home.' Darren was talking more often in the past tense these days. I wondered if he was thinking of leaving. There'd been some trouble in Germany recently, when he'd ended up stabbing another neo-nazi during a slanging match against C18. 'Now it's all Special Branch and dawn raids, murder, an' all that. But she was close to Chris [Castle] as well, so she understands.' Darren was adamant on this point. I thought there must come a time when that bond would snap. Just a year or so later, though, they went on to have a kid together.

On that day of rain, grime and beer, Darren had told me how supportive Jackie was of Will. '"Keep your chin up, chicken," she says to 'im!' Even Darren laughs. 'She has a Celtic attitude to things, but don't take no grief off of 'im.'

Since the murder, she'd become 'very hard inside. But she's a genuinely nice, decent person. Whereas Maxine [Charlie Sargent's partner] is a two-bit working-class scrubber.'

Nick looks at him quizzically. Darren says, 'What? What! I ain't said nothing wrong.' He ends on a strange note. 'Did you know Will calls Jackie "Jacqueline"? Yeah, he does, 'coz he's such a snob at heart, Will.'

What was she doing with him? It's not as if they have a quiet life, I think. She's the one person who can stand up to him and live. And in his own way, it sounds like he loves her too. At least, that's what Darren said.

Darren once talked about the time he'd had to remind Will to get Jackie something from Duty Free. They were on their way home after one of the trips across to the Continent, on Movement business. 'Why, what for?' replied The Beast. He was genuinely dumbfounded, holding his bag of twenties and fifties.

'Well, because that's the sort of thing you're supposed to do for women, Will,' Darren said, trying not to laugh.

'Oh,' he grunted, and they went into this cosmetics shop. According to Darren, Browning couldn't bring himself to look up while at the perfume counter, worried he might get contaminated perhaps, thinking maybe the person behind it was eyeing him up, or something. Darren said he tried to pull him away, but then strolled off. Let him get on with it, no point being too close to him in this mood, he thought. Anyway, what could go wrong? Later, on the plane, Will showed him what he'd bought her. A lovely bottle, Darren agreed, yeah, pricey . . . except it's aftershave, mate. The Beast just looked at him for a while, said, 'Are you taking the piss?' No, replied Darren, laughing inside, knowing better than to push it.

Another time they'd been in Belgium. This skin they were staying with 'had this lovely black bust of Hitler, a huge fucking thing, solid iron, it was,' chortled Darren. Got to have that, says Will, how much? Probably made by the score in some Turk's sweatshop in East Germany, but the geezer ums and ahs before finally relenting after a bit of hard bargaining (wondering about this crazy Englishman's reputation) and settles on an extortionate price. Will calls Jackie, tells her he's got something for her, she'll love it. Her all surprised, excited when he turns up, this huge box under his arm. Then he turns around and pulls out this small pack of choccies, which he'd just picked up in the 7-Eleven round the corner. 'These are for you,' he grunts, mindful of Darren watching. He keeps the bust for himself.

* * *

Listening to Nick and Darren makes me think about their world. It's all wrapped up in Respect. Just like Charlie told me. The ritual of Respect, you could call it. That's what it was – showing us who's boss. It's a play carried out from the knee-cappings of Northern Ireland to the basement cells of Beirut. Staring at your own short future in someone else's flint-like eyes. No mercy, mate, is the message.

I suppose it's about showing the other guy you're a Somebody. About knowing he'll push a bottle in your face without a second thought. And that you'd do it to him as well. Respect. Not some gang word from the ghettos, but very real, alive, carried by these men, born on ugly, soulless estates and cul-de-sacs.

White, working-class, English-style respect is just your pub/fight culture taken to its logical extreme, says Nick. Respect the toughest geezer in the pub, the one who can hold his own with a pool cue or glass. Not fists, just the meanest cunt there is, as Charlie would say. It's pure animal.

You don't like him, you may not even look up to him – but you fear him. And that counts for a lot in the Movement. As fat Charlie said to me, you don't think before taking on those three gypsy brothers, you just get fucking stuck in, take an ashtray to the side of the head and carry on. It's not a time for rational debate, is it? The question hangs aggressively in the air the way Charlie puts it.

It almost reeks on their breath – this world they live in, where you drink in the violence, drugs and pure maleness like beer. Bit of coke here, bit of blo' there, other dealers persuaded by bricks and bats to move on. Men fighting for a second of belonging, of being somebody in this shifty, lonely, frightening world.

'Here's a guy,' Nick says to me, 'who's been boxing since the age of nine – something his mum made him do, to calm his aggression – and who's spent his childhood from ten up, in solitary confinement from one institution to another. Yet he doesn't drink, hates smoking, goes red when

47

he has to watch a stripper with the lads in the pub on "collection" Sunday, and has this weird, dangerous sense of honour.'

Nick had first heard of him back in 1991: a man with so much hatred inside him, who fills the room with such sheer physical presence that you can't help but be intimidated. The late afternoon sun is beginning to tinge the sky red. We've decamped to the nearby McDonald's and are sitting opposite a 1950s convertible parked inside the restaurant. Elvis stares down at me from a poster on the railing above. 'He's only five-ten [5 ft 10 in. tall], but broad, with powerful arms and chest, and a washboard stomach,' Nick continues.

I know the rest. I've got a copy of his photo with me. He comes complete with dark, brooding furrows stitched on his brow, short brown hair, and a rumbling voice used to guttural outbursts. He's a loner with dozens of followers in tow. A fanatical book reader, but uncomfortable with displays of emotion. It's all cocooned inside the exoskeleton of that huge green bomber jacket.

Back when I'd still been meeting Charlie, there'd been the time when Browning had fallen asleep with the gun in his lap, waiting for the police to kick in the door. Darren said there'd been some sort of tail following them, then a chase, in which they'd lost the other car. It was after the Danish bombs. He'd looked over at his friend Wilf, and was surprised to see how relaxed he was. Knowing the end was coming, The Beast was at peace.

Nick and I talked about their paranoia, though. How they tried to make up for what they lacked in power to change and shape life, through fear and physical force. Perhaps it was us journalists who had the real power, instead? We would listen. Maybe that's why some of them talked to us. And why they feared us, too.

* * *

The flow of people through the McDonald's could be a thousand miles away for all I know or care.

I remember Darren back in the Finborough talking of Will's rather bizarre attitudes. He seems to have accepted them without much problem. Perhaps the price for attaching himself to the cause. 'If we're sitting in the front room and Jacks swears at something, saying, "Oh, for fuck's sake", he'll say to her, "Don't swear, Jacqueline, it makes you sound like a common whore." He really don't like all that. He's a right tart, Will. Don't like no smoking, either.'

'Or football,' Nick adds. Darren goes off to get a round. He comes back, settles the glasses carefully, like a child doing a puzzle, on the table.

'Thanks Darren,' I tell him.

'No worries, you're like a mate now anyway,' he says. 'Plus you're gonna give me copies of this book when you're finished, aintcha?'

'Er . . . yeah,' I say. 'Anyway, I want to know more about Will. Is he quite eloquent?'

'Yeah, more so than most people give him credit for. 'E's more intelligent than Charlie or Steve. Reads a lot. Loads on dietary stuff.' Nick laughs. 'He's obsessed with stuff he's interested in,' Darren continues. 'But he's scatty as well. He'll repeat something he's said to you 30 minutes ago.'

'So, does he relax?'

'Yeah, he's got a weird sense of humour. He'll never come out and tell a dirty joke, but a lot of it revolves around violence, rather than actually doing it. Very dry.' How would Nick describe this, he asks.

'Very puritanical,' is Nick's two-word answer.

Darren jumps back in: 'He'll say he's got nothing against strippers an' that, but if one of these girls sat on his lap when we're on a night out, he'd just say, "Get this slut off of me" and go spare and throw her away.'

Apparently he 'used to get dribbling drunk, shag loads of birds and go down the nightclub' until he was about 19 or 20.

'Really?'

'Oh yeah,' Darren asserts, raising his eyebrows for emphasis. 'He stopped drinking after a concert in Brandenberg, when he made a right fool of himself.'

'Yeah, but I don't understand why he's so puritanical.'

'Maybe it's because he spent so much of his time banged up an' that.'

'Was he abused, then?'

'Nah, nothing like that. Maybe he's just an angry bloke by nature. He's been banged up since 13. Expelled from schools since 10 or 11. He don't talk about it that much.'

'There was that conviction which prevented him joining the Marines,' Nick adds. This was for an assault against a gay man in London. 'That was his lifelong dream, joining up, so this only seemed to fuel his resentment towards everything.'

'What?'

'Society, humanity, the State perhaps.'

'I still don't understand the puritanism.'

'Strange that, I know,' admits Darren. 'Maybe he just doesn't do things by halves? For all his faults, though, he would never do the dirty on Jackie. That would be wrong or disgusting in his book. But he would do other things that most of us wouldn't.'

'He'd do quite well in a Muslim country,' I joke. They both laugh.

'He just doesn't like women in the scene,' Darren says.

Our talk turns briefly to the nature of nationalism. I relate the story of the novel *England Away* by John King, how the British hooligans in it don't want to hang out with German neo-nazis. It puzzles me, these loyalties.

'They're English first,' says Darren, 'and they'll stand for England first. Mind you, if there was a left/right demonstration, then they'd stand with the others against the left.' I think this is an important point that many of the American extremists I'm to meet later don't understand.

I get in more drinks. 'No doubt about that,' Darren continues, returning to the main topic. 'Wilf would do anything for you. He's very honourable.'

'But extreme?'

'Well, most of our lot are extreme. But look at their [Steve Sargent's] lot. They're all weirdos. Cross is just a freak. That's probably why he's in the scene. Charlie – well, you just run out of adjectives for him, dontcha?'

* * *

The night is beginning to draw down. Nick and I are walking back towards Whitechapel. A dozen colours wander past. A hundred languages drift through the cooling night air. High above us, a jet stream burns white across a vivid scarlet backdrop.

I decide not to push my luck. Perhaps another day, another time, The Beast and I will keep an appointment. But not today. He's drawing into himself, I've heard. The death of his friend, Catford Chris, has hit him hard. And the loss of loyalty from his international crew. He's becoming isolated. His life revolves around revenge, a bittersweet obsession with the Sargents. Others are beginning to circle, particularly around the music business. Things could turn violent again. It's time I moved on.

THREE

ACCEPTABLE AND ELECTABLE

OCTOBER 1998

Life seemed to be returning to normal. The phone had slowly stopped ringing. The sweltering, humid city months gave way to an Indian summer. Darren had disappeared and would not resurface until the following year. Much later, he'd end up working as a mole for *Searchlight*. But, for now, he was silent.

The Beast seemed to have disappeared, too. I heard rumours about his plans and the direction of the new C18. There were vague whisperings about a European bomb plot hatched among the continent's various neonazi groups. British names were mentioned. Others from Germany and Scandinavia were also involved. There was talk of a meeting out in the Czech Republic or Slovakia.

The security services seemed to be taking few chances with The Beast. C18 had worked well when its members were poorly known and the hooligan world they inhabited little monitored. Now they'd gained a reputation, and their activities made it hard for them to become invisible again. Many on the left – and now on the right, too – were claiming it was some sort of State or media creation, designed to entrap and entice.

One piece of gossip even suggested that an agent, perhaps from Special Branch, had walked right up to Browning in the street. Apparently he'd grabbed the mobile phone from The Beast's outstretched hand and had deliberately smashed it on the ground. A way of telling him they were still watching.

He couldn't breathe without being followed. Still, it hadn't stopped him from pushing his increasingly one-man revolution. His new magazine, *Strikeforce!* had a cover proclaiming, 'It's This Easy!', next to a picture of the Oklahoma bombing. He claimed to be right no longer, but revolutionary. I sat looking at it on the Tube, engrossed, ignoring the womb-like heat. Did this represent a new, dangerous direction for the extremists? As we pulled into Brixton station – the very heart of black Britain – where I was visiting a friend, I had to fold the magazine away hastily, suddenly aware of the looks I was starting to attract. There would be a link, soon enough, between these two worlds.

The grapevine suggested, too, that Browning was beginning to lose control of the music business. Many of the bands were frightened by his increasingly erratic and violent outbursts. Rival organisations were raising their heads. Blood & Honour in Denmark and Germany; Nordland in Sweden; and the Hammerskin nation, an international network originating in Texas.

I'd heard nothing from Steve. Nick Lowles told me he'd probably retreated to the wilds of Norfolk. If so, he'd be living with his elder brother, Bill, the former British Movement heavy and avid dog fighter. I guess plastering was more on Steve's mind now than Aryan revolution. I hoped he'd taken my advice and got out of his pathetic little movements. He was still taking time, though, to churn out his pamphlets. Of his vaunted National Socialist Movement, I'd heard nothing. It would be a year or so yet before it hit the headlines.

* * *

Nick and I caught up one blustery afternoon at a favoured haunt in north London. I was late, as usual. I saw him at a table in a quiet corner, a mineral water in one hand, a sheaf of documents in another. A pair of glasses rested halfway down his nose. His face was locked in concentration, lending unusual and normally unapparent lines to his youthful features.

'Hi Nick, sorry I'm late. Drink?'

'Nah, not yet.'

We were both steering clear of alcohol. Too many months with the neo-nazis had taken a toll on our waistlines. I settled in opposite him. He seemed more preoccupied than normal. I thought he might be worried about another meeting. Most of our rendezvous ended with him having to rush off to a secret encounter.

A small sigh escaped from his lips. 'I'm going to meet Myatt.'

I looked up. His eyes searched mine for comment. Perhaps the surprise showed on my face. Nick leaned forwards, took a sip from his glass, then laughed nervously.

'Don't worry, I'll be taking some protection. Got my friend coming along. You know, the mountain runner?' His voice dropped, as he glanced at a gang of youths drinking at the bar. A mask settled back over his features, and he turned towards me. 'Says he'll sort them out, if only I'll let him.'

'What? That might not be the best idea, Nick . . .'

'Only joking,' he said, slapping his palms gently on the table. He was referring to a former SAS buddy who often worked as a close protection detail. 'It should be fine,' he added, more slowly. 'It's just an insurance policy, in case the mad monk's carrying anything.'

My interest was piqued. Officially, I'd left the white supremacist world behind. I was working on other stories. But something had lodged inside me and wouldn't let go.

'So, why the sudden interest?' I asked. 'Something new about our friend in the wilds?' We joked about Myatt, but there was something unsettling about the man. Rumours seemed to hang about him like circling vultures.

Through Nick, I'd learned more of his early beginnings: the diplomat father, who'd settled the family in Tanzania, then the Far East, but spent a lifetime yearning to return to Africa (and later died there). The highly intelligent son had spent much of his early life in overseas boarding schools, which contributed to 30 years of wandering and instilled a deep loneliness. The teenage Myatt had joined Colin Jordan's British Movement, then dropped out of Hull University, where he was studying Physics, to form the National Democractic Freedom Movement. It lasted less than a year, but its members were involved in attacks on trade unionists, socialists, and black people. Myatt was sent to prison as a result. Later, after travelling through Africa, he would return and write deep tracts on Western civilisation and National Socialism, which he saw as having religious, philosophical and spiritual dimensions.

Now an invitation from the man himself had arrived on Nick's desk. We discussed whether he should take the chance to meet with him. Nick was pretty sure Myatt would be taking a weapon (it was rumoured he carried an SS dagger with him) and was concerned about his safety.

'You'll meet him somewhere public, though?'

Nick nodded. He didn't look convinced or reassured.

'Here, have a look at these,' he said, handing over the printouts.

'Order of Nine Angles' jumped out at me, halfway down one of the first sheets – the satanic group to which we thought Myatt had belonged (and which he has always denied). Nick told me Myatt was the High Priest of the ONA, something he was obviously keen to conceal from his neo-nazi friends. This belief in Satanism was not linked to simple devil worship, rather derived from the Greek word for 'adversary' – in this case, opposition to the present order.

One section referred to the arduous physical rites of passage, including spending three months living rough in a forest, that were necessary to move up the ranks of initiation. Others described the deep sexual nature of the rites: for example, where a priestess (the Mistress) 'takes the person she has chosen and indulges herself according to her desire' whilst the congregation eat consecrated cakes containing marijuana, then sacrifice an animal. I read this oddly disturbing and fascinating material later that evening, by the light of my bedside lamp.

I checked different sources on the web. It was clear the network stretched to various parts of the globe; at least one contact was in New Zealand. The whole thing triggered memories of a powerful series of interviews I'd conducted, for a special investigation into child sexual abuse. The experts had told me that some abusers would concoct occult rituals to mask their activities. Few would openly acknowledge the ugly reality of their sickness; it had to be something 'greater'.

One section of the papers talked of the means by which a victim could be selected. How they could be given a chance to redeem themselves if they acted 'honourably' in an incident observed by an ONA member. For example, whether they would intervene to save a woman threatened by violence. Of course, it was the ONA member who decided whether you had acted honourably. And it was they who would sometimes set up the incident in the first place. If you 'failed', you were deemed guilty and therefore deserving of the punishment selected for you. It could be a knife in the back, or being pushed in front of a car. It didn't have to look like murder or take place on some sacrificial altar.

Another tract mentioned how it was necessary to infiltrate other organisations, such as fascist groups, in order to rule from within. Then there was the call to cull opponents. Journalists sat near the top of the list. Even the 'official' Church of Satan, in America, shied away from these guys, as was clear on their website.

'He's living with a guy who calls himself "Christos Beest",' Nick said, suppressing a chuckle. 'They're out in Shropshire, on some sort of smallholding.'

That made sense, I thought. It was Myatt, after all, who'd set up the National Socialist Alliance and had drafted the plans for the Aryan Homeland.

Nick thought a few more ONA members were dotted around the country, including a female teacher, but that they numbered less than a dozen. He told me Christos' real name, as well as a disturbing account of one of the rituals a former convert said he'd had to endure. I had to lean in close to hear him over the background chatter. I saw small bags under his eyes, woven with intricate veins, and our tiny square of table felt over-exposed in this bland, crossroads bar. A welter of regional accents bubbled around us. The drifting layer of smoke formed a cloying taste at the back of my throat.

'There's something else, too,' Nick said. He cocked his head slightly. 'There's stuff happening in the BNP. Rumours of a leadership challenge.' The British National Party was the UK's largest far-right political group. I'd yet to encounter it, although many of the C18 people had once been members. They spoke of it in highly derogatory terms.

'John Tyndall's on his way out.' Nick leant back, slowly. He was referring to the party's current leader, an infamous international extremist who'd been on good terms with figures such as William Pierce.

'How do you know that?'

He paused and swirled his drink. 'Oh, I've got my sources,' he replied nonchalantly. I had no idea who these were, or how accurate.

'So why's this of interest to me?' I knew very little, still, about extremist politics. 'It's not quite as – elemental – as the gang, either, is it?' I was wondering how I'd be able to sell an article from this.

'Oh, I think it'll be worth it.'

My attitude would change, slowly, over the next few years, as race riots shook parts of the country. I'd see the ugly heart of ignorance beating all around me: in newspapers, among friends, in enemies, in quiet suburban neighbourhoods, here and abroad. Via my BNP contacts, the white supremacist world and its international connections would soon begin opening up.

It was then that we talked about Nick Griffin, the new face of the BNP.

* * *

Two years after the F111s departed, it was a dangerous time to be in Libya. But the three young British men were not to be deterred.

'Margaret Thatcher is a war criminal,' they stated, 'guilty of aiding and abetting mass murder by her terrorist friend Ronald Reagan.' They wanted support from the regime that had previously shipped arms to the IRA and which they had first approached shortly before WPC Yvonne Fletcher died outside the Libyan Embassy in London, shot by a Libyan agent.

In the end, all they got were 5,000 copies of Colonel Muammar Gaddafi's *Green Book*. But it wasn't the first time they had been in touch with pariah regimes and extremist groups, seeking alliances and support. Only a few years earlier, their leader had spoken warmly of Ayatollah Khomeini's Iran. Through their Libyan contacts, they had already approached Louis Farrakhan's militant Nation of Islam, claiming 'we share a common struggle for the same ends'. Overtures to the PLO were rebuffed, but it was clear these men had a radical, international agenda.

Who were they – members of a splinter Irish Republican movement, or Islamic militants? Not quite. These were the leaders of the National Front, the UK's most infamous far-right organisation. The NF at one time had some 17,000 card-carrying members. When it fell apart in 1989, most disappeared into obscurity.

Except one.

Nine years later, it's a cold, wet autumn day when I see him standing alone by the station. Rain slides over the window and obscures the hills that rear up so suddenly as you cross the English border.

'All right, mate!' he calls out affably, if slightly self-conscious. The wind whips his words quickly away.

He stands partway down the narrow platform, his left arm resting casually against a railing. A crumpled-looking blazer is wrapped about his body – once slim, now with a touch of soft around the midriff – and a tie is teased into the air by the squall. A grey layer of cloud presses down, quilting the small valley town.

'Nightmare journey!' I stutter, seeking to break the ice. I'm nervous. Not as bad as before, but dreams and images have plagued my sleep recently.

He grips my hand in a warm, moist handshake. 'Well, we do like to keep the riff-raff out,' he jokes, snappily.

There's a slightly odd, almost fixed stare as I walk up to him. I notice his boyish haircut, the sort you had when you were ten years old: a black mop, short-back-and-sides. His voice sounds oddly familiar, dropping from thin, sensitive-looking lips.

We clamber over a small walkway, side by side past the old station building. He's chatting easily, directing me to the local pub and telling me something of the history of the tiny Welsh town. He has a smallholding some 20 minutes away. He seems excited, eager to please. To impress, perhaps. I'm one of the first representatives of the mainstream media to come to see him. Within a few years, there will be a flood.

Nick Griffin's manner is, indeed, charming and urbane. After I'd written a letter to him, he'd written back, keen to get in touch (we'd end up emailing each other many times over the coming months). The script was polite, neat, with no hint of anything untoward. I didn't know what to expect. I hadn't met a suit-and-tie fascist before. His dress suggests something of the country squire or gentleman schoolteacher. Boyish features belie his age; he's 40 next month. Clearly well educated, there's little at first to separate him from his image as a pillar of the community. It's a description he likes to use when talking about himself, discussing his relationship with his neighbours, farmers mostly, dotted across the isolated valley. Except for the mention of Jewish influence, violent Islam, and betrayal, I'd hardly notice him among the pensioners and country folk strolling outside.

But then Griffin is a man of many layers, moving and talking on another level entirely to the C18 crew, though his words carry to my ears much the same message. There's a clipped, smug tone to his voice as we settle down to our interview. He starts by telling me: 'We're living in a Second World country. Heading to be a Third World country.'

'Er, just what are you referring to?' I ask, trying to be polite.

'We'd be here all day if I enunciated all of the reasons. But it's not just the immigration issue,' he says, quickly, sensing the shift in my posture, anticipating my next question. 'It's far, far greater than that. If there wasn't a single immigrant in this country, we'd still be in the same position with police corruption, crime, political corruption and people's dissatisfaction with the way things are.'

I know a thing or two already about Griffin. He has a controversial past and, in his own words, he's hoping to create a political earthquake, using journalists like me to pass on his message. It's a key part of the 'new' right strategy. Get the media whipped into hysteria, and they'll do the job for you. They love scare stories. The broadsheets more than most, preaching to their flocks of already-converted.

Griffin's being widely tipped as the next BNP leader. He doesn't seem shy of the fact, either. Ambition positively leaks from him. Staring straight at me with that odd lopsided smile, he states clearly that he wants to put the party, and the extreme right, on the electoral map. I can feel his ego bloom and blossom, watered by my words and interest.

Britain is still one of the few European countries without a sizeable extreme right political movement. Our race problems are slowly building, though. The murder of a black youth, Stephen Lawrence, in south-east London in 1993, revealed the institutional racism of the Metropolitan Police. No one was ever convicted of his killing, in a sloppy, bungled investigation. And violence between white and Asian youths is beginning to spill onto the streets of northern mill towns such as Oldham, near Manchester. But for now, the media ignores most of it – except the tabloids, of course, which are obsessed with 'fake' asylum seekers.

Griffin's smooth, clipped voice brings me back to the present.

'If we managed to produce one MEP [Member of the European Parliament],' he tells me animatedly, 'if you think of the fuss Derek Beackon caused with one tiny council seat on the Isle of Dogs, one MEP would really be something utterly spectacular, an historical earthquake.'

The idea of a single electoral success is something of a Holy Grail, beckoning and dominating their lives. I say it'll never happen. But in some parts of the country, it's already becoming a distinct possibility.

* * *

When I first heard of the BNP, it was as blows were being traded between left- and right-wing gangs in Millwall, south-east London, the area I'd visited to trace The Beast. The violence followed Derek Beackon's electoral success in 1993, when he won a seat to the borough council in Tower Hamlets, one of the most deprived inner-city areas in Europe.

The old East End whites were moving out, replaced – as they saw it – by a new wave of immigrants from the South Asian subcontinent. They felt under threat and, in a prescient warning to the Labour Party, turned not to the Conservatives or Liberal Democrats, but to the racists. As Maggie Thatcher had spotted a decade earlier, the white working class can be the most conservative constituency out there. Although the BNP's success was short-lived, the reverberations were felt throughout the local community. Racist attacks went up some 300 per cent in the three months after the election, according to a local monitoring group.

As the party's self-styled 'director of publicity', Griffin says these days are coming back. He's come out of self-imposed political exile and is talking of 'the electoral road opening up'. He desperately hopes these next European elections will give the party a huge boost and shake off the violent extremist images of the past. They'll be the first to be held under proportional representation, a system that offers smaller parties a greater chance of a seat – one reason Continental Europe has larger Green and neo-nazi movements. Crucial, too, is the funding for TV broadcasts and mailings that comes with these elections. For Griffin, this is key. 'We won't get any seats this time round,' he candidly admits. 'But such a huge throw-out of publicity will inevitably produce a serious crop of recruits.' His eyes are shining.

The BNP has been around since 1982, yet has never managed to break out of the political wilderness. Its uncompromising stance on racism, insistence on forcible repatriation for non-whites, and anti-Semitism, plus its shambolic organisation and the violence of many attracted into its ranks, have kept it to the fringes of British politics.

Matthew Collins, a member of the National Front and undercover mole for *Searchlight*, remembers walking into its 1991 annual rally and being told: 'Welcome to the Nuremberg Rally, Bethnal Green style!' He adds that: 'The bar emptied out onto the floor, and the audience was whipped into a frenzy by chants of "Leader, Leader, Leader!" which turned into foot-stomping in time to "Führer, Führer, Führer!"' He also recalls a vicious attack on a public meeting in Welling Library in 1990, during which a well-known BNP member stamped on a local Labour councillor's face.

As I listen to Griffin's soft, smooth words, I reflect that, to your average member of the public, the BNP's supporter is still more likely this Sieg-Heiling skinhead than the small businessman or graduate Griffin tells me he's now so keen to attract. It's a difficult image problem, given that the party also spawned Combat 18 at the beginning of the decade. I remember how Charlie and the others talked about John Tyndall. Steve had spat something about him 'owning some fucking yacht or other, down in Brighton'.

Later, during another encounter, Griffin admitted that he knew the former C18 leader and that Charlie had threatened him with a knife, somewhere deep in the bowels of London. The fat man had chased him into a McDonald's, he said, and forced him to leap behind the counter, defending himself with a kitchen implement. It sounded comic. Almost.

'The party's not running on all cylinders,' he admits now. He adjusts his tie, presenting an image a world away from those days. It'd be easy to be taken in. He tucks in with gusto as we sit down to a Thai meal. We've moved up the road to a small, secluded hotel. The owner and his Thai wife regard us coolly, suspiciously, seeing my tape recorder sandwiched awkwardly between the crockery and the crisp white tablecloth. 'We need to shake out the dead wood,' adds Griffin between mouthfuls.

'Meaning?'

'Those that are inefficient will be replaced by those that are,' he declares, the words slightly muffled as fat white pieces of rice drop from his lips.

The idea is to shed the East End image and appeal to more respectable elements of the community. For all the charm and persuasion, this is still a notoriously white, working-class, male-oriented party. Attending BNP events and seeing supporters close up – people Griffin calls 'beer patriots' – you can't help but be struck by the sheer number of misfits and weirdos the right seems to attract. Griffin claims its natural support has left the cities and formed 'white flight' areas in the suburbs and rural communities. Similar language to C18. I don't believe him – yet.

'You can't go into a village round here without meeting someone with a Birmingham accent,' he says. Behind us, the verdant valley spills as far as the eye can see. Am I really seeing such hate, here? 'And if you talk to them for five minutes, they make clear they left because of what was happening, in ethnic terms, where they used to live.'

I'm the first to hear one of the main changes: the BNP will publicly drop its policy calling for forcible repatriation of immigrants. It's a clever, even obvious tactic. Although Griffin privately maintains that he still agrees with the line ('I'm sure many of them are clamouring to go back to somewhere where they belong'), he states simply: 'It's a vote loser.'

John Tyndall, the current leader, doesn't think so. It's one of the main policy platforms he introduced. Griffin sits back, undoing the napkin from his shirt, looking pleased with himself. 'It's one of the main obstacles to becoming acceptable and electable,' he adds with a shrug of his shoulders. It's a phrase that stays with me. Griffin's party will use fears over asylum seekers (and this phrase is often interchanged with 'immigrants' or 'Muslims') to garner votes in less affluent, predominantly white areas.

To achieve this end, the ex-NF chairman has been quietly building a power base within the BNP, readying his leadership challenge. Tyndall, though highly respected as an orator and elder statesman of the right, is well into his 60s. Rumours of Griffin's imminent rise are rife in the pubs and working men's clubs frequented by the BNP's supporters.

Under his influence, the party has already begun to look for new voters among Britain's disenchanted communities. He seems particularly keen, at this moment, to dwell on the plight of the farmers and the decline of the rural community. They've been badly affected by the BSE crisis and a huge drop in farming revenues. One of his BNP publications, *The British Countryman*, speaks out against the big bosses supposedly running the National Farmers Union (NFU) and a hostile European agenda. A typical article is headlined: 'The "Silent Majority" Finds Its Voice Again!' and claims, 'Middle Britain is waking up! We're sick of . . . New Labour's attacks on country sports, on farmers, on the green belt, on cottage hospitals and on our children's right to a traditional education.'

Another leaflet, 'Who Is Culling Britain's Farmers?' talks of cuts in support grants, pressure against exports, the BSE crisis, and the power of 'economic and political lobbies which [want] the destruction of the family farm'. The leaflet targets the supermarkets, so-called 'free trade' politicians, the EU and large landowners as responsible, and speaks of the BNP as the 'British Farmers' Party'.

It's pure opportunism, which later fails to bring in new votes. Why on earth would a party that invests so much time and effort in race be relevant to a farming community? No, the BNP power base is still in the cities and those white-flight suburbs. But his language can sound persuasive, even seductive. 'Some farmers,' he says in a soft, insinuating tone, 'are literally suicidal. In part because they can see no hope, and also because there's nothing they can do to regain some self-respect.' He pauses and shifts self-consciously, for effect: 'But we can provide that.'

What's going on? 'They have apparently turned up at livestock markets in the past year,' says the NFU's head of parliamentary affairs, Barney Holbeche. 'I subsequently learned after the event that there was a big group of them at Blackpool football club last year [coinciding with the Labour Party conference]. Had I known it, I would have shown them to the door. Presumably the British National Party think they can somehow take advantage of the undoubtedly dire state of British agriculture at the moment, and people going out of business, and perhaps stoke up some xenophobic resentment towards Brussels – which seems to me to be a pretty cheap way of garnering votes. But that's what they're about. We certainly hold no candle for them in any sense whatsoever.'

It isn't just the farmers Griffin has been targeting. Worried mothers on one estate suddenly found a campaign springing up over the rehousing of paedophiles, led by the BNP. A couple of years later, there'd be riots by white youths in Portsmouth, trying to burn out what they mistakenly thought were abusers in their community.

Such opportunism doesn't seem to bother Griffin. He's also tried to create his own roads protest movement, in a 'Stop The Building' crusade. I stare at the flyers he's sent me announcing this campaign, the evening I get back from our meeting. Cunning. But virtual. Say all, do little.

Most of this, though, is one or two men, bashing away at a word processor or website, late into the winter evenings. It becomes part of a trend that sees the BNP trying to create influence 'circles', for example targeting pensioners and war veterans. Often it's designed to get people like me to write about the party's rapid modernisation.

Another example, the Media Monitoring Unit – to refute accusations that the party is 'Nazi' or 'fascist' (something Griffin admits holds it back) – is basically a one-man operation run by Griffin from his farmhouse. This same naked ambition has led him to court the remnants of the National Front, in order to secure the infamous NF name. Such a move would create a great stir, leading to plenty of media coverage.

Nor are these ideas unique. The model is inspired by the phenomenal success of far-right groups abroad, particularly in Europe. These range from Jean-Marie le Pen's Front National (FN) in France, which also saw a power struggle between the old and new guard, and Jörg Haider's phenomenally successful Freedom Party (FPÖ) in Austria. In the USA, former Ku Klux Klan leader David Duke tried to reinvent himself as a mainstream politician and was nearly elected as Governor of Louisiana in 1991. Duke's supporters are extremely close to Griffin and his cohorts, as I was to learn later. In Australia, chip shop owner Pauline Hanson achieved notoriety with her anti-immigrant One Nation Party. Griffin says they've also been looking at Italy and eastern Germany for inspiration.

In France, the FN has attracted up to 15 per cent of the national vote (this drops when the party later splits). It once held over 2,000 local council seats and polled 4.5 million votes in 1997 elections. One Nation secured 11 seats in Queensland's 89-seat parliament in 1998, taking nearly 23 per cent of the vote. The BNP polled only 25,000 votes in Britain's May 1997 general election, which shows just how far it has to go in order to break out of the wilderness.

* * *

Griffin is relaxed now, confident that he can run rings around me. I'm not a threat. His words pour out liquid-quick, clever, sometimes unwise. He's predicting that their first real council success will come in a couple of years, in an area dominated by Asians, 'where there is a problem with Asian gang violence against white people'. He even claims blacks in east London will vote for the BNP, for much the same reason. A tumble of words and vitriol presage an attack on Islam, hinting that most Muslims are religious fanatics.

To me, his words ring false. But then, I'm not a potential BNP voter.

'Are you trying to ape the FN's success?'

He smirks and sips at his mineral water. 'I wouldn't say ape them. It's a matter of looking at what they've done and looking for parallels. For example, they've got a very effective paramilitary operation in France, which is regarded as completely normal and legal. That level of militancy is not part of the British tradition, so we're not trying to copy it.'

'But is it realistic to hope for their level of success? Surely the right's fractious nature here will always hold it back?'

He admits that until it has one real success, it will have difficulty raising its profile. 'A senior member of the FN told me that the first ten years are like crossing the desert.'

'But the BNP's been around for 17 years!'

He coughs. 'It's a long desert! We can take a few more years yet.'

In fact, when I meet him, Griffin has just returned from an FN-sponsored international fair in France, and talks enthusiastically of One Nation's success and of his hopes of going on a speaking tour to Australia later in the year (which the Australian government refuses). Of One Nation he says: 'They've sprung from nowhere to become a serious political force – and we're not nowhere. We're far in advance of where Hanson and her party were a year ago.'

As Griffin talks, I study him. The one major odd feature is his left eye. It's placid, still, a different colour to his right. Small deposits of crusty goo collect at its edges. It's fake, I realise. He alludes to it later, telling me he lost it 'in an accident in France'. One rumour suggests there was an accident with a gun.

Overall, his manner is friendly, even cultured. But there's an undisguised intellectual arrogance about him. I feel I'm talking to someone who sees himself on a different plane to those around him.

He was born in Barnet, north London, the very same suburb which had spawned the Sargents. His father Edgar was a right-wing Tory councillor, who took his son to his first National Front meeting at the age of 15. Politics was a key part of the family's life. A Young Conservative at the time, Griffin soon became hooked.

'I suppose in a way it's family,' he reflects. His parents 'were both on the right wing of the Conservative Party. They actually met at a Communist Party meeting, which they'd gone to heckle, shortly after the war.' He sniggers.

Talking of his encounter with the NF, he says: 'We all went along, my parents came along, and my sister too. They said, "Oh, that was interesting", and I said, "Well, I'm going to join." There was some concern about it, but that was all. I was allowed to make my own decision, and it carried on from there.'

Studying History and Law at Cambridge University, he became the NF's national student organiser. After university, he rapidly rose through its ranks to become vice-chairman (and briefly chairman), before helping to split the party with an increasingly erratic agenda. In particular, he and his comrades tried to form alliances between the NF and the rabidly anti-Semitic Louis Farrakhan, Libya's Colonel Gaddafi and Iran's Ayatollah Khomeini. The alliance (and Griffin's attempts to sell Gaddafi's *Green Book*) did not go down well with the average NF supporter.

Next, he formed the International Third Position (ITP) with ex-NF colleagues and an Italian fascist named Roberto Fiore. Fiore had belonged to the group linked to the bombing of Bologna train station in 1980, although he himself never took part. The two men became close friends, with Fiore running a successful property agency in London. He's now part of an international network of extremists, heading a fringe fascist party back in Italy. The ITP advocated (and still does) a mix of neo-fascist, back-to-the-land, anti-Semitic and fundamentalist Catholic views. Griffin left it in 1990.

For a few years, he concentrated on raising his four children and working on his smallholding. I learned that his wife, a nurse, had herself been an NF committee member. Griffin resurfaced into extremist politics during 1993 and was admitted into the BNP only a couple of years ago, after papering over a series of clashes with John Tyndall, himself an ex-NF leader. The two men hated each other, Griffin admits. Others say they still do.

His most recent public activity, prior to our meeting, was to receive a suspended prison sentence for racist material produced in his personal magazine, *The Rune*. To some, his response to this case – producing a commercially available tape of his interview with police officers – was further proof of an unbridled arrogance. It didn't help when he was secretly taped by an undercover TV programme, *The Cook Report*, saying that his former Member of Parliament, Alex Carlisle QC, was 'this bloody Jew . . . whose only claim is that his grandparents died in the Holocaust', after Carlisle had reported the magazine to the police.

When I push him about all this, he simply laughs. 'I would have had a much more comfortable lifestyle if I'd gone on to become a lawyer!' He cites what he calls his defence of free speech as an example of his commitment to his politics: 'I believe in the things I say and write. It's a matter of personal pride and dignity. I talk about real problems in real areas, rather than use airy fairy terms.'

He likes to see himself as a family man. Stubborn (seeking to explain his attraction for the political extremes), yet someone who enjoys working on the land and is heavily involved in local campaigning issues, such as keeping the local school open. He believes his neighbours view him as a decent, righteous person. For a moment he sounds almost normal: 'Like any young family, we stagger from crisis to crisis.' Then he claims, 'I even have some things in common with liberal journalists!' His tongue seems to recoil over the phrase.

But weren't you the same man, I ask, who wrote of the need to create a strong, disciplined force, with the ability to back itself 'with well-directed boots and fists'? Didn't you advocate creating a European martial arts federation to train the right's street soldiers and, as the bricks and broken bottles were being traded on Millwall's streets some five years ago, said that 'when the crunch comes, power is the product of force and will, not rational debate'?

But I begin to see that Griffin is nothing if not a political animal – a man for whom inconvenient history does not stand in the way of personal ambition.

'My past was an experience, primarily,' he tells me, unfazed, settling comfortably opposite. He's smiling, though with little warmth. 'There were some ideologically crazy periods, but I hope I've learned from my mistakes.'

'Such as?'

He shifts slightly. 'Allowing my youthful enthusiasm for perfect ideas to run far beyond what's politically possible. That's the main one.' The tone is smug, final.

There's an almost schizophrenic character to Griffin and others on the extreme right. You talk to one man on the surface, yet view another beneath. For example, one of Griffin's closest allies in the BNP, Tony Lecomber, tried to bomb the London headquarters of the Workers Revolutionary Party in 1985, and has a conviction for attacking a Jewish schoolteacher on the Underground. When I finally see him, I'm surprised. He's a nerdy, slight figure with glasses, who holds respect within the party because of his more 'physical' past. Griffin himself has struck up a relationship with William Pierce, arguably the world's most infamous neo-nazi.

'Pierce is clearly an exceptional mind,' Griffin tells me.

'What about his reputation, though?'

'He isn't a terrorist,' he replies. 'He wrote *The Turner Diaries* as a piece of fiction, about what would happen against the Weathermen. And for that he's been hounded, which is ridiculous.'

'So he didn't inspire anyone?'

'No. Well, if he did inspire them, he didn't mean to inspire them.' On a journey to the US years later, I'd read tracts written by Griffin in Pierce's newsletter, and Griffin's men would try to take me to see the old man himself.

In 1997 Griffin also wrote *Who Are the Mindbenders?* about Jewish figures dominating the media. It's part of a personal obsession. He is associated with a loose collection of individuals and international extremists belonging to the Holocaust revisionist movement. This jars with the cloak of respectability he's tried to don. Many revisionists are in reality Holocaust deniers. I met quite a few on my travels – Brits, Canadians, Belgians, Swedes, Germans, Americans – often introduced to me by Griffin's network. They may tell you that a few hundred thousand Jews, at most, died during the war – and often only of disease and malnutrition. After that, they'll probably go on about Allied treatment of the Germans and Stalin's purges. Griffin himself bangs on to me about the bombing of Dresden. It's reminiscent of the controversial historian David Irving, whom Griffin and many of his supporters admire. 'Certainly, not so many died,' Griffin utters confidently, when I ask him again about the scale of the Holocaust.

I know, too, that Griffin boasted to the undercover *Cook Report* that he had updated Richard Verrall's controversial book on the Holocaust, *Did Six Million Really Die?* and that he has regularly written in BNP publications that dropping anti-Semitism from their policy is 'the kiss of death'. Yet he denies being anti-Semitic.

I didn't know then just how close his association had been with the whole revisionist movement. I accepted his description that he was (a classic extreme right refrain) 'anti-Zionist'. The forces of extremism seek to link their hatred to the very real problems in the Middle East. I've lived and travelled in Israel, as well as parts of the Arab world. Yet I don't develop a personal obsession with Jewish identity the way the Holocaust crowd do. Even if that community did exercise any power, I can't quite see why it's such a burning issue for the strange, introverted individuals I keep meeting. What reality, if any, does this exercise on the estates and projects of Britain and North America?

I decide to go direct.

'Do you believe in a Jewish conspiracy, as so many on the right argue?' I know I'm being inflammatory, seeking to invoke some rabid outburst, and I'm surprised how easily he brushes it off.

'It's cowardly to pretend it doesn't exist,' he says, arguing that there is a powerful 'lobby'. He agrees that it is 'something beyond the ordinary experience and interest of most people'. More importantly for him now, though – speaking to the media – is that 'it has no place in electioneering'.

A chill draught blows around my legs, raising a creeping tide of goose bumps. I shiver and pull my jacket around me, as Griffin drones on about the world of conspiracy that surrounds him.

He's talking now about the British Board of Deputies and how he claims they've pressured people not to reveal that the NF had Jewish members. He's still speaking low, swift, darting to and fro amongst my points, gliding through and ignoring the more difficult areas of my questions. He mentions that Gerald Kaufman, a prominent Jewish Labour MP, calls the Board of Deputies a 'lobby not self-representative of Jews'.

'They wanted to be able to portray to ordinary Jews that it's [the NF] hostile to them, that it's going to pack them all into the gas chambers,' says Griffin. 'Therefore keep on voting as you are, keep on supporting us, give us your money.' He's hardly paused for breath. For the first time, I see some colour settling into his blanched, rounded cheeks. 'Clearly, Jews are very talented people.' That cold, glinting eye stares straight at me. I watch the white mucus collect at its corners. I wonder if he changes it regularly. 'But when they see non-Jews wanting to preserve their people, they interpret it as a threat.'

The mask of respectability is starting to slip. I don't even need to prompt him now. He starts to liken all this to a gay power bloc in the media, my world. 'They watch each other's backs, and when there's a conflict of interest, they will go for one of theirs,' he says, his voice a high-pitched whine, buzzing in my ears, irritating now.

In common with many on the far right, he seems obsessed with homosexuality. I can't understand why. I have gay landlords, gay friends, have drunk in gay bars – all without any problems. No one has 'converted' me against my will. Later, after many encounters with the extremists, I begin to wonder why it's gay *men* they have such a problem with. 'It has no place in electioneering,' Griffin adds, maintaining that he would remove their pension rights. 'But at the same time, to close your eyes to it is ludicrous, cowardly.'

* * *

Because, as Griffin tells me, a lot of these opinions are 'vote losers', helping to keep nationalism in a ghetto, they won't be presented to the British public come election time. But that doesn't stop him speaking at length to me about how Islam is a 'violent religion' and how Asians are pursuing gang violence and ethnic cleansing against whites – until I point out that he has associated himself with figures such as Louis Farrakhan in the past.

Then there's the almost inevitable right-wing paranoia about global conspiracy, about how global capitalism is The Enemy: 'There are groups which control what goes on – there's the government, the agro-chemical industries, there's the big landowners who control the NFU, and the European Union.' It's disturbing, familiar language. I've heard it before, from friends and in meetings I've attended in the Green and direct action movements. There will be times when the decentralised structure of these communities allows both far right and far left to infiltrate. According to Griffin, his tactics have already seen an exponential growth in membership (although he won't show me the figures).

'But by targeting these disaffected groups, aren't you just being all things to all men? Manipulating people's very real fears and worries as a cloak for respectable fascism?'

'Absolutely not,' he states, steepling his fingers, adopting the manner of an adult lecturing a child. 'We're just articulating things and offering them a political choice, to be active against a monolithic bloc which gives them no choice except economic suicide. We're offering people hope where they have none.'

'So there's no racial violence trailing in the BNP's wake? It doesn't whip up racial tension?'

'No,' he says. 'It just so happens that those tensions already exist – it's natural when you get different groups of people living together. Every time a multiracial society has been tried in history, it's ended in horrible bloodshed. All we're doing is trying to motivate people in a political direction.'

I'm starting to know what to expect. In Griffin's view, society is already at 'breaking point'. All the BNP is doing is recognising this 'fact', and trying to look after the interest of its 'own' group.

To me it's sad, unappealing language. Unless you're living without hope on some estate somewhere, in an area where different communities rarely mix. Where the council has for years overspent its budget on ill-conceived schemes and pushed a liberal agenda, whilst ignoring very real, ground-level problems such as housing, job creation, and poverty. When riots strike towns in northern England a few years later, it transpires that young whites and young Asians have very little understanding of or interaction with each other. I see the same thing for myself, mixing with the grim, violent East End BNP/C18 mob, as they fight a 'rearguard' action against recently arrived Asians.

'Young white kids have no pride in themselves,' Griffin goes on to say. 'They are constantly being done down, and see members of ethnic communities boosted up. When that goes on, I understand why white youngsters become, in crude terms, race haters.'

'Hang on,' I cut in. 'Wasn't the far right active for some time in Eltham, [the area in south-east London where Stephen Lawrence was murdered]? Doesn't the BNP bear any responsibility for that?'

The persuasive, seductive language, which sounded so reasonable a minute ago, starts to unravel. 'No,' he says calmly, unmoved. 'It just shows that multiracial societies don't work.'

To my ears, it's a stunning, callous denial. Over the years, as we encountered each other, I learned it was a classic Griffin trait. Simply deny what doesn't suit. 'Most people I talk to are sick of hearing about Stephen Lawrence.' A smirk flits across his thin mouth, flickering before he turns back to me and calls the coverage the murder received an 'outrageous distortion'. His features are quite calm, as if he's said the most natural thing in the world.

Then his face twists, as he suggests that Lawrence may even have been carrying a knife when he was attacked, and (countering my protest) that the media fails to take note of much worse Asian gang violence against whites. 'And the media don't allow that, do they?' His tone is aggressive now. This leads him into an animated spiel about Asians deliberately pursuing a high birth policy, which he calls an attempt at ethnic cleansing.

Why don't I think like this? I'm well-educated, got a degree, have travelled widely. What's the difference between us? To him, even with the Cambridge degree, life seems quite literally black and white. At the moment, I wonder if even he fully believes this stuff. Then, I think, this is a man who's been in this movement since his mid-teens. Who's never had another job or career. Married a woman who was inside it all, too. And it's not as if he came from the same background as Charlie and Steve. Yet this cancer is ingrained. In some ways, I can better understand the world of the estates and hooligans than I can this hollow man before me.

He keeps talking of 'our people', as though there were some static, inherent nation. 'Race is more important than the transient nation. But you cannot talk to people about the moral threat to the survival of their race – which is a fact – because it's beyond their ken. You have to take human nature as it is,' he quips, quickly, 'so you have to address everyday issues.'

He speaks with little charisma. Griffin is not a natural orator or rabble-rouser. His attempts to be jocular seem forced, his tone too snide, his voice too high. Which is why I'm surprised so many want to follow him. There's no presence about the man, no gravitas or depth. In fact, it's more than that. I just don't like him. I feel I'm viewing a hymn sheet with no words. There's little about him that leaves me convinced. But I know I'm not part of the target audience. Trapped on some sink estate, forgotten about by New Labour and the Tories, I might find this sort of stuff enticing.

Right now, the future seems pretty uncertain for Griffin and his buddies. 'You only have their word that they're growing,' says Nick Lowles, back in London. 'They may be growing in South Wales, where Griffin is based, but in other traditional areas, such as London, they're actually shrinking. In fact, there were only 300 people at their annual rally last November. The whole problem for the BNP is race. By its own admission it supports racial nationalism. It can bang on all it likes about the woes of the farmers, or small businesses, but racism is what makes it different, what distinguishes it from the likes of the UK Independence Party.'

With the official interview finished, we walk back through the centre of Welshpool, ending up in a small, traditional-looking bar. Relaxing, pint in hand, Griffin seems less self-assured, less confident about the future. 'I've been more or less at the top before and believe me, it's a lonely place,' he confides.

Yet as quickly as he's said it, he scrambles to reassert the earlier bravado: 'The BNP is going to win Euro seats, and you'll see BNP councillors established in local areas within five years. We've got potential mass support in every part of the country.' He adopts a prophetic air: 'Look, there are simply patent racial differences which go beyond skin colour.' He sighs, melodramatically. 'All the BNP is doing is looking out to sea, looking at the weather and saying there's a hurricane coming. But the media say we're creating the hurricane, which is nonsense.'

FOUR

THIRTEEN DAYS

17 APRIL 1999, SOUTH LONDON

Tomorrow I travel to a war.

It'll be my first time in the Balkans since 1993. Meeting men turned slowly mad, trapped in small towns, defending schools and mosques with ancient rifles against artillery and tanks. Walking through the fragile rubble of villages, hugging thin central highways, few faces greet you. Just the perfectly patterned splatter of tank shells, marked on the side of each house.

I can recall the ugly, tight twists of shrapnel lingering beneath the bullet holes. As you draw in near a refugee camp, small boys run up to you, offering mortar and artillery shells, tripwire and mines as souvenirs. I wish some of my fascist and neo-nazi buddies could see these delicate-looking gifts, before they go out on the hustings preaching separatism, or petrol bomb an Asian councillor's house. It's not as if we don't know where this ends up. Even here. Just look at Northern Ireland.

I'm not the only one going down to the war. Apart from scores of wannabe writers and photographers, several of the extremists end up travelling to the conflict, too. The true nuts, from a host of European countries. Many have already been out there during the Bosnian war or the Serbo-Croat hostilities that preceded it. They sign up for either the Croats (if they're Catholic) or the Serbs (if they're Protestant). Some C18ers have had contacts with the White Eagles, a Serb paramilitary group which is linked to Blood and Honour.

In a strange way, perhaps this is a dry run for the Asian lads who take their fight out to Afghanistan two years later (indeed, some have already fought for the Bosnian Muslims). The call of Al-Qaeda and the Taliban seems to be a potent elixir in the faceless suburbs of this country and others. Is it the same call of those edge cities that draws the neo-nazis?

We live in a time when individual identity can be swamped. A time of aggressive individualism, when community is a bad word, and the freedom you have is that of the consumer. No wonder many living in the old Soviet states wish to return to the certainty of their former lives. Rapacious capitalism has done much to destroy their beguilement with the West. Many of us are prepared to forgo certain ideas of freedom if it means stability.

But down there in the war, you see it for what it is. Life is more *black and white*, the way the extremists like it. The stumbling, stinking lines of refugees, living in their own filth, are the legacy of warlords like the infamous Serb paramilitary leader Arkan – the kind of guy Charlie and his pals would admire. Dozens of Kosovan refugees would tell me about evictions and attacks led by such paramilitaries, pumped up on booze and drugs, looting and raping. Egging each other on as they step into the blocks of Soviet-era flats. Family men who refuse to see families as they kick in the doors.

Even if you're only an observer, this experience leaves you changed. You can't communicate to the folks back home the indelible stain, even excitement, that it leaves imprinted on your soul.

* * *

Something crashes into my shoulder. A young black face glares at me. I'm shoved sideways into the road, stumbling, blinking and amazed. The figure strides on, angry, purposeful, leaping the barrier that fences off the dark tarmac. His taut, muscular back runs across the road and down past the Tube station entrance.

Clapham Common. I'd forgotten how close we are to Brixton, to all the junkies, crackheads, prostitutes, beggars and religious nuts. I'm on my way to see a close friend, a last bit of normality before I leave tomorrow, when the military transport will dip down towards Tirana, dropping steeply towards the city's twinkling coal-fired lights, banking to avoid the missiles that could come flashing up at any time. From there we'll take a helicopter, then the long twisting drive up into the foothills and mountains, past the ruined Soviet-era factories, bribing the different mafia clans, and on towards that much-photographed border.

My friend's lived in Brixton for the past few years, drawn to the vibrancy of the place. I remember first going there, during an evening out at one of London's biggest gay nightclubs. I'd wandered, amazed, watching the pills being quaffed, meeting members of the protest/rave community at a Celtic dub night. It was my first real introduction to a subculture.

I think my friend was also woefully ignorant about the true face of the area. Not the bars and restaurants, but the crime and mental illness, the drug use and poverty. Houses might be trading for £300,000, but it's still an area where some of Europe's poorest citizens live.

It's also the spiritual heart of black Britain, home to many original West Indian émigrés. They started arriving on ships such as the *Windrush* after the Second World War, encouraged by the government of the day. Listen to people like Nick Griffin, and Brixton and the *Windrush* often crop up in

70

their conversation. Blacks now make up only about half the area's population, but the influx of different nationalities continues. I'm told you can hear over 100 languages being spoken there. The black and white communities tolerate each other, rub shoulders in the shops and markets, yet barely mix. Massive race riots tore the place apart in 1981. Everyone's desperate to make sure it doesn't happen again.

* * *

The slight-looking figure had been standing there, stick-like, hands thrust deep into the pockets of a blue jacket. A baseball cap hid his features. The twitch of a tiny dreamy smile played above a pale, almost smooth chin.

He appeared to be staring up Clapham Park Avenue. Perhaps following in his mind's eye the journey down through Acre Lane – past the small grocery stores, the Caribbean bakery, minicab firms, takeaways, timber yard, and on past The Hope and Anchor, then the newly built supermarket – his surprise a small grunt, on seeing how many white faces pass him.

Down into Brixton. Straight into the heart of hell he's just created.

A crack of thunder peals overhead. I have to pull the hood of my sweatshirt up quickly, as the rain starts to piss down. It soon works itself into a sweat-drenched lather, lashing the hapless Saturday shoppers. I've got to walk the 20 minutes from Clapham yet. Brixton station is closed off. No explanation why. Must be the bloody engineering works again. The foul, tepid air of the Tube is expelled in a constant whoosh, tugging at my clothes, as I struggle past the crowd.

At the corner of the Common, I angle through the 'sheep'. That's a word he would use to describe them. They don't know what he's done. Yet. But they will.

* * *

'You can't go any further, son.' The cop's stern tone might have sounded patronising. Not today, though. His dark-sleeved arm is a firm but gentle barrier. A look of anxiety, perhaps even panic, struggles to surface beneath his professionally set features. 'What . . . ?' I start to ask, but I'm pushed away, others surging around and past me. The policeman is overwhelmed for a moment by the sudden flow, before two colleagues join him in pushing back the crowd.

I double back, behind Lambeth Town Hall and out onto Brixton Hill. I squint, screwing up my eyes to peer through the sheet of rain, willing the scene to focus. I hear sirens, and dark rumbling thunder overhead. It sounds horribly close. The rain drums down hard.

I start walking towards the Tube.

There's a hum, a sort of energy. People are walking up and down Acre

Lane, and even here on the Hill, chattering, pointing, looking. The town hall clock tower chimes out. No one even seems to notice.

A helicopter suddenly buzzes overhead, its angry whine left ringing in my ears after it's passed. Christ, it's flying low. Water hits my open eyes. There's another – I can hear, rather than see, the approaching rotors – coming from the direction of the prison. What's going on?

'. . . omb . . .' I catch a half-heard snatch of phrase, spoken by a deep Caribbean voice. A group of black youths are running past. It's repeated, then taken up, travelling between the shocked, blanched faces of those stumbling about me.

Slowly, I make my way back towards Brixton Road, trying to work out what's happening. I wonder if my friend's come out yet. Was she shopping at the time? Have the IRA targeted Brixton for some reason? For the life of me I can't think why. There's no significant military target. All Brixton's famous for is its black population . . .

A siren shrieks past. A riot van full of cops screeches around the corner, powering towards the police station. Near the crossroads, marked now by a thin stretch of red-and-white tape and a cordon of police bikes, the usual Saturday crowds are absent. To my right, the neon light of the recently renovated Ritzy cinema glows comfortingly.

My gaze is drawn downwards by a sharp crunch beneath my heel. Glass litters the street. Shrapnel of various kinds glints softly. Metal, and something else: red, shredded, torn. Near me, someone's crying. Someone else wipes a thin trail of stale vomit from his ashen face and clothes.

A finger lies in the road.

* * *

The TV crackles silently in one corner of the room. On the screen, I see flames licking under the hood of a car, tightly parked in a narrow street. Black smoke curls upwards, drifting past the Victorian buildings. A couple of brown-faced figures run past. Overhead, here in Albania, the sound of helicopters and jets bounces over the city above me.

I remember her face, crying, on that day. They'd only just got her sister into the Tube. The 7-Eleven next door was crowded. People jostling and shoving, muttering obscenities, desperate to buy their papers, drinks, and candy. The usual Brixton crowd; the usual high level of tension.

Then it happened.

An enormous bang, a crash followed by the telltale 'crump' and shockwave. For one small second, she stopped. They all did. But as she later told me, she knew instantly it was a bomb. 'Judy!' she shrieked, hands flying to her mouth, tears already starting to course down her face. 'No!' She turned to her partner, mouth open, her legs beginning to move her away from the counter.

A wave of dust and glass billowed over the street. There was a moment of silence. The teller smiled at her nervously. Then she rushed outside, ignoring the cries of alarm from behind her, thinking the Tube had been targeted. Where her sister had just gone.

'Get out of here, get the fuck out of here!' A plain-clothes cop, stomach rippling out over a flapping shirt, waved his hands furiously at the shocked pedestrians. 'Move! It's a bomb!' screamed another, water streaming over his head and down onto the glinting badge. She was pushed backwards, but could see the station was still untouched. Fifty yards down the road, though, was another story. Wounded shapes, some missing limbs, others with nails sticking from eyes, fingers and other parts of their bodies, writhed in agony on the ground. Bone protruded from flesh. Nearby, someone stared silently down at his foot. It pointed backwards.

Then the screams started.

Run. That's all she remembers now. A blur. I must have turned up 20 minutes, maybe half an hour later. We missed each other. It wasn't until I returned from the war that we met up again.

Thirty-nine men, women, and children injured. Lives torn apart by a vicious, crude nailbomb, stuck in a holdall, next to an Iceland supermarket. Every year, I'd go back and stare at the small plaque that was later put up to commemorate it, a half-noticed reminder of some sick fantasist's dream.

And now this. A week later, another device, this time in the heart of London's Asian community, Brick Lane. Odd to think how I've ended up in one war, and seem to be watching another back home. Thirteen days of terror. No one knowing where and when the next attack will come.

The TV anchorman is saying that a group calling itself the White Wolves has claimed responsibility. I've never heard of them, but then it could be a C18 cover (I later hear they've claimed it, too). I bet there'll be raids going on all over the country now. If it is a racially inspired campaign, it'll be the first in Britain. The people of Brick Lane are lucky, though. The boot of the car has contained much of the blast (it's a nailbomb, like the Brixton device). Only six people are injured.

I'd talked to Nick from my mobile as I sat at the airport waiting for my flight out. 'What do you think? Could it be them?' I asked. I was half-joking. Perhaps there'd be some other explanation. Animal-rights extremists, fringe Republicans. 'Dunno yet, too early to say. Might be, though. Good luck,' he added, wishing me a safe journey.

The more I thought about it, even from that first day, the more worried I became that this was linked to people I knew. Had someone from The Beast's crew finally committed to practice what they so often preached? Maybe we'd been following the wrong people all along – could William Pierce's cold influence have reached across the Atlantic, helping to ignite the first round of a race war?

Six days later, and the Admiral Duncan pub in Soho – London's gay heartland – dissolves in a flash of light, powder, sulphur and nails. Three people are killed, including a pregnant woman, and a further sixty-five injured, including a friend of my landlord. I watch, silently, on CNN, as beer trickles down my throat. Only this morning I've seen an entire town crossing over the border from Kosovo.

I used to use that pub as a meeting point with other journalists. What the hell's going on?

* * *

'Yeah, they're all down to me. I did them all.'

The 22-year-old spoke the words openly, without surprise, to the two plain-clothes detectives sometime after midnight. Most people had already gone to bed. Cove, a small suburb of the prosperous commuter town of Farnborough, Hampshire, was quiet.

David Copeland stood, bare-chested, dressed only in tracksuit trousers. Although he was short, the Flying Squad officers could tell that he worked out. Most surprising was his openness. He didn't seem surprised to see them at all. Behind him, a large Nazi flag was pinned to the wall of the bedsit. A loaded crossbow sat on the bedside table. Unknown to them, explosives and fireworks were wedged in the bottom of his cupboard, tucked into the corner of the tiny room.

'It's him!' the cop exclaimed, looking from the photofit image back to Copeland's face. 'It's him, the bomber.'

* * *

When I got back from Albania, the rumour mill was already rife. No one seemed interested in the foreign conflict anymore. Everyone had a pet theory about the man they were calling 'The London Nailbomber'.

The tabloids were busy speculating about neo-nazi gangs and terrorist networks. People I'd never heard of were suddenly being quoted as experts. The so-called White Wolves and other (fictitious) organisations were also doling out warnings and claiming responsibility. Some thought it was the work of a mad loner, like the random killings seen more commonly in the US.

Copeland's admission of guilt seemed to suit the Metropolitan Police quite well. 'There is no suggestion at this stage that the arrest is linked in any way to the extreme right-wing groups that have claimed responsibility for these attacks on innocent people,' Assistant Commissioner David Veness said. 'There appears to be no trigger event or specific date that sparked these attacks, which were clearly the responsibility of the same person. The man is not a member of any group that made claims of responsibility for the bombings, nor did he make any of the claims using their name. It is understood he was working alone, for his own motives.'

And that's what most journalists printed.

That summer, riots overtook the heart of the city. Anti-capitalist protesters stormed into the Square Mile on 18 June, launching a day of action based on the protests which had recently taken place in Seattle. Other demonstrations shook capitals around the world, in a loosely coordinated but amazing movement.

I watched, entranced. What had happened to the dedicated but fluffy Green movement I had come to know well? Even down on the road protest camps I had visited, I'd rarely seen stuff like this.

The City of London police were taken completely by surprise. Offices were stormed (including an attempt on the Stock Exchange), a luxury car dealership smashed, and taunts thrown by City workers, waving their wads of cash at the assembled crowds. The police panicked, batoning those around them and running over a woman.

This new movement had no hierarchy as such. It seemed to have been born from the frustration of the roads protest movement – which I knew well – but the resultant alliance was not something I'd encountered before. I was shocked, elated and worried all at once. Different websites and email lists had helped coordinate the action on the day. The tabloids, even the broadsheets, went into overdrive, desperate to prove some form of 'secret' leadership behind the whole thing. Even in the fascist networks I heard whisperings of admiration for what had been achieved. Striking right at the heart of global capitalism. The Enemy.

I signed up to different lists, left, right and anti-capitalist. My inbox overflowed with congratulatory messages about the day of action. Suddenly, the whole left/Green situation was energised. One list carried messages of particular admiration. It seemed interesting; there were links on it to pro-life, vegetarian and animal-rights movements. The group behind it controlled charities in England, owned property in northern France and a village in Spain, and ran training camps in eastern Europe. It was called Final Conflict, based on a magazine of the same name.

I looked closer. The parent organisation was the International Third Position – Nick Griffin's old group.

I sent them an email.

* * *

Much of what I now know about David Copeland came from my conversations with Nick Lowles. Nick was determined to discover who the bomber *really* was (you can read his excellent account in the book *Mr Evil*, co-authored with Graeme McLagan). So I knew a lot about him even before the trial proceedings began the following year.

Copeland was the first 'lone wolf' I encountered in my journeys. A baby-faced, boy-next-door killer, inspired by the twisted rhetoric of the extremists around him. A man who destroyed, yet was merely a pawn in a greater game. There was nothing, outwardly, to mark him. Small, nondescript, average. Invisible. No tattoos or street-fighting background. He would have stood, unnoticed, at the back of the BNP meetings he once attended. An underachieving loner. How many more like him are out there?

You could argue that he was already mentally ill. Indeed, his trial later centred on whether he was 'mad or bad'. He's now held under indefinite detention at Broadmoor Psychiatric Hospital. But without the template of the extremists he encountered, perhaps his path would have been different. From Pierce to Griffin, the extremists provide the oxygen that ignites the torments within the Copelands of this world. And I feel the pain they cause more deeply, because it was my friends that this sad, inadequate little fucker tried to kill. And he didn't even know what it meant.

That 'race warriors' and Aryan heroes often turn out to be such pathetic losers, mentally ill and unstable, is hardly a glowing testament to the cause. But try convincing the extremists that their 'holy' warriors are simply mad. They even have a phrase for them, coined from the Identity fringe. It's called the 'Phineas Priesthood', based on an Old Testament hero, Phineas, who slays a fellow Israelite for sleeping with a foreign woman, by thrusting a spear through both of them. By doing so, Phineas turned away God's wrath from the nation of Israel. And by the nation of Israel, they are referring to the 'white' nation, not the Jews, whom they consider deceivers. For the political fundamentalists, however, the excuse of madness is a convenient cloak for their activities. They can't police the Copelands of this world, they argue.

Sick or not, Copeland was following a stated aim of many neo-nazi wannabes: to ignite a race war. It was the same thing Charlie Sargent had written about. The fact that Copeland didn't know there were white people living in Brixton – which he claimed in his police statements – even though he lived just an hour away, reveals how naive many of the racists can be. With Copeland these ideas, put forward by a network spanning continents, had come home to roost.

In the end, it was ironic. This young man had put into deeds what all those C18 guys had failed, despite all their posturing, to achieve. Even people like The Beast. Under the ice-white glare of publicity and state attention, C18 shrank back into the shadows. People were falling backwards to dissociate themselves from the movement. In fact, few of them had even heard of the guy. He hadn't been seen in their boozers or out on the terraces. The NSM – a group to which Copeland belonged, after leaving the BNP – fell apart even faster. Myatt would disappear back into his woods, resurfacing as a Muslim called Abdul Aziz. I received an email from him, threatening me with a duel to the death the following year, after publishing allegations about his Satanism. In a reply to my query whether this was *really* necessary between two civilised gentlemen, he wrote: 'However convincing "evidence" may seem, it does not prove anything in the final analysis . . . In respect of involvement in and adherence to Satanism, my own conscience is clear and God is my witness. I do not have to prove anything in respect of these decades old allegations and rumours.' Steve was back-pedalling at the same time, putting out a hurried statement claiming NSM leader (and former ITP member) Tony Williams had hit the bottle, then suffered a nervous breakdown.

So much for the Aryan revolution.

But what drove Copeland?

* * *

As Copeland's story unfolded, with Nick digging deep into his background, my journey took another strange twist into the past.

I'd recently written an article about hate on the Net, for *The Guardian*, in which I mentioned a US organisation known as the World Church of the Creator, whose network seemed to be entirely 'virtual'. Their site advertised the *White Man's Bible* and even a women's group. But they weren't a church as such. In fact, they were overtly hostile to Christianity, being distinctly neo-nazi in their leanings. A poor man's rival to William Pierce's National Alliance, if you like.

When you signed up to the Church, you became a 'Brother', reporting to the 'Pontifex Maximus', a nerdy individual named Matt Hale, an Illinois law graduate in his mid-20s. The group's original founder, a notorious supremacist named Ben Klassen (who'd committed suicide several years earlier) believed that your race was your 'nation'. It was that simple. And it drew hundreds of responses via the Net.

Later, I'd encounter these same white supremacists on their home territory. Hale in his own house, too. For now, though, they seemed to be another set of closet weirdos, locked in their sad tirade against the powers of ZOG, protected as ever by the Constitutional right to freedom of speech. Harmless.

Except that the Church's chief lieutenant suddenly went on a two-day killing spree across Illinois that summer, leaving two dead and nearly a dozen wounded over the Fourth of July weekend, before killing himself. Like his close friend Matt Hale, he was a criminology student and had attended one of the top private schools in the state. He had an exemplary, privileged background. More people would have been killed, had he not been such a bad shot.

This was something of a coincidence: just after Copeland, another set of random neo-nazi murders. This time, as I found out, there was a much stronger connection between the killer and the leader of a white-supremacist organisation.

It wasn't the first such example, either. Timothy McVeigh and his co-conspirators had earned notoriety and, among some, a cult status for the terrible bombing of Oklahoma City in 1995. McVeigh had close links with the militia movement (and some ties to an Identity group called Elohim City), plus a copy of Pierce's *The Turner Diaries* on him when he was arrested. The bombing was almost identical to a plot described in that book, written in 1978 under the pseudonym Andrew Macdonald and considered by many in the white nationalist movement to be the modern-day equivalent of *Mein Kampf.*

In it, the fictional Earl Turner leads an underground army, The Organization, that initiates a race war during the 1990s against a Jewish-controlled government (ZOG, of course). The secret leadership of this army, known as The Order, oversees a truck bombing against the FBI headquarters and a mortar attack on the Capitol building. The Organization splits into small cells, with the whites eventually winning, murdering Jews and minority groups, taking over Southern California and nuking Tel Aviv. Although not particularly well written, it's been translated into several European languages and has sold over 200,000 copies worldwide.

One group inspired by its message of violence was White Aryan Resistance (VAM), in Sweden. In 1991, four VAM members raided a Stockholm police station, stealing 36 Sig-Sauer automatic handguns, while other activists raided military dumps in search of explosives. The group's leader was Klaus Lund, who'd been sentenced for the killing of an anti-racist activist in 1986 and also helped carry out a bank robbery in 1991.

Such was Pierce's myth and pulling power that even the BNP – supposedly a party now embarked on mainstream politics, according to Nick Griffin – had invited him to speak at its annual rally in 1995. One day, John Tyndall himself would tell me about his meetings with William Pierce.

Another figure of infamy and myth is Eric Rudolph. He's on the FBI's most-wanted list, being suspected of the Atlanta Olympic bombings in 1996 as well as anti-abortion extremism, including murder. He was another loner, another follower of Christian Identity. Both figures featured prominently in David Copeland's thoughts, as he read *The Turner Diaries* and plotted his campaign of destruction from his bedsit.

Then, at the beginning of August, a burly former Aryan Nations security guard goes on a shooting rampage in Los Angeles, spraying a Jewish community centre with more than 70 bullets from his Uzi. Half a dozen young children are hit. Trying to make an escape, he shoots dead a Filipino postman who happens to get in his way. When arrested, Buford Furrow said that the man was a good target because he was non-white and appeared to work for the government. The previous October, he'd tried to get himself committed to a psychiatric unit in Seattle, saying: 'I'm a white separatist. I've been having suicidal and homicidal thoughts for some time now . . . sometimes I feel like I could just lose it and kill people. I also feel like I could kill myself.' He was refused treatment after pulling a knife on a nurse.

In October 1998, a gay student was found beaten to death and crucified on a fencepost outside the small college town of Laramie, Wyoming. Matthew Sheppard, 21, had suffered a severe skull fracture and been burned in the attack. Police said he'd begged for his life after he'd been picked up by two men in a bar. He was found 18 hours later, in the freezing cold, by a passing motorist. At first he thought that the figure on the fence post was a scarecrow. He died the next day in hospital.

Forty-nine-year-old James Byrd, a black man, was dragged to death behind a pick-up truck in Jasper, Texas, that same year. He'd been picked up by a group of men on his way home from a party. He was beaten, chained behind the truck and dragged for three miles along a remote country road. Byrd was alive when the dragging began and had used his elbows to prevent his head from hitting the road, but he was decapitated when his body slammed into a concrete sewer.

Prosecutors said one of the accused, the unemployed and nondescript 24-year-old John King, was a hate-filled white supremacist who planned to form a group called Confederate Knights of America, Texas Rebel Soldiers. They showed the jury racist tattoos on King's body – including one with the words 'Aryan Pride' and another with the Nazi SS symbol. Police also found a cigarette lighter with a Ku Klux Klan engraving at the scene. That the men, all of whom were alleged to have had white-supremacist sympathies, were so careless speaks volumes for America's new breed of race warriors. Various hate sites champion their cause.

Suppressing the disquiet gathering in the pit of my stomach, I roamed through William Pierce's National Alliance website, browsing among the hundreds of extremist books for sale and reading the text of his weekly radio address (he has his own station). I listened to his broadcasts via RealPlayer, hearing the old man's waspish, crackling voice lament the perils of Mexican immigration, the power of the Jews, and the 'liberals' – pronounced long and lilting, with that same 'you know what I'm talking about' tone as Griffin – whilst warning of a general meltdown. It was both crude and clever. Pierce could remonstrate against the use of violence by white nationalists, then claim he 'understood' how people might react like that if the country was being invaded, for example by Mexico. The fact that he spent most of the broadcast talking about violence seemed to impart a pretty clear subtext. White nationalists in the US are continually talking of an 'invasion' of their country by Hispanics and of the eventual disappearance of the white 'race'. Pierce's style also reminded me of some of the more extreme Protestant ministers in Northern Ireland.

Listening to Pierce, there seemed nothing he'd like more than a societal breakdown. Easy to say when you live on a remote mountain commune and run what's effectively a personality cult. Later I read an article which said he had a penchant for East European mail-order brides. This seemed a source of amusement for some of the extremists I met. By the time I got out to the States, Pierce was on his fifth or sixth paramour.

Something else caught my eye, too. An article from the German magazine *Stern* revealed how extremists were infiltrating left-wing and anti-fascist chat rooms, then tricking the activists into swapping addresses and phone numbers. One 20-year-old, using the monicker 'DavidLane' (after an infamous US member of The Order who'd coined a well-known white supremacist phrase, the '14 Words': 'We must secure the existence of our people and a future for white children') was suspected of posting at least two death threats on the Net, then offering substantial rewards for the murder of named individuals. Another neo-nazi was posting addresses onto his own site, which was hosted abroad to avoid stringent German laws. Meck88 (the numbers standing for the eighth letter in the alphabet, 'HH' or 'Heil Hitler', a common neo-nazi greeting) said: 'This is a page where I publish the names, addresses, telephone numbers etc of people who have earned a proper beating. If an activist who is prepared for violence sees this, then he doesn't need to hesitate in finishing off these people in any way he can.'

German *Oi!* even offered a page called 'The Small Explosives Master', an extensive programme giving tips on how to fabricate and use explosives. There was a search facility for different types of bomb-making equipment and an illustrated guide to making various devices, placed on the Net via US provider Geocities. At the same time, Nick Lowles was telling me about David Copeland's search for bomb-making instructions on US websites.

Such concerns about online extremism were not new. Back in the 1980s, the infamous Aryan Nations, a paramilitary group associated with Christian Identity and based in a compound in Idaho (until successfully sued by the anti-hate group the Southern Poverty Law Center), sponsored a computer bulletin board. One of the two men who helped set it up was Louis Beam, the Vietnam veteran who'd suggested the idea of 'leaderless resistance', after The Order was destroyed by the FBI.

In 1985, not long after the launch of Aryan Nation Liberty Net, another white supremacist, Stephen Donald (Don) Black, was being released from prison. He'd been arrested whilst taking part in an armed revolt against the government of Dominica. It sounds amazing, particularly as Black looks very much the respectable father and businessman. I met him during my travels in the States; he's tall, youthful-looking, powerfully set, with a thin mouth and a shy, reserved tone. It was while serving his jail sentence that he became one of the first white supremacists to understand computers and the power of the Internet.

It was Black who would launch Stormfront, the first major extremist hate site. 'There is the potential here to reach millions,' he said at the time. 'I think it's a major breakthrough.' He likened it to having his own TV show, saying: 'I don't know if it's the ultimate solution to developing a white-rights movement in this country, but it's certainly a significant advance.'

Initially, Black could find only a handful of other sites that reflected his anti-Semitic, racist message. Today hundreds of sites, chat rooms, newsgroups and e-lists promoting a variety of philosophies have joined Stormfront on the web. Stormfront still remains the granddaddy of them all, and it's guaranteed Black international notoriety. After we later met, he even let me sign up to it.

Even the tired old BNP was staking a web presence, launching a kids' site and offering various press releases online. As Nick Griffin later told me, it was their perfect antidote to a hostile mainstream press.

Nick Lowles told me Copeland had visited a small Internet café near Victoria station several times, seeking something greater than the lacklustre race warriors he'd found inside the BNP. It was during these trips that he'd come across the website of Steve Sargent's National Socialist Movement and written off to their UK box number. He'd also downloaded bomb-making instructions, including something called *The Terrorist's Handbook*. I visited that same café myself, trying to imagine what had been going through the young man's mind at the time.

Nick Griffin's group had proved too dull for Copeland. He'd been to a few branch meetings during 1997, after moving up to London from his father's place in the village of Yateley, Hampshire (his parents having divorced). He found his way to the Christian Identity heresy via the Net, too. In fact, this was key to his descent into extremism, providing in his and others' eyes a divine right to racial violence and intolerance. When I met Identity believers, I wondered how many had ever seen a religious war. Algeria and Bosnia are not something I want to witness again.

Identity traces its roots to a British Empire movement called British Israelism. Started by one Edward Hide in the nineteenth century, this movement held that the 'white' races of Europe were descended from the Lost Tribes of Israel, sought to explain why and how the white man was superior, and provided racial and divine support for the Empire.

Under Identity readings of Scripture, Eve was seduced by the Serpent – the Devil – and bore a son, Cain, who then slew his brother Abel. According to one ideology, this seedline developed into the race today known as the Jews, who are therefore eternally damned. Unsurprisingly, Identity followers tend to be virulently anti-Semitic. Adam's other descendants founded the 'true' white race, eventually making their way to Western Europe and beginning the different nations found there. Other races are often referred to by Identity preachers as 'mud people', deriving from a lower form of life, without the necessary divine spirit of the white man. American Identity adherents often claim the Pilgrims aboard the *Mayflower* were Adam's descendants, making America God's Promised Land.

To them, the Bible provides a mythology of the nation's origins. Their interpretations of the Scripture can get fairly tortured, but their hope is that the Kingdom of God will come down from Heaven to rule here on Earth. Until then, they must do everything they can to prepare the way, hence the need for a Phineas Priesthood. Men and women would be divided in role by their gender, races would not mix and homosexuality would be outlawed. Laws would derive from the Bible, not from politicians. I've been quoted reams of Scripture by stern-faced, middle-aged men claiming their divine kingdom will free from fear all these beautiful, blue-eyed children. All so simple.

Identity preaching differs quite strongly from mainstream Christianity. Identity followers genuinely believe that the Bible condones racial separation. According to them, mainstream Christians can be agents, even unwittingly, of the Antichrist. One of the key Identity preachers I later visited – a man introduced to me by the American Friends of the BNP – spoke of them with loathing.

This man ran Kingdom Identity Ministries, one of the pre-eminent Identity organisations, based in Arkansas. It runs long-distance theology courses to followers around the world and, like the National Alliance, has a radio station, book and mail-order business, and links to dozens of other supremacist movements. It has a particularly strong following among white separatist prison gangs, such as the Aryan Brotherhood. Prominent prisoners like David Lane have been among its followers.

We know from his police statements that Copeland visited the Kingdom Identity site several times. Its mission statement makes its beliefs pretty clear:

> We believe that as a chosen race, elected by God [whom they refer to as Yahweh] we are not to be partakers of the wickedness of this world system, but are called to come out and be a separated people. This includes segregation from all non-white races, who are prohibited in God's natural divine order from ruling over Israel. Race-mixing is an abomination in the sight of Almighty God, a satanic attempt meant to destroy the chosen seedline, and is strictly forbidden by HIS commandments.

Young extremists like Copeland often discover the right via white-power sites, many of them dedicated to Ian Stuart Donaldson, the near-mythical lead singer of Oi! band Skrewdriver, who created Blood and Honour (taken over by C18) before dying in a car crash in 1993. With the growing popularity of MP3 music files, it became possible to download white-power tracks from bands like Skrewdriver, almost anywhere in the world. The violent US music organisation the Hammerskins also proudly boasted the existence of a new British chapter from its colourful web page.

After my *Guardian* article is published, I receive a deluge of angry emails proclaiming my betrayal of the white race and my servitude to the liberal establishment. Another 'lazy journalist', part of the ZOG power structure. Amongst the nuts and conspiracy theorists, one piques my interest. It's from a close, personal friend of Ian Stuart himself.

He wants to meet me.

* * *

As I delved into the workings of these extremists, David Copeland was telling police interrogators that his family 'fucked me up'.

'I'm just a nazi who likes killing people,' he boasted. The notoriety he craved had finally arrived. Yet he hardly seemed to have understood the implications of what he had done. Even the murder of a pregnant woman caused only momentary regret. He hadn't considered that anyone but gays might have been in the Admiral Duncan, his final target. And if he hadn't been caught, he had planned to launch a further campaign against the Hindus and Muslims of Southall, in west London.

It had all started so innocuously. Copeland had been born into a typical suburban environment. His father was an engineer, his mother a housewife. They'd moved from west London out to the cheaper 'burbs in Hampshire, where they had more space to raise their three boys.

Copeland was a late physical developer, and it seems much of his inferiority complex stemmed from his small size. He had underdeveloped testicles, too, and resorted to using prostitutes when older (he only ever had one girlfriend). One of the preoccupations of his teenage years was the worry that he was gay. Apparently, his family used to enjoy watching *The Flintstones* on television and singing the theme tune together. With the line 'we'll have a gay old time', he seems to have believed his parents were sending a message about his sexuality.

In his later years at school, he grew his hair long and started listening to heavy metal bands. His dour demeanour earned him the nickname 'Mr Angry'. Perhaps earlier bullying contributed to this feeling. No staff now seem to remember him from that period. He was, to all intents and purposes, invisible.

Drug and alcohol abuse followed, and he seemed to have a troubled relationship with his brothers. This even led to violence and petty crime, including a conviction for assault. A string of failed jobs seemed to contribute to his developing racist views. He blamed immigrants for taking the best positions and, mirroring later BNP statements, said local authorities were favouring them with better treatment than 'native' whites.

The hooligan violence surrounding the 1996 European Football Championships excited him enough for him to get a large 'England' tattoo, much to his father's chagrin. The two were slowly drifting apart, although Copeland senior would get his son a job working with him as an engineer on the Tube. Other graphic pictures that summer showed the horror and panic at the Atlanta Olympics, after the bombing of Centennial Park. It led Copeland to wonder what would happen if a similar device were set off at London's Notting Hill Carnival. This became his first plan; it could have been devastating. As Nick Lowles writes in *Mr Evil*, 'Coupled with a strange pleasure, this [developing interest in racism] may have provided him with a calling, something to aim for, a direction in what until then had been an unhappy, unstable life.'

When he came to make his devices, packing them with nails (having purchased ingredients quite openly in fireworks shops and from chemists and builder's merchants), he'd already given up on the BNP. By now, he was Hampshire organiser for the NSM (a laughable title, given the group's tiny size) and intent on pursuing the race war he saw espoused in David Myatt's and others' writings. I reflected now, sadly, on Myatt's comments to me about raising up his skinhead warriors.

I soon discovered that Copeland wasn't the first British nazi to launch a bombing campaign. During his BNP days, he would no doubt have come into contact with Tony Lecomber, the party's East London regional organiser, who later rose to, then fell from, the position of deputy leader under Nick Griffin. Lecomber is of average height, wears glasses, has a rather square haircut and, when I saw him, sported a distinctly unfashionable raincoat. He'd begun his political life as a teenager in the National Front, then followed John Tyndall out of the party and into the newly formed BNP in 1982. After changing his name a couple of times, fearing it sounded too foreign, he began producing a hardline racist and anti-Semitic youth bulletin called the *Young Nationalist*, which dismissed the Holocaust as a lie, praised Hitler as a hero, portrayed blacks as monkeys and promised a race war.

In 1985 Lecomber went one step further. He was arrested while trying to blow up the headquarters of the ultra-left Workers' Revolutionary Party in London. Unfortunately for him, his homemade bomb short-circuited in his car, leaving him with minor injuries. When police later searched his home, they discovered crude grenades and bomb-making equipment. After being released from a three-year prison sentence, he was jailed again for attacking a Jewish schoolteacher who'd been removing a BNP sticker on the Underground. When he emerged from prison the second time, Nick Lowles told me he'd promptly received a beating from The Beast, perhaps part of the BNP/C18 power struggle.

That autumn, as Copeland sat in his remand cell, there was another little-reported arrest. Stuart Kerr was a 20-year-old skinhead living in the prosperous, blue-rinse town of Chichester, West Sussex. Like Copeland, Kerr was an underachiever, a sheet metal worker obsessed by race. Like Copeland, he lived in an area with a tiny number of ethnic minorities. And, like Copeland, he had mental problems. He ended up waging a one-man campaign against an Asian shop-owner. He was caught on closed-circuit television, trying to hurl a petrol bomb through the shop window. When arrested, he had a Nazi flag in his room – just like Copeland – and the same kind of C18, BNP and US extremist literature. He had associated with racist hooligans from West Ham football club. Even the manner of his arrest as he slashed his arms in the police station car park, desperate to gain attention, bore the hallmarks of a sick and sad mind.

FIVE

GREEN AND UNPLEASANT LAND

SUMMER 1999

Another skeleton station, another bleak, rain-soaked landscape.

This uninviting vista is not the Derbyshire I know, the county of spa towns and rolling hills, but a large, grim-looking village. Langley Mill, where the Midlands merge with the north of England, seems cold and unwelcoming. Derelict hoardings flutter as I walk past, under the shadow of a dark railway bridge. A figure waits for me outside the pub.

'Sid' – not his real name – has been sending me emails ever since my piece in *The Guardian*. He's been pretty hostile. But my replies – I told him I was genuinely interested in what he believed – have produced an agreement to meet. His email address – a forwarding device only, of course – reflects his views. It's based on the name of a Second World War German battle tank. He's a racial nationalist and original member of C18, he says. He has a thick Derbyshire accent. In one email, he mentions something about problems with the 'missus' and having to look after several cats. A working-class bloke, with a keen interest in (German) war history. I'd guess he's somewhere in his 30s; intelligent, self-educated. Not part of the football crowd, but probably still handy.

Meeting him in person, I'm taken aback. A camouflage jacket drapes his shoulders and roughly hewn dark hair falls toward his shoulders. It's shorter on top, long at the back, a biker's cut. No baseball cap or Stone Island gear for this one. With his dirty boots and ancient Land Rover in the pub car park, he's not at all what I'd expected.

As we walk along the dirty grey road, then clamber into the old vehicle – I can see jerrycans of petrol behind us, slopping away and making me nervous – I keep thinking this is a set-up. He just doesn't look the part. And I'm miles from anywhere, looking down at the rough tarmac and gravel. Sid's appearance seems closer to an Animal Liberation Front extremist than a C18 heavy. He seems surprised by my reaction; after all, he tells me, he was a close friend of Ian Stuart. And on the right, that's near god-like status.

He's adamant that he's been part of the scene, although 'not as active as I used to be'. Like Griffin, he calls me 'mate', but this time with a more honest, open inflection. I shake his hand – a strong, firm grip, noticing his blunt mechanic's fingers, oil ingrained into the nails – and I tell him he can check me for any recording equipment. He's been very specific about this, no photos or tape of his voice, but he says no, he'll trust me. After all, I've given my word. And it's true. I've brought nothing but a notebook with me.

We drive through the rain, across the hills and dales, in his battered jeep, freezing our nuts off as we visit different pubs throughout the afternoon. It's a tour of all the old haunts Ian Stuart used to frequent. In the tiny public bar of the Red Lion, one of Stuart's favourite pubs, we share pints of Mild and discuss politics, bombs and race.

We talk about Copeland, too. I have to be careful not to give any of my information away. At this point, everyone's denying he had a connection with the right. Sid seems adamant about this. 'Just a loner, mate, another one of them mad blokes you get from time to time.' The same reaction has come from the BNP. It's only with publication of a photograph in *The Mirror*, showing Copeland standing behind a bloodied John Tyndall during a demonstration by anti-fascists, that the truth starts to come to light.

Toying with a beer mat, checking the other side of the bar for onlookers, I decide to ask Sid about Ian Stuart. So much has been written about him, so many websites seem to be dedicated to the man, it's very hard to understand who he really was. An Aryan hero?

'He would 'ave hated all that,' says Sid, back to the wall, cramped onto the small, upholstered bench opposite me. The maroon fabric has seen better days. I hate this bloody drink, too; I keep thinking, bloody dishwater, as I listen to him speak.

'Yeah, I got to know Ian fairly well, 'specially after he came back up here from London [after Stuart had become disenchanted with life in the capital]. Y'know 'e had his fingers fucked up by AFA [Anti-Fascist Action]? Yeah, with an 'ammer. He didn't want to go through that kind of thing any more. Also, 'e was getting pressure 'coz his mom was ill an' that at the time.'

Sid mentions his disgust with the whole 'business' surrounding the white-power music scene. Is he into this kind of music then? *Oi!* stuff?

'Not really, I'm not into the rock that much now. More folk and the like.' That seems a surprise. I don't realise there's a burgeoning nationalist folk scene developing, moving away from the skin bands. In Germany and the States, even here in England, former white-power musicians are returning to their 'roots'. Then something Sid later says, as we're getting out of the Land Rover in front of a different pub, surprises me. It's after we've been talking about war memorabilia and Nazi Germany. 'Yeah, mate,' he remarks, 'y'know that there's one of us in the metal movement, don't ya?'

'No,' I say. 'Who?'

He mentions the name of a famous heavy rock star.

I lift my eyebrows. 'Really?' Bloody hell. If that got out, and was true, it could be dynamite.

'Yeah, serious,' he replies. 'He's a collector like me,' fingering an SS insignia badge.

'Very nice,' I utter, my tongue clicking nervously against a suddenly dry mouth.

Sid turns back to the jeep. 'Aw, fuck it,' he exclaims, trying to clunk the defunct handbrake into a closed position.

In another pub, down the road in another town, he talks of the pits that have closed, the miners who used to come drinking here. He seems very grounded in the area. 'Here's where I committed me first crime!' he jokes, pointing to a back alley, cutting through a housing estate, where as a teenager he undertook some minor form of delinquency. Then he recounts that some of their bands used to gig in the very same pub, an ugly, 1930s-style brick building, replete with brass farmyard instruments and stained red carpet. The place oozes nicotine and the barmaid calls me 'duck' as I collect our drinks. Sid refuses all but a single pint from me.

'We call 'em fake Blood and Honour, now,' he says, referring to the 'new', non-C18 organisation, which has recently moved out of The Beast's control. It seems it's split into two organisations. He admits that he's been to see a band from 'the other side'.

Every time we mention Stuart, Sid talks of his hate for what's going on now. ''E wanted to leave, y'know? Get out, while he still had a chance. Not many people know that.' What, leave the movement? The man who's now a demigod for all these young skins round the world? 'Yeah. He was fed up with it. Pretty depressed about it all, really. All the violence, the hassle. He was starting to doubt it all. But it was the others that wouldn't let him go. People like Charlie and that.'

The picture Sid paints of Stuart is of someone depressed, wishing for a simple, uncomplicated life, a person used by the movement as a figurehead and money maker. He sounds as though he was pretty intelligent, too, from a middle-class background here in Derbyshire, interested in poetry. A former punk, too. He would have been an interesting man to interview.

Sid drops me off, but I miss my connection home. I spend the evening stuck on my own in a grim little pub, slowly getting drunk, aware of my accent and waiting for the lights of the train to come like a beacon through the dark.

* * *

My path takes me to Nick Griffin once more. Twice, in fact, before the end of this turbulent year.

I've been ruminating, meanwhile, on the split within the Front National in France. Led for decades now by former paratrooper Jean-Marie le Pen, it's a seminal movement on the far right. Almost every other European group has looked towards the FN for inspiration. Its annual festivals have hosted extremist and ultra-nationalist politicians from across Europe. I met German, Flemish, English and Italian nationalist politicians who had attended such events, or linked up with the FN in other ways. Now Le Pen's deputy, Bruno Megret – a more modern, suit-and-tie figure, whose wife was mayor of the FN-held town of Vitrolles – was claiming he led the group. In the end, Megret ends up with a new party, the Mouvement National Républicain (MNR). The only real loser is the far right, as the nationalist vote is split.

Emails buzz back and forth between me and Griffin, himself an ardent admirer of the French nationalists. In good time, one of his key men will offer to introduce me to the MNR. All in all, he seems keen to talk. The forced pleasantries of our first interview seem to be relaxing. Of course, the revelations about Copeland have yet to come out, and the BNP have so far denied any knowledge of him.

My burgeoning, what? – friendship? relationship? – with Griffin is going to see me introduced to a network of international extremists, within 18 months' time. He's hoping I'm going to write something which will propel him into the limelight. Soon, however, he won't need to worry about me.

Warm air lingers in the skies over the English border town of Shrewsbury, the last threads of an Indian summer, gauzy and thickening. Griffin is wearing a crumpled white shirt, sleeves rolled up, a little less formal than before. He seems in remarkably good humour. Surprising, given that he's just been 'outed' by a former senior comrade in the National Front. A news-sheet has been circulating from Martin Webster, an openly gay extremist, claiming he and Griffin shared passionate liaisons during a four-year affair. There have been several such rumours about Griffin. But he's also just won the party leadership, ousting John Tyndall by a two-to-one majority. Little seems to dent his enthusiasm. It won't be long before he's a household name.

'Come on, I've just got to pop in the post office,' he says, setting off at a stride I imagine he thinks will wind a city boy like me. As we walk, he points out the medieval buildings around us, talking about the town's Civil War history and the part the Welsh have played in the region.

'Have you seen what Jörg Haider's been doing in Austria?' he suddenly slips in. There's an interesting change to the tone of his usually bland voice. I look sideways at him, my foot scuffing the cobblestones of the road, and I nearly trip. A little smile plays rapidly on his face. I spot a slight twitch as he speaks, and I can see the lines etched just by the corner of his mouth. 'Pretty impressive. That's where modern nationalism can go today.'

I'm aware of Haider. He's been storming the polls in Austria, a prosperous, conservative country that has been ruled by a conservative/social democratic two-party system since the 1950s. Haider's Freedom Party – which has controversial policies on immigrants and family planning, along with Haider's less than subtle comments about Nazi-era war veterans – is about to step into coalition government, with around 28 per cent of the national vote. It will send shockwaves around the world and cause a temporary freeze in diplomatic relations with Israel and the EU.

Haider is Griffin's ideal role model, as he outlines in various emails: a multilingual, highly educated and media-friendly frontman who can appeal to the respectable voter. Similarly in Switzerland, the nationalist, anti-immigrant People's Party achieved the largest share of votes in recent elections, under the leadership of Christoph Blocher.

We end up in one of Shrewsbury's many ancient pubs. A wooden floor raps to the sound of our feet, whilst oak beams stretch above us, solid, speaking of stability and history. Only the garishly dressed barmaids and thumping Ibiza hits serve to remind me I'm in the twentieth century.

Griffin is keen to steer the discussion, even before I've had a chance to get the beers in, talking about his much-vaunted reforms of the BNP, of the new influence circles he's created (he's just launched an ex-servicemen's newspaper), and of the Internet revolution within the party. He talks of 'flattened hierarchies' and adds, with a smile forming, 'We've decommissioned the boot.' He sounds pleased with his choice of words, allowing a hint of that undisguised arrogance to creep into his voice. His conversation then meanders, again, into the territory of blacks taking over the inner cities, talking of a past when 'a black person in London was so unusual it used to turn heads in the street'.

We start to argue each point, bantering, playing mind-games. The tempo slowly builds. Liberals want to breed us out of existence, he says, and the reason we've got so many Nobel Prize winners is that we're somehow racially special. We're more inventive than others, apparently. Something to do with developing in an Ice Age. Otherwise we'd all still be Neanderthals. But journalists like me, looking down on this kind of argument, are dissing their own people. 'Liberals,' he taunts, 'people like you, are to blame if populations don't get along.'

'In what way?'

'For the drastic reduction in civil liberties, for one.'

'What are you talking about?' I respond. 'This isn't paradise, but it's a damn sight better than many countries I've visited.'

He stops for a second. You can see him stumbling, verbally, for a moment. His mouth sits half-open then quickly snaps shut. He's obviously used to trotting out a line, then moving on to the next issue.

'Look, you don't need to try and prove something with every point. It's clear that if we simply separated groups out, we'd all get along fine.'

'Really? Like Bosnia, perhaps?'

He denies this, then adds: 'People like the Nation of Islam and I get along fine.' Yeah, well, they're fellow racial extremists, I think. It's the people in between you have a problem with.

For a man who wants to talk of modern politics, of local issues affecting local people, there are an awful lot of racial overtones to his words. When I ask him about his Green credentials, from the ITP days, and how this sits with his statement about our advanced nature leading to industrialisation (meaning: progress), his reply is simple: 'The people who first created the mess should sort it out, rather than people who never invented the wheel – because living in Africa they didn't need to.'

'That surely can't stand scientific analysis,' I tell him. 'And anyway, what's that got to do with greenhouse gases?'

He leaps straight on the point – the wrong point, of course. Australian aboriginals have developed differently to their environment, he says, which is proof of our racial differences.

His words turn to the *Windrush* – he's mentioned it before – and how immigration is 'a form of strikebreaking'. Then he says something even I find surprising. Arguing about the nature of fascism, he says the British state is a 'Big Brother', whilst his views are closer to 'an anarchist position'. I can't believe that no one but me seems to be questioning him about these amazing statements. Who would vote for an anarchist to run their government – even a local council?

Okay, I think, time to change tack. 'You're simply not representative of your party, are you? With your fancy words and Law degree?'

'Yeah, that's probably true,' he reluctantly admits.

'Most of your pals are racist thugs, aren't they?'

'I don't accept that, no. Well, some may exist, but they don't direct the party or its policies, and it's becoming less true by the month with the kind of new recruits we're getting. They're on a totally different scale and attitude to those I've seen before in nationalism.'

'So what about Tony Lecomber then? How does he fit in? It's not exactly a great CV, is it, for this new party image of yours?'

'No, it's not,' he says swiftly. 'Indeed not. But it's a fact, and he can't run away from it. He's repudiated that past and knows it was idiotic. He and I have discussed it.' Griffin strokes his face carefully and says Lecomber now lectures on his experiences, telling people that violence is counterproductive. 'Someone like Tony, because of his past, has more chance of getting those youngsters to be political, than some toffee-nosed git like me!' He takes a quick swig from his pint. I watch his Adam's apple move up and down, before the onslaught begins again.

'What's more important than me, than all of this, is violent Islam.' He's smooth again, back on the rails. 'If you walk in parts of Oldham at night, you'll be attacked because of your skin colour, because you're white, and that's going on night after night after night.' That clashing undertone of aggression is back, lacing its way through his words. Partly because of my own ignorance, I fail to take on board the significance of these comments. Massive race riots will later ignite in the town of Oldham, catching all of us liberals off guard.

There's something particularly prescient in his smooth, snide words, talking of how communities are deliberately divided in Northern Ireland, by walls or a park or an industrial estate, and that this must be the way forward up and down the country. 'Separating them out just a few hundred yards, that's all it takes,' he smiles. Later, it does indeed come true.

I point out that he's talked many times before of being a 'British' nationalist, not 'English', which has nastier connotations. Then why is it that the word 'white' seems to slip into his conversation so easily, as his guard drops? 'Why is it always that whites are always guilty?' I've heard him ask many times.

Then I tell him he just wants easy answers to difficult questions. 'C'mon,' I point out – leading slowly to Copeland – 'some people just want an excuse for violence or to blame their problems on others.'

'Yes, I would accept you're right there,' he admits. 'There are nasty undercurrents to human nature. Those base things exist; they cannot be wished away. Therefore you have to make your policies on the basis that there is this nasty undercurrent, and if you don't, you're asking for these things like Sarajevo to repeat themselves. It's as simple as that.'

Okay, I think, enough of the pleasantries. 'What did you make of David Copeland, when you met him?' My eyes sparkle with innocence.

'I didn't meet him.' His voice is flat, although I'm straining to detect a peppering, a little soupçon even, of aggression. A thin strand of spittle stretches across his lips. His eyes glare straight back at mine. I deliberately shift my gaze from that strange glass stare. He's an odd-looking bloke, I think suddenly, at the back of my mind.

'Who did meet Copeland, then? He was in the party, wasn't he?'

'A few people from East London.'

I notice a slight edge – desperation? – creep into his voice. But no, he claims Copeland only ever came along to a few meetings. 'It obviously wasn't his cup of tea.'

'So why did he come in the first place? How do you think this sounds to your average member of the public?'

'It doesn't reflect well on us, yes. But it's the media that ends up sensationalising these things.'

I take two long sips from my drink and think on the next question. 'Isn't the right a clearing house for nuts and loons?'

He doesn't answer directly. It's the 'liberals' that attack them, so 'the reason that the right has a disproportionate number of oddballs is that they have less to lose'. The suggestion is that the 'normal' supporters are too afraid to come out with their views. We 'liberal totalitarians' are to blame.

'What's weak-willed about joining a party where you stand a good chance of being beaten up, losing your job, or your children being bullied at school and your windows going through? No one involved in that is weak-minded.'

'Hmm,' I mutter quietly. I'm saving the best for last. I regard my fingers drumming silently on the table. I flip a beer mat between one finger and thumb, puncturing it.

'What about yourself?' I say. 'You've got a past you don't want to come up again, haven't you?' He knows, instantly, what I'm talking about.

'No, I haven't got a past; I've got someone saying I have got a past.' He draws in a quick subtle breath. But I'm thinking back on his comments at the time of the nailbombings. It didn't exactly help his 'new' image when he wrote (referring to victims' solidarity marches) that 'gay demonstrators flaunting their perversion in front of the world's journalists showed just why so many ordinary people find these creatures so repulsive'.

'Hey, Nick,' I jest, seeking a crack in the armour, 'that's not exactly a normal, balanced response, is it? Why the vitriol?'

'It's a classic fit-up. Webster hates me because I got rid of him from the NF in 1983. And he's got a terrible temper. He's a vindictive old queen, a stereotypical old queer.' Loathing is clear in his words now, dripping, as though tasting shit. 'He's always wanted his revenge – it's not unknown for homosexuals. But I'm happy, I know my past, I'm not homosexual. It's a smear campaign. A pack of bullshit. I don't blame Webster for it. He's being used.'

'So why not sue him?'

'He's a man of straw; he doesn't own anything. I could only clear my name by bankrupting him.'

We dart around the point, then swiftly drop back to the fake pleasantries of before. Despite the rancour of our little debate, Griffin agrees to meet with me again.

* * *

Next time, back at his farm in Wales, it's freezing, dark and unwelcoming, a real Celtic winter's night. I leave behind the city's Christmas rush and travel through to the small town of Welshpool, up through the twisting farm roads, to Griffin's smallholding.

On the steps of the cottage I meet his wife, a stern-looking, solid, blonde-haired lady who folds her arms and regards me with open hostility whilst two of their girls run past. Griffin beckons me forward, and we walk under a trellis framing a narrow cobbled pathway.

It's cosy inside the small farmhouse. A fire burns in the hearth. It smells, and feels, homely. Normal. Making me a cup of coffee, Griffin smiles and seems relaxed. Maybe he trusts me now. Or, at least, believes he can use me.

This time, he's pressed into a leather jacket and faded black jeans. A slight paunch sinks over his belt and, unusually, his hair is ruffled. Meeting 20 minutes earlier, in town, he'd stood with his back to a small, red Fiat Panda, the seats removed. In the back was a pig's carcass. It barely fitted.

'Can you give us a hand with this?' he'd asked, as I looked with incredulity through the window. 'I have to drop it into the butcher's, and he'll make it into sausages, chops, that kind of thing. We pay him with some of the meat.'

'Oh, er, okay then.' I felt pretty unsure of things. Was this some bizarre initiation, perhaps, checking whether I was Jewish? But soon I found myself up the road, leaping out of the car and helping carry the pig down a side alley to the butcher's. The animal's greasy, bloodied legs kept slipping from my fingers, and I feared I'd drop it.

Later, we spend the evening picking up one of his girls from an after-school music club, crashing over cattle grids and winding through dark woods. He tells me of his recent contacts with the shadowy Bloomsbury Forum, a collection of extreme-right intellectuals that includes elements from the Conservative Party. Again, this apes continental developments. There's even talk of a 'New Right' project which, according to Griffin, would incorporate a publishing house and produce training seminars and CD-Roms. Targeting public schools and the Oxbridge circuit, he says it will provide the BNP with 'a fifth column within the Establishment'.

I've heard, too, through Nick Lowles, that the BNP's name might be changed to the Freedom Party, presumably to take advantage of the Austrian situation. It's later launched by exiled BNP members, as a rival organisation.

Back at the house, he talks more of his past and childhood, about his father and a 'conventional and happy' upbringing. I savour the pleasant aftertaste of wood smoke at the back of my nostrils, taking time to relax and look around. He shows me the kids' rooms and the area where he works with his computers. His dad lives just down the road, he says. Edgar Griffin is still an active member of the Conservative Party. In fact, the blurred line between the two parties will later prove extremely embarrassing to a new Tory leader.

We leave politics behind us, and I allow him simply to talk, watching and studying his face. Griffin is relaxed too, I think, trusting me and reminiscing about a time when 'everyone felt safe back then'. We discuss the private schools he attended, his time growing up in rural Suffolk, other kids he knew, and his earliest memories – such as cycling down the road during election campaigns in the 1960s. He takes pride in telling me how he boxed for his college at Cambridge.

As night falls, the butcher's assistant drives into the muddy courtyard, through the three different gates that bolt off this hill from the uncertain outside world. The van clangs past the last cattle grid, spraying thin, manure-coloured drops high in the air. The guy's on his way to help slaughter another pig. Watching the animal – holding my nerve, Griffin observing me all the while – I tell him about my idea for this book. Will he help me?

'It shouldn't be a problem,' he says. 'I think we can do that.'

'Really?'

'Yes.' And that's it. Then he mentions, with a sudden 'Ahh,' as if he'd almost forgotten, that David Duke, the infamous political racist from Louisiana, is planning a conference in Russia next year. It'll bring together all the top people from the extreme right. Perhaps an invitation can be wangled for me, he suggests.

I walk inside the main cottage again and take time to talk to Jackie, his wife, while mulling all this over. My adrenaline level is running high. Too many cups of coffee, too much play-acting. But I count my breaths, calming myself, invisibly, with the chi kung breathing techniques I've been taught. It works. Slowly I relax and talk with this woman. She warms to me. I like her. I genuinely don't want to hurt this family. But, I have to remind myself, I vehemently disagree with their beliefs and with where they could lead us.

* * *

LONDON, WINTER 1999

Victoria Station is dark against the winter night. The wind whips among the commuters. These cold evenings draw close early, uncomfortable and unwelcome this time of year. Crowded, yet lonely. You feel the true soul of the city here. Rush-hour stress, antipathy for fellow humans, invisibility.

I'm standing next to the large newsagents, my back to a dozen people. I've chosen the best corner possible, aware of my vulnerability. Dressed in a red fleece, though, I stand out. That should be enough for him to see me.

The wait is fierce agony. Anticipation, eagerness, the copper edge of fear eating at my nerves. My eyes blur in the sharp, freezing air. Rubbing them, I still can't see anyone; well, no one I could spot as a neo-nazi. Every young face, each baseball cap; I peer intently, temples pulsing, seeking his face. I wish he'd hurry up. I wonder whether I've got enough time to make it to the toilet. These meetings always make me nervous, crossing between the worlds.

I've been receiving the Final Conflict email newsletter for several months now. It's a bizarre mix of opinions, some revisionist, others anti-abortion. Many concern 'poofs' and 'faggots', usually a re-edited piece from a national newspaper, taken out of context. Neo-fascism, of course, and the 'evils' of race mixing, feature high on the agenda. You can follow links to interviews with the leaders of the NPD – Germany's most extreme neo-nazi party – or read about the 'lies' of the Israeli/Palestinian conflict, which somehow always descends into 'international Jewry', or pick up hints of the Asian and white-gang violence starting to surface in some of Britain's northern cities.

I feel uncomfortable at having this stuff on my computer. I shade the screen with my body every time my girlfriend walks in. But it also becomes almost second nature to have a quick look at this strange collection of views each day. It's proving useful for keeping tabs on the fascists. They seem to have such good links to the rest of the extremist world.

There's another reason for my current interest in the International Third Position. They've been in the news. I've read allegations that one of their English charities is diverting funds from a shop for political use. The *Evening Standard*, a mass-market London-based tabloid, has broken the story. It could be argued that, given its own right-wing leanings, there's some irony in this and that it's these 'middle England' tabloid papers that are doing more damage than any fringe gang or political party, stoking tensions and fears, an oily murk of opinion that suggests we're facing a 'flood' of asylum seekers. Half the time it's young blokes like me writing this nonsense. Even they don't necessarily believe it, but it sells. Still, the *Standard* and its associated papers, such as the *Daily Mail*, have earned the enmity of this strange little band of nuts and, through them, of their wider circle of associates across Europe, Russia and the USA.

A Spanish newspaper has also just broken a story about the group, revealing that they've bought a near-derelict village in northern Spain. Is it some secret hideaway, or training area, for a clique of white supremacists and neo-nazis? A few months later, there are massive anti-immigrant riots taking place in the south of that country. North African migrants bear the brunt of the attacks. Final Conflict buzzes with reports. Coupled with their extremist views on usury, abortion, green issues, ultra-nationalism and opposition to materialism, plus international links to a host of violent neo-nazis, it's sent the press into a temporary feeding frenzy. Still, no one seems to have met, let alone interviewed, any of these guys. Are they just cranks?

They loathe the press, and *Searchlight* too. Gerry Gable is a personal enemy. It seems their battles stretch back to their earliest origins, crawling from the primordial muck of the NF. My entreaties to meet with them are greeted with silence; initially at least. When a reply finally comes, after my second meeting with Nick Griffin, it's formal and wary. A short sentence or two from the Third Position in England, telling me I'll be referred upwards. Wait, it tells me. It doesn't seem to hold much hope.

My gaze passes the same businessman perhaps a dozen times. I'm holding a copy of the newspaper I've agreed to carry. Our eyes meet again. No, I think. Not him. But after a while, I walk over all the same.

'Er, excuse me. You wouldn't be from the ITP, would you?' I ask, my voice sounding too high, feeling foolish. I've already had one false alarm. I'm hoping, if I'm wrong, it will sound like an innocent enquiry, as though I'm waiting to meet someone from a corporation.

'Ah, Mr Ryan, yes, hello,' he answers, formal, stilted, looking down towards the paper. 'Sorry I'm late,' he says, thrusting out his suited arm and gripping me with a cold handshake. 'Trouble on the train.'

I look into his pale features. The face is early 40s, with a dollop of brown hair sitting squarely over pasty white skin. A slight doughiness hints at the first onset of middle age. An unfashionable moustache clings to his upper lip. A touch of grey in his hair is offset by a largish pair of spectacles magnifying intelligent-looking eyes. With the smart suit, briefcase and polished shoes, the image reminds me of a business traveller. Like the city around us; there, but invisible. As far from Charlie and Steve as you can get.

Until now, my contact with the network has been entirely virtual. Unlike most other groups I've encountered, they refuse to communicate with me in any other way. And even then not direct, but forwarded from other shadowy figures abroad.

We dither a moment, as I try to recall where we can talk. After a fruitless few moments, we make our way up the escalators at the back of the station, towards the heavens of this clinically lit urbania, into the beckoning mouth of a fake Irish pub.

'Derek Holland, by the way,' he offers, politely. 'Pleased to meet you.' Then he stalks off, in a stiff, odd stride, towards the bar, offering to buy me a pint. A minor but pleasant surprise.

I stare at his back, then turn again towards the table, trying to appear casual. The name is infamous. Excitedly, I tap my pen on my leg, wishing I had my tape recorder. Holland was one of the leaders of the National Front, with Nick Griffin. The two ended up living in a village in Normandy with the rest of the ITP cadres, during the late 1980s and early 1990s. I have a picture of them standing in front of a wall painting of Colonel Gaddafi in Tripoli. Holland's now one of the dominant leaders of the ITP and has close links with extremist figures in Italy and other Catholic nations and, via the Internet, to just about every other white-supremacist organisation on the planet.

Even after this evening, he remains a shadowy figure. Like Ian Stuart's friend 'Sid', he's insisted on secrecy and anonymity. No tape recorders or even notes. In fact, the sole purpose of the meeting is to have me 'checked out'. To see if I really am worthy and fair enough to be introduced to his pals. It's been difficult. Already, they've seen one of my articles on the BNP, written for *The Times*. A hostile message had surfaced one day – to my personal email address – claiming the piece was horrendously biased against 'Mr Griffin'. The formality of the tone reminds me that these sometime friends are now implacable enemies. Internal politics exist even (especially) here in this twisted little world.

Settling into a tight corner of the pub, my eyes scanning the bar around us, Holland tells me he's just got in from Italy.

'Oh, really?' I enquire.

'Yes, I come over from time to time.'

'But you don't live here any more?'

'No, I moved out some years ago. My wife's Italian. I still have family in Ireland, though.' He was born there, he adds, although I can detect no sign of it in an otherwise neutral accent. That gives us something in common, at least.

We banter for the next hour and a half, me polishing off three pints of Guinness along the way. We talk about abortion and his strong critique of globalisation (like me, he finds it interesting that this issue links him with radicals and Greens). He also discusses his days with Griffin, the powers that be, and his ideas on 'distributism', a philosophy dreamt up in the early twentieth century by writers such as G.K. Chesterton, centring around a 'back-to-the-land' approach: reducing the size of communities, favouring rural life over urban.

It's clear a strong intellect lurks behind those intense eyes, although I still sense there's something very wrong with all this, as I chew my lip and listen to his steady rant. It's more a kind of empathy I develop, after meeting these fellows, that they're simply too intense, too repressed, and too certain they're right. It's easy to imagine them gathered in their tiny groups, plotting and waiting for the day that never comes.

I keep thinking back on the pictures I've seen of this now genteel-looking man. The nervy, fiery-eyed youth, longish straight hair, unfashionable specs. The body in those images is taut, thin, repressed. I'm trying to place that image over the stolid, grey figure I see before me now.

'Why should we talk to you?' he says, suddenly. The friendliness is gone; hostile suspicion has crept in. His eyes flash behind those glasses, catching the light and seeming to silver over. Vitriol seeps into his words. A familiar feeling; I should have expected it. The paranoia is too great.

'All journalists are the same,' he snaps. His stare fails to falter for the several seconds that I look at him.

'I'm not,' I answer. 'I mean, I want to tell the real story. That's who I am, how I work.'

'That's what they all say. No one's ever given us a fair hearing. We don't need anything from journalists. We never benefit. They just print their lies whatever we say.' The stare continues. 'Why should you be any different?' His sentence ends suddenly, as though cut off for effect. A silence descends on the table.

I must admit, I'm not prepared for this. I had imagined the group to be more ready to talk. After all, compared to most writers, I at least give them an open hearing. But this simply shows my naiveté.

For the next 45 minutes we circle each other, verbally crossing swords. At one point he says: 'Aren't you afraid?'

'Of what?' I ask, bemused.

'Me.'

'Er, no. Should I be?'

A look of – what? – annoyance crosses his face. 'I could have someone outside right now, ready to follow you or knock you off the minute you leave.' His skin glistens in the artificial pub light, even through the wafting smoke. I smile back, saying nothing. I can sense the frustration eating at this man.

'I could have someone waiting for you too,' I bluff. He sits back, momentarily silent. 'What's to stop me having some AFA guy waiting in the wings? If I wanted to do that, though, I'd hardly have been so obvious or open with you, would I?'

'How do I know?' he says. 'I don't know you. You could be with the Other Side.' He's barely touched his drink. I can see the hint of stained ivory poking through that half-opened slit of a mouth, grinning back at me.

Still, I won't get very far if these hostilities keep up. Turning the beer mat around in circles, I think hard for a moment. 'Well, what should we do [I'm about to call him Derek, but then think again], Mr Holland?'

'It'll be very hard to convince anyone to speak with you – unless you can do something for us.'

Ah.

'What?' I steeple my fingers together, placing them under my chin and adopting what I hope appears to be a serious demeanour.

'We might be able to grant you an interview – if you write something positive about us first.' He wants me to produce an article extolling the virtues of the ITP. Crazy. No one would ever publish it. But that's the line he sticks to. If I do this for them, they might be able to introduce me to the NPD, for example. That could be a real coup. I keep chipping away, twisting, trying to come up with other reasons or possibilities for them to talk to me. It doesn't occur to me that our very meeting in this place is already a clear enough hint of their organisation.

Suddenly, he checks his expensive-looking watch. It glints in the subdued light. 'I need to get going,' he says. Shit. We haven't even agreed anything yet.

'Look, I'll try and do what I can,' I say, stalling. 'Surely there must be some way we can sort this out. What do you suggest?'

'Hmm . . . is there any chance you can get over to Italy?' he says. He's looking off to the side, seeming distracted, as though mulling a sudden idea. He picks absent-mindedly at his nose.

'Dunno,' I reply. 'Bit expensive for a freelance.' Like everyone else I met, he seems convinced I have money to burn. He probably imagines, like all the rest of them, that I'm working for the State or *Searchlight* or both.

'If you can get out there, we might be able to introduce you to some people. Perhaps in the spring.' I imagine he's referring to Roberto Fiore, one of the founding members of the ITP and a former member of the Armed Revolutionary Nuclei (NAR). Fanatics from this group bombed Bologna train station in 1980, killing 85 and wounding 200 others (Griffin dismissed my comments about the NAR, saying 'Everyone was a radical in Italy during those days'). This infamous Italian neo-fascist has just created a new political party called Forza Nuova (New Force), based on extreme Catholic views. A bomb that destroyed the offices of a left-wing newspaper in Italy, in 2001, was planted by a member of the same group.

Thinking back on it now, it's amazing just how many organisations the ITP is, or has been, linked to. At one point it was trying to draw close to the highly conservative Catholic order, the Society of St Pius X. Former members have been associated with a group called the American Front – their post office box was in the same Arkansas town where I discovered various Christian Identity ministries and a KKK leader – and with a 'new' force of National Anarchists. Through this latter connection, they came into contact with the Green and protest movements. Alternative Green, a movement set up by former *Green Anarchist* editor Richard Hunt, has had close relations with a tiny splinter group called the National Revolutionary Faction, headed by former member Troy Southgate.

Holland's cold, amphibian voice brings me back. He's muttering, '. . . need to get hold of someone . . . supposed to meet . . .' He's fumbling for change in his pocket, so that he can use the payphone. I end up lending him my mobile, watching him turn his back and chatter away to someone in Italian. When he hands it back, I store the number he's called – just in case. It's here in central London.

With that, he says he must go. He hands me a sheaf of papers and documents, including the ITP's infamous rag, *The Voice of St George*, which they later delight in seeing when shown during a documentary on racism by black commentator Darcus Howe. You can almost imagine the secret thrill this motley bunch of men draw each time they appear in the press, despite their inevitable outrage at 'misrepresentation'.

One day, I'd sit in former NF leader John Tyndall's home, hearing him say in sad, resigned tones: 'Ah, Derek Holland . . .' as though mentioning a failed pupil. Tyndall had been a mentor to people like Griffin and Holland. Now he considered them responsible for the destruction of his creations.

But at this moment, that day is long away. Another meeting with Holland will fail to clear any introductions. They're insisting on this piece of PR about them. It's impossible. Other doors are beginning to open, though.

I swallow the dregs of Guinness and walk off into the freezing night.

SIX

OUTSIDERS

JANUARY–DECEMBER 2000

My life among the zealots began to make sense.

Travelling the crumbling and colourful wasteland of modern Britain, I was encountering the 'new tribes', groups of individuals bound together by common cause, searching for identity, purpose and belonging.

In the last few years, I'd lived with environmental protesters in tunnels and treehouses; joined pagans in neo-shamanistic ceremonies; dealt with the extreme hedonists of club culture, seeking a spiritual brotherhood in dance; followed evangelical Christians proselytising among drug addicts and dropouts; and met members of a violent neo-nazi subculture. Disjointed communities, yet linked by the same powerful forces. Convinced there was a wider theme at work, I set about creating this book.

The year itself started on the streets of London. Bloody Sunday happened nearly 30 years ago, yet was still a raw wound. An inquiry was underway into the events that led British paratroopers to shoot and kill 13 Catholics and wound many others (one of whom later died) in Derry, Northern Ireland, that fateful day. It was guaranteed to bring out the neo-nazis chanting against their hated enemies, the IRA and Catholics (did this include Derek Holland's ITP? I wondered). And, this year, me.

The march was ragged, loud, and colourful. The tricolour of Eire floated in the steady drizzle. A drum banged in time to a tin whistle. Here and there a black armband surfaced through a sea of sombre, hard-set faces. This was the second march I'd attended. Last time, I'd been surrounded by men from the newly created NSM – loyal to Steve Sargent and David Myatt – as I watched the ritual of insults hurled between the far right (pro-Protestant and pro-British union) and the marchers (left-wing and Irish Republican groups, often Catholic, and relatives of those killed on Bloody Sunday).

This time I mingled, unseen and silent, as the marchers assembled near the Embankment, next to the Thames. Through Nick Lowles, I'd heard rumours of a possible clash between The Beast and the marchers. But, unknown to me, it was more complicated than that.

I followed the march into the centre of London, noting the worry on the faces of the tourists I passed. At first, the thump of the drum and fluting sounds of the whistle reflected, simply, a very Irish sound – to my ears, the call of home. But then you saw the banners and the hangers-on: the large, gap-toothed fellows wearing combat jackets and spoiling for a fight.

The first confrontation took place along Whitehall, near the entrance to St James's Palace, Prince Charles's official abode. A small, screaming band of crop-haired National Front supporters chanted, 'No Surrender to the IRA!' and other insults. With their skin hairstyles and ranting faces, I kept thinking these could be gay blokes shouting to each other across a noisy dance floor. The more serious figures loomed, suddenly, once I got up along Oxford Street. The direction of the march had been changed this year, and I scouted ahead. There – half a dozen guys wearing baseball caps, thickset hands thrust into pockets, being herded off the pavement into a van by uniformed police.

I doubled back, rejoining the march. I felt horribly exposed, in case anything did go off. We rounded a corner towards the final destination, a rallying point at the University of London.

Yellow-jacketed police were suddenly in force. To our left, a gang of 30 or 40 men peered silently, snarling in our direction. I recognised several people, including Andy Frain, a leading member of the Chelsea Headhunter football hooligan gang. Nicknamed 'Nightmare', he had a reputation for psychopathic violence. He was later caught boasting, on an undercover TV programme, how he had slashed an off-duty policeman's throat. Many such stories floated in the underworld of the hooligan scene.

The group surged forward, but the cops were there first. A senior officer began talking to them, face to face. I was too far away and couldn't hear what was said. Clearly, though, he was taking no nonsense. They remained, tense and strained, where they stood. With the turn of another corner, the march ended. Was that it? I took myself off into Tottenham Court Road, somewhat confused. Only later, talking to Nick Lowles, did I learn that a major clash had been averted.

The Beast had allied himself in recent months to the ultra-violent Loyalist Volunteer Force (LVF) in Northern Ireland, an offshoot of a larger paramilitary group, the Ulster Defence Association (UDA). The newly formed British Ulster Alliance (BUA) was still allied with this older group (in fact, Steve Sargent had offered to introduce me to the UDA's London network), and one of its leaders had been heard to say that Browning would soon be 'whacked'. Both groups had drawn their supporters together that day, in preparation for a clash. Only good policing kept the men tied down in different pubs and prevented what could have been a bloodbath. The Loyalist links would surface again in my travels, when a leading BNP member told me he could arrange a meeting with the BUA leadership.

During the spring, a Boston-based librarian proved crucial in helping me shape this book. David Goldman ran a unique web operation called Hatewatch. A university librarian by day, at night he and a team of volunteers maintained a wary eye on extremists using the Net. Our conversations and emails slowly shaped the template and the groups I should approach in the US. It was my first foray into the world of international extremism, away from Britain.

At the same time, I was searching for a potential lone wolf, another David Copeland, Eric Rudolph, or Timothy McVeigh, someone I could actually meet. Goldman mentioned the name Alex Curtis. 'I know someone, a professor, who gave an anti-racism lecture,' Goldman told me by phone. 'He got a call from this guy Curtis later, telling him exactly what he'd been wearing and what he'd said. He told him he'd been in the front row of the lecture. He must have been sitting in the audience all the time, without any of us knowing. You should be careful with someone like him, though. He's unpredictable.'

But Curtis could have been my conduit to the deepest level of the subculture. I'd seen his site, which he ran from San Diego, hoping for a violent revolution which would topple the American 'Jew-occupied government'. He talked of lone operatives, chipping away by their 'daily, anonymous acts'. Detailed diagrams seemed remarkably similar to works produced by former Order member David Lane. Curtis said he was just a propagandist in all this, advocating the use of any and all means to succeed. Of course, I sighed. You wouldn't want to be there with the gun yourself, would you? But Goldman had said he was being watched as a possible future leader, or more likely as an ideologue for others.

Or as someone who could topple over the edge.

I found a picture of Curtis on the web. He looked remarkably similar to Matt Hale, leader of the World Church of the Creator; the same intense, shadowed features, glaring, fixed eyes, hair too neatly combed and pressed down onto an elongated head. I emailed him and waited for a reply.

I read that hate crimes were on the rise both here and in the US. London's Metropolitan Police had just released new figures showing a near doubling of racially motivated crimes. We had one of the highest levels of racial assaults in Europe, yet one of the most emasculated extreme-right political movements. Come here for hooligans; just find your racism in the mainstream parties. Still, even that was about to change. New laws were announced, cracking down on asylum seekers. Middle England was appeased, for the moment.

I began emailing Heidi Beirich of the Southern Poverty Law Center (SPLC), another person who proved extremely helpful in my quest to uncover the soul of the radical right. Like Nick Lowles, Heidi was involved in difficult undercover operations and was a specialist on groups such as the

National Alliance. The SPLC was very well known in the US. From its Alabama base, this civil rights group and its founder, Morris Dees, had successfully sued a number of prominent white racists, a unique tool in combating what Americans call 'hate crimes'.

Curtis emailed back, turning down my request to meet. Within a few months, he was arrested and given a three-year sentence, during an FBI operation known as 'Investigation Lone Wolf'. He'd been harassing and intimidating several figures, including a US Congressman, leaving fliers, telephone calls, and even a live grenade to get across his message.

In April, the controversial right-wing historian David Irving, a cause célèbre to the intellectual right, lost his libel trial against Penguin Books and author Deborah Lipstadt. After considering the case for almost four weeks, Judge Charles Gray ruled against Irving, saying he had failed to prove his reputation had been damaged. Irving, who outraged survivors of Nazi death camps, had been seeking damages over Lipstadt's 1994 book *Denying the Holocaust: The Growing Assault on Truth and Memory*, which he claimed had generated waves of hatred against him. Lipstadt and Penguin Books both denied libelling Irving by branding him a 'Holocaust denier'.

Mr Justice Gray said the charges he had found to be substantially true were that 'Irving had for his own ideological reasons persistently and deliberately misrepresented and manipulated historical evidence' and 'for the same reasons, he had portrayed Hitler in an unwarrantedly favourable light, principally in relation to his attitude towards and responsibility for the treatment of the Jews'. The judge also said that Irving was 'an active Holocaust denier; that he was anti-Semitic and racist and that he associated with right-wing extremists who promoted neo-Nazism'.

There scarcely seemed time to draw breath before other zealots entered my life again. On May Day, an American journalist and I watched as a ragged mob of anti-capitalists let fly its rage at the city's police force. It was a terrifying few hours, visceral and fear-laden. People charged up and down the backstreets and alleys off The Strand and Whitehall, seeking escape. Black-clad riot police forced them back. Young men with balaclavas and kerchiefs held cans of lager, smashed in windows and screamed abuse at wealthy foreign tourists. 'I fucking hate you, I really fucking hate all of you!' shrieked one young hooded guy at an Italian lady, rocking her car back and forth with three of his mates. It was an uncomfortable reminder of my encounters with the far right, although this guy would probably be the first to claim he hated the 'fash' (fascists) too.

The group planning the May Day protest was called Reclaim the Streets (RTS). Initially it had been created more as a 'theme' by the wider Green/protest movement, as in 'let's do a Reclaim the Streets', and would literally take over a section of road for a party. It had been phenomenally successful in the mid-1990s, aiming to bring attention to the campaigns against new road building by the previous Conservative government.

Since the violent protests of 18 June 1999, RTS meetings had suddenly grown, swelled by the ranks of grim-faced militants from the extreme left and anarchist groups. There'd been no talking to media, and no cameras allowed (in fact, I'd heard one guy telling his mates to seek out and attack any cameramen they saw). Infiltrators were sought out. Nor was there any 'leader'. RTS proclaimed on its website that it promoted 'disorganisation' and non-hierarchical structures.

Suddenly, the old liberals and 'Greenies' were being shouted down, gradually pushed out at these meetings. An organisation sprang into existence, a coalition of mild-mannered direct-action protesters and extremists bent on overthrowing the System. Anti-capitalism proved a convenient bandwagon for the once tired and flagging fortunes of the militants. And it was clear that many militants were there, including the Socialist Workers, Green Anarchists – the same organisation linked, via its former editor, to the ITP (I chatted amiably to the *Green Anarchist* paper seller outside the protesters' meeting hall) – Black Flag, the Revolutionary Communist Party, even Iraqi and Kurdish Communist groups. Since the hard left and anarchists began taking over, the violence had increased and millions of everyday Britons – who should have been allies in a battle against the excesses of big business, climate change, genetically modified crops and so on – were excluded.

For a network that claimed it had no organisation, a clique very clearly had emerged in the anti-capitalist movement. A network the militants and zealots could never build on their own now existed across the country and beyond. That seemed both the strength and the weakness of rebellion: it united disparate groups with very different agendas. Fights began breaking out between activists, as arguments raged over the movement's future direction.

Meanwhile, in the north of England, the BNP was slowly pounding the streets of Burnley, Oldham and Bradford, campaigning on local issues and preparing for the elections. If the party faithful were fazed by David Copeland's trial, it didn't show, despite *The Mirror* picturing John Tyndall with the London nailbomber. But the court case electrified most of the nation for a few short weeks in early summer. The young man sat placidly, pasty-looking and unhealthy, in the dock. The confidence and bravado of his arrest were gone. He'd been undergoing psychiatric tests and treatment.

What shocked most of the victims and their relatives was his inanity. They found it hard to square this image with the terrible and senseless deeds wrought just over a year before. His Brixton attack had left a baby boy with a 10 cm nail in his head, not to mention his murders at the Admiral Duncan. Insults were screamed at him. He showed no sign of having heard them.

Arguments raged between legal counsel and psychiatrists. Most of the experts seemed to think he was delusional, suffering from 'religious, grandiose and persecutory components'. Copeland had described how he was 'a prophet' acting out 'his Mission', claiming his bombings were to be the first of many and would result in the Apocalypse. Believing he was special, he quoted scriptures to justify and explain his actions and claimed divine intervention would sweep him from the courtroom up to heaven. 'It is my opinion he is likely to be suffering from a schizophrenic illness,' Dr Gilluley, a psychiatrist, concluded.

One voice stood out against this otherwise consensual medical opinion. Dr Philip Joseph, a consultant psychiatrist at St Mary's Hospital, west London, argued that Copeland was suffering from a personality disorder rather than any form of paranoid schizophrenia. His religious beliefs were simply a crude articulation of Christian Identity. Few people have heard of this obscure doctrine. Having seen much of the political and religious material found in Copeland's possession, Dr Joseph concluded that he was simply repeating what he had read. He contended that the other doctors had formed their opinions because 'they were not aware of the literature he had'.

In the end, Copeland was found guilty and given six life sentences. The rest of his life was going to be spent in Broadmoor.

After the trial I received a call from a contact in the BBC, keen to talk about my experiences with extremists. I mentioned my encounters with the ITP, and their fanatical anti-abortion beliefs. Which is how during summer I came near the clutches of the Right Hand of God, as the fanatical end of the anti-abortion movement likes to style itself.

A terrifying 1,750 violent assaults and 50 murders have been attributed to pro-life groups in the past 25 years in the US. The scene was characterised by lone gunmen and by groups of extremists forming picket lines and blockades at clinics. This was where Eric Rudolph, the Olympic bomber, started out. Leaders and former leaders from these extremist organisations had shown up in recent years in both the UK and Ireland.

I spent several weeks making calls throughout the British Isles, learning about these groups. The most vociferous had been Precious Life (UK), a spin-off from Precious Life (Northern Ireland) and Youth Defence in Eire. Jim Dowson, a former member of the ultra-Protestant Orange Order, led the group in Scotland. He'd promised all sorts of shock tactics against clinics, sending the press into one of its familiar frenzies. Dowson had also composed a song in support of a Loyalist bomber. Another, more shadowy group was Crusaders for the Unborn Child, an offshoot of the ITP based in Manchester.

In Ireland, abortion was illegal except when there was danger to a mother's life, and about 7,000 Irish women travelled to Britain for abortions each year. Controversial US figures had made appearances and were believed to be funding and training the Irish activists. Pro-choice workers I spoke to worried that violent attacks, or even US-style kidnappings, could come to Ireland, particularly if abortion was made legal in the constitution.

CARE (Christian Action, Research and Education) was a more mainstream pressure group, but some still thought it controversial. It had a member on a government advisory body, but they were 'homophobic bigots', according to one gay Labour MP. One of their people took me out to lunch in an Italian café once popular with former Prime Minister John Major. These new Christian soldiers – well organised, well funded, disciplined, committed – had assiduously courted those in power. They were also anti-abortion, pro-family, supporters of Section 28 (part of the Local Government Act of 1988 which forbids the promotion of homosexuality by local authorities, particularly in schools) and so on. It was not a world I was familiar with, but it seemed to hint at battles to come.

Many of the campaigning techniques dovetailed with the American experience, where the Moral Majority movement ensured that 'pro-family' religious opinion was heard at the centre of power. Using many of the same methods – mass letter-writing, forging close relations with politicians, courting newspapers, producing policy papers, plying sympathetic government officials with information – Britain's newly emboldened Christian movement had given the country its first whiff of morality politics.

I decided I needed to get out. England felt too small, too familiar after all these experiences. I spent August in Lebanon. Under a beautiful Mediterranean sun, I wandered through Roman and Phoenician ruins, seeing the same cedar groves that once supplied ancient kings and empires with their building materials. It was hard to believe this place had torn itself apart in such a terrible civil war. The heart of Beirut was being rebuilt and Arab tourists were arriving from all over the region to enjoy what used to be called 'the Paris of the Middle East'.

On a hot, dusty day, on our way back from visiting an ancient Christian grotto, my taxi driver stopped on a hill near the city of Tyre. We parked on the side of the twisting mountain road, looking down onto the coastal plain and the glittering sea beyond. There was a crowded settlement below. It seemed to be walled. Narrow twisting alleys sewed a labyrinthine course through fluttering lines of washing and tiny, flat roofs were soaked with dirty grey puddles. 'Look there. There is all the criminals, the thiefs, bad men, gangsters,' he said, pointing. 'We should get rid of them. All of them. No good. Phah!' he snorted, waving his hand in disgust, before flinging open the car door and getting back inside. I hadn't even asked him to stop. He seemed to feel it was necessary to do this. I looked again. I asked him what it was. It was a Palestinian refugee camp, he told me. Probably been here decades.

In Lebanon, I soon discovered, the Palestinians really were third-class citizens, unwelcome these last 50 years. Inside those camps were no fewer than 17 different Palestinian factions, all vying for control and prepared to fight it out with deadly force. Young kids carried kalashnikovs, even old men sometimes. I saw it with my own eyes.

The poverty in those camps was mirrored in some of the poorer southern suburbs of Beirut, and on towards the border with Israel, where we saw the yellow and green of Hezbollah flags everywhere: by the roadside, on the border, on top of houses, on the backs of buses. Hezbollah was a guerrilla force of Islamic fundamentalists, partly funded by Iran, hailed as heroes by many folk. And now a political and social force, too. At one of their shops, we stopped to purchase a souvenir of our trip. To many in Israel, these people would be 'scum'. On the Lebanese side, too, there was an area where you could symbolically 'throw' a stone at the hated Israelis – the Jews – who had invaded their land. In 1990 I'd stood on the other side, watching Israeli tanks crossing the border. The soldiers had spoken with contempt of the 'Arabs who don't know how to die'.

In Beirut's prosperous northern suburbs, we sat talking with young Maronite Christians, men and women who saw themselves closer to Israelis and us 'Europeans' than to their own countrymen. They bitterly resented the presence in their country of so many Syrian troops, who stood on numerous street corners (ironic, as the Christians had called them in). A raucous pool party thumped away in the five-star hotel behind us, as we sipped expensive cocktails. The scene was one of prosperity and urbane chatter. We could have been in Florida or at an expensive resort in Greece. Yet the Maronites and their Phalangist soldiers had been responsible for some of the worst excesses and massacres of the war, including the rape and wholesale slaughter of civilians.

Travelling after that in Australia, I learned that young Lebanese kids were themselves being blamed for a crime wave in Sydney. A police chief in the city's western suburbs was attributing a series of robberies and rapes of young white women to gang members of Lebanese origin. In the end, he had to retract his statements in the face of conflicting evidence.

Australia had a much-vaunted way of life. I'd lived there in 1990; this was my third trip, and things were changing fast. Oriental faces told you it was starting to look towards Asia, not the old motherland. Like America, there was a certain isolation, too. It was developing an unenviable reputation for its treatment of asylum seekers (one later emulated by Britain). Subject to mandatory detention, they were often locked up far out in the bush. These detainees had been sewing up their lips to refuse food, whilst the government shipped Afghan refugees off to tiny Pacific island states. The practice was condemned by the UN, but seemed to have had little impact on popular opinion. Pundits instead claimed these policies enabled Prime Minister John Howard to see off the threat from Pauline Hanson's anti-immigrant One Nation party.

In the hinterlands of New South Wales, I rarely saw a black face. The Aborigines had still been refused an official apology for their treatment at the hands of the settlers, and many now were condemned, like Native Americans, to poor education, alcoholism and early death. In the past, babies had been forcibly taken from their parents, in order to be raised in a 'proper' Christian manner. Many had tried to hide from the government men, often unsuccessfully. There were official charts on the 'whiteness' of Aborigines, and how colour could be bred out. Some of this was still going on into the 1950s.

I saw a group of Aborigines near a gas station, in a small town I'd chosen as a back route from the main Pacific highway. Barefoot and obviously poor, they sat on the steps of a few nearby buildings. I was in a cramped shop that seemed to serve as the town's convenience store. As I bought a drink, a young Aboriginal woman walked in. The attitude of the lady serving me changed instantly. 'Waddya want?' she snarled aggressively. Her accent was much thicker than the Sydney-siders I'd got used to. 'Two packs of fags, missus,' the young Aboriginal replied. The first woman, in her late 30s perhaps, but heavy and doughy, threw the cigarettes on the counter, then made a point of counting each cent she was given in return. As the dark-skinned woman turned and left, the shop assistant muttered under her breath. 'Bloody Abos . . . sorry about that, love,' she said, turning back to me. 'Now where were we?'

The US election was boiling away on the TV screen, with the dry Al Gore and the much-lampooned George W. Bush slugging it out in front of a largely apathetic audience. The result was too close to call, and recounts had to take place in Florida. There was some evidence of a swing to a third party. Not the right, though, but the Greens. Ralph Nader did more than upset some Democrats with his newfound partnership in this corner.

Meanwhile, a fiery former Reagan and Nixon speechwriter took the helm of the Reform Party, campaigning on an isolationist, ultra-right agenda. White supremacists were found within his headquarters, and for a while the far right proclaimed him a true saviour. Then he appointed a black female running mate and crashed to disaster.

My BNP contacts eventually would lead me to the man himself.

SEVEN

THE MESSENGER

DECEMBER 2000

The nerves are starting to bite. It's becoming real, at last, this odyssey of mine.

Behind me, I watch his back stride off into the night. Nondescript jacket, balding head surfacing above hunched shoulders. The fingers, surprisingly slender, sink into hands mapped out with veins across weathered skin. The mouth drops ever so slightly at the corner – a consequence, perhaps, of a frequent no-nonsense expression. His voice is gruff. He can be a difficult man. A passionate soccer fan. Yet a fierce intellect and hidden sensitivity lurk beneath hooded brown eyes.

Graeme Atkinson is a unique figure, one of the foremost anti-fascists of his generation. A former teacher, Graeme has lived for many years in Germany, going undercover and helping expose various neo-nazi figures. He's one of those who helped film David Irving, showing him at gatherings of the extreme right, speaking fluent German. He's also survived a murder attempt by neo-nazi gang members in Sweden.

We've just met in the cramped café of a freezing station. Our voices were hushed, even in these anonymous surroundings. I drank weak, over-boiled coffee and unwisely chose a plastic-tasting Danish pastry for my dinner. It was late, cold, wet. Other travellers sat nearby, waiting like me for the last train from this soulless crossroads.

Soon, Graeme and I will be preparing to travel to Berlin together. For the first time, I feel totally out of my depth. Few people can help me. My partner thinks I'm mad, and so do my parents and friends.

Before we set out, Graeme tries to brief me. This is just a scouting mission, but he doesn't want to mislead me. The scale of extreme right and neo-nazi activity is high in Germany. This is not simply a few nuts from the Internet. As he explains during our second meeting, one cold evening before Christmas: 'I had to talk to some of the left back in England. Y'know, about what was going on in Germany and the like. The scale of it, y'know, that's what I was trying to impress on them. Then this one clown,' he says, tutting in his deep northern accent, 'he says let's go over there with a coachload of the boys. I said, what, I don't think I heard you properly from back there. Can you repeat what you just said? And he did. Bloody crazy! But they just didn't get it. How are you going to take one or two coachloads of people, carrying baseball bats, and take on the thousands of voters who've put political parties into regional government?!' He shakes his head and looks down, then lifts his chin and starts laughing, as if he can hardly believe what he's just told me.

But it's no laughing matter. According to Graeme's contacts in Berlin, there have already been 134 deaths directly attributable to extreme-right violence since the Wall came down. He speaks slowly, his voice measured. I try not to let my nerves show. According to an interior ministry report he also hands me, racist crimes have shot up by over 50 per cent in the past year. It makes my experiences in England seem trivial by comparison.

Earlier this summer, as I was travelling across the UK, a pipe bomb exploded in a station in a suburb of Düsseldorf. Ten foreign students were injured, including a pregnant woman. Six were Jews. The targeting seemed deliberate. 'Bombs go off because people can't imitate Haider over there,' says Graeme, sitting at his kitchen table. He seems to pour coffee by the gallon. 'The majority of violence comes in where political representation [of the far right] is less.'

I don't know what it's like to be of Kurdish, Vietnamese or African descent and living in some east German town, invited over when the West wanted workers and the GDR had close relations with other communist states. To be someone like Alberto Adriano, who didn't have a chance. A German citizen, of Mozambican origin, Adriano was kicked to death on the streets of the east German city of Dessau earlier this year. His racist attackers stripped him naked, screaming 'nigger pig' and 'this is the march of the German resistance', as they caved in his head with their steel-tipped boots.

The murder was part of a fresh wave of racial violence sweeping Germany. German police are investigating nearly 16,000 racist attacks in the last year alone. The 85,000-strong Jewish community has borne much of the brunt of these attacks and vandalism in recent weeks.

Graeme hands me various papers, photocopies and Internet reports detailing these events. They're arrayed in a neat, clinical set of boxes stored in his attic. Düsseldorf synagogue, which serves a congregation of 6,300 people, was firebombed on the evening of 2 October this year. No one was hurt and damage was minimal, but the attack 'left deep spiritual wounds', according to the city's chief rabbi, Michael Goldberger. In the wake of the Düsseldorf attack, a Jewish cemetery in Schwäbisch Hall is daubed, windows at another synagogue in Berlin's Kreuzberg district are smashed and a Jewish cemetery in Potsdam is defiled. In Halle, swastikas are carved into the gate of a memorial at the site of the city's former synagogue.

As I talk with Graeme, we hear that the government has just banned the German chapter of Blood and Honour. It's their response to this rocketing level of neo-nazi violence, but does little to dampen enthusiasm for the white-power music scene. It's funny to think back on my meeting with Ian Stuart's old friend Sid, in that tiny Derbyshire town. It was Stuart who created Blood and Honour back in 1987. From there it passed into the hands of C18. It's an international movement, particularly strong in Scandinavia and Germany. Perhaps, for dispossessed white youth, it represents rebellion. Certainly, there's a huge market for white-power bands. The scene in Germany is second only to the USA, where millions of dollars now change hands.

Only ten days after the ban, there's a concert in the northern town of Lüneberg. When police turn up, acting on a tip-off, neo-nazis retaliate with massive violence. Forty-six officers are injured, two seriously. Thirty-two extremists are arrested, but most walk away untouched.

There are numerous attacks on foreigners. The clock tower at the former Buchenwald concentration camp is desecrated. And a birthday party organised by anti-fascists is raided by a squad of young nazis, in the east German town of Wurzen. The attackers, wielding knives and baseball bats, wreck doors and furniture, smash windows, and leave three people badly wounded.

One incident in particular lives in infamy, leading The Beast, Will Browning, to compose the song *Barbecue in Rostock* with his band, No Remorse, eulogising the destruction of an immigrants' hostel in the north-eastern city of Rostock. During a three-day campaign of terror in 1992, the hostel, housing mainly Vietnamese immigrants, was subjected to a calculated and brutal series of attacks. In fact, it lay virtually under siege for nearly those entire three days, with little help from outside authorities or the community.

I watch the events unfolding on a film called *The Truth Lies In Rostock*. During the increasingly severe attacks on the building, locals are seen applauding youths as they become ever bolder, eventually clambering onto balconies and leaping into windows, hurling petrol bombs and chasing terrified residents onto the roof. Flames begin to lick at the lower floors. The police arrive late, outnumbered, and are pushed back. Their one water cannon runs out of water. Old men and women can be seen cheering the arrival of outside neo-nazi organisers as hostel workers try desperately and in vain to call the police. Eventually, they clamber across the roof to the adjacent building. The hostel is completely torched. Afterwards many locals claim they saw nothing, and that it was the immigrants who were causing all the crime and problems in the area.

During my stay, I also watched another film, *The Truth Shall Make You Free* (after an old Nazi saying), which Graeme had co-produced. His collaborator Michael Schmidt had penetrated deep into the country's far-right gangs, and what he revealed was truly frightening (his book about these experiences, *The New Reich*, is well worth reading).

'What's going on?' I ask Graeme, my eyes widening as I turn from the TV. He's working on a case for the Canadian government, buried deep in a set of notes. The adversary this time is an infamous revisionist, Ernst Zundel, a German who emigrated to Canada and set up his 'Zundelsite' web operation several years ago. The courts have since been trying to close it. He's another whose path I would later cross.

'Jeez, Graeme, this is monstrous in scale!' I say.

He lifts a tired-looking face from the documents, pulling his glasses off his nose and rubbing the bridge between his eyes. 'Yeah, well, now you know why I laugh at some of the stories I read about what's happening in Britain. It's nothing – nothing – in comparison to what's going on in other parts of the continent.'

There's a question of identity at work in Germany today, Graeme believes. It ties in with my own thinking, but there's an added factor. In Germany, there's the question of being a 'blood German'. It's something deeply ingrained into the national psyche. In some people's eyes, you can't be black, for example, and also considered German. You can be 'born' German, by blood, not 'become' one, no matter how many generations of your family have lived in the country. In the birthplace of Nazism, the rise of intolerance is a worrying sign.

There's a sombre tone to Graeme's words. Germany already has three extreme-right political parties. There's the Deutsche Volksunion (DVU), the Republikaner party (REP) and – my quarry – the Nationaldemokratische Partei Deutschlands (NPD). Even the Christian Democrats – former Chancellor Kohl's party – are said to have become much more right-wing and anti-immigrant in an effort to shore up votes. It's a move mirrored elsewhere on the continent. Conservative and even liberal politicians react to greater economic insecurity, linking this to an increasing influx of migrants. This in turn seems to create a fear in much of the mainstream populace – the workers and even the middle classes – that we're being 'swamped'.

Graeme says the NPD has become a breeding ground for neo-nazi extremism. It has organised street demonstrations across the country and has virulent views on race and immigration. Yet it's been infiltrated at many levels by even more extreme, street level neo-nazis. These local *Kameradschaften* (a term taken from the Nazi era meaning 'comradeships') are right-wing social networks which have sprung up all over the country. Comprising mainly youngsters, they're responsible for stoking up and organising much of the tension in poverty-stricken areas suffering from high unemployment and rapid change. Easterners have, in general, been less well placed to cope with integration than the West. Indeed, a form of racism exists even between these two halves of the country. I remember meeting west Berliners whilst living on a kibbutz. Though they were clearly left-wingers, they spoke in often highly derogatory tones about the 'easterners'.

The Kameradschaften have been instrumental in declaring some neighbourhoods, even small towns, as 'NBZs' (National befreite Zonen) or 'liberated zones'. That is, free of foreigners and any left-wing opposition. The German government has started moves to ban the NPD – even though it's a legally registered political party. It's an almost unprecedented move; the last such group to be banned was the Sozialistische Reichspartei, a National Socialist party in the 1950s.

The evening draws on. The village sleeps around us, as Graeme calls his contacts first in Norway, then in Chicago. Exhausted, we end up speaking of Haider's success in Austria, and of the less noted but equally powerful changes taking place in Italy, Scandinavia, and Belgium. These changes are far more noteworthy, Graeme believes, than the growth of fringe neo-nazi groups. In Belgium, for example, the ultra-nationalist Flemish party, the Vlaams Blok (VB), is raging up the polls. Most of these organisations and movements tend to feed on a diet of anti-immigrant rhetoric (often anti-Islam, too) and deep conservative politics. 'Traditional' and pro-family values are high on the agenda, along with a desire for those mythical 'better' days of the past. Russia also has several burgeoning ultra-nationalist movements, as do Slovakia, Hungary and other central and eastern European countries.

Such changes have begun to inspire nationalists and far-right politicians across the continent. 'There's an organic political connection between all these groups, but not necessarily direct, physical contact,' says Graeme. He recommends that I visit the Vlaams Blok, instead of my planned foray into France and the remnants of the Front National. They'll be more relevant and more amenable to discussion, he reckons.

And he's right. What I'm to find in Belgium, next spring, is startling. An ultra-nationalist party, surging right in the very heart of the European experiment.

* * *

We arrive late in the evening, a few days before Christmas. Below zero, the air is crystalline. Short jets of exhaust steam from the passing traffic. The hum of electricity and clatter of metal grinding on rails herald the passage of yellow-and-white trams. The roads unfurl, Roman-straight, wide and well planned. A quick bus ride to the nearest station, between huge, grey apartment blocks, and we're silently riding on the U-Bahn into Berlin.

This is where it all began, I think. We exit the U-Bahn, looking up at the rails stretching overhead, following the old shape of the Wall, snaking off into the distance. 'C'mon, hurry up,' Graeme snaps, eager to get inside.

As we walk, bitter gusts of wind chill the pale, almost dead-looking flesh of the passers-by. The language I hear on these streets seems harsh, guttural, unfamiliar. I'm used to travelling in countries where everyone accommodates me by speaking English. To me, this is very much an alien place.

We struggle across a huge, old imperial bridge, leaning over the Havel River. I pass dour east Berliners, Turks and Oriental faces. Tailgates of passing taxis glow through the sleet. Even the city's odour is subtly different to my native England, the shops and bars we pass permeated by the smell of cooked sausages.

We fetch up in front of tall, dark, wooden doors. We ring the bell, Graeme lets forth a sharp burst to the disembodied voice within, and soon we're circling up a wide stone staircase.

Rolf greets us a few flights up. A genial-faced man, with a frizz of greying hair, he greets me in excellent, slightly accented English, shaking my hand loosely. 'I lived abroad for a few years,' he explains. Rolf is not his real name, but as a dedicated member of the anti-fascist movement (or 'Antifa' as it's called here) he needs to preserve his anonymity in one of the most dangerous countries for right-wing violence.

For three days we sit at the long pine table in Rolf's small kitchen, drinking endless cups of whisked coffee and talking of the country's neo-nazi scene. I shuffle back and forth between the apartment and one of the main anti-fascist archives. What I learn exposes the huge scale of right-wing activity. Although the Republikaner party has enjoyed some electoral success, it's recently suffered internal splits. The DVU remains the largest of the three far-right parties in electoral terms, but it's the NPD and *Freie Kameradschaften* that everyone is watching. The NPD has only a few council seats in different states, but it's been mobilising thousands of skinheads for several years now. Most of this activity is organised by hard-core nazis from the former Gesinnungs-gemeinschaft der Neuen Front (GdNF), a notorious (and banned) neo-nazi umbrella organisation. Most recently, the party organised a controversial march through the Brandenburg Gate. Anyone who knows Second World War history understands the significance of that act.

One figure is key in all this: frequently convicted Hamburg extremist Christian Worch. He's been active since the 1970s, when he was chief lieutenant to Michel Kühnen, one of Germany's seminal far-right figures. Kühnen, who created the GdNF, was a closet homosexual and died of AIDS in 1991. Worch lifted his mantle, and today forms a bridge between neo-nazi youth and cadres who've secreted themselves within the NPD. He also has links to other national socialist movements across Europe, such as the Danish National Socialist Movement (DNSB) in Denmark, the National Socialistik Front (NSF) in Sweden and the pan-European Blood and Honour network. As a result of his influence, a power battle is raging within the

NPD, between Worch's men and the old guard leadership who favour greater respectability.

According to Tammy – another pseudonym used by a female friend of Rolf's – Blood and Honour Division Deutschland remains the most influential organisation in a burgeoning extreme-right youth culture. Late one night in a bar, she tells me of her visits to the 'liberated zones' in the east of the country. It's extremely dangerous work. Despite the recent ban, Blood and Honour has been publishing its own newspaper. The Berlin section of this violent gang is the strongest, but sections in Brandenburg and Saxony continue to stage illegal concerts and are regularly seen at marches organised by the NPD and Freie Kameradschaften, she says.

In particular, the group acts as a crossing point between organised criminality – protection rackets, drug trafficking, and selling banned music and publications – and militant paramilitary activities. It sounds disturbingly like what I've already encountered in Britain. The Freie Kameradschaften also have a share in this. The latest example is an interview in *Hamburger Sturm*, in which an anonymous neo-nazi argues in favour of building illegal armed cells. Significantly, this publication is put out by people around Christian Worch and another infamous extremist, Thomas Wulff. My old friends from Combat 18 have been active on the scene, too. The Beast seems to have a personal connection to (what Graeme labels) 'a psycho' called Thorsten Heise. German, Swedish and British C18 members, plus those from the international Blood and Honour network, have recently met in Norway.

Tammy seems tired, but as a favour to Graeme has agreed to this late meeting. At the Norwegian gathering, she says, this network agreed to coordinate their international activities and step up attacks and intimidation against anti-fascists, journalists, and representatives of the State. It's not the first time this has happened. Thomas Nakaba, the Danish neo-nazi who created C18 Copenhagen, led an international bombing attempt fostered by British and Scandinavian extremists. Nakaba's trail would soon lead me abroad once more.

Tammy tells me it's going to be very hard cracking into this scene, and potentially quite dangerous. This is very different to the 'Hollywood Nazis' I'll see in the States, she says, with a wan smile. Here, people die. I'll spend months negotiating directly with Worch in his Hamburg base, as well as with key figures within the NPD.

Before I leave, Rolf and his network of secretive contacts agree to help me when I return. We stay in touch over the following months. They'll accompany me on a dangerous trip right into the heart of the nazi resurgence here in the West, deep inside a 'liberated zone'.

* * *

EARLY SPRING 2001

Fat flakes of snow drift past the window. My face pressed against the cold inner surface, I look down as we tumble beneath the cloud level. Then I lean back into the deep, soft leather seat. This is the way to travel, I think. The Scandinavians have the right idea when it comes to comfort.

It's been a busy few weeks. Since my last trip, I've managed to establish direct contact with William Pierce in the States. A curt email from the man himself has arrived, agreeing to meet me. It's labelled 'Chairman'. Christian Worch in Germany has agreed to meet with me too, after several faxes. In uncertain English he tells me about his busy schedule organising demonstrations. Over the years, Pierce has made direct connections with the NPD and in the music scene, as has Worch. (When I tried calling Worch, all I got was an answering machine playing Def Leppard.)

Leading neo-nazis from the Blood and Honour network in Sweden have also issued a tentative yes. Erik Blücher, a well-known Norwegian extremist and key figure in the international music scene, will see me at his southern Swedish stronghold of Helsingborg. Members of the National Socialistik Front (NSF) have agreed, too. *Searchlight* hand me pictures of them, in their uniforms; one even legally changed his name to 'Himmler'.

I'll have to tread carefully. The scene has gone off the scale recently in Sweden, with a spate of killings and bombings, and mass outrage amongst mainstream opinion. An investigative journalist has been car-bombed with his young son; two policemen have been executed and two caught in a booby-trap blast; a trade unionist has been shot dead on his doorstep. One of the leading members of *Searchlight's* sister magazine, *Expo*, has narrowly missed being hit by a sniper's bullet. It's like The Order all over again. One of the guys arrested for the police killings belonged to the NSF. All four major national newspapers have published identical covers, listing the names and addresses of 54 suspected neo-nazis in a show of public revulsion at these killings.

Now, though, the trail has led back once more to Combat 18 – but not to England, to Charlie and Steve or The Beast. At least, not directly. This time the trail leads to Denmark, land of social democracy.

When I arrive, Copenhagen is reeling from a recent rampage by English football hooligans, but still seems resplendent in its island setting. Tall spires rise from the flat landscape, punctuating a rolling, grey sky. Avant-garde sculptures perch boldly next to canals. And tucked into little inlets nestle bars filled with flushed-faced locals. It reminds me of my childhood visits to Amsterdam.

From the window of the space-age train, gliding in fast and sealed from the airport, I count block after block of neat, six-storey buildings. It's more uniform than I'm used to. This is not the chaotic, drab, Victorian cityscape of England. I crick my neck from side to side, sip my coffee and think more on my quarry.

Thomas Nakaba: the name haunts my journey. Another lone wolf? Perhaps like Copeland, inspired by stronger figures around him? That's how it seemed at first.

I know he's currently rotting in prison, here in Copenhagen. And the next few days will prove something else for me: how Nakaba once was the linchpin of an international neo-nazi terrorist campaign. He also was part of another British-inspired export, the huge international growth of Blood and Honour. Few people seem to know much about this twisted, introverted young man – not even those he tried to kill. I feel his presence around me.

As it turns out, Thomas Nakaba and his former friends in Denmark's leading extremist group, the Danish National Socialist Movement (DNSB), also had close contacts with many other organisations I'm soon to meet: Christian Worch; skins in Blood and Honour Deutschlands; members of the NSF in Sweden; Will Browning and Darren Wells. And he had a fervid obsession with William Pierce's writings.

Outside, it's bitingly cold. The sun gilds a sudden break in the cloud cover. I wander past a Somalian or Ethiopian couple. They hold hands, she pregnant, he short and looking up towards the station noticeboard. I wonder what it's like to be an immigrant here. I'm told one reason neo-nazi and far-right political groups are on the march in Scandinavia is a sudden and recent rise in immigration. These countries never had a multi-ethnic 'empire', as such. Nor were they founded on the basis of America's New World-style immigration. My sources tell me that around 10 per cent of the Danish population are now migrants. For a significant minority, this change seems to cause problems.

In Norway, such tensions have led to the creation of the Progress Party; in Sweden, the Sweden Democrats; and here in Denmark, the Danish People's Party (which gets 12 per cent of the vote by the end of the year and enters into coalition government). All are far right, anti-immigrant (repatriation schemes are a common theme) and anti-Islamic, claiming the churches will soon be converted into mosques. Anti-globalisation links them, ironically, with the left. But it's the foreigners, as ever, who attract much of their attention. And all three parties are growing.

* * *

I nearly bump into Erik Jensen before I see him. The station draws majestically up around us, cavernous and booming. 'Hello,' he drawls slowly. 'Nick Ryan, yes?' His voice is surprisingly soft, the sentences drifting off at the end. He offers me a gloved hand. An attractive red-haired woman stands next to him. She beams a radiant smile, shakes my hand, then turns quickly and leaves.

'My apartment's not too far away,' Erik says, his craggy face framed by white hair and a genial beard, yellowing nicotine stains painted into his whiskers. He leads me off down crowded steps, out onto a narrow platform below. We make our way through rows of office workers, many of them holding bikes. We jump silently onto a train and ride the short distance to his local station. The cold air is fresh, invigorating after the dirt of London.

Erik is a founder and leading member of *Demos*, a sister organisation to *Searchlight*. He's been active since the 1960s, when the anti-Vietnam War movement led him into left-wing politics. We've never met before now, but I recognise his face. Scandinavian neo-nazis have put out a caricature image, showing him targeted in a sniper's scope.

'Oh yes, they've tried to break down the outside door, smash the windows and target our offices,' he says, casually, when I question him about it.

The pleasant aftertaste of wood smoke and pipe tobacco bathes the back of my throat. The freezing air is banished once more as we enter a small, crowded apartment. Shafts of sunlight occasionally break through the windows. We're near the top of one of the six-storey blocks, overlooking a railway siding. The rumble of passing trains is a gentle undertone to our disturbing conversation.

Without speaking, he points to a kettle with one end of his pipe and indicates I should prepare myself some tea or coffee. I take off my shoes and walk gingerly over the pine floor, past row after row of books, most of which concern the right. I wonder if he has a copy of *The Turner Diaries*. 'Oh yes, in there somewhere. You should read it for your research. It doesn't take long. Otherwise, I wouldn't bother with it, though. It's not a very good book.'

As I clatter around the kitchen, the old man turns his back, wrapped in a thick cardigan, and seems to hunt through a collection of cardboard folders. He grunts and pulls out some glossy black and white photographs. 'Have a look at these,' he orders. His voice sounds tired, but the ice-blue eyes are sharp and inquisitive as he peers at me through a tumble of eyebrows. I lay some of the pictures next to an old PC.

Shaven heads. Leather jackets. Tattoos. Blood and Honour banners. Scene after scene of skins and their girlfriends. A *Who's Who* of Europe's neo-nazi clans.

I hear the click of a lighter, then a puff of smoke drifts across my view. 'One of our people has just taken these,' Erik says. 'It's the funeral of Marcel Schilf.'

In Nordic and white-power music circles, the name is legendary. Schilf was one of the key figures in the Blood and Honour network. A Dane born in Germany, he forged an almost father-son relationship with Erik Blücher in southern Sweden. The two occupied the same building for a while, a place called Club Valhalla in Helsingborg. The young nazi ran NS88, a CD and video firm, then another outfit called NS Records, operating in tandem with Blücher's Ragnarok Records.

Schilf became a hero to the young neo-nazis of Scandinavia and

Germany. He was a key figure in the creation of Blood and Honour Scandinavia, linking various neo-nazi operations in 1997. Only after this move were individual chapters set up in each country. They often ended up in close competition with other white-power businesses, bankrolled by William Pierce. That tension would lead, at times, to violence.

Erik rolls off a litany of names present in each picture of the funeral and asks if I recognise several British figures. Schilf had died slowly, as his lungs collapsed from cystic fibrosis, leading Blücher to post an almost tearful eulogy on the Blood and Honour website. I'd have to be careful talking about it with him.

The old left-winger also tells me something of Erik Blücher's background: how the Norwegian has spent much of his nearly 50 years in this movement, meeting former members of Hitler's regime and working with the longtime right-wing publisher Anthony Hancock, in a printing press back in Brighton, England, in the early 1980s. Blücher had always remained secretive about his connections – until 1997, when he suddenly revealed himself as spokesperson for Blood and Honour Scandinavia. Another link in the C18 web. He once wrote that the neo-nazi skins he found around him were 'the new SA [brownshirts]'. Blücher and I keep swapping emails throughout the year – even when his father dies. I'm extremely nervous about meeting him, but determined to try. Sweden seems an epicentre of hate that I must visit.

Erik then shows me a picture of Jonni Hansen, who is in jail after running over a protester outside his party's headquarters. For a while, he was Denmark's leading – or at least most public – neo-nazi. His Danish National Socialist Movement had its own headquarters, a radio station, a website, and an electoral strategy. A traditional 'Hitlerist', Hansen developed close ties with Christian Worch in Hamburg and with the NSF in Sweden. These groups would often be seen at the Dane's headquarters, and vice-versa. White-power records were even recorded in the garden of the DNSB commune.

Erik explains the difference between these political groups and Blood and Honour. 'B&H is an ideology. You don't have a party; it's a brotherhood.' (There's a Nordic term, 'bootboys', which is often used for their members.) 'You can't be a member; there are no membership cards. It's only your merits which can gain you a place in the informal organisation. So in terms of organisation, and how to get power, they are very different.'

Blood and Honour is also inspired by the US notion of 'leaderless resistance'. There's a strong undercurrent of paganism and Norse revivalism in its philosophy. But its original model was Combat 18 in Britain. In contrast, Jonni Hansen, Christian Worch, and perhaps also Erik Blücher, favour the creation of a party – a nazi party – which could be legalised in a country such as Germany. The end result? Build it up, just like Hitler.

A strange, almost comic-looking figure from the US, Gary Lauck, helped bring the men and their networks together. When I visited Lauck's website – trying not to laugh at the image of the small, moustachioed man in his brownshirt uniform – I found links to dozens of other organisations. Some, like Sweden's NSF, were not a surprise. Others, in a welter of European languages, were. Lauck had served prison time in Germany for his views, so I guess he's pretty serious about his aims. Or perhaps he's just another American wannabe, who doesn't understand the difference between US and European cultural sensitivities. This gulf in understanding was something I encountered time and again on my travels.

I stand outside Erik's apartment on a bridge, gripping freezing metal and gazing down into black water. I've come outside for a break. I ponder the events that seemed to lead Thomas Nakaba down into his spiral of hate. It was only 100 metres from where I'm standing, in the next apartment block, that he put together his bombs.

And it wasn't far from here, either, that Nakaba and Will Browning met for a second time, in the DNSB's compound. Browning and Charlie were highly impressed with Jonni Hansen's set-up. Perhaps the DNSB operation helped convince The Beast of the plans for an 'Aryan Homeland' back in England. The two men, together with Steve Sargent and a number of others, formed a group which planned to kill a Swedish neo-nazi. Known as 'Pajen' ('The Pie'), he was a key member of Nordland, a white-power music business based in Sweden and in bitter competition with Blood and Honour. Pajen had also been mouthing off against The Beast.

The first encounter between Browning and Nakaba had taken place in the town of Roskilde, in 1995, during an annual commemoration march for Hitler's henchman Rudolf Hess. This event regularly draws thousands of neo-nazis from across Europe. Browning had let fly against left-wing protesters and a TV camera crew, with characteristic rage and violence. The young Nakaba was so impressed that he set up a C18 chapter here in Denmark and embarked on his doomed and self-destructive course.

I'd first heard his name whispered by Nick Lowles, during Charlie Sargent's murder trial. About the letter bombs sent from Sweden and the targets back in Britain. In fact, what began as a power struggle between two men soon escalated into a deadly international conflict. From the heart of Essex – the very centre of the 'Aryan Homeland', in those same streets of Chelmsford I had roamed – a rivalry between Charlie and The Beast spun out of control and spawned a new kind of neo-nazi movement. Unknown to me, it took place right under my nose.

* * *

The story is outlined slowly during the days I spend locked deep in discussion with *Demos*'s underground network. I walk through the cold, cobbled streets, exploring and trying to understand this city.

Rasmus Juel walks by my side, dark-haired and fresh-faced, intelligent eyes glittering. Like most Danes, he speaks excellent English. We visit his girlfriend, the same red-haired woman I'd met at the station earlier, and spend time chatting in a Chinese restaurant. He reminds me of Nick Lowles, the same pleasant features and youth. He's also invisible; you'd never pick him out from a crowd. Guys like this are the antithesis, in a weird way, of the lone wolf. And they exist in each country I visit.

I've been staying on a couch in his apartment. It's an unusual communal set-up, shared by a mix of left-wing individuals. One, a geographer, bakes apple dumplings as he jokes with me about 'your diseased isle' (referring to our BSE problem). During the night, I gaze up at the twisting, gilded steeple of Vor Frelsers Kirke. From the apex of this seventeenth-century church, reached by a spiral staircase, you can survey most of the city.

Rasmus and I discuss Nakaba's life. Few people seem to know much about who he really was. There are rumours of a difficult childhood and a growing obsession with people like William Pierce. But there appear to be few I can talk to about this; they're either in prison, or have disappeared, or would try to kill me.

The bone-numbing cold does little to dent the free spirit of Christinia, a hippie haven left over from the early 1970s, built on reclaimed military land. The wooden shacks, jewellery stalls and once-derelict warehouses are subject to their own laws and communal living. We pass small fires burning beside stalls, the flickering flames illuminating small packets of hash and grass, openly for sale. Incense and patchouli oil waft across my nose and vision. We settle for some kind of healthy wheatgerm kebab, then sit on a freezing wooden bench and talk, as the sun sinks below the horizon.

* * *

The time was October 1996, just a month before my first encounter with Charlie Sargent. David Myatt, the former monk and Satanist, had been writing of the need for a terrorist struggle in the extreme right.

'The primary duty of all National-Socialists is to change the world,' he wrote, in one of his verbose outbursts. 'National-Socialism means revolution: the overthrow of the existing System and its replacement with a National-Socialist society. Revolution means struggle: it means war.' He went on to produce a template and guide for these attacks, talking of raising tensions within 'enemy' communities to incite a backlash against whites, and calling for 'covert action groups' to infiltrate other organisations and to prepare for direct conflict with agents of 'the System'.

Charlie's much-vaunted race war had yet to materialise. Darren said, during an interview for a TV programme: 'We wanted people to take notice of us, to move onto the next level. Some in C18 wanted to be a proper terrorist organisation.'

The gang was attracting more police attention. There'd been raids on their CD and print operations. The Beast was waiting for a possible prison sentence, for his part in these activities. Others in the extreme right were lambasting him and C18, calling them 'soft'. All this contributed to his desire to create a small, radical cell. When his band released its album *Barbecue in Rostock*, he wrote a letter to accompany the CD, which began: 'When I hear the do-nothings, the money makers and traitors of the scene slagging off C18 and spreading lies, it makes me mad.'

Mad enough, it seemed, to organise a bombing campaign.

Thomas Nakaba apparently felt the same way. The young Dane became the fifth member of Browning's cell. By now, he'd also made a close friendship with Darren Wells, who had helped me understand The Beast. The two had met during what became an abortive attempt to locate and kill Pajen, in Sweden.

Darren started a relationship with the best friend of Nakaba's partner. By now, the Dane had moved to Pivo, a small commuter town. He was living in state-supplied housing because Anya, his girlfriend, was pregnant.

In September of that year, he'd travelled to England, attending a meeting on the Homeland project with The Beast and Darren, hosted by Charlie. Browning became incensed when Charlie read out a list of ISD Records debtors, against his express wishes. These included his friend Marcel Schilf, who owed £20,000. His mood further worsened when Charlie stated that C18's main aim was going to be increasing paper sales. In Browning's view, ISD Records had been created to fund terrorist organisations.

The Beast and his new clique reached a decision. He would keep money away from the ISD accounts and funnel it into terrorist activities. Nakaba himself suggested using Denmark as a base. It was close to most of mainland Europe, yet also sufficiently remote, and had more tolerant laws. One of his close friends had helped fit alarm systems to many of the country's military dumps. The gang would be able to raid these with impunity, collecting heavy weapons for their struggle. Swedish neo-nazis put the same theory into practice when they raided such dumps to launch their terror campaign in 1999.

Browning and Wells travelled to Denmark at the end of that month. They'd just given up on an attempt to find, and possibly kill, a rival member of the British Movement. The Beast had also overheard, for the first time, a phone call from Charlie claiming he'd stolen money from ISD Records. It only fed his rage.

The decision had already been made to shift ISD to Scandinavia, away from Britain. Browning and Wells took the ferry from Copenhagen to Helsingborg, in southern Sweden, to visit Marcel Schilf. Rasmus told me some other details about Schilf: he'd been an amateur bomb maker and a computer hacker, and had been raided by police after a left-winger was killed by a letter bomb. A dozen devices and a manual were found, but despite help from Scotland Yard, no evidence could be found linking him to the crime. When more letter bombs were sent to targets in Vienna, he was again high on the suspect list. Austrian police thought the Danes had helped German extremists manufacture the devices. Again, no charges were brought.

The men met in Erik Blücher's Club Valhalla, passing the pastiche façades of Helsingborg's tall beachside houses. During the discussions which followed, Schilf agreed to act as head of ISD's Scandinavian operations. Thomas Nakaba was to become its sole beneficiary, receiving funds for his operations in a specially created bank account. Browning would also have access, but the main purpose was to help purchase weapons and equipment.

The men also discussed the first leg of their operation: sending letter bombs to targets on the right and left. Nakaba was to be the instrument that sent these 'messages', as they became known, of righteous retribution. It seemed disturbingly reminiscent of The Order.

In the tawdry surroundings of Pivo, the three men celebrated and toasted their plan. The town, about 40 minutes from Copenhagen, had become a cheap dumping ground for the poor. In one of only two restaurants, Tony's Pizzeria, they discussed their plot. Outside, the snow was unusually thick for the time of year.

Darren remembers Nakaba taking out several sticks of dynamite and the men starting to giggle nervously. 'Like kids in a candy store,' Darren said later. There was sudden consternation when Nakaba told them the explosives were extremely sensitive to heat and cold. Trudging back to his cramped flat, the men had even begun playing with lumps of plastic explosive.

In December, Nakaba flew to London for three days. The attacks were being brought forward, before The Beast went off to prison, as a warning to his opponents. A list of targets was drawn up: the London address of Anti-Fascist Action; British Movement leader Micky Lane; *Searchlight*; the mailing address for the British Hammerskins (by now, I'd learned that Hervé, the French skinhead, who was part of Steve Sargent's mob, was working for the Charlemagne Hammerskins); and former Olympic swimmer Sharron Davies, whose crime was that she had a black partner.

Browning handed Nakaba a design for a detonator, copied from a guerrilla warfare manual, then left him to his own devices, to set the plan in motion in mid-January. Browning agreed not to speak about the bombs on the telephone, but when several weeks passed and nothing had happened, he became frustrated. After a number of attempts, he finally raised Nakaba on the evening of 16 January 1997.

'Have you sent me the messages yet?' he asked, using an agreed code.

'Yes,' Nakaba replied, hesitantly. He found Browning's London accent somewhat difficult to understand. And he was reluctant to go ahead with the plan, it seemed.

'You promise?'

'Yes.'

'You promise?' The Beast repeated, ever suspicious.

'Yes, I told you,' the Dane replied.

'Fucking brilliant!' said The Beast. 'There's only a few of us. The rest of them are wimps, they're wankers. When we've done this, then we'll go on and do the more important stuff.'

Unknown to them, Danish police were already listening in on the conversation. Nakaba was being watched, too. The plan would be stillborn.

Nakaba had not yet sent the bombs. He was trapped. If he didn't send them soon, The Beast would find out. He faced a difficult choice: risk either jail or The Beast's wrath.

What followed was a rapid series of journeys. Nakaba phoned his brother-in-law, telling him he would be around the next day. After a poor night's sleep, he set out on his quest – watched all the time by Danish police. They'd already received a message from the British authorities, telling them that Browning had brought a gun and C4 into the country. (Erik Jensen says Browning bought these in Poland, but didn't realise that he was sold training explosives.)

Nakaba bid goodbye to his young partner – now with a baby – and spent the day buying parts and making preparations for the big event. His brother-in-law and a friend were both sympathisers. They helped him fetch the explosives (hidden in the cellar of a family house), whilst Nakaba tried to fashion a home-made detonator. After four failed attempts (he kept shattering the light bulbs he was using), he had to go round to another contact's house and buy a set of proper devices. Not before he let several off, though, in a churchyard, in full view of the police surveillance teams. His friend went out from his cluttered, dirty flat and purchased the final components: a pack of padded envelopes and some new bulbs.

Leaving the flat, Nakaba made one last call to Anya, who told him there'd been a threatening phone call from an anti-fascist organisation. He told her to go to her brother's place, where he would pick her up later, and reminded her of what to do if he didn't come back.

In the early evening hours, with the temperature dropping violently – just like now, Rasmus said as he related the story to me – Nakaba zipped his jacket over his nazi tattoos and made his way to the hydrofoil terminal. But it was closed. He had to take a bus service to the ferry port at Dragor, then catch a boat for the 55-minute journey to Sweden.

The fear and adrenaline were beginning to tell. Despite the cold, he was dripping with sweat. When he disembarked he made his way to Linhamn, near the city of Malmo. Ice caked the streets, making the concrete buildings seem even more stark in relief against the glittering night sky.

His steps took him past a letterbox. He carried on walking, then doubled back. According to statements Nick Lowles saw, he began thinking about his family: of his mother, who hated his political views, and who had married an American of Japanese descent soon after he was born, then a man of Pakistani origin when the first husband left. The second disappeared soon after, though not before fathering his mixed-race sister.

Unhinging his shoulder bag, Nakaba took out, then carefully posted the three packages he carried. Each contained a videocassette, inside which was a small piece of wiring. This would detonate a piece of plastic explosive when opened. They were addressed to AFA, the BM and Sharron Davies. 'She's a race mixer and should be taught a lesson,' Browning had said. In the extremists' eyes, it was the cardinal sin.

As Nakaba walked away, the plain-clothes officers who had been following him all day signalled to waiting colleagues. The postbox was isolated, and the packages were soon made safe.

At five o'clock the next morning, the police kicked down the door of his Pivo apartment. The neo-nazi managed to get off one shot from his gun, hitting one of the officers in the groin, before being swiftly overwhelmed.

In reality, it was over before it had begun. The whole terror campaign was stillborn.

Then they went after The Beast.

* * *

I spend my last afternoon walking for hours, pacing my own demons and those of my quarry.

My journey takes me down through Strøget, the world's longest pedestrian mall. Through a curtain of driving snow, I glimpse the majestic ramparts of the Tivoli funfair. There's a sad, yet graceful quality to the rusting ironwork, even if the old dippers and swings remain silent, swaying gently, almost playfully in the dead winter's breeze.

Tivoli and its gardens are Copenhagen's grand architectural memorial. The gates are locked, but I can sense the thousands of souls who've passed through here. I walk round the walled outskirts, my head slowly plastered with a damp layer of melted snow. Then I give up the quest for an entrance and set off at a brisk pace for the south of the city.

Who was Thomas Nakaba? I ask myself again. Not just the bomber, but the man. Just another faceless psychopath, one of life's losers? What set him on this course? No one can tell me. I wish I could meet his family or friends, but even they seem to have sunk away, beneath the surface of daily life.

What was the meaning of his actions? I'd been told that the previous January, around the time my first article on Charlie and Steve was published, a letter bomb containing two cubes of dynamite was intercepted en route to the Swedish Justice Minister, Laila Freivald. It had been posted by a Swedish C18 sympathiser. Why? These questions crowd my aching head. I miss my partner at moments like this. Why is it only hate that brings me on this journey? The cold burns deep into my scalp.

I pull my coat closer around me. It's much calmer here than back in Britain, I muse, stepping between two passing cyclists. Not as 'ordered' as Germany, but quieter, more polite, clean. I laugh inwardly as I watch everyone patiently waiting for the 'green man' signal before crossing the road. In England, everyone – even the cars – seems to jump the lights. I encountered the same in Berlin; rows of people waiting to cross these large open roads that are often devoid of traffic.

Erik Jensen said that Nakaba carried out his operation more as a favour to Marcel Schilf than to the Brits. Schilf was raided straight after the bombs were posted. But we can't ask him, because he's dead. Ten thousand Deutschmarks were found in his ex-girlfriend's apartment. Much of Nakaba's material was printed by him. But that, in itself, wasn't a crime. Erik said he knew Nakaba was unpopular with members of the DNSB. Very much a 'hard nut', he'd wanted to hang out with semi-criminal gangs, not 'Hollywood-style Nazis' who dressed up and sang old Reich songs.

Yeah, I said, but who was he really? Eventually, after musing over his pipe, Erik replied: 'I never met him personally. I only saw him in the court, and at demonstrations in the past, when the fascists used to fight with the punks.' He took in a husky breath and said that at one of these demos, a young skin had 'spat in my face, called me gay, then threatened to cut off my cock'. As for Nakaba, Erik remembered: 'He was not very tall, but liked to act macho. A policeman said to me that he had tried for eight years to become a Hell's Angel, and they wouldn't have him. And therefore he took the next best thing.'

Was there any significance to any of this? Thinking back on his answers, I pass endless six-storey apartment stacks, finally coming to a junction partly obstructed by roadworks. Standing in the lee of a small café, I take out my map and look for the southern suburbs. Erik said this is where Nakaba spent much of his teen years. The map ended. I take a guess and turn left.

'The significance of the case was that the public and police suddenly took them [Combat 18] seriously. Before that, they were only clowns.' But the race war they'd wanted hadn't happened. Like the London nailbomber after them, most of the right went to ground. 'From that point of view, it was counter-productive for them,' agreed Erik.

I walk beneath a graffiti-strewn concrete bridge, beside the freeway. Several old ladies regard my passing with surprise – probably because I'm walking, where most people would drive – as I stalk through a bus stop. The landscape is industrial. I move slowly past a brewery, thin chimneys pushing out clouds of steam. 1930s-style apartments creep up; their dirty red brick passes for what can be called slums.

I wander in and out of these backstreets, aimlessly, past fading barbershops, into small newsagents, around rubbish skips. Lorries rumble by. By Copenhagen's standards, this is a poor area. By mine, and by England's, it's fairly respectable. The streets are wide, folk seem polite. Back home, I would be likely to get turned over by some crackhead junkie or harassed by smackheads trying to grab my Tube ticket.

This is where Thomas Nakaba grew up.

Rasmus had spoken of the scale of neo-nazi violence in Denmark. 'It's very isolated here, and in Norway. Apart from people like Nakaba, of course. You'd have to search for it. Which is why it was hard to identify Nakaba beforehand. But in Sweden, it's a proper subculture. You'd come across it in school, for example.' He stared intently at me, across his kitchen table. 'To a large degree, it's a very international movement in Scandinavia. Also, because some of the groups are very small, they try to form an international network. Like the left. They travel from country to country to attend concerts.' He showed me a copy of *Resistance* magazine. The Swedish organisation behind it, Resistance Records, has recently been bought by William Pierce.

I come near to the water's edge, where I can see the radio masts and conning towers of large container ships, standing like cliffs on a spume-tipped sea. I hear English being spoken, over the harsh cry of sea birds.

Back in England, Nick Lowles has been telling me about rumours of a Millennium Bomb. It never came to pass, but people like Thomas Nakaba were supposed to be the vanguard of this effort, a trailer for an explosion of orchestrated violence across the continent.

EIGHT

THE CALL

I drank in the sound.

The smartly dressed youngsters around me barely paused, their designer gear a uniform. Perhaps they adjusted a bulletproof vest, or shifted the cradle of an Uzi. An unconscious gesture, seeking comfort as dusk approached. Then, as the Shabbat drew near, the young Jews went back to their friends and drinks in this popular bar. We hurried our way through the streets of the Old City, accompanied all the while by that plaintive, wailing cry: the call of Jerusalem.

The same noise had echoed through the cheap plaster walls of a hotel-cum-brothel in Damascus, a sweltering warren, half-open doors revealing intimate sounds and the cheap mingling aftertaste of perfume and sweat. At 5 a.m., long after the bouncers had ejected their now-silent human cargo, we'd be woken by the harsh, but enticing, call to the faithful.

Further to the west, in the desert of the Western Sahara, I'd watched the men and women pray in lines, angled to Mecca. The Imam called out the start of the prayer, '*Allaahu Akbar*' – God is Great – as nature dwarfed and surrounded us.

In Tripoli, near the northern border of Lebanon, I stood in an old Crusader castle, hand resting on dust-coloured stone, basking in hot light as the mullahs duelled from their minarets during noon-time prayer.

I miss that sound. It holds no fear. Rather, it draws me towards the mysteries of another continent, even when I hear it criss-crossing the roofs of Brick Lane in London.

* * *

MARCH 2001

The two young men sit across from me. They look tired, stressed. But then so do I.

The first figure leans forwards, arms held arrow-like on the large, oval table. He's slim, with raven hair and a sallow complexion. The open neck of his sweater reveals a matt of wiry curls. We've met a couple of times before. An understated man, he can be full of sharp, bubbling wit. Today, there's a tension about him, evident in the thin film of sweat and grease shining from the bridge of his nose.

The other is taller, with a slight flush to his jowls. Glasses offset his affable, nondescript visage. It's a familiar face. His teeth flash white when he cracks into an occasional smile. He shifts first backwards and relaxed, then suddenly towards me.

A sheaf of papers lies between us.

'We want you to go to Beirut.'

The words hang for a moment. The room is dark, even with the tall window framing London, moving in the world beyond us. Shadows mirror the shifting cloudscape above. I laugh. They don't. 'What – do you mean seriously?' The surprise must show on my face.

'Yes. It'll be a one-off which might never be repeated.' Steve, the first figure, is talking. Fast. His stubble moves up and down on his sallow jaw as he speaks. 'It's going to be one of the biggest meetings for years. The first time that the Americans, and European heavyweights, have linked up with the Arabs.'

'Meeting of what?' There's a pained innocence to my voice. Perhaps I can sense some of what's coming next.

Nick pushes the papers towards me. The letters 'IHR' stand out, printed in bold capitals. Beneath, in parentheses, the words 'Institute for Historical Review' are framed in a smaller, neater font.

'Beirut . . .' Steve is repeating. But I miss the rest of the sentence. I know what he said. It's just that I don't want to hear. The words only half-penetrate.

'What's this got to do with me?' I try to tone down my response. I can feel pinprick patches of sweat oozing into my palm.

'Well, it'll be totally unique. And you know them. You can play the naive journalist. It's the perfect way to get in,' Steve says.

'To *what*?' I snap. I don't like being dropped in it. 'What are we talking about?'

'Revision and Zionism,' says Nick, cutting across my words. He unfolds another set of documents, which he shoves along the table, like a drink across a bar top. 'That's the name of the conference.' His phone begins to bleep, but quickly – and unusually – he silences it. A muffled chirp is all I hear, as he tucks it back inside his jacket.

'It's going to be a massive meeting of Holocaust deniers and Islamic fundamentalists. Unique.' He takes a second to gauge my reaction. 'And we want someone on the inside.'

Wonderful. I'm barely a few days back from Denmark. Now it seems I'm about to jump into the fire all over again.

I pause, breathing carefully. 'Why me?' When I speak again, my voice sounds dispassionate, deep. 'I don't know if I want to go back there. What am I supposed to do at this thing? What if something goes wrong? Who's there for back-up?' There's no immediate answer. 'And what about security? It's not as if I can call anyone for help when I get out there.' I'm serious. Although I've dealt, briefly, with Hezbollah and deniers like Nick Griffin, I really don't want to fuck around in a place like Beirut. Death or disappearance would be easy, even though the civil war is over. It's only a few months since the Israelis have pulled out. Surely, they wouldn't be too happy with some of the world's most rabid anti-Semites gathering on their doorstep?

Steve's reply is light in return. 'Because you can do it. Because it'll be useful for you, and for us. They won't suspect anything. And you are a journalist, so there's no reason to cover that up.'

'Okay, but what about the event? Is it likely to be allowed to go ahead? Won't I get problems trying to come into the country? Maybe I'll have to use a tourist visa to keep things quiet. I don't want to get into difficulties because of that.'

'It's all been cleared at top government level, with the Lebanese authorities,' Steve says, upbeat. 'I don't reckon you'll have any problems.'

He pauses. Nick takes up the reins. It's like a hard cop, soft cop routine, this. 'We want to know who's coming over from the Arab countries, and the Islamic groups in Europe. There's an increasing amount of Holocaust denial coming from fundamentalist groups here in London, too. It's been quite an interesting development. It seems they're using the Holocaust, talking about the Holocaust "lie", so it's becoming a convergence of interest between them and the right. It's like they're saying, "Here you are the Jews, you've played up the Holocaust, the Holocaust didn't happen, so you're talking it up to help create the state of Israel." In their mind, the state has been created so they can persecute the Palestinians.'

I've seen the results of Israeli bombings, so I'm no great fan of theirs. But the idea of a convergence between the far right and anti-Zionist groups is worrying. Later on in my travels, someone framed this kind of problem. 'Why are there all these tight controls in Europe on freedom of speech [about the Holocaust], when the majority of material published comes from, of all places, Japan?' Even I was taken aback by this claim. All sorts of lies can turn into twisted truths, given time and lack of debate.

'There's going to be at least one major figure from Russia,' adds Nick. 'One of the speakers, I think.'

'What's the connection there?' I ask. I've just heard that David Duke, the former KKK leader turned politician, has relocated to Moscow. Maybe this has something to do with it. Nick Griffin and I have been emailing each other about Duke. Griffin has said he's passed my name to Duke's main people in the States. Perhaps I'll be able to get an invite to Russia, he says.

There are already several paramilitary groups out there, some of them linked to the attempted coup that brought Boris Yeltsin to prominence in 1991.

This is turning into a bloody Tom Clancy novel, I laugh inwardly.

'The right is on the rise in Russia,' Nick says. 'There's increasing links between the figures there and some of these Islamic groups over the question of Zionism.' He has no real idea as to the extent of these contacts. But consider this, he adds: 'How will National Socialism mix with the Islamic world, which are threats to each other? You should ask them this: How will this mix of opposites play out?' Both Steve and Nick reckon these guys will openly claim the Holocaust is a lie.

I look down at the papers again. A mix of Nazism and Islamic fundamentalism. And me in the middle.

'You don't have to do it, you know,' says Nick.

I'm torn. I hate travelling alone into this kind of world. Pretending, acting. Going into that heart of darkness, again. But I do have to go. I know that. So does he. Or at least he's counting on it. Ever since those 18 months I spent after college – trapped in Kuwait, caught in an earthquake, mugged, attacked by British soldiers, and nearly sunk in a typhoon on the South China Sea – I've been determined to live my life and face my fears.

'Okay, I'll think about it. Give me the details and I'll bell you later.'

I set my city mask in place, muscles locking into a familiar frozen routine, barring all strangers.

Then I walk back out into the real world.

* * *

That evening I collapse into a living-room chair, depositing myself in front of the news. I sigh. After a few seconds, I struggle up again and pour a glass of malt whisky. My partner tries to talk to me, but I'm snappy and irritable. Then I feel guilty. I apologise to her, oblivious, however, to the damage my obsession is causing, and head upstairs to my study.

I call forth all the old Final Conflict newsletters from my PC, chewing on the side of my lip and sipping from my glass. Searching through the morass of hate and buffoonery, I turn up several references to the Institute for Historical Review. I rub my eyes and lean back. I'm working too late. I wish I had someone I could talk to about all this. Maybe I should have done something else with my life. Then a link catches my attention, and I hunch forward again. There's a piece from last May about the world's first online revisionist conference, sponsored by the IHR. It's too late for me to listen in, but the advert speaks of live audio feedback over the Net, as the speakers took the podium. A puff piece tells me that:

Founded in 1978, the Institute for Historical Review is a not-for-profit research, educational and publishing center devoted to truth and accuracy in history. The IHR continues the tradition of historical revisionism pioneered by distinguished historians such as Harry Elmer Barnes, A.J.P. Taylor, Charles Tansill, Paul Rassinier and William H. Chamberlin.

The Institute's purpose is to 'bring history into accord with the facts'. The IHR is at the center of a worldwide network of scholars and activists who are working – sometimes at great personal sacrifice – to separate historical fact from propaganda fiction by researching and publicizing suppressed information about key chapters of history – especially twentieth century history – that have social-political relevance today.

For a body that declares itself interested in all aspects of history, there's an unhealthily obvious slant towards the Holocaust. One line proudly trots out a quote from the *Los Angeles Times*, describing the IHR as a 'revisionist think tank that critics call the "spine of the international Holocaust denial movement"'. A few lines down, it says that 'the orthodox Holocaust extermination story . . . plays an enormously significant role in the cultural and political life of America and much of the world'.

I still find it odd, this tide of hatred. Obsession with the Jews at every corner. A fixation with proving Germany was the greater victim of the war, and that other figures in history have been 'worse' than Hitler. Why this great need to keep disproving the Holocaust?

As I search for the IHR site and for contact details for this Beirut conference, I remember that David Irving has had several contacts with the organisation. Perhaps I'll be meeting people like him in Lebanon. Following a link from a search engine, a rather plain-looking site surfaces onto my screen. The Beirut details are held under a thick black line. I click.

The new page speaks of a growing level of cooperation between revisionists in the West and in Muslim countries. The whole thing is being organised by a Swiss revisionist organisation called Association Vérité et Justice, in conjunction with the IHR. Arabic, French and English speakers will be present. One chilling line refers to 'measures [which] have been taken to insure [sic] complete security for the event'. Some sort of ex-special forces types or Syrian intelligence, no doubt. What if they suss me out? I don't like the sound of this. My natural reaction is to pull back. No one can make you do anything you don't want to do. But this will be an unrivalled opportunity. I have to get into this world somehow.

A guy called Jürgen Graf seems a key figure. He's Swiss, on the run from the authorities in his homeland after being given a 15-month prison sentence for his views. Several editions of his works on the Holocaust have been banned in European countries. He's now living in Tehran, at the invitation (so the site says) of Iranian scholars. My mind jumps to Nick Griffin and the ITP. Odd, how the right seems happy to link with extremists from other causes.

A man named Mark Weber, at an address in Newport Beach, California, calls himself 'director' of the IHR. He's a historian, he claims, who has studied and taught in Europe and West Africa and carried out extensive research into the Holocaust whilst living in Washington, DC. Or so I read. Other descriptions I find elsewhere on the Net are less kind. One civil rights group calls him a 'professional denier' who edited the National Alliance's newspaper back in 1978. Then he worked for the infamous Liberty Lobby and arch-right-wing supremo Willis Carto. Carto's tale stretches back to just after the war and a friendship that became a rivalry with William Pierce, both seeking to be the top dog in white-supremacist circles. Carto founded the IHR but was ousted in a boardroom putsch, led by Weber, over financial irregularities. The two have been locked in court cases ever since, as the IHR tries to regain millions it suspects were sunk into Carto's other organisations. Weber has written on the lesser achievements of non-whites and on his concern for the future of the white race. All very scholarly, no doubt.

I later discover that Weber is an integral part of an international revisionist and extreme right network and has close connections to members of the BNP.

I fax off my registration that same evening.

* * *

Another special day, this one. I'm moving back into English nationalism, to the heart of the 'new' BNP, to meet one of Nick Griffin's up and coming stars. As I surface from the hot breath of the Northern Line, slanting drops smash against the soot-encrusted pillars above. The rush hour mob surges through the rain, a tide of humanity shrouded in black and grey. London Bridge. I like this area of town. Lots of old buildings around here weathered the Blitz. TV and film companies tend to use it as a base for period dramas. A couple of ancient pubs even survive from Dickens's day.

I've called ahead to Paul, telling him when I'm coming. He's one of Nick Griffin's wonder boys. Not even 20, and the party's new director of publicity. The kind of guy Griffin wants me to meet.

On the train, towards the commuter lands of Kent, I gaze at the passing landscape. Mothers with babies, life trundling on around me. There must be hope in this world, I think. Why go through life consumed by angst, or abusing others? I remember a teacher asking us to write an essay about what we'd tell a Martian visiting our society. I knew it was an artificial exercise, but I tried my hardest to explain the world, as I saw it, around me. Now, I'm not sure what I'd say. That 12-year-old was a happier, more innocent person than I am now. What would I tell an outsider about my world? About us? After my travels, I've seen how mean, twisted and introverted we can be. Can we offer no better than these puerile extremes of religion, ethnicity and political beliefs? Why do fear and hate rule so much of our lives – not just in the war zones I've seen, but here, too?

Station names flash past. The first few I recognise – Lewisham, for example, dubbed by some brash estate agent 'the new Notting Hill' (it isn't). Then we trundle through places off the map. Or at least off the Tube map.

A sign for Eltham blurs through the rain, as we judder onwards. The suburb where black teenager Stephen Lawrence was murdered in 1993. Everyone knows it was a racist attack by a white gang. But no one's yet been convicted, despite compelling circumstantial evidence. A friend of mine, when he invites me around to his new house in the area, becomes visibly frosty and defensive at my mention of Lawrence, as though I've insulted him personally.

I step out at Bexleyheath, on the nondescript border between London and Kent. No man's land. It's deadly quiet. A tiny station, forgotten in the middle of the day. The soul of this place, if it has one, is sunk at the moment in the heart of the city. It'll come back to life between five and seven, when the workers return.

I take out my mobile and call for directions. 'Paul? Nick Ryan, the writer here.' Pause. 'Er . . . you okay?'

'Yeah,' he says. His voice is direct. Not clipped, exactly, but too firm. Maybe my imagination.

I turn around, trying to keep the mobile dry from the pelting rain. 'How do I get to your place then?'

The south London accent directs me as I begin to walk up the railway siding. There's no one else around. I'm surrounded by houses and parked cars, yet feel alone.

I follow his instructions, holding a thin, tattered umbrella against the battering elements. It turns inside out, and I junk it in a passing bin. The journey takes about 20 minutes at a stiff walk. Over a bridge, the dark Victorian brick stained and immutable. Ancient graffiti speaks of youth long past. Down a long, narrow stretch of road, identical semi-detached houses stretch each side of me. The pebble dash facades feel typical to London: pre-war, depressing, drab. The smell of cat shit persists, despite the breeze.

I reach a crossroads and call again. I move over the highway, past a café, a newsagent and a car accessory shop. Songbirds call out through the streets. I start to relax and notice sycamores lining my path. Is this the kind of place the right is targeting? Seems quite pleasant.

* * *

I'd noticed how the BNP had finally revamped its web presence, merging its many amateurish sites. Slowly, clear sections appeared: contacts for the media, press releases, articles refuting unfavourable coverage and links to dozens of other ultra-right groups. It obviously borrowed heavily from nationalist sites abroad, such as the French Mouvement National Républicain. Nick Griffin's face ended up plastered right across the top.

'Fanks,' says Paul Golding, facing away from me, down towards the screen. From this angle, his still-rounded, baby-faced features are hidden. I've just complimented him on his work redesigning the BNP site. His cheeks are flushed, perhaps embarrassed. 'I'm still workin' on it.' His fingers tap furiously, then rest on the scratched surface, grime caked under the nails. 'There,' he says contentedly. A Union Jack appears on the screen, and strident, patriotic-sounding classical music thunders away from a stereo. His fingers float over keys again, an intense flurry, then I see a status bar flashing. He leans back.

'Impressive,' I say, half meaning it. 'Do it all yourself?'

'Yeah, taught m'self while going to college. Just picked it up really.' He wants to shrug his shoulders in a show of modesty, but seems to suppress the movement. 'It weren't that difficult, like, after a while.' But he seems suspicious, perhaps surprised by my positive comment.

'What do you use?'

'Dreamweaver, and raw HTML.'

I could be talking to any teenager. But there's something off-centre about his image. As with Griffin, it's not something you can instantly define.

His crinkled, wavy hair is slicked back and plastered onto his skull. I detect streaks of blond, deep beneath the gel. A thin mask of acne cream vainly hides swelling spots. From the smell of cheap soap and aftershave, along with crumpled dark trousers – dog's hairs forming tiny lines of grey over the creases – and polished black shoes, I'd say he's made an effort to dress up for my arrival. Pity I didn't do the same.

We settle onto his tattered leather sofa in one corner of the room. A photocopier squats nearby. Net curtains hide all from casual view. I nearly trip over a box file as I sit down. His back remains ramrod straight. Clearly, he's ill at ease.

I should take him seriously, though. In his native Northend, a little suburb up the road, the BNP gained over 26 per cent of the vote in local elections last year. It was a warning shot for the powers that be. A couple more per cent, and the party would have been in. Paul's too young to stand for election yet, but with his conviction and intelligence, he might prove attractive to the voters. I can see his eyes light up when he talks about it. Clearly, it's going to be an aim of his.

'So, tell me about the problems we're facing, then, Paul,' I start. 'Round here, maybe,' I indicate with a nod of my head. I probably sound patronising and formal. I start to untangle the cord of my recorder. His mouth gapes for a second, momentarily hesitant, then the flow begins.

'I'd say one of the main problems round 'ere was the asylum seekers. Since the last few years, I'd say. The council's trying to stick them in, while we've still got problems for housing for our own people.' He proudly tells me about a campaign that he helped lead against converting a disused pub into a temporary hostel. 'That was where we really showed how the BNP's community politics worked, like,' he beams.

References to 'the asylum seekers' pepper his conversation. How the government, through the local council, is trying to force hundreds of these people onto the streets of his little homeland. 'Our people are just becoming a minority,' he says, in all earnestness. I can see little sign of it when I walk around the area myself.

'The fing about asylum seekers, though, is that they're not our problem. We shouldn't 'ave to deal with it. It's Tony Blair, and before that the Tories, who did this to us.' It's interesting, how he reserves his greatest venom for the Conservative Party. 'They just talk tough, people like [then-Tory leader William] Hague, in order to get votes. Our people are in danger of becoming a minority,' he repeats, staring straight ahead. I notice a sheen to his skin; grease or sweat.

'So, should we encourage others to go back home?'

'Yeah, but the real issue is to stop them comin' in, in the first place.'

'Everyone?'

'Well, we could still allow other Europeans in.'

'Why?'

'European culture is the same, basically.'

'Come on, that's not true,' I answer. 'I've lived over there. Try telling a Frenchman he's like a German.' Perhaps I sound too dismissive. His body language shifts; I can sense the barriers coming up.

'It's true. I've been over to France recently, they say the same fing. It don't matter whether you believe it or not. We do, and I know it's goin' on. So do all the people round 'ere.' His gaze never leaves my face. I keep trying to think of how to make him smile, crack the ice and get to the real bloke beneath.

'What do you believe in, then?' I think quickly. 'Am I British, with an Irish dad?'

'Yeah,' he answers, pulling at the collar of his white shirt, which looks newly pressed into service. 'Some of my ancestors at some point came from elsewhere, too.' But this was part of the British Isles, he maintains. It reminds me of the Conservative politician Norman Tebbit, telling the well-known black interviewer Darcus Howe that Howe was 'British', not 'English'. Even though Howe was raised in a British colony, under an English education system, and – as an English Literature degree holder – was more educated than most white Brits. It didn't make any difference, said Tebbit. Howe could never be English.

'What about Frank Bruno?' I say, meaning the famous black boxer. 'Would he be considered British?'

'Naw,' he replies, steadily.

He talks of 'differences', then mentions 'God'. I feel myself freeze inside. I've met so many nuts and fanatics who hide behind that name. Perhaps he doesn't know about or share Nick Griffin's pagan beliefs. 'God made us like we are,' says Paul.

What I realise later, after all my travels, is that I'm dealing with Belief. It doesn't matter if I can disprove what he's saying; he still believes it. It's like religious conviction, or like a Maoist during the Cultural Revolution. Until something comes crashing into that world, or causes the walls to fall down, the converts don't want to change. The complex, confusing and sometimes tortured personal realities are now slotted into a neat structure.

Paul's gone to the extremes of that belief. Many of us around him, though, are also taken in, swallowing simplistic platitudes about crime and refugees, or a lack of discipline in kids. That's what worries me more, as I listen to this young man talk. He really believes what he's saying.

'What else do we need to put right, then?'

'Crime's out of control in this present system. We need to bring back capital punishment. The judges are just too soft today. And there should be less degeneracy on TV, too.'

Zeal burns in his comments. At only 19, he's already concerned about sex and violence – even though, as I point out to him, he's got several Hollywood action blockbusters lining his video shelf. 'Er, yeah, hah . . . well, apart from them . . . But ya see what I mean, though, in a general sense, don'tcha?'

'Oh, yes.'

We start talking about the concept of identity. To me this is key, but not just on a national level. When Paul starts saying, 'We've got to bring back our national identity', I think he's missing the point. Perhaps he's well-intentioned. I'd be wrong if I said he was simply a race hater. There's a more complex, subtle mix going on here. But identity keeps surfacing in my mind. As he talks deferentially to his girlfriend from a mobile phone, seemingly under-the-thumb to her insistent chatter, I'm reminded of how curiously old-fashioned he seems.

He flips open the CD player and pops in the music from the film *Gladiator*. Russell Crowe's face sends up a cloud of dust from the top of the machine. Crowe played a violent skinhead in the raw Aussie film *Romper Stomper*. Pointing toward the bookshelves in the far corner of the room, I ask how he feels about National Socialism.

The sheen on his forehead glistens, his eyes remain locked to mine, his temple pulses. 'Nah, we're not National Socialist,' he quips, the deep accent bouncing through his words. 'What I am, and you can quote this if you like, is a Patriot. That's 'ow I'd describe m'self.'

'What does that mean, exactly?'

'I'm patriotic. I love my country, my people.' He snorts, trying to clear a blocked nose. Taking out a handkerchief, he carefully wipes the side of his nostril, then folds and places the cloth back in a pocket. My foot is drumming up and down. I feel penned in. I wish I had a camera. You should see this, you, my friends, who laugh so much.

'Yeah, but I've seen that kind of patriotism before,' I tell him. 'At the hands of Charlie Sargent and the bombs from C18.'

He has an answer for that one, too. 'C18,' he says – the 'eighteen' becoming 'ate'een' – 'was set up by the State to destroy the credibility of nationalism.'

'Set up by who?'

'The security services.'

I pause to draw breath, to ask another question, but he slams right on: 'It's like there're these lobbies, right, that are workin' to destroy Britain. Right naa, it's Liberalism. Before that, it was Communism.'

'Really?'

'Yeah, that and global capitalism. Immigration serves those economic interests. The British people di'nt vote for immigration; it was done by the Establishment.' The words, parrot-like from his youthful lips, sound just like Nick Griffin.

He shifts, standing up and walking to the bay windows. 'We can see what's being destroyed. White countries.'

I offer to take him for a fry-up and coffee. It's the least I can do, to thank him for talking to me. As we walk into the clinical little room smelling of cleaning fluid and chips, Paul's nose wrinkles at the drifting cigarette smoke. He refuses anything but a couple of slices of toast and some baked beans, though I've offered to buy him more. I almost feel sorry for him. He seems slightly lost. Not a bad sort really. But then, I reflect, that's the danger: if I react like this, how will some housewife respond? Probably by voting for him.

I watch him shovel in the beans, slowly, carefully, precisely. He's a curious chap. I kind of like him. Or respect the energy he's throwing into all this. He tells me about his family in Brixton, his school years, his fiancée. She calls him frequently during our conversation, and he goes all quiet and embarrassed and tries to get rid of her.

'M'granddad was a Communist.' My eyebrows raise. Two ladies chat, oblivious, a constant monotone through which I snatch half-heard pieces of conversation – 'So Dave says 'e wasn't seeing 'er, if that were so, 'ow come I found this number?' Paul tucks into his beans, studiously picking his way through the sauce, cutting the crusts from pieces of milk-white bread.

There's a suppressed nervous energy about this young man, an old-fashioned kind of seriousness. Something evident in a fierce, fiery stare he's locked onto me since I first walked into his house. If I weren't used to extremists, I'd find it unnerving.

Still, I'm not sure yet what to make of him. His accent reminds me of Steve Sargent. But when I mention C18 he says, vehemently, 'We don't need scum like them.' He's adamant about that. No, he doesn't seem the football type, then.

We walk back to his house. I keep swallowing a recurrent piece of phlegm down into my throat. I hack, cough and excuse myself to go into the bathroom and spit out the detritus. It's a short walk across the landing, the threadbare, greying carpet scuffing under my feet. The place needs a vacuum. The bathroom itself is another clue: a tip, stinking of piss with foul, wiry hairs stuck to the rim of the toilet and onto the remnants of a bar of soap. A sad, elderly, male atmosphere pervades this place. I know someone else is downstairs, and I can hear a large dog bashing itself against a door.

I return to Paul's room, where I've left my stuff as a sign of trust. He can look into my notes for all I care. I'm making it clear I have nothing to hide, or any undercover intentions. I'm about to ask him a question, but as it frames in my mind, I pause for a split second, struck suddenly by the images on the faded walls around me.

This is Griffin's new man, who clearly hero-worships his leader. Yet this tumbling, ramshackle, dirty old house seems more like Steve Sargent's place all the time. Inside this stale, stuffy box, flags smother the walls: a Cross of St George, the dragon of Wales, the Union Jack. Some sort of Viking princess above the bed. Books on the Third Reich and Hitler crowd cheap whitewashed shelves. David Duke's work is up there, too. It speaks volumes about identity. Which is ironic, given the name of the magazine Paul helps Griffin edit.

This is a depressing little place. I think of my father, over from Ireland and growing up, three families to one terraced house, in the early 1940s. It was never like this.

Paul's brows draw together, his expression earnest, nervous yet determined. I ask my question: How many members have they got around here? 'About 300 in sowf-east London,' he answers. He's a full-time worker for the BNP, he announces proudly, as if daring me to contradict him. No dole scrounger this one, at least.

By the end of three hours, we're warming to each other. I've a job to do, though, so I push another button. I know where to look now, for these code words. Global capitalism has already been broached: read, moneyed interests, the Jews. 'What about old George Bush's phrase, the New World Order? What does that mean to you?'

'There is a New Wald Order,' he replies. 'It's a developing battle between nationalism on the one 'and, and internationalism on the uvver.'

'Are you talking about the Jews?' My voice is level, blunt.

'There's extreme Jews, the Zionists, but I don't know how much they influence things day to day.' He doesn't want to talk about it any more. The phone suddenly rings, cutting across the conversation. He chats away for a moment, then turns back to me, a half-smile tentatively forming on his lips.

''Ere, you'll never guess – you'll probably think this is a set-up – but that was a black bloke, West Indian, said 'e'd read something about us, and wanted to know if he could join. Did you know we 'ad an ethnic liaison unit, naa?'

'Get a lot of calls?'

'Quite a few, yeah. You'd be surprised 'ow many actually. There's a Turkish bloke, well, 'alf-Turkish, we've already got signed up.' He pauses for a second, thinking how to make this sound good. 'I'd say we get two to three calls a week with enquiries like that.'

The conversation drifts on for a couple more minutes, then he checks the time and says he has to get back to his work. I ask for one final favour.

'You know Tony Lecomber, your deputy leader guy?'

'Yeah?' he replies.

'Erm, well, I've been trying to reach him, and he hasn't replied to any of my requests for an interview.'

'Oh, I'll call him now for you, if you like. Do you want me to?'

I lick my lips. 'Okay, yeah, thanks.'

Golding cradles the phone against his neck and punches a swift flurry of numbers. After a second, he starts speaking, 'Yeah, Tony, it's Paul. I've got someone 'ere wants to speak wiv you.'

He hands me the receiver.

'Hi, Tony?'

Silence.

'Er, this is Nick Ryan, the journalist doing the book about the extreme right.' I hear an intake of breath. 'I've interviewed Nick Griffin and quite a few of the others now. Perhaps you've heard my name?'

'I don't talk to journalists.' The voice is flat, a monotone. I imagine some petty bureaucrat sitting at the other end.

'Well, I have got permission from Nick Griffin, and it would be really interesting–'

'I'm busy.'

'Okay, but we don't have to meet right now. What about in a couple of weeks' time?'

'I'm always busy.'

'Always?'

'Always.'

My entreaties fall on deaf ears. I gingerly pass the receiver back to Paul and hear an angry bark of words. Paul looks flummoxed.

'Sorry about that,' I say.

'Oh, don't worry.'

We shake hands and, to my surprise, he agrees to meet again.

The setting sun leaves me in a pensive mood. I'm starting to travel inside the political right. It's different to everything that's gone before, at least in my experience. What I don't realise is just how similar it will become.

* * *

Surprisingly, as the days pass and I renew my previous contacts with Nick Griffin and the BNP, Mark Weber and I strike up a virtual conversation.

During our first exchange, he thanks me for being so cordial with my registration request to the Beirut conference. Good; my tactics have worked. Then he tells me he's 'intrigued by your outlook and the project you described'. I send a polite reply.

A few hours later, the inbox flashes again. I'm in! Excellent. Then a crashing wave of worry swamps me. I call Nick Lowles. 'I'm in, mate.'

'Aha, jolly good. Give me a call later on, and we'll talk about what you need to take.'

I rummage through the message from Weber. Details of the conference location are secret, right up until the last minute. Extensive security precautions are being taken, and I and the other delegates will have to fly in to Beirut then call a number from the airport. It sounds dodgy, like a spy novel, or one of those illegal raves back in the 1990s. I'm feeling edgy.

My partner notices the change. I'm more moody, quick to lash out and to blame others. I withdraw into myself and the project, further into this nightmare world.

My chats with Weber continue. I tell him I simply want to understand more, that I'm a dispassionate observer. Which is honest, up to a point. He tells me Horst Mahler, a founding member of the left-wing terrorist Baader-Meinhof Gang in Germany, will be attending. Bloody hell, that'll be a coup, I think, sipping on a fiery glass of malt. I swirl it carefully, aware that the bottle is getting low.

I find references to Mahler on several sites. Most are in German, but I learn that he was a brilliant socialist lawyer who looked for ways to turn his Marxist theories into practice. His idea was to form a band of 'urban guerrillas' to foment revolution. After a long spell in jail, he renounced his former comrades and reversed his politics, becoming an ardent nationalist and high-ranking member of the neo-nazi NPD.

A week on, Weber sends through a general email detailing how the World Jewish Congress, the Anti-Defamation League and the Simon Wiesenthal Center are demanding that the Lebanese authorities ban the conference. It almost seems as though the IHR is boasting about it. There are even reports that the US government is preparing to step in.

I go ahead and buy my plane ticket anyway, after being reassured by both Weber and Nick Lowles that it will go ahead. Then I reserve the same hotel I stayed in last year. It was used as the unofficial British embassy during much of the civil war and has its own pub, complete with traditional British-style furniture and images of the countryside. A home away from home. That'll suit me fine, I think. Beer – and I can escape to the press corps or UN troops who frequent the place if anything goes wrong. I put a quick call through to Nick and Steve at *Searchlight*, confirming the details. We'll run through a final checklist in a day or so. The hotel faxes me back, saying they're looking forward to my arrival again. I swallow another dram of whisky, feeling satisfied with my progress. My partner wanders in, running her hand over my neck and shoulders, twisting me round and planting a kiss on my lips. Slowly I relax, then reach behind the computer and hit the 'off' switch.

* * *

There's been a massive uproar. Fourteen prominent Arab intellectuals have all signed a letter deploring the *Revisionism and Zionism* event. Other bodies have joined in the criticism from around the world. The only ones who seem somewhat muted are the Israelis.

'That's because this'll be an excellent time for them to do some spying,' explains Nick. 'Think of it. When or where else are they going to get all these folk gathered together in one place, with their Middle Eastern enemies? And on their doorstep, which makes it easier to get people in?'

'Guess you're right,' I say. I'm still dubious about the safety and sanity of all this. 'Wish me luck, then.' There are only a few days until I leave. Nick and I hook up in another of our usual bars, this time in west London, to go over last-minute details. We discuss how I can speak to these groups, like Hezbollah and Islamic Jihad. I'm terrified, but I've agreed to go.

'Ah, it'll be fine,' reassures Nick, sipping his mineral water. The pint in my hand looks large and enticing. I gulp about a quarter of it down in one go. 'Still, there's some other good news just in. Massimo Morsello has just died.'

'Fucking hell, really?'

Morsello is one of the founding fathers of the ITP. He'd left Italy for England, after spending several years in jail for his neo-nazi activities. Final Conflict sent out an email obituary for him, trumpeting his songwriting and musical skills, of all things.

'Yeah, cancer. He'd been ill for quite some time. He was certainly a player in his time.'

Death comes to us all, I muse, regardless of the 'truths' we espouse. Worth bearing that in mind.

A week later, it's all over. The Lebanese authorities have banned the conference. The pressure seems to have been too much to bear. The White House has been leaning hard. A great weight lifts from my shoulders, but I curse all the same.

I feel oddly deflated. I'm spared the potential dangers, but strangely feel empty and disabused. I've lived the last few days on the knife edge of stress, losing weight and sleep. Then, suddenly, it's just gone.

My girlfriend's happy, but I can't get a refund for my tickets. Various e-lists buzz with the gossip. The IHR releases long-winded complaints – this, of course, is how the 'New World Order' gangs up against 'honest' scholars. 'Free Speech: Shot Down in Beirut' scream the headlines.

THE CALL

Around 11 o'clock the same day, a scrawled fax arrives from a secretive Belgian contact, listing the names of two members of the Vlaams Blok – Flanders's burgeoning ultra-nationalist movement – I should approach. The words 'Don't use my name!' are underlined twice at the bottom of the page. Trawling the web, I discover the VB's site, with its proud Lion of Flanders crest. I wing off a message to the VB, writing and rewriting as fast as possible. I need to be subtle with this one. I can't tell them of my links to C18. Probably not even the BNP. These guys are in another league.

NINE

INDEPENDENCE DAY

1 MAY 2001

'Eigen Volk Eerst! Eigen Volk Eerst!'
– *Our Own People First! Our Own People First!*

The roar shatters the tranquillity of this early weekday afternoon. For a second or two, it's quiet. Then the cry comes again: 'Eigen Volk Eerst!' It's like a tide, a deep undertone beneath the overcast spring sky. Perhaps 200 or 300 'skins', lion tattoos engraved into their heads and arms, roll along the narrow street, herded by the canal to our left. The red flush of alcohol bulges through thick corded veins. Voices rasp hoarse.

The ancient cobblestones rattle with vibration. The chants of the crowd, four or five thousand strong, echo across the old market town stalls and bounce between medieval buildings. I've never seen anything like this. The mood is infectious. Intimidating, too. I feel as if I'm one of them, watching the outside faces, North African youths, glaring in, hostile, from the side alleys. But apart too. Any minute now, someone will shout 'Impostor!'

This is the heart of Europe, the very centre of the EU experiment, just half an hour from Brussels. Yet I'm transported back to an earlier, darker era, one my grandparents might recognise. Drawn along by a march with thousands of extreme-right sympathisers. Not only skinheads, although they're here too. Respectable folk: families, kids, the elderly. All screaming:
– *Our Own People First!*

* * *

I'd wanted to travel to France and meet members of the Front National. But everyone had told me the FN was a shadow of its former self. Even the new MNR, which Paul Golding had suggested I visit, seemed small fry. I needed something new, a different kind of movement.

I pondered Nick Griffin's words: When thousands of people vote for you, you can't be considered neo-nazi. Was this where we were headed?

Now it seemed I'd found a unique independence movement, one that hailed from the right rather than the left. The Vlaams Blok (Flemish Block) had spent much of the 1990s storming the polls in the northern half of Belgium.

This tiny, flat country is actually two nations: southern, poorer, French-speaking Wallonia, and a richer, Dutch-speaking majority based in the north, Flanders. This latter region is culturally distinct and, in the VB's eyes, ripe for independence. Belgium's capital, Brussels, is also a former Dutch-speaking city (now 85 per cent French-dominated), and once the Flemish capital. The VB wants it back.

Members of the Flemish Block claim a proud seafaring heritage, their own language and traditions, and economic superiority to their French-speaking neighbours. They also point out that they form some 60 per cent of the population of Belgium. Yet they feel overruled, despite considerable regional autonomy. They resent the huge subsidies which pass from the north to the south.

Despite the image and relative prosperity of modern-day Belgium – I remember visiting my dad, when he worked there in the 1970s, and marvelling at the trains and buildings – it seems a substantial minority of its citizens want to break away. Some even want Flanders to join up with Holland, to form a 'Greater Netherlands'. The VB has, in effect, been campaigning to destroy the Belgian State, with worrying success.

The party also wants a tough crackdown on immigration and repatriation of all illegal immigrants. About 10 per cent of the country is made up of foreigners. This issue is the real reason the VB grabbed my attention. An article by Dutch academic and extreme-right expert Cas Mudde claimed two-thirds of the VB's supporters voted for the party because of its stance on immigration. Fewer than 20 per cent said the real reason was the push for independence. (Another 30 per cent used it as a protest against the established political parties and system.) Almost half the VB's supporters were 'ethno-centric', i.e. they favoured their own kind over others. Almost one-third were actively racist, believing in the superiority of the white race.

Many of us Brits saw Belgium as the heart of modern Europe. Home to the EU and NATO, a place we joked about. Full of 'Eurocrats' trying to pass judgement on the correct size of bananas. A waste of taxpayers' money, perhaps, but not some hotbed of racism.

The VB's rapid growth has led to furious exchanges with the liberal media and opinion in Belgian society, including accusations of far-right and even neo-nazi beliefs. Until I arrive, I don't know whether this is true or not. At the very least, it's an odd image I digest: that the rich, well-educated Flemings might be xenophobic and ultra-nationalist.

The party hit the news recently, when one of its founding members claimed, on Dutch TV, that the Holocaust death tolls were exaggerated.

There's talk of links between some VB officials and veterans' associations, members of which fought in SS battalions during the Second World War. There are rumours of connections to elements of the NPD in Germany and the old apartheid movements in South Africa.

The party's been promoting zero tolerance law and order policies, and (in a strong Catholic country) 'family values'. Like Haider's Freedom Party, it wants to help mothers remain at home and thus increase the Flemish birth rate. Like some of the ultra-nationalist groups with which it's been associated (the Front National in France, Lega Nord in Italy, the Danish People's Party), the Block has frequently been accused of other extremist beliefs: homophobia, strong anti-abortion sentiments (again, partly around the notion that immigrants have higher birth rates and are breeding the Flemish out of existence) and of being 'undemocractic'. VB supporters deny many of these claims. The party members I later meet claim it's the Flemish who are discriminated against and who support the rest of the country – those with 'Latin tendencies' – with massive subsidies.

This fierce contest, in the very heart of federalism, fascinates me. Graeme Atkinson is right; this will be an interesting encounter. How, and why, could such a party be on the rise? Why wasn't more written about it outside Belgium? Here was something far more successful than my native BNP, seeming to share many of the same views. The ruling powers, even other Flemish parties, seemed so worried that they had created a 'cordon sanitaire' – an agreement not to cooperate with the VB on any level. Only by means of this ring fence has the VB been prevented from stepping into regional power. What was going on?

Everything I read about Belgium said it was a vibrant liberal democracy. Few guidebooks mentioned the rise of a new extreme-right movement. Even if they had, calling it 'new' was a bit of a misnomer. As I later discovered, the Flemish had a history of collaboration with Germany during the First and Second World Wars. Much of the VB's – and its predecessors' – early angst had circled around pardons for these people.

Despite all this, only last November more than one in three people voted for the party in Antwerp, the country's second-largest city, famous for its Jewish community and diamond centre. In some suburbs, the VB already had over 40 per cent support. It held 10 per cent of Belgium's parliamentary seats, as well as members in the Upper House (Senate), the Flemish regional parliament, and various regional and city councils. The joke was that if it ever got enough votes, it would join up with the government – but only to vote the Belgian State out of existence. 'The first Belgian government we join will be the last!' went the joke.

This was like nothing I'd ever encountered. I wondered if this was where Nick Griffin was heading. Would I see the suit-and-tie fascists walking around my neighbourhood, garnering votes on a platform of resisting 'foreigners' and the forces of globalisation? If so, would they cease to be extremist when people voted for them? If they weren't fascist or far right, what were they? Anti-immigrant, xenophobic, ultra-nationalist? What did these labels mean? Was it just a protest vote, or something more serious?

The VB and the BNP seemed to share a fascination with Jean-Marie le Pen's Front National in France. My Flemish contacts told me how the party's leader, a charismatic former journalist named Filip Dewinter – nicknamed 'the new Haider' – had crafted many of the VB's phrases and policies around FN slogans. Odd, given that the Flemings often despised their French-speaking countrymen.

* * *

Brussels is a dirtier, more 'real' place than Copenhagen. Pollution, traffic, noise, street stalls. Even a few homeless. Somehow familiar; somehow . . . English.

My first meeting with the Kurds wasn't far from here. *Wired* magazine had sent me to the small, sleepy town of Denderleeuw to cover an amazing experiment. The Kurdish diaspora, for the first time in its 3,000-year history, was coming together.

From a satellite broadcasting over central Zaire, MED-TV beamed programmes across Europe and the Middle East, in the three main Kurdish dialects. What was so special about that? In several countries, even writing the language was forbidden. Turkey was particularly harsh in its repression. The station became subject to jamming, correspondents were killed or beaten up, European governments became embroiled in diplomatic rows, offices were raided. Yet I met dozens of young Kurds willing to volunteer for MED-TV, tears in their eyes as they thanked me simply for writing about them. I was at once moved and confused. But this was a fight I could understand: violence, repression, poverty, the attempt to assimilate an entire nation. No matter what the extremists of the right told me, I didn't think theirs was a fight on the same level.

* * *

I speak on my mobile to Geert Van Cleemput. He sounds upbeat, his English excellent, hinting at education and intelligence. I haven't encountered anyone fluent in so many languages, at least not anyone considered a zealot. He has a deep American accent and a slight lisp. He's open, polite, keen to help, and shows none of the arrogance and superciliousness that my other encounters with the far right have led me to expect. Perhaps he isn't an extremist at all.

Later, I learn that Geert's not a trained media relations expert at all. He's been chosen to deal with the foreign press because of his language skills. A Greek philosophy lecturer, he was raised in a family deeply involved in

Flemish politics. He's been back in the country less than two years, after 16 years studying and teaching in the States. There, he sang in a gospel choir, was the only white member of a soccer team and voted for the Democrats ('George Bush is such a loser!').

Geert's turn on the news. Back in Britain, the police are gearing up for anti-capitalist protests. In the north, there's already been rioting by football hooligans charging through Asian areas of Bradford. The tabloids are whipped into hysteria by a supposed racial attack by Asian youths on an elderly war veteran.

I stroll from the doors of my faceless hotel, leaving behind CNN and the locked world of my Internet connection.

A dog runs ahead of me, stopping to piss against the pitted façade of a church. I shoulder my way through tourists, passing Turkish and North African faces, before stopping in a bar, ordering up *moules et frites* and strong blond beer. The chime of ancient bells tolls through the background noise. I narrowly miss a couple just entering the bar as I wander down into the Grand Place.

The Beast has been here before me, as have BNP men. I've seen pictures of them at the annual commemorative rallies at the Diksmuide war memorial, set up to commemorate Flemish dead of the Great War. The August festival is a gathering point not only for the VB, but for neo-nazis and ultra-nationalists from across Europe. Nick Lowles told me he was nearly lynched by some skinheads there, saved by the British hooligan crew with him.

A strange place.

* * *

Brussels is quiet. The train pulls through grey, decaying suburbs, north towards Antwerp.

Back home, the crowds are gathering in central London. Oxford Street is a heaving mass of humanity. Not shoppers this time, but anti-capitalists. Riot police and youth, facing off down the narrow side streets.

The train slows down at last, half a dozen stops out of the citys, and we pass beneath a lattice of steel girders. Mechelen station seems over-large; few people are around. My footsteps echo loudly as I search for the exit, wandering through a tiled, concrete landscape. I check the change in my pocket then walk outside. Coach stops and a bus station. No crowd, no noise.

After 20 minutes, a battered Renault 25 pulls up, swerving round fast, tyres screeching, right in front of me. The metallic coat glints dully in the muted afternoon light. Then the side door swings open.

'Hi!' A wide, smiling face, framed with glasses, leans over the passenger seat. 'Nick, right?' The driver thrusts out a hand, straining against the seatbelt. An open leather jacket reveals a pale shirt. He looks momentarily bemused, trying to reach towards me, then glances down, tuts, clicks open the belt, and leans towards me again. 'Sorry I'm late. You weren't waiting too long, were you?'

Geert. He looks younger than his 41 years. 'No, no problem. I was just enjoying the air, really!' I jest. He seems puzzled, but the smile, with the hint of a gap tooth, remains as he motions for me to hop in.

For these next few days, Geert will be my guide, chaperone and personal spin doctor into the world of Flemish nationalism. He flicks a hand through the fronds of his fine, mousy hair. His teeth shine. The smile is a permanent fixture, but his eyes are quizzical, as though thinking through every comment, each nuance.

'So, do you do this often?' I ask.

'I'm sorry?' he says, the lisp apparent.

'Collecting foreign journalists?'

'Oh, hah, this! Er, not very much actually, though I have dealt with the BBC's Jonathan Charles on a documentary last year.' He pauses, eyes fixed to the road. 'They weren't very fair to us, though.'

I glance at the racing scenery. 'Do you mind talking to journalists?'

'Not at all. It's interesting to speak to other people and practise my language. No, there's no problem. As long as they're fair to us.'

I have to stick one hand onto the dashboard, to steady myself as we make a sudden turn. Geert's muttering. We double back. I look through the rear window and see the detritus of Coke cans and other debris lying around the back seat.

'I don't actually live here. I'm based in Antwerp, so I don't know Mechelen so well,' he says. It's clear we're lost. He turns back to the map for a second. 'They said take a right here.' He looks up and swerves again. I glance down at my watch. The hour for the march is approaching.

We crash over tram tracks. 'So, where is everyone?'

'Good question,' he answers, fumbling through the street map. He navigates with one hand on the wheel, steering with his palm whilst glancing occasionally at oncoming traffic. The noise from the cobblestones and iron tramways is a constant juddering buzz as we zoom over the road, trying to find the right place to turn. Many side alleys are already sealed off by police tape or patrol cars. A helicopter buzzes overhead.

Eventually we pull off the ring road and swing down into a small street. We park the car and, just as I'm stepping out, a teenage girl runs past us, nearly bowling me over. She has a Middle Eastern complexion and is screaming. A plump, balding white man wearing a flapping checked shirt runs after her. A boy follows him, also shouting. Geert and I look at each other. Counter-demonstrators are gathering on a flyover bridge above and behind us. I don't like this. Ahead, the canal traps any further progress.

'We should do something,' Geert says. I squint at the man. He's clearly out of breath and angry. He calls after the girl. She screams abuse at him. People start wandering past us, small groups, in dribs and drabs. A police car crawls slowly down the road. I can hear the milling crowd now. The man catches up with the girl. She's fighting in his grasp. I walk slowly ahead, not sure whether to get involved.

'I'm sure it'll be fine, Geert,' I say. I'm worried about joining this march, that we might be trapped by left-wing protesters. Geert doesn't reply, but trots over to the police car and launches into earnest conversation with the cops. They call the man over. An exchange follows, then Geert runs back to me, looking relieved. 'He's her social worker. Says she's absconded from care and he has to take her back.'

That dangerous sense of unreality is creeping in again. We turn the corner and the narrow road rolls out towards a leisure centre. Pleasant-looking apartments squat to our left, the canal to our right. A crowd is gathering directly ahead. Banners hang from the protesters' hands. A large stage is set up at one end of a car park. Video screens, set against the backdrop of a huge Vlaams Blok poster, frame a solitary perspex lectern. A cameraman sits high up on a crane, surveying the scene.

'I didn't realise there'd be this many people!' Geert says, raising his eyebrows. He scans the crowd and appears to recognise a couple of people, moving up to them and shaking their hands. They look like business types on a weekend outing. We're probably too late to hook up with his other buddies from the research division of the Block. Instead, we settle in at the back of the march, as it prepares to move off.

I look around. I'm hanging near the back, which seems to be the gathering point for the skins and hooligans. A group of bulky men, muscles packed into black jackets, walk just ahead of us. I spot a Blood and Honour T-shirt. I try talking to one guy, slightly older, in a denim jacket and holding a flag, which says he and his buddies are from the town of Aarschot. Sideburns are carved across his vein-cracked cheeks. In broken English, he says, 'We just wants our free homeland, our own land.' His pals glare suspiciously at me. 'It's difficult to explain, my English is not good.' He exchanges words with Geert, then says: 'Yes, speak to your friend, he can tell you better than me.' As a skin girl wanders past us, Geert looks uncomfortable. There's a pervading smell of booze amidst the tattoos and denim. I'm guessing Geert would prefer to be nearer the front.

'Everything all right?' I ask. This is where I want to be, at least for the moment.

'Yeah, no problem, you just go where you want to go,' he replies, somewhat unconvincingly. 'You might get better interviews up front, of course, with the leaders, but if you want to stay back here, that's your business. I'm just here to help.' He doesn't sound pleased or relaxed. I get the impression he's fuming. I smile inwardly.

As we walk along the canal path, a great cry rises: 'Eigen Volk Eerst!' It's taken up, up and down the line. A sea of banners sways past us. Fists punch the air. Along the alleys beside our route, silent immigrant kids are cycling and holding back behind policemen, staring at us in fear or hostility. The black-clad skins in front of me begin snapping the poles of their banners, breaking them down into sticks, ready for a fight. The young toughs swig from cans of beer. Across the canal, North African teenagers hurl insults at the guys surrounding me. Bottles, bricks and pieces of wood are hurled at us. The police charge the groups, which melt and reform further up the way.

The adrenaline's pumping. 'Eigen Volk Eerst!' comes the cry, louder this time. The air is thick with banners and curling moustaches. We seem to be catching up with the front of the march. 'Eigen Volk Eerst!' 'Eigen Volk Eerst!' Over and over comes the cry. Geert leaves my side to have urgent words with the VB stewards. He wants them to rein in the hooligans before this gets out of control. I ask him what the skins are chanting – some new phrase – but he claims not to understand.

As we turn away from the canal, in towards the medieval heart of the city centre, people cheer us from window sills. Well, most of them. One young group has a sign saying 'Vlaams Blok = SS' hanging from their window. They laugh down at us, exchanging insults with the skins. One skin, a Lion of Flanders tattooed into the back of his skull, obviously wants the blokes to come down and fight him. Fingers are flipped, and the march moves on.

I lose Geert for a moment. Then he comes back, leading another man towards me. 'Nick, I want you to meet a good friend of mine. Dr Hermann Pol. He's a councillor for us in a suburb of Antwerp.'

'Pleased to meet you,' we greet each other, simultaneously. Pol navigates between a mum and her pushchair, to come closer to me. He's short and balding, somewhere in his 50s, a managerial type in a dull brown raincoat. Geert urges me to hurry up, as he tries to manoeuvre us towards the front.

Pol says the hooligans are a minority. I'm surprised he isn't more scared of them. I've learned that most people here can speak a semblance of English, and our conversation can likely be overheard.

'We are a, how do you say, rightist party? Yes, rightist, but not extremist. Look around you. Apart from these guys,' he gestures, fearlessly, at the skinheads, 'most of the people here are families. Although we are attracting a lot of votes from younger people now. It's because most people are fed up with groups like the Christian Democrats and the Socialists. Also the high crime caused by immigrants, of course.'

As we chat, Pol tells me he's a doctor, a general practitioner. He's a former lifelong Conservative, who voted for the Christian Democrats. In the district he represents, 50 per cent of the electorate voted for the VB.

'How do you see yourself?' I ask.

'As a Flemish nationalist,' he answers, looking straight at me through a rounded pair of spectacles, as his eyes lock beneath the v-shaped furrow of his brow. He wraps part of his coat around his arm. 'As a Christian, too.'

'So what's the main problem you're dealing with?'

'Immigration. Uncontrolled immigration is causing a lot of trouble. These illegals are stealing into the most poor areas, and then pushing out the locals, and this is causing a lot of problems.'

'Really?'

'Oh, yes. These people find it very difficult to integrate, and they often come from the lowest social classes.' He doesn't speak with vitriol. He tells me about the many patients he treats, several of whom come from Moroccan backgrounds.

His manner reminds me of my dad, discussing a serious topic in quiet, business-like tones. It's interesting that he doesn't mention independence as the primary issue.

'Are you a racist, then?' It's becoming hard to shout over the crowd.

'No. No, I don't think so. I'm not against immigration, as long as we can absorb them in a decent way.' He explains that he's worked outside the country, in a multinational firm (later, he became a senior executive in Belgium's national cancer society), so is used to dealing with different nationalities. 'But most of these people are from another culture. It's Islamic.' I'm left to ponder these words a few months later, after 11 September. If they feel this way already, how will the Flemish react to that? Similar comments begin coming from a new right-wing party in the Netherlands, Leefbaar Nederland (Liveable Netherlands), and one of its offshoots, Leefbaar Rotterdam, which takes 17 of Rotterdam's 45 seats in spring 2002. The leader of that local party, Pim Fortuyn, is to crop up again ominously at the end of my journey.

Pol is easy to talk to. I've met a thousand people like him. If the right is attracting men like this, something must be going on. Either the problems really are as bad as they say – or else respectable folk are being driven by fear.

He's just the sort of guy that Griffin, back in England, would love to have on his side. This very fact already makes me doubt whether the Block is anywhere near the BNP or the other groups I've seen. It certainly seems to have mass support. And not just from the working class, although they're much in evidence today.

Pol, Geert and I stay together for much of the rest of the afternoon. We wend our way through the small streets, in what seems a fairly well-to-do town centre. As we move past the cathedral, I ask a marcher what they're shouting. 'Nothing for Belgium, everything for Flanders,' he says, a grin on his whiskered face. We're near the front now, where the leadership is gathered, soberly dressed in suits and smart tweeds. Geert's talking to me about the corruption of the Belgian government and how the press censors itself (against the Block, of course). He regales me with scare stories on immigration – how one travel agency in Kazakhstan, for example, was selling refugees tickets to Belgium. When I later communicate, secretly, with investigative journalists and Flemish academics, they tell me this is a standard VB tactic: paint an apocalyptic scenario of the world today, then portray yourself as a victim of hostile outside forces. That's a constant theme of the right, and of protest parties in general.

Only when we get back out towards the suburbs does the town start to look more drab. I hear sirens and see riot vans parked near the roads leading to the leisure centre. Back at the rallying point, a woman approaches me, a journalist, she explains, and warns me to be careful. The skins are mainly hooligans from the soccer club, Beerschot, she says. 'Mechelen is not a dangerous city. Certainly not as dangerous as they [the Block] have led people to believe. Make sure to write that.' Before I have time to ask her a question, she's gone. Two old ladies stand by the kerb, clapping vigorously for us.

We gather in front of the stage. The roar of the helicopter drowns out the early speakers. Then the party leadership begins taking to the plinth, head mikes crafted to their skulls, and the TV crews move in. Geert attempts to provide a translation, but the words don't mean much to me. As I stand there, hemmed in by the crowds at the side of the stage, he presses my hand into greetings with various VB politicians, including the party's latest Senator. Dramatic music sweeps over the crowd from the huge speaker stacks. I spot Filip Dewinter, a youngish, smiling figure, chatting with a journalist nearby.

The party President, a trim, tanned, handsome man named Frank Vanhecke, is taking the stand, talking about the power of the Freemasons, when all hell breaks loose.

Two riot vans shoot up and start offloading cops. A couple of helicopters hover over a field at the back of the leisure centre, and suddenly all the skins – and others – are running towards the VB marquee, behind the stage. I hear shouts and cries, even over the stirring music.

I tear myself away from the speech makers and try to find out what's happening. People are pushing and speeding past me. I sniff the air. There's an odd odour – smoke from the burger stalls, and something else: tear gas. I press on.

A sizeable crowd has gathered in front of the marquee, against the temporary fence that separates us from the remainder of the playing field. Roaming North African youths hurl over missiles from the other side, whilst the skins taunt them and try to clamber over the railings. Several figures are carried past me, rivulets of blood traced across their alcohol-flushed faces. Ambulances edge through the crowd. VB leaders shout for calm. I turn and see Geert behind me.

'Why aren't you listening to the speakers? I thought you'd be interested to hear what they have to say?' He seems hurt, but I guess he doesn't want me to see this fracas. A young skin charges past me, followed by two girls. With his shirt open revealing tattoos and muscles, and a beer can dangling from one hand, he seems a pastiche of a 1950s rebel. He joins a huddle of his fellows near the fence.

'Sorry, Geert, I just want to see what's going on. You don't mind, do you?' It's hard to speak over the noise.

'I just want to help,' he replies. 'We'll try and get you interviews with some of the party's leaders. There's some really good people there. I just hope that, at the end of the day, you'll be fair to us. This isn't representative, you know. I can guarantee, though, that when the news comes on this evening, that this is all they'll show.'

He steers me towards a stocky figure who looks like a kindly old schoolmaster: dark-haired, bearded, with a friendly grin, glasses and a tweed jacket. His trousers are tucked into his socks. 'What's your name, again?' I shout over the din as we shake hands.

'Oh, my name will be double-Dutch to you!' he jokes, in decent English. 'Francis Van den Eynde. Here, have one of my cards. I'm Vice-President of the parliamentary party, and what you call an MP for the town of Ghent.' He smiles, but I can't read his eyes.

Later I'm told he's a former leader of Voorpost, an infamous, militant activist movement which has had links to groups in South Africa and with extremist networks in Europe. Some called it neo-nazi. It still exists, but the VB is trying to pull away and present a more moderate, modern image. Geert doesn't seem keen to discuss it, when I ask him later.

Another of my secretive contacts, a man I'd meet later in Ghent, informs me that Van den Eynde was actually raised in a French-speaking socialist family. He'd changed his name from François, organised pro-apartheid meetings, and mobilised activists to disrupt anti-apartheid protesters. Apparently he once was beaten quite badly by skinheads. My contact also claims he's a pagan.

'How did you get involved with the party?' I shout over the sound of generators and the helicopter. Something whizzes past my head: a piece of paving stone.

'I'm involved since 30 years,' he says. 'Since I was 14 years old. At first I was in the old nationalist party, the Volksunie [a more liberal independence movement, from which the VB split in 1977].'

I explain I'm an outsider. 'Why does the party have such a controversial reputation?'

'In my opinion, because we are the only party that asks the independence of Flanders.' I can hear shouts building in the background, behind the chain link fence. The police seem to be moving in. Several dozen North African youths are chanting behind police barriers. 'But they try to catch us about the problem of the foreigners in this city. Well, not only this city, this country. Because we have a big problem with, ah, immigration. In our opinion, enough is enough. We don't want to take all the multicultural society.'

I ask him what this means. 'The problem for us is that they never mention what is a multicultural society. Our opinion is that everybody who lives here has to respect our language and our culture. And if they do that, they are welcome. No less, no more.'

'Are other parties elsewhere similar?'

'A lot of [them] are similar in different ways. If you ask me which parties I admire, hmm . . . then in the East, the Legas [Lega Nord/Northern League] in Italy. And Sinn Fein in Ireland.' These two groups encompass the political spectrum: extreme right and left, I point out. 'For us, both are very interesting,' says Van den Eynde, adjusting his spectacles with a thick finger.

Although he maintains that independence is their original aim, others claim immigration/foreigners is really their first issue. 'In fact, our first aim is to save our own identity. And that's the reason why we have problems with the immigration. We have no home rule, at all. We have a kind of federalism in this country. We want independence. In this time of globalisation and mongrelisation, we try to save our own identity. Everybody in the world, even when he is black or yellow, who is struggling to save his own identity, is our ally.'

He seems fired up. 'This is the world of McDonald's and Coca-Cola. It's very important to be against globalisation. It's one of the major problems. In the future, that will be more and more the big problem. What is it?' he asks, rhetorically. 'It's the One World philosophy.'

'Does the concept of a New World Order exist – you know, as George Bush senior once said?' This is a coded question that Nick Lowles has suggested I ask political extremists.

'Yes, and I'm against it. For us, it's very important that everybody could be himself.'

'Are there interest groups using the New World Order?' I'm hunting for a flaw in the argument. Perhaps some reference to the Jews.

'Yes, of course. In particular, what you can call international capitalism.' Strange, how this language links him with the anti-capitalists now hemmed in on London's streets. Then, as a cold wind settles in: 'For us, the struggle is not over,' Van den Eynde smiles.

A hand clamps on my shoulder. Five steel-like pincers lock into muscle and bone. Shit. A spurt of unintelligible language bursts from behind me, aggressive and demanding. The genial figure in front of me looks momentarily nonplussed then his bearded mouth begins moving, in what seems like slow motion. A sudden burst of 'Eigen Volk Eerst!' rises again. A flare shoots across the sky. Cobblestones land near the marquee.

I'm facing a blunt-faced, heavily built skinhead, his head completely shaved and garbed all in black. I explain that I speak only English and that I'm a journalist.

'Who are you?' I ask.

'I'm just someone, a Fleming, fighting for my country,' he answers,

155

leaning in close. I can taste his breath and see his solid, stone-like grin from close quarters. His teeth are stained and his eyes shocking blue.

'What's your name?'

'Ah, I don't give my name. I'm just here to support the Flemish people.'

'Are you a member of the Vlaams Blok, then?'

'No, I'm not a member of the party, because of my job.'

'What's that?'

'I'm a soldier. We can't get involved in politics.'

'So what are you doing here, then, if you can't get involved?' I cup my hands together, to speak over the noise.

'I'm just here to fight for my country. And to keep the cool, to make sure the young people don't lose it so much.'

'Fight for who, though?'

'My country. When it's necessary, that's what I'll do. It goes back a long way in my family. My grandfather fought in Stalingrad.' He tells me he supports the IRA and ETA, the Basque paramilitary movement and that he's been four times in Croatia with the UN. I know many extremists have been down to that area because of their political beliefs. Catholics – Flanders is a strong Catholic area – would naturally side with the Catholic nation of Croatia.

'What about the people around us – your friends? Are they neo-nazis?'

'You see all the people, they are believing in a Flemish cause. You have them, too, er, the right, extremists who want to fight.'

'Is that you?'

'No, no, no, I'm just for a Flemish cause.'

A flurry of conversation takes place between Geert and the skin. A few days from now, in Antwerp, Geert will urgently discuss the skinhead situation with the party leaders. It's proving a difficult image problem for the party.

* * *

A sign surfaces into my field of vision, The White Horse. Stuffed to the gills with Turkish men playing cards and dominoes, the bar seems both familiar and alien. I think about walking in. But I'm becoming aware of my whiteness, afraid I'll attract the wrong kind of attention. I make eye contact with one of the men inside, then turn away and continue up the street. When I look back, the faces are just a dark blur.

The Vlaams Blok headquarters is housed in a large, shabby tower block. It's reminiscent of Eastern Europe, a pharmacy and sandwich shop on either side of the entrance. Inside, past the security buzzer (the building was bombed not long ago) a cramped, old-fashioned lift takes you to the third floor. I have a flashback to my travels in south-eastern Turkey, sleeping in cheap concrete buildings, trying to avoid the secret police.

Then the door swings wide and I'm spat out into modern office surroundings.

Geert seems relaxed, a blue shirt open at his neck. Sunlight streams in through large plate-glass windows as he walks forwards. 'Hi Nick, good night?' His manner is genuinely friendly. I like him. I feel bad that one day I'm going to write things he might regard as a betrayal.

He introduces me to a guy I saw yesterday, a gangly, scholarly-looking bloke, slightly ungainly, jacketed in tweed. His name is Derik, one of the party's lawyers. Two other men, one a sandy-haired economist, the other the head of the unit – sporting a beard with no moustache – regard me suspiciously from their desks.

Geert tells me to join him in his office whilst he calls up to the party's President for an interview. Close in he looks tired, as he removes his glasses and chews the ends. The small room is cluttered with filing cabinets and stacks of paper. 'Sorry, sorry, take a seat,' he motions, embarrassed.

As we wait, he admits that the night classes in law are taking a toll. But he must do them if he wants advancement. That's the only way up in politics, he believes. I decide to quiz him about these beliefs. He talks about the growing sense of alienation and frustration building up in cities like Antwerp, and his support for a 'Greater Netherlands' project. He also mentions the need to build strong family units. I smile and ask him – if he doesn't mind – about his own marital arrangements.

'I have a partner,' he says.

'Flemish?'

'No, she's Greek,' he says, quickly. They cohabit. I stay silent. 'But this is a party of choice, too,' he remonstrates. 'We don't want to tell people what to do with every aspect of their lives.'

The corridor outside is a flurry of activity. Most of the people here are preparing one of the biggest challenges the organisation has faced in years. A government-funded anti-racism centre has lodged a suit, alleging that the VB incites racial hatred. If successful, this would mean a withdrawal of central funding and potential destruction for the party.

'So far as they fight racism, excellent, that's a fine thing,' Geert says in his American accent, fixing me with those wide eyes. 'But they have taken it upon themselves to really attack us. They say we are a racist party, and they are suing us so that we will lose our party funding.' He thinks they could potentially sue every member of the party. 'They are trying to kill the party, that's the intention.'

As he talks, he thumbs through a book which has been critical of the VB. I struggle to keep my face straight. I'm already secretly in touch with the author. Geert tells me he's preparing a critique of this work and sighs that the party is always being misquoted. That's why he's keen to read a first draft of my chapter (a request I politely sidestep).

When we talk about race, he claims, 'I can't just go to the States. I need a permit from the US. And if I don't behave while in the US, I'm out. That's not racism.'

'Aren't we just trying to turn the clock back, though?' I suggest. 'Refugees aren't going to stop leaving countries, are they?'

'That's the sad thing. We need to invest and support those countries, so people feel they have a reason to remain.' His manner is persuasive, the language of liberalism.

'So what's the biggest issue facing Flanders's potential independence? Wallonia – the French – or [as I suspect] immigration?'

'Oh, Wallonia, no doubt. Of course, there would be tensions about immigration in an independent Flanders,' he admits. 'It's a nationalistic issue also. If we allow members of other cultures to keep all of their cultural values, like their languages and certain non-democratic practices, that affects us too. If indeed Turkish and Arabic become official languages, and if people from abroad know that, that will affect immigration even more. And that to us is unacceptable.'

It all sounds so reasonable. And I think Geert is genuine in his beliefs. I'm beginning to question my own thoughts, listening to all of this. I wonder how I'll surface from my odyssey.

* * *

Whirlwind days follow.

After meeting the tanned, suave Frank Vanhecke – an eloquent multi-linguist who denies any link between the Block and extremism – I'm whisked through the smart, carpeted corridors of the Belgian parliament. Many of the Block's MPs are young, only a few years older than myself. Curiously, the one female member – born in Ireland, and a native English speaker – refuses to meet me. We have a tense, embarrassing encounter outside her offices, Geert speaking low and urgently to her. She grins nervously at me. I can't work out the problem. As we talk, I see the shuffling, lumbering figure of Francis Van den Eynde walking into an office, then speaking loudly on the phone, as he leans back in a large chair. He, too, makes his excuses when I ask Geert to set up a meeting. It seems odd after our initial encounter. Geert acts bemused. Maybe someone's found out about my *Searchlight* contacts. Or maybe they've seen that email I forwarded to the Voorpost website.

Nationalism and identity: this is where it ends up. Is it so bad? I don't know yet. The VB paints a persuasive picture of a modern party. Is this part of a sea change across Europe? If so, why haven't I seen it back home? Where people can't vote in a Haider, then you get the violence, Graeme had told me. Which was worse?

Back in a sweltering, glass-fronted room at VB headquarters, I meet Johan Demol, the party's law and order spokesman. He's a former police commissioner, much championed as an advocate of zero-tolerance policies. His words become a blur, and an unhealthy film of sweat coats his pasty-looking skin. He talks about the Mafia's growing power among Belgium's ruling classes. I'm more taken with the tacky John Wayne statue sitting on his window. His small, beady eyes narrow as he reminisces about cleaning the streets of prostitutes and drug dealers. Near the end of our interview, he mentions a meeting he had with the MNR leader, Bruno Megret, in his stronghold town of Vitrolles; another link in the international network.

Geert and I spend more and more time together. I end up temporarily based at the third-floor offices, hanging out with his colleagues. We eat pizza in the building's basement and travel together to his native Antwerp. On a Friday afternoon, we're crammed into a hot, stuffy carriage, with all the other returning commuters. Perched on the North Sea coast, this old trading centre oddly reminds me of towns in Eastern Europe, China, even the Middle East. The smell of the sea and decaying ozone. Tug boats and barges wending their way towards the open water. It's a place of memories, history – and sudden change. A place of peeling decay and faded glories. I spend much of my time wandering through the old cobbled backstreets.

I'm billeted next to the station in a grubby, block-like hotel, a depressing vista of neon lights and billboards framed through the bent aluminium and glass of my tiny window. Jewellery stores, with racks upon racks of diamonds, grace the puddle-strewn streets. This is the Jewish area of the city, and it's interesting to see the stern-faced men opening their stores in the morning, as last night's prostitutes melt away.

That evening, I bid farewell to Geert and slip off unnoticed. Time to seek a new quarry. In the city centre, near a McDonald's, I find an Internet café, where I contact *Searchlight*, check my emails and send off speculative notices to Voorpost and the VJM – the Vlaamse Jongeren Mechelen – a new, more extreme Flemish movement. It's based in Mechelen, where the demonstration was held the other day. My contacts have told me they're closer to the networks I find in Britain: younger, streetwise, unafraid of confrontation. Later, on my first night back in England, they email me an invitation to a soccer match between themselves and their Dutch counterparts.

Checking behind me, I set off across a large square, dodging buses and moving between ever-decreasing pools of light. This is a seedier end of town, and I'm aware of potential danger. If the Block find out what I'm doing, things could get sticky. Neon glows from the tall, stark edifice of a five-star hotel. The shops are closed, and red tailgates are the only signs of life. Every now and then, something shuffles and stirs in a dark doorway, so I pick up the pace and hurry on.

'Must be somewhere around here,' I mutter, cursing that I have to pull out the street map. Choosing a side alley, I fetch up in front of a shadowed, metal door. An earnest-looking young man answers and a welcome beam of light spills onto the cold stone steps.

'Come in, come in,' he says. Marc Spruyt is a friend of a friend, part of a worldwide network of journalistic contacts. He's responsible for two books, so far, on the Vlaams Blok, as well as numerous articles. A Fleming himself, he's not convinced of their message.

'They are a right, revolutionary party, Nick,' he says, handing me a beer. The apartment is well-ordered, numerous files secreted neatly on pine shelves. A wooden floor creaks beneath my feet. His wife walks through the kitchen, picking up their baby and singing him to sleep. We lower our voices. 'They want a mono-cultural, and – how do you say? – mono-racial society.'

He lists a litany of problems associated with the VB. One of their major antagonisms with the left has been their antipathy towards the trades unions. 'Think of them as at the centre of a far-right web; you have kids' groups, student organisations, activist groups like Voorpost, even links to veterans' associations.' We talk late into the night and he mentions that he's trying to sneak into a veterans' meeting the next evening. 'We think that one of the main VB guys is going to come down there,' he says.

That night, I flick through the static on my broken TV, finally finding a French channel. It shows a Jewish cemetery that's just been desecrated.

* * *

Geert waits for me at the party's headquarters, down the long, wide boulevard of America Street. He hovers over and around me as I talk with Gerolf Annemans, the party's parliamentary leader, and Filip Dewinter (who I learn has changed his name from Philip, to sound more Flemish).

Annemans is a bearded, eloquent figure, sitting in a little pool of light from the angle-poise lamp on his desk. He compares the Belgian state to East Germany and complains about the party's treatment from the press, as he carefully toys with the leather writing pad on his desk.

Dewinter arrives late and flustered. He has just a touch of grey eating at his temples, the first real sign of age on the young orator's face, and sports a neat V-neck pullover. His eyebrows meet in the middle. Much of our conversation concerns the economic situation of Flanders. Other matters, like immigration, are couched in seemingly reasonable language. With Geert looking on, the whole thing feels very 'managed', very Haideresque. Annemans admits he's met Haider, as well as Le Pen and Umberto Bossi, head of Italy's separatist Northern League. Dewinter claims the Italian right is a source of inspiration. In just a few days' time, both the Northern League and the former fascist party, the Alleanza National, will enter into coalition with Silvio Berlusconi. Two parties of the right, helping to govern Italy. Things are changing.

I press Geert to take me to a traditional Flemish bar, somewhere I can see 'real' or 'normal' Flemish nationalists. 'Take a look around you, Nick,' says Geert. 'One in three people walking past voted for us. Just stop anyone in the street.'

Marc Spruyt had told me to go to the Leeuw Van Vlaanderen (Lion of Flanders), an infamous Flemish nationalist pub, traditionally popular with harder elements of the movement. Gerolf Annemans said that many journalists called it 'The Beast'. Geert is uncomfortable. By now, I've learned that he doesn't drink or smoke, and he seems ill at ease with some of the more zealous signs of nationalism. But I twist his arm, eventually.

He sneezes constantly, rubbing tired-looking eyes as we drive through the twisting streets. He apologises for coming down with a cold, but I feel bad too. The guy has put himself out on my part. After parking near his old Jesuit school, we enter the narrow, snaking alleys and paved lanes of Antwerp's old town. Heavy metal music blasts out into the street from an Irish bar called Molly's.

The Lion of Flanders itself is tiny and nondescript; a brown façade that seems trapped in time, surrounded by newer, brasher restaurants. Old newsprint papers the walls. The wizened bartender, sporting a beard with no moustache, takes our order with a quizzical, suspicious eye fixed on me. Geert blurts out something in Flemish – telling the guy I'm a journalist, he explains to me in English – and suddenly everyone in the small room is staring. I gulp down the strong lager and ask for another. The barman pretends he can't understand English, so I'm forced to point at the beer tap.

In the corner sit two long-haired guys wearing blue, white and orange sashes. Dutch students from a nationalist organisation, Geert whispers. I think he looks more out of place here than I do. He's hardly touched his beer. Still, when the others learn Geert is a prominent member of the VB, they suddenly break into smiles and begin chatting and slapping backs. I swallow hard, feeling relieved.

As the guy next to us blows cigar smoke into my face, the barman grins and says, 'Hey, English, look here!' He removes several glasses from a shelf. Behind it are dozens of different stickers, from all kinds of nationalist and national liberation movements. Groups in Sweden, Corsica, Cuba, Sardinia. Near the door, fading pictures show members of militant groups, many now swallowed into the Vlaams Blok. Then the bartender reveals the pride of his collection: a Sinn Fein emblem from Ireland, with a Lion of Flanders inside it. He rewards me with a gap-toothed grin, as I mutter what I hope sounds like appreciation. He regales us with stories of how he'd been coming to this place since 1958. He used to go around the countryside, he says, painting out all the French signs. Later, in Ghent, I'd see how the nationalist students had gone round spraying graffiti on the medieval university walls.

Geert and I leave the pub, to share one last meal together. We dine on spaghetti in a trendy restaurant called Travel, served by a Thai waitress. Saying goodbye, I feel a twinge of sadness. That evening, I stride aimlessly through the streets, melancholic and alone. This strange, schizophrenic place.

The next morning, over coffee, Hermann Pol tells me about his marriage break-up, his new wife, and his sons, and invites me to stay with his family. I'm touched. We swap emails for much of the rest of the year.

* * *

My trip ends in the medieval city of Ghent. Another demonstration: a sea of banners fluttering against a backdrop of old buildings and churches. This time, the action involves both the VB and members of other Flemish movements. Thousands have turned up, and there's little or no visible opposition.

At my side is Wim Haelsterman, one of *Searchlight*'s many contacts and a protégé of Graeme's. He's my age and has been working undercover in this area for several years. I've been staying at his house, learning that not all Flemings have swallowed the Block's message of mono-ethnicity.

Only yesterday, I was meeting the senior leadership of the VB. Now I feel apart again, back in the world to which I belong. Watching some of the same faces – there's Luc, the skinhead from Mechelen, whom I shadow for the next hour – as well as most of the leadership, I snap discreetly with my camera, feeling strangely exposed with Wim by my side. I'm nervous. An enemy now, no longer a friend. There's little chance the Block would have allowed me inside their party, had they known of my contacts.

TEN

PEACE LINES

MAY 2001

England erupts. The north is burning.

C18 gangs have been on the rampage, led, in part, by my old contacts. The BNP is much in evidence too, stirring up tension. It seems an unholy marriage of convenience. Nick Griffin invites me to witness events for myself. I'd say yes, but for the next mission I have planned – one he's just cleared on my behalf.

Events unfold as I finish my last-minute preparations. Within a few days, I'll be on a plane to Washington, DC. I've spent the past couple of weeks talking with Mark Cotterill, a well-known British extremist and head of the American Friends of the BNP (AFBNP). With strong links to the National Front, the Conservative Party, the Bloomsbury Forum and Loyalist groups in Northern Ireland, Cotterill has been steadily building a network of white supremacists on America's East Coast. His contacts stretch from the Identity movement, through to Holocaust deniers, David Duke's network, Pierce's National Alliance and Pat Buchanan's Reform Party. Much speculation surrounds his role and final intentions. How the Americans have reacted to him, I have little idea. I'm about to find out. I'll be staying at his apartment, after all. As far as I'm aware, this is unprecedented access into the world of white supremacy.

In England a white mob gathers on the edge of Oldham, early in the morning of 26 May, then attempts to march through a largely Asian area. They constantly regroup, seeking to outmanoeuvre police, using taxis and mobile phones. Asian anger boils over, fuelled by years of poor education, housing, high unemployment and tensions with the police. Dozens are injured in the riots that follow.

Each side seems filled with hate. A gang of white men calls for a taxi, then ambushes the Asian driver. Asian youths build burning barricades, attack the police and firebomb the offices of the local newspaper, which they blame for racist articles. Nick Griffin is in the area, too, and a meeting takes place between him and C18 hooligans. My old friend Darren threatens to 'do him' during the encounter that follows. By this time, though, Darren is already working undercover for *Searchlight*, informing on the gangs to the police. It's dangerous, unforgiving work. But it stops even greater problems. In just a few months, he'll have to flee the country.

Tensions rise in other cities. On 24 June – by which time I'm meeting Griffin's contacts overseas – Burnley goes up. The same happens again to Bradford, on 7 July. A notorious racist hooligan almost single-handedly goes out of his way to rile anti-Nazi protesters and attack passing Asians. The result: an explosion of violence.

This is not the Britain most of us know. We're ignorant of the lives of millions of our compatriots, it seems. We watch travel programmes on TV and worry about the plight of animals in far-off corners of the world. How many of us are prepared to explore the underbelly of our own society?

You can't recreate community with anger and hate. People I'd met in the most adverse of circumstances – in wars, in refugee camps – had a stronger sense of family ties and belonging than many of the white English I knew. Kurds, who lacked the aggressive sense of individualism that surrounded much of my life, lived and breathed community. Like the network, they considered me a Friend. Sahawaris, too, fighting for their very survival in the Western Sahara.

But a certain section of white English males, and their women, were blindly groping for explanations. Why had their world changed? They didn't know and they were lashing out because of this. Like the poorer Afrikaans speakers in South Africa, they were watching the old order slip by, feeling abandoned whilst their former servants – sometimes better qualified and educated – took the jobs that 'by right' should have been theirs. What would it take to recapture 'Englishness' from their grasp? Why was it that I flinched when I saw the Cross of St George – one half of my own heritage – but not the Irish tricolour, which represented the other?

And now the riots are spreading, on the eve of our first General Election since the Labour Party came to power. Nick Griffin talks of dividing races; soon enough, it happens. 'Peace lines' – iron fencing – are erected in Oldham, to keep warring groups apart. Belfast, on the streets of mainland Britain.

The National Front keeps threatening to march in different cities, and the left responds by seeking confrontation, playing into the hands of the extremists. Nick Lowles has already called, wishing me luck for my journey, but also to warn me privately that the BNP may put in a strong showing.

I join Paul Golding and the BNP men on the campaign trail. Slade Green is a target area for the right, a white flight heartland, part of the Northend ward near Bexley, in Kent, where the BNP obtained 26 per cent of the vote in the last local election. If they're to break through and become a continental-style, anti-immigrant party, this is where they might do it.

With a colleague, I arrive late in the morning at Slade Green station. It's a soulless, decaying place, a landscape of first-time buyers' homes, vandalised ticket machines and lounging kids. As we walk down the platform the sky tarnishes, loosening rain.

Golding and I exchange warm greetings, as he pulls up in his battered little car. Three others are with him. The first is bland-looking, dressed in a suit, jowls hanging, broken veins, thick, wet lips, and a prominent nose. Another is hard-faced, no-nonsense, blunt features set off with a short back and sides. The last is heavy-set, chubby and tattooed, a pouting lower lip moulded into bulldog features. They regard us suspiciously.

'Awright Nick?' says Golding, as we shake hands. The baby-faced guy is pleasant and open, the others less so. The no-nonsense guy gives me a sneer and a light, grudging handshake.

Paul pipes up: 'See that there?' he points, nodding towards a tumbledown former pub. 'That's what we stopped 'em from turnin' into the asylum 'ostel.'

I tell them that if it's all right, we'll just tag along behind them, as they go leafleting on the estates. 'I dunno what you're looking for,' says the grim-faced guy – Jay Lee, I learn – 'but unless people like ANAL [a derogatory acroynym for the Anti-Nazi League] turn up, it'll be pretty quiet. You'll find that most of 'em around 'ere support us.' His accent is broad Mancunian. He tells me he's a train driver, but won't reveal for which company. 'Still, you're a journalist. Shouldn't be too 'ard to make someit up, should it?' He grins, hard and flat, straight at me. I protest my innocence, but he seems unconvinced. Oddly enough, he's one of the extremists I end up liking the most. At least he's honest.

A short ride through faceless streets and estates, and we pull up in a lay-by. Colin Smith, the puppy-faced leader of the pack, steps out. His manner is pleasant, not defensive, as my previous encounters with the right have led me to expect. He's the official BNP parliamentary candidate for the area. A suit nearly – but not quite – hides a series of Mod tattoos emblazoned on his wrist. A cheap gold watch sits above them. I can see the word 'Specials' carved into his skin. They were a Two Tone band. Not exactly Nazi stuff.

'Right lads, take these,' he says, handing out a wad of leaflets to each person. Then we split up.

Paul and I wander through the flat, modern estate. It's very quiet, and most of the doors are closed. There seem to be few people about. It seems quite a nice area to me, newly constructed houses and small blocks of flats. In the distance, Dartford Bridge hangs above water-logged fields.

The newly laid tarmac makes barely a sound as we walk. At each door Paul knocks, earnest and polite, introducing himself as part of the local parliamentary team. His patter is well-rehearsed. It usually starts with a quick introduction 'as representing your local parliamentary candidate', then quickly descends into 'we're concerned about the asylum seekers, 'ow they're takin' all the 'ousing round here'. To my surprise, about two-thirds of the people we encounter murmur in agreement. This isn't some terrible battleground, a hotbed of racial conflict.

'We're worried about crime too. The local police are doin' nuffink, as our people are going 'omeless into B&Bs, whilst the asylum seekers get everyfink,' says Paul to one middle-aged lady. Only after lambasting the 'Kosovans' does he talk about other issues, such as the lack of youth facilities. My colleague seems even more shocked than I am. I suddenly worry. Perhaps my guard has dropped too much? God, I'm not even reacting to this – it's starting to sound normal. I'm brought round by the woman's voice, agreeing with Paul. 'Oh, I know, love,' she says, hovering at the edge of her door. 'Don't worry, I'll be voting for you this time.' It's a scene I see repeated dozens of times.

My colleague watches as Colin encounters an Indian woman on her doorstep. He literally recoils, thrusting a leaflet towards her, then backs off and moves to the next house.

This is the white flight heartland, the dying dream of England's old guard. Unable, unwilling to cope with change, shifting ever outwards, searching for the mythical past that never was. Or maybe I'm just wrong. Perhaps most people want to live like this.

The only real sign of extremism I see is an open garage, with a Millwall FC sign pointing inside and faded Millwall stickers in front of net curtains. As I move in for a closer look – noticing the garage interior full of professional builder's equipment – a car horn toots behind me. I jump in shock. 'Oi, mate, you won't find no coons in there. Try looking next door.'

'What?' I gulp.

'I said, if you want to find a spade, there's one in next door.' A heavy-set figure in a white T-shirt and shorts, with thick, pale legs and a glinting earring, smiles at me. He nods towards the door of the block of flats next to his house. 'You won't find much luck with 'em, though, eh?' He obviously thinks I'm one of Them, the BNP. I smile weakly back, nod slightly, and say, 'Yeah' under my breath. He jumps into his 4-wheel-drive with his young son, and speeds off. An England motif is wrapped across the spare tyre on the rear bumper.

Later, we chat with these men in a nearby pub. Asylum seekers are clearly the main issue. 'It's the political arrogance we can't stand. Why shouldn't we protect our independence? Who would choose to have crime in their neighbourhood?' Colin Smith is quite erudite – considering, as Nick Lowles tells me, that he has a dozen previous convictions. Still, after 20 minutes or so, they begin opening up about their beliefs, fears for their children, and hopes for the coming elections. Some interesting things crop up in the conversation. Colin says his sister was one of the founding members of the Green Party. His blue eyes open wide as he talks. He seems, almost, like a nice local lad, the boy who never grew up. Someone close to his mum, perhaps. When I ask if he has a partner, he answers, 'No', slightly embarrassed. The suit-and-tie image of the businessman jars, too, with his work as a security guard.

'It don't matter what the liberal establishment say, we know we're right,' says Jay. 'I know I'm right. I've read a lot of stuff on this; I started out on the left, you know.'

'I'm a JT [John Tyndall] man,' he adds later, telling me he once lived in the party's former headquarters in the suburb of Welling. He came down from Manchester originally, after spending time in the army, to go to university. What did he study? 'Physics,' he spits, dull and flat. 'Then I changed to politics and economics. But *they* got rid of me in the end.' He draws the words out into a sneer. He claims he made political speeches, which got him into trouble with the professors and lecturers. I get the impression there were difficulties with his family, too. Anger wells inside him, vented in sudden, fervent, fundamentalist bursts. Abortion seems one of his causes. He's very neat, too. As he talks, he carefully wipes his glass of lemonade with a small, folded napkin. Eventually, we chat about his family. He claims that most of them are left wing in their beliefs and don't speak to him any more. 'And my mom's married a Jew,' he laments. He tells me about his kid, and his dad ('you did fuck all, ya cunt, just sat around talking shit') now living in Australia. When I mention my visit there, he offers to get his dad to put me up. It's extremely kind of him, and odd, too. He hardly knows me. I find it difficult to judge my own thoughts on this. Despite myself, I find it hard not to form bonds with these people. I don't want to betray them. I really don't. I don't want them to feel as though I've seduced them with fine words then set out to destroy them.

We walk outside and I take a series of snaps, the BNP men leaning happily against a set of railings. The Labour Party candidate passes us, on the back of an open-top lorry, canvassing support from his loudspeaker. Our guys call up, laughing and catcalling. 'We know 'im quite well,' says Colin. The Labour man laughs and shouts back.

As Paul drives us back to the station, his face takes on a serious, troubled look. 'Nick?' he says.

'Yes?'

'I saw you'd written an article in the past, with Nick Lowles.' My heart leaps into my throat for a second. I smooth my hands down, deliberate and slow, onto the creases of my trousers. 'Do you know 'im, like?' There's a studied innocence to his words.

'Not really,' I reply. Just like any other journalist, I call up *Searchlight* from time to time. I tell him that the newspaper in question added his comments to mine later. Which is kind of true.

'Oh,' he says. 'So what does he look like then?' I can feel my colleague shifting uncomfortably on the back seat.

Not really sure, I say. I'm in a real quandary. I don't want to lose Paul's trust, but neither can I betray Nick. Not for any devious reasons of my own – most of what I'm saying is true; I'm not working for *Searchlight*, nor am I in daily contact with them – but I don't want to fuck around with someone else's life and security. We usually talk by phone, I tell Paul, and only from time to time. I try to arrange my body language to appear casual and unconcerned. C'mon, c'mon, I'm thinking to my friend, say something and change the subject.

He does, and we witter away the next couple of minutes on minor matters, until we're disgorged back into Slade Green.

My pal is incredulous. 'I can't believe they opened up so easily,' he says. 'Right after you started talking to them. We didn't really have to encourage them at all.'

'No, well, if you know these guys, you know which buttons to push, I guess.' I pause. 'That's what I've been doing these last five years.' Still, I'm worried. It might not be quite so simple in America, far from help.

ELEVEN

NEW JERUSALEM

JUNE 2001

'Sir, this way, please.' A squat man of Middle Eastern appearance is trying to take my bags. I shouldn't bother with the unmetered taxis – it'll be a guaranteed rip-off – but tonight, of all nights, I don't want to be fumbling around and haggling. Best to go in luxury and stop worrying.

'Summer's Bar please,' I tell him. The heat turns into a cooling balm, as the Mercedes air con bathes the back of the seat.

My driver is a Palestinian, holding down two jobs and supporting a family. I chat to him briefly in Arabic. He listens intently, as we reminisce about the Middle East.

Traffic is light. We swing towards a junction, then under a freeway bridge, somewhere on the outskirts of Washington. The city rises, modern and vast, around us. The twilight brilliance reminds me of my visits to Sydney, halfway round the world.

Ahead, a small bar glints in the night. I can just make out the words on the sign. A large, mostly empty car lot stretches off to one side.

I step from the taxi. Struggling to carry my bag, I hear an English accent. A young man, with shaven head and shorts, is sitting on the kerb speaking into his mobile phone. He wears England's soccer colours. I remember: there's a game today between England and Greece. Strange, though, seeing such things so far from home.

The light brick and cheap pine of the squat building remind me of a Pizza Hut. It's called a 'sports bar', a soulless US phenomenon, which I've seen creeping into parts of the UK and Australia. It's packed. The familiar prickle of nerves blisters over my skin. I shiver, the sweat cooling despite the heat. I stumble down steps, searching through the haze and chatter for the face I've seen only on websites.

There: a red England football shirt; a pair of shorts; the military, repressed-looking moustache; dark, neat hair; a flushed, rounded face. His pink, hairless legs encased in white socks and trainers dangle beneath the tall bar table. I slowly shoulder my way through the crowd.

'Hi, Mark?' I shout through the din. He doesn't seem to hear me. A solidly built guy with bleached hair sits next to him, tattoos running up and down his legs. He gazes intently at the soccer game, on a TV at one corner of the bar.

I repeat myself. The first guy looks up, pulling a cigarette from his mouth. 'Oh . . . hi!' He seems surprised. 'You're Nick Ryan?' Obviously, I don't fit my image. 'I thought you'd be a bit older,' he shouts. I think I detect irony in the voice, but with all this noise, I'm not sure. I offer my hand and we shake. 'I didn't expect you quite yet. You're early.' The second man stares at me, then flicks back to the soccer screen.

'Come on, come on, sit down,' orders the guy I take to be Mark Cotterill. He's formal and, over the racket, I detect a West Country accent. He looks up for one second, making eye contact from the dark pools beneath his brows. But most of the time he listens with his head down, as though pondering each point raised. He seems relaxed now, beer glass in hand.

The second guy introduces himself as Carl. 'Carl Clifford. All right? Just call me Cliff, that's what most people do.' He smiles.

Between snatches of the game, drinking cold, piss-weak beer, we chat. Cliff has been in the country for 11 years now, Mark for six and a half. They've been told by Nick Griffin himself that they can trust me. I don't reveal my other connections. When I ask what they've got planned in the next couple of days, Mark leans in close, sweating, and says in a deadpan voice: 'We thought we'd take you down to the annual conference of the Council of Conservative Citizens. It's in North Carolina this weekend.'

It sounds like some corporate function, perhaps for a retirement group. But I know better. The C of CC, as it calls itself, is one of the US's largest white-supremacist organisations. It's a powerful pressure group, born from the White Citizens Councils, a reaction to school desegregation and the growth of the civil rights movement in the 1950s and 1960s. It was the middle-class white supremacist movement, whereas the Klan was for the working class. Klansmen, Holocaust deniers and National Alliance members all have been members. Even Republican Senate leader Trent Lott spoke to the group.

'I'm not coming,' says Cliff, in a curious Anglo-American twang. 'I can't leave the cats for too long. But you should get to meet all types of people from the movement there.'

* * *

Late into the evening, I sit in Mark's apartment. The French windows are open, but there's little breeze. The air outside is moist and warm. Crickets chirp in the undergrowth. Inside, the rooms are infused with a certain smell I can't quite place.

Mark says he's just been hosting several members of the NPD, over from Germany. 'A bit surly,' is all he really says about them. They've driven off now, five hours over the mountain roads to William Pierce's compound in West Virginia.

A young German called Hendrik Möbus – a convicted killer and a leading figure in the black metal scene – had been hiding out at Pierce's place, helping him gain further credibility with the youth in the movement. People thought he'd been advising Pierce about the music business. Eventually, the FBI arrested Möbus near the compound, breaking his arm in the process. Extradition proceedings are taking place against him when I arrive.

'We're going to take you there, too,' Mark says. 'You'll have to drive, and pay for the hire car of course.'

'Of course,' I answer, dry-mouthed, thinking on my feet.

'Cliff might come with us, too. Won't you, Cliff?'

'Ah, yeah, I haven't been up there yet,' he replies, in his weird part-American accent. 'It should be quite interesting.'

Mark says he's been there before. 'I used to edit his magazine, *Resistance*, albeit only for one issue,' he mentions, mysteriously. It seems that the American Friends of the BNP and the National Alliance have quite a bit of crossover.

This is even better than I'd hoped for. These guys are going to deliver me right to Pierce, with their personal recommendation. Only later did I realise that few of them were as enthusiastic about Pierce in private. Many referred to him as a cult leader, albeit one with a strong intellect and fanatical cadres. Most thought that on his death his organisation would fall apart and dissolve into factional infighting.

Fighting jet lag, I watch Cliff at work on the AFBNP website. Sipping on diet Coke, he seems almost the archetypal techie. But he's also been in the US Army and now works for a contracting firm, developing compression technology for battlefield medical use. His wide face is friendly and open. Later, he shows me a certificate to prove he's been ordained some kind of minister. When we drive back up to Falls Church, the suburb of DC where Mark lives, we pass an army base where he says he used to work. He still has a pass for it.

Most of Mark's friends seem to drive him around. He has yet to pass his test, he admits with a sullen shake of his head, looking out the window and avoiding eye contact. The lack of a car is strange here, where you can hardly walk across the road without having to cross a freeway. The sight of fat Americans, wedged with their tiny legs into cruising automatics, makes a smile surface onto my lips.

'We're the only whites in this place,' Mark says over his shoulder, turning the key in his condo door, inside a huge brown-brick complex. 'Well, apart from one other guy.'

'Who are the rest?'

'Um, mainly Hispanics.' His voice is deadpan again. But the way he paces and structures his words conveys deep disapproval. It's a clever way of speaking. Perhaps it's natural. He rarely launches into overtly racist language in front of me, at least not at first. But he makes frequent references to 'homosexuals' and 'negroes' in a cold, overly formal, distasteful manner. There's something not quite right, ill at ease, in this strange-looking 40-year-old.

Inside, the place is simple and clean. Very ordered. Cheap fittings and bare, whitewashed walls, not much stuff around. An improvement on Steve Sargent, at least. I later learn that Mark is acquainted with my former chums. In his files I find a picture of him with Charlie Sargent. Perhaps the order is the sign of a woman's touch? But Mark says his wife decided to leave him only a month ago. But when I ask one of his close friends about Mark's wife, he tells me: 'I didn't know he had a wife! I've never seen him with one.'

'Help yourself to a beer,' he calls out, going into the bedroom to find me some bedclothes for the spare room. When he comes out, he looks down at a cheap white phone and answering machine. 'Nuts,' he mutters, letting the messages play out, deleting most with a quick press of a button.

I gaze around at neat lines of AFBNP videos and various books about the right. Watching some of the tapes later, I'll see Nick Griffin sharing podiums with members of David Duke's network, the National Alliance and Pat Buchanan's Reform Party campaign. Volunteers go round holding buckets to collect donations.

I sit up well into the night. Mark seems to trust me completely as I stand over his shoulder and casually glance at the emails he sends. There's no encryption programme I can spot – unlike on my laptop – and I can quite easily see what he's typing, and to whom. He's in touch with a couple of British folk from the left, one a journalist, the other an anarchist conspiracy theorist. He also communicates regularly with Paul Golding, whom he sometimes dismisses in private. He admits that he even calls Nick Lowles from time to time. He has a copy of his book. I learn, too, that Mark's place is used as a stopping-off point for many extremists travelling to the East Coast. In what seems to be an informal network, it doesn't seem to matter much what your official group is; you know that in certain towns there'll be someone like this, at the hub of the network, who can put you up.

The next day we begin what becomes a routine, taking a bus to the nearest Metro stop, dropping in at an 'all you can eat' diner for an unhealthy breakfast before Mark heads off to work, for 'a doctor, one of us, a sympathiser,' he mumbles reticently when I ask him about it.

In Britain, the General Elections are taking place. Mark is fired up – but not as much as his English colleagues. He seems more cynical than others in the BNP.

'Ah, if we see anything, it'll just be a protest vote. It happened with the NF back in the 1970s,' he says loudly, as we sit on a public bus. Most of the faces around us are black, Asian or Hispanic. I feel as though eyes are boring into the back of my neck. 'Still, there's a certain amount of optimism, so I hear, back there.' He seems keen to hear my news from England. I get the impression he misses it. He's been fundraising solidly for the party these last couple of years. My contacts at the Southern Poverty Law Center estimate that as much as $200,000 might have been collected in that time.

That afternoon, I follow Mark into an office block. Setting a bundle of papers at my feet, he tells me, 'I just have to drop something off at the printers.' I make a note of the name and number of the address – just in case.

Cliff collects us near Dupont Circle, one of the few roundabouts I see in the US. Mark walks up fast, powering stiff-legged and intense, towards the car. He looks faintly ridiculous in his unfashionable shorts. We head back out to Falls Church. The high-rises give way to hilly suburbs; low housing creeps up on either side of the road. Having pulled off the main freeway, we head into a grocery store. A blast of frigid air shoots down my neck as we enter. Collecting several packs of beer and crisps, we bump into one of tonight's first guests.

Mark is planning a get-together of his little network to watch the British election coverage on the C-Span TV channel. 'Don't look now,' mutters Cliff, 'but here comes one of our nuts.' Mark turns, shoes squeaking, and spots the figure about to enter the store. 'Oh God, he's right. With any luck he won't see us,' he says, ducking.

Too late. The soft, shambling man walks in, wearing a pink sweater. In a strong voice, Mark calls out: 'Hey Bruce, how's the struggle going?' There's an obvious inflection of irony to his voice.

'Hey Mark, Cliff,' replies Bruce, almost childlike. 'I was just coming in here to get some stuff, y'know, for tonight.'

'Right then, we'll see you back there,' says Mark curtly, shooting out the door and into Cliff's car.

'Who's that?' I ask.

Cliff pops the central locking, clicking on the handle and looking up for a moment into my face. 'You don't want to know, Nick!'

Back at the apartment, Bruce taps on the window, asking to be let in. We've already cracked into the first beer. Mark chimes up, too loud again, with the false pleasantries. 'Hey, Bruce!' His voice booms. I look across at Cliff, who winks at me. 'Ah, Bruce, I see you've still got your device . . .' He's joking about a silver tie pin – at least, that's what I think it is – wedged near the top of Bruce's pink shirt. 'Is it still keeping the EMFs away?'

Bruce smiles nervously back at him and mutters something too softly for us to hear. Behind his back, Cliff is cracking up. 'It deepens his voice, too, apparently,' he whispers to me.

'Hey, Bruce, back when I was a kid and we used to go into the synagogue, we had to take off our shoes,' Mark quips. He glances down, obviously, to Bruce's feet. 'Are you going to take yours off?' A devious grin plays on his mouth for a moment. Clearly, he's having a joke at Bruce's expense. Bruce just smiles and says, 'Oh Mark . . .' in that soft, high-pitched voice.

The entry buzzer goes and a portly guy wanders in. 'Oh, hey Mark!' he calls out. A double chin bounces on his thick neck. I look down and see skinny legs protruding from his shorts. A bunch of cans dangle from his hands. His frog-like eyes are sandwiched in an expression of permanent surprise, goggling behind large-framed glasses.

I'm introduced. 'Hi, Jeff Anderson. I run separatist.org.' He thinks I'm one of them. A business card pokes from his fingers. Mark takes pleasure in the discomfort the sudden mention of my profession causes in those around us. 'Nick's a *liberal* journalist, you know,' he says, his voice deliberately lilting up at the end. It's as though he were speaking to the hard of hearing. 'He's come to write all about us.' The words are being paced, and spaced out, again for effect. 'So you'd better be careful what you say. We don't want him to say we're extremists, do we?' he grins. 'We're not supremacists – are we?' He laughs. I laugh too, trying to blend in, my sensibilities dulled by over-exposure.

Jeff and I chat much of the night. The C-Span commentator refers to a possible large showing for the BNP tonight. Jeff pulls carefully on a bottle top, cursing as he spills some beer onto the plastic table. He tries to talk to me at the same time. 'Immigration is not the problem,' he says. 'Only non-European immigration.' He calls me a 'fellow Euro' and goes on about the injustices visited on the Germans after the Second World War. He can't understand why different European countries would ever fight each other, 'because they're white, right?' He seems genuinely mystified. I tell him that in the UK, without the First Amendment, the kinds of things he says here would never be tolerated. 'That just shows how much democracy has been eroded over there,' he says. 'Why don't you ask Tony Blair why he's destroying the British people?'

As the evening progresses, more and more figures surface out of the night. Men. Waddling in, occasionally striding confidently up, perspiring. Most amazing is the sense of euphoria, little giggles breaking out, as they watch the screen. Eager anticipation seems pressed onto wet lips, as handkerchiefs dab brows. Many are former supporters of Pat Buchanan, who left the Republicans to stand as presidential candidate for the Reform Party. They all curse his weak showing of only 0.4 per cent of the vote. Many blame his choice of a black female running mate. No matter that she was a strong Conservative herself; her skin colour seems to have cost him a lot of votes. When I mention my pending interview with Buchanan, they all say I should ask him about this. They seem quite upset.

Pizzas turn up and are wolfed down. Mark watches, silently, as others consume his share. He mutters under his breath, remaining rigid. His anger is palpable, eating into the air around him. No one else seems to have noticed.

Much of the night, the others circle around him, like nervous schoolkids. His constant response to their questions is to place his chin in hands, look downwards, and mutter 'um hmm' in reply.

The TV suddenly announces that Nick Griffin has won over 16 per cent of the vote in Oldham, and a great cheer erupts. Some punch the air; one or two rise up from their seats. On screen Griffin is parading on the stage, wearing a symbolic gag over his mouth. Mick Treacy, the BNP candidate for the second Oldham ward, gets over 11 per cent. A corpulent professorial guy, with thinning hair and a smart burgundy jacket, clenches his fist together, exclaiming 'Yes!' over and over again. His name is Joe. He seems a nice bloke, intelligent, well-versed in international affairs (we discuss Italy and Australia). Is he some kind of academic, from the nexus of intellectual extremists I've started to meet? Mark tells me later that he does indeed work at Georgetown University – as a car park attendant. 'You wouldn't believe it to look at him, would you?' he says, swigging from a bottle of beer.

Amidst the euphoria, Mark's phone rings. He steps outside, through the French windows. A minute later he steps back inside, furtively, and fixes me with a serious expression. 'Nick, could you come out here for a minute?' There's a no-nonsense tone to his voice.

Mark stares straight into my eyes. 'I've got a call here from one of our top people,' he says, shifting for a moment to indicate the mobile phone. 'He says he wants to speak to you, but only on condition of anonymity. Will you agree to that?'

'Er, yes, I guess. What's this all about?'

But his lips are sealed. He simply hands me the phone and steps to one side.

'Hello?'

'Hi. Tell me what your business with us is.' It's a demand, not a question. I think quickly, wondering who this is, and make up something about modern nationalism and identity. I hope it sounds serious, businesslike. 'If I tell you my name, you must promise not to repeat it,' he says, after listening silently to my groping explanations.

'Okay.'

He tells me, then continues. 'Listen, I come from a very senior Republican family.' (I later learn that his father was a state majority leader of the Senate.) 'And I have been a White House press officer. So you can understand why I want nothing to come out.' The last sentence has been spoken at high speed. The guy sounds highly educated, deep-voiced – and intense. 'I can help you, give you interviews, or introduce you to some top people. But I've opened my mouth before, and it led to getting thrown out of the University Club [a famous DC establishment]. I can't afford another incident. You understand, don't you? Don't you? I can't force you to sign anything, but if you give me your word as a gentleman, an English gentleman, that'll be enough for me.'

When the others inside hear the name, there are a few moans. I'm not sure why. This guy sounds like a top player. Mark just looks at me, an eyebrow raised. 'Er . . . okay,' I reply again, my voice dropping to a whisper. 'Whatever you say.'

I hand the phone back to Mark.

* * *

The next day begins early. We're at the airport by 6 a.m., bleary-eyed. Mark refuses my offer of a Danish pastry, sticking to black coffee. We're waiting for the chap I spoke to last night, checking our watches and worrying about the boarding time.

Another contact wanders up, a tough-looking fellow with a real lived-in kind of face. His long black hair is held back by a bandana; he looks like a Vietnam vet. When he speaks, it's through the crushed larynx of someone who's smoked most of his life.

'Hey Fisheye,' the guys call out to him weakly. His eyes are somewhat large and bulging. He looks a bit pale, but quickly downs two coffees. 'Hi,' he says, shaking my hand, as Mark introduces us. His glance is not untrusting, his accent thick from some part of the States I don't recognise. 'Journalist, you say? I'm always careful around journalists.' He pats a camera case. 'Something of a photographer myself. This trip for me is business.'

Just before we check in, our man finally appears sprinting down the corridor. The others curse under their breath. Why, I'm not yet sure.

'Hi, oh hi,' he says, shaking my hand vigorously in a sweaty grip and flashing a set of perfectly aligned white teeth. He's dressed smartly, in what seem like tailored clothes. Mark goes through the routine of explaining who I am. His eyes light up with recognition and, perhaps, nervousness. He's younger-looking than I had imagined, permanently tanned, with his fine blond hair cut into a neat preppie style. A crisp striped shirt is held at the wrist by personalised cufflinks. His initials are stitched just above them. I see them on every shirt he wears over the coming days.

'Mark and Fisheye do some work for me, from time to time,' he says, when I ask how he knows the others. He runs a consultancy of some kind. He talks fast, animatedly, hyper – particularly for this time of morning – and seems very well-travelled. 'I met that guy Taki, you know, from *The Spectator*,' he grins. 'In a club in London called Annabels, I think it was called.' He lets slip that 'I'm a good friend of Dr Pierce, you know.' I stop dead. The tickets are being checked just ahead of us. 'He's stayed with me at my house.' Mark reveals later that this guy took Pierce along to the

University Club, which seems to have been what got him thrown out ('I'm suing them for $6 million,' he keeps repeating).

I make a mental note to ask him more about Pierce. But he doesn't seem to need prompting. On the plane, he starts telling me how he helped set up the deal for Pierce to buy Resistance Records. I nod politely, trying to appear only moderately interested, clicking the belt shut. My hands are trembling slightly. First he helped Pierce's arch rival, Willis Carto, buy a substantial number of shares, he says. He had worked for Carto in the past. 'I made him thousands – millions!' he exclaims, sounding bitter. Carto ran something called The Liberty Lobby, a radical right think tank and pressure group. He also published America's largest-circulation far-right newspaper, *The Spotlight*, which had some 360,000 subscribers at its height. My friend set up his direct marketing operations. When Carto needed cash, Mr Anonymous arranged himself as a go-between with Pierce, helping purchase and transfer the shares. And that was when he and Mark ended up editing *Resistance* magazine, after Pierce had bought the business.

From the corner of my eye, I can see Fisheye – whose real name is Ed Cassidy – looking at Mark and raising his eyebrows.

I turn back to my newfound friend, who is now holding forth on the death penalty, how homosexuals should be shot, how laws should be relaxed to make it easier to buy guns. I find it hard to square his comments with the erudite, educated, Establishment image and voice he presents. For someone who doesn't want to be noticed or quoted, he certainly is loud and forthright with his views. He asks about the rest of my trip. When I mention Pat Buchanan, he says: 'Oh, say hi to Pat for me.' I blink, in surprise. I catch a glimpse of a hip flask of some kind. 'We had lockers next to each other at the gentlemen's club. PJB is a really nice man, but he shot his election to pieces when he put that black woman in as his running mate.'

* * *

The conference takes place in a featureless, 'identikit' Holiday Inn in Asheville, North Carolina. I look out the window at the rolling green hills around us, baked hard by the summer heat. Well, the scenery is nice. An Interstate highway carves through the inclines, past the occasional billboard or flashing neon. Mostly, it's wide open spaces. We miss the protesters from Anti-Racist Action (ARA), although Fisheye later shows me the pictures he snapped of them. I leave the relative comfort of air con only once, as we step from the courtesy shuttle into the hotel lobby. The sunlight is blinding for an instant, then we're inside once more.

The atmosphere seems jolly, with a lot of hand-shaking and reminiscing. Most are middle-aged, male, soberly dressed. I spot a few Baptist ministers, tall and flamboyant, in ten-gallon hats. A woman who seems to have seen the side of a surgeon's knife swans past, arm attached to one ageing minister. Confederate flags are much in evidence. Everyone has a name badge. There's a programme of events, stickers, fake leather conference pads.

Someone bumps into my secretive friend at the entrance. An exchange of words follows. 'Did you hear that, he called me a son of a bitch?!' He has just given an interview to the magazine of the Southern Poverty Law Center, an organisation that is anathema to most US racists for having sued many of their prominent leaders.

Mark and I chat. There's still a lot of euphoria, and handshakes for him, as the Americans come up to congratulate the BNP on its success last night. Although he proudly wears a Union Jack on his clothes, Mark still thinks, privately, that Nick Griffin's success was a protest vote, thanks partly to the recent rioting. 'Don't worry, we know what he really means,' he told me, drunkenly and obscurely, last night.

I move down the corridor, swimming pool to my left, cafeteria to my right. The grey-looking salads and fried chicken do little to stir my appetite. Elevator music drifts out from hidden speakers. Mark veers off from my side to go straight up to a tall, well-built man. 'Hey, Don, nice to see you again!' As they shake hands, I move in closer and recognise Don Black, one of America's most infamous white supremacists. His website, Stormfront, which he's run since his release from prison back in the 1980s, is a clearing house of bulletin boards and gossip for international extremists. I hope he hasn't read my article in *The Guardian*. Black has a youthful face, thin tight lips and dark sparkling eyes. His wiry black hair is carefully cropped. With his business suit, he seems more politician than stormtrooper. He's good pals with David Duke – used to work for him, in fact, then ended up marrying Duke's ex-wife.

A podgy, middle-aged woman approaches me and says, 'Hey honey, here you go, here's your conference ID and pack. Now, what's your name, and who are you with?' Mark rescues me, and I go in officially as a guest of the BNP.

Later, after sitting in boredom listening to speeches (there's a lot about the battle to keep Confederate flags flying in Mississippi, and how AIDS is going to kill the Africans), I move outside to stretch my legs and chat to Mark at his little stall. A well-groomed figure pulls up, short, middle-aged, somewhat stocky, with carefully slicked hair, a smart suit and gold rings on his fingers. A gold-tipped cigarette hangs from his mouth. In his wake follow a group of elderly and middle-aged hangers on. One looks like a heavy. Another has his dolled-up wife in tow. The foundation is slapped on thick and, by the way she walks, I wonder if she's been enjoying the hospitality suite.

'Gordon, pleased to see you again!' Mark calls out with some obsequiousness. They chat for a moment, then the figure moves on. 'Gordon Baum,' Mark explains to me. 'He's CEO of the Council. A powerful man.'

After lunch, I collar Baum during a smoke break outside. 'So, you're the reporter?' he drawls. The southern accent is thick, but confident. He looks like an attorney or ageing movie star. 'Have you seen anything here to send you back with a fright, Mr Reporter?' he smiles, coldly. I spend the next ten minutes being lambasted by tales of media distortion, with the good old boys around him smirking and laughing when he makes reference to the breeding of pigs on some family farm (a parable, I'm guessing, for race mixing). One of the guys says their 'darkest hour' has arrived, with the liberal forces seeking to pull down Confederate statues. This means little to me, but I shake my head in concern, all the same. 'See, we have nothing to hide!' Baum exclaims, gesturing widely with his hands.

After about five minutes, a tall, intimidating man steps out through the fire exit. I keep glancing at him to my right, trying to concentrate on taking notes. A dark crew cut is set above narrow, chiselled features. He eyes me coolly. Steven Barry, Mark later whispers in my ear. Former special forces sergeant and military adviser to William Pierce and the National Alliance. Now he runs his own extreme-right magazine, *The Resister*, dedicated to other special forces guys with similar beliefs. He doesn't seem to blink once as he observes me.

Making my excuses, I end up inside the hall again and hear Glayde Whitney, a professor of psychology from Florida State University, rant about an 'egalitarian elite' deciding gun controls. He rolls off a list of Senators involved. They all clearly have Jewish names. The next evening, I'll be helping him – too drunk to stand – in and out of a station wagon.

As I sit down at a table in the café outside, an overworked waitress asks for my order. 'Sorry darlin', we're a bit stretched today,' she says. 'Say, are you from a church group?'

* * *

I find a dimly lit niche in the hotel bar and order a beer. The table service is not something I'm used to. Nor tipping.

'Excuse me, you're Mark's friend, aren't you?' I turn to see a small man offering his hand. He's smartly dressed, with dark hair turning to grey and a tight little moustache. A friendly smile is stitched to his mouse-like face. By the look of the suit and tie, he must be some sort of professional. 'Peter Gemma,' he says, offering me his business card. It says he's a political lobbyist. I order him a beer. Would he speak with me? I ask. 'Yes, but I don't really like to be quoted.' I cajole him. He agrees.

It turns out he knows Mark back in DC; they belong to some of the same political circles and appear at the same discussion clubs. As we chat and I tell him about my travels and project – he nods, eagerly, and seems genuinely interested – he suddenly says: 'Are you sure it's wise? You know, staying at Mark's place?'

179

'Why not?' I ask.

'Well, you know, his connections, that kind of thing.' He goes quiet.

Switching quickly, I suggest he tell me something about himself. Soft rock blares in the background, across my tapes. 'I'm what you might call a' – he pauses, smiling to himself for a moment – 'moderate extremist.' He grins. 'In a previous life, I was a former Republican Party campaign manager and fundraiser.' I lift my eyebrows.

'I had a good, pretty stable background, kinda liberal. I started out with the George Wallace campaign in '68, then went more mainstream after that.' How old is he now, then? 'Fifty.' He looks younger. He's sweating, despite the air con. He loosens his tie. 'Then I became one of the original Reagan supporters.'

I sip from my beer. Gemma says he became a close personal friend of Pat Buchanan, whilst the two were still in the Republican Party, and remembers taking Pat to Israel on a fact-finding trip. 'I took his place on *Crossfire*, too,' he adds, referring to the CNN political discussion programme, on which Buchanan became a regular.

With Buchanan, he defected to the Reform Party, because 'Pat was the only one talking about immigration.' He says he became his Vice Presidential campaign manager – which is interesting, because when I eventually meet Buchanan, he sounds hazy about Gemma's name. Even more interesting is that someone associating with white supremacists was helping run the campaign for Ezola Foster, the black woman Buchanan chose as his vice-presidential running mate.

Gemma is still on the party's leading council, despite the fall-out that's occurred since the election debacle. 'Did you know about Mark's story there?' he asks suddenly. Mark had found himself work in the mailroom, part of an attempt by the AFBNP to infiltrate the campaign. Pat's sister, Bay, who seemed to run much of the campaign, kicked him out when she found out who he was. Gemma sounds a bit wistful about it all. Fisheye later tells me that he himself was one of the Buchanan campaign photographers. And I was to see other pics of Fisheye back in the 1960s, dressed in his American Nazi Party uniform. Obviously not everyone with a white supremacist connection was discovered. Fisheye just smiled when he told me, and proudly held up a picture of him meeting Buchanan.

I order up a second beer and Gemma follows suit. He's a likeable fellow with a sharp intellect. We've travelled in many of the same parts of the world. He's represented many Arab interests via his consultancy and tells me, 'I will support just about anyone or anything that basically believes what I believe.' A big fan of the former Rhodesia – 'I went there, you know, met Ian Smith,' – he's modest too. Much later, I saw one of Mark's AFBNP videos, in which National Alliance members were speaking. Gemma is caught for a second on camera, then dashes sideways off the stage, covering his face.

He lets slip that he went though an 'awful divorce'. I wonder what on earth he's doing here. He seems far too sensible, too well connected, to be at such a gathering. When I hint at this, he just smiles ruefully. We while away quite a bit of time chatting – like me, he seems little enamoured with the speakers and events – and I feel I've found a fellow soul amidst this sea of extremism. It could all be a front, of course, but I doubt it. Even when he mentions that he's a friend of David Irving and has met Nick Griffin, I barely pause. Or that he ran a pro-life committee and campaigned on space defence issues. Only when he tells me that he holds William Pierce's intellect in high regard do I begin wondering again. I should be careful about letting my guard down. Even Gemma's amazed that I'm not using a pseudonym. I look up. Several faces around us are regarding me with equal amounts of suspicion and interest. Obviously, word has got around about me.

Gemma's suddenly called away, so I take to walking the corridors. Each TV set I pass is carrying news about Timothy McVeigh's coming execution. It's weird, stalking this banal place, seeing all these white misfits around me. I slip unnoticed back to my room and log onto my laptop. There are about a dozen emails from different 'brothers' in the World Church of the Creator. Matt Hale has been singing my praises to the faithful.

I end a surreal day by having dinner with Don Black, Mark, Gemma, Fisheye and others. Mark's eyes are pink-speckled; he hasn't slept the whole of the previous night. 'I don't need to,' he states, simply. We drive down the highway to a German Black Forest restaurant. Fisheye keeps snapping away, making pointedly sure to get a picture of me in there. 'Insurance?' I joke. He just smiles, saying nothing.

Despite Black's fearsome reputation, he remains mostly quiet, stiff-backed, almost nervous of company, unblinking. Our anonymous friend more than makes up for his silence, however, rapidly getting drunk and cracking numerous racist jokes. He hardly ever seems to stop talking. Odd for someone so concerned with his privacy. Several of the guys seem preoccupied with eyeing up the women in the restaurant, talking in salivatory terms about a 'bikini contest' later back at the hotel bar.

Barely awake, I sit up with Mark and the others, including a ginger-haired guy called Bruce. Bruce is a silent, serious fellow, seemingly ill at ease with his fellow extremists. He seems to mull each point before speaking. 'I don't like to talk too much,' he says when I ask if he'd like to do an interview. 'I really don't want to be quoted.' He shakes his head – shyly perhaps. I see him back in DC several times. We become quite pally after a while, although I learn very little about him (he's something to do with the Navy, I'm told).

Meanwhile, Mark downs his usual poison, which seems to be rum and Coke. A glass is grafted to his hand most of the weekend. 'You don't get this back home, eh? Don't worry, I won't tell your missus!' I look up. There's a pearl-white grin carved across his usually dour features. The gathering ogles the local women as they dance on the tables and strip down to their bras and panties. Thumping hip-hop accompanies each strip. Mark seems on edge, focused, smoking and drinking in time as the dancers gyrate. Some of them seem barely out of their teens. Back in the bar, he keeps denying any formal Loyalist connections – despite the stickers I've seen on the fridge back in his condo – but admits having met various London members of the UDA. Then, for some reason, we get to talking about his wife. He shouts in my ear, over the noise: 'Sex with someone doesn't mean anything.' Then he proceeds to chat up two fat women, holding cigarette and beer in the same hand, trying to get one of them interested in me. I can't tell if he's joking or serious. I find myself laughing. This is just too weird.

* * *

The next morning, with another hangover, I sit with Sam Francis drinking weak, over-boiled coffee and vainly trying to get some service. A huge, potbellied man, Sam is a close friend of Mark's. I meet him several times over the following days, often in Mark's company. He's one of the intellectual heavyweights of the extreme right in the USA.

A former columnist for the *Washington Times*, Francis is a friend of Pat Buchanan's. His writings on race and isolationist politics have made him a major figure on the extreme right. I didn't know it at the time, but I was later told he'd been helping edit Buchanan's latest book.

Initially, though, it's his appearance that strikes me. He's a giant, extremely rotund and often waspish to the fame seekers hanging around him. Still, as we spend more time together, I come to like him. He has a razor-sharp wit, and he seems to believe genuinely in his cause.

'I studied Brit history,' he tells me, when I ask about his background. 'That's what I got my doctorate in.' Before going into journalism he worked for a US Senator, and for a think tank called the Heritage Foundation. 'I was fired from the *Times*, yes, that's true.'

'Why?'

'For saying that Southern Baptists shouldn't have to apologise for slavery.' This drive for an apology and compensation for slavery has become an obsession and target for many of the supremacists I meet.

'So, how do you define yourself, then?'

'As a right-wing nationalist,' he says. 'And from the paleo-conservative wing of thinking.' Then he launches into an attack on 'neo-conservatism', a force he says has been growing since the 1960s. A force that welcomes immigration, to help big business.

'What kinds of things are you concerned about, then?'

'Oh, without a doubt, the racial issue is overwhelming. Race and multiculturalism have been rediscovered out there. There needs to be a stop to immigration, and to this whole multicultural experiment. Otherwise the racial darkening of the country is going to continue.'

I later see him speak at an after-dinner club, about racial genetics. He's not a naturally confident speaker. But he's intelligent and the issues clearly get him fired up, such as when he talks in all earnestness of the 'balkanisation of America'. If the most erudite thinkers are getting so fired up, what about the less controlled individuals? That's often why the left and civil rights groups believe people such as Francis and Cotterill are more dangerous; they help inspire other extremists.

Francis's belly hangs over his belt as he folds his arms and huffs. Isn't this all about fear, though? 'Fear is a great factor in some of these speeches, yes,' he acknowledges. He wobbles his great head and shifts his blubber, as he squirms on his chair. He becomes quite agitated as yet another person interrupts us. I didn't realise just how much of a figure he is in this scene. Mark speaks of him fondly and familiarly, as 'Sam'.

About 20 minutes into our chat, he checks his watch, apologises and stands up. Still sitting, I find his size even more impressive. How does he keep walking and eating? I dread to think what his doctor must tell him. We swap a couple more anecdotes about our upbringings – his father was a salesman – then he waddles off to give a speech.

I walk into the hotel bar. It's quiet this time of day. I spot the anonymous guy, sitting near a stern-faced individual at a table at the back. This severe companion looks up through dark glasses, his blond hair cut into a military-style flat top. A shiny, dark suit, creases perfectly in place, is settled around a broad-shouldered frame. He sees my tape recorder and says: 'He's not recording me at all.' It's an aggressive command, not a request. 'I won't be recorded. I don't want my name written anywhere.'

Mark appears at my elbow. 'Nick, this is Lawrence Myers.' Myers slowly removes his sunglasses and gazes at me impassively. 'Lawrence is a good friend of mine,' the anonymous guy gushes, slugging back his drink. Swallowing nervously, I offer my hand. He looks down, then slowly grips my fingers. I notice an open briefcase to one side.

'There's been a bit of a problem,' Mark states, simply. 'It's been cancelled.'

'What?'

'Your visit to Hillsboro.'

'What?!'

'To see Pierce. We got a message through which says they don't like what you've written in a *Guardian* article.'

I want to run. 'The good doctor won't be seeing you,' Myers states simply. His voice is deep, deadpan, impassive. 'You want to write about nationalism, right? We know all about you, about your book, who you work for, how much you're being paid – $40,000, right? – and your connections to *Searchlight*. We've read all about it.'

Mark looks on, extremely concerned. 'Hey Lawrence, what's going on?' says the anonymous guy. Myers repeats what he's just said. 'No way, no way?!' our friend exclaims, looking at me as if I'm some diseased animal.

I begin to tremble.

'We've seen your articles,' Myers repeats. His voice is ice-cool, the threat certain, hanging just below the surface. I gulp, stuttering that there must be some mistake, that I haven't got all these connections, hell, I'd love to have $40,000! 'We don't get things wrong. I've worked in this game a long time. We have our way of checking these things.'

There seems no way out. Mr Anonymous is slugging back his drink and watching me with pity. Mark simply stands there, looking down at Myers. Any minute now, I'm going to be thrown out of the whole thing. Or executed, beaten up, something. The tall figure of Steven Barry wanders in and makes eye contact with Myers. Myers nods back.

I pile on the platitudes. I admit that I may have spoken with *Searchlight* once or twice, but only as a journalist. I resort to pleading, sweating in terror, my heart pounding. I feel my face flushing, like a naughty schoolkid. Myers lifts the cigarette to his mouth, blowing coolly from the side. He'd make a good interrogator, I admit, in some small part of my mind that's watching the event and almost laughing.

The charade continues for what seems an interminable time. Later, Mark tells me that some people say Myers is a former intelligence figure and Pierce's chief lieutenant, heir to the empire. He's based out here, not on the West Virginia compound. That's how Pierce likes it apparently. Mark dislikes him and thinks he's working for someone else. That's what he tells me later. But at this moment, I don't know that. I just feel horribly exposed. My only comfort is that perhaps they don't know everything. They got the size of my advance wrong, anyway. Maybe they're confusing me with someone else?

Myers remains silent. Perhaps this is some kind of power game to him. Mark just seems to accept that he won't be going to the compound. It's only when I talk to others on the scene that I discover the rivalry between the two men, and the growing antipathy between their networks. Perhaps Pierce is starting to view Mark's AFBNP as a threat. For his part, Mark appears quite dismissive of Pierce and his men at times. 'Pierce's people can be easily offended,' he says. 'They see people like Bob Matthews and The Order as Robin Hood. It's like a cult, with the absolute allegiance of the younger adherents to Pierce.'

When I desperately seek advice from both my right- and left-wing contacts, secretly tapping away on my laptop, many mention this as a possible problem. Maybe the real issue is some kind of power struggle. Or maybe Pierce is just cranky. 'He can be like that,' Mark says. 'I wouldn't take it personally.' And it doesn't stop him from letting me remain with him.

Either way, some sort of divide seems to have opened up in the right, in front of my eyes.

Much of the rest of my trip is spent trying to email Pierce and his confidants. I'm desperate to get the meeting back on.

'I've got you a meeting with someone else who's big on the scene,' Mark says, as I stumble eventually from the bar.

'Who's that?'

'Jared Taylor.' He gives me a room number.

Perhaps if I keep myself busy, it'll all be okay.

When I knock on the door, a pleasant voice with a Southern twang says, 'Come in, it's open.' I enter. The bathroom door opens and out steps a fit-looking man, probably in his late 40s or early 50s, with a towel wrapped round his midriff. 'Don't mind if we talk while I dry myself, do you?' He throws a stack of papers onto the bed. 'I've got to run through my speech for this afternoon, too, so I hope you don't need too long.'

Taylor is a Yale-educated racist who lived for 17 years in Japan. He talks enviously of their 'mono-ethnic culture'. He runs an intellectual network centred on a magazine called *American Renaissance*. I remember now: Mark introduced me to one of its editors on election night, a guy called Jim Lubinskas, a sales manager of some kind with a large, snazzy car.

Taylor paces up and down the small room, speaking as though to a great crowd. He uses the same language as Pierce, but in more soothing, persuasive tones. 'Mah greatest concern,' he says, 'is the survival of mah people, which Ah think of as Americans of European extraction. We're the people who built this nation.' He talks of Mexico invading the US ('What if?') and accuses the Establishment of 'intolerable double standards'. 'Whites have to wake up,' he says.

'Listen, Nick, race is one of society's great faultlines. Whether we like it or not. I used to think a bit more like you, until I went to Japan. But I've learned, through experience, that people think with their blood, not their passport.' He sits down in front of me, in a cross-legged pose. I'm not really listening. I'm still reeling from the encounter with Myers, waiting for the door to fly open and some skins to come in and grab me. 'Most whites have an unconscious sense of their own racism, if that's what you want to call it.' He smiles, in a friendly manner. 'But they deceive themselves, with this white flight behaviour. Moving out from the cities, into the white suburbs and towns. There's a huge amount of hypocrisy surrounding the multicultural society.'

He continues with talk of this white 'exodus' and how they are 'refugees in their own country'. His magazine often links in crime statistics with the argument, or suggestion, that certain races are more 'prone' to committing crimes than others. He rebuts many of my arguments, suavely turning them on their head. A natural orator. He pulls out reams of statistics from his briefcase, prepared for his speech. The science of pseudo-science. Even I start believing this stuff. With all this fear eating at me, I don't know what I believe any more.

I try to calm myself, to focus on the words being spoken. Near the end of our conversation Taylor reveals, somewhat surprisingly, that he hitchhiked around Africa in his late teens. At 19 he was in Liberia, then studied economics in Paris. Hard to think of that, sitting here in this strange, colourless hotel, surrounded by these misfits and weirdos, probably about to be lynched.

Later that afternoon, I skulk in my room and in the side corridors. Mark has passed word that Myers apparently called Pierce again, to check whether he might change his mind about meeting us. 'No' was the answer. 'Then again,' Mark says, 'Myers's finger could well have been down on the receiver all the time.'

A whisper through the corridor crowd suggests that Ernst Zundel, the infamous revisionist, has put in an appearance. I seem to miss him, but end up drinking with a tall, shockingly blond man who turns out to be David Duke's number-two guy.

Duke is a former Klan leader who donned a suit and tie and in 1989 shocked America by winning a seat in the Louisiana House of Representatives. A year later, he was very nearly voted to the US Senate, capturing 44 per cent of the vote. In 1991, with his popularity at its peak, he ran for Governor of Louisiana. He garnered more votes in the primary than the sitting governor, but lost the race in a bitter run-off. He's now in Russia, where it's rumoured he's building a network of contacts with the ultra-right. There's talk of a sealed indictment back in the US, relating to a potential fraud investigation. He remains a hero on the US radical right, though. He's also a close friend of Nick Griffin, and both Duke and Pierce have spoken at AFBNP events. Duke represents the political wing of the white supremacists, and Pierce the neo-nazi hardline. Both have a worldwide reach, and their followers are often friends – or happily belong to both networks. They often closely associate with Mark, too. It seems clear that the links I'm uncovering point to an attempt by the AFBNP to become a leading group among the US and international far right.

Roy Armstrong fits the 'spook' image, with his dark, crumpled suit and aviator-style Ray Bans. He looms over me, seeming capable of violence. Despite the fears, I laugh, thinking to myself he looks like a renegade from a '60s spy movie. Most of the time, though, he simply chats, in a slightly awkward manner. He's driven here all the way from Duke's house in Louisiana, he tells me. His gaze shifts out to his battered car outside, plastered with racist bumper stickers. I feel pretty uncomfortable, knowing that people will see us together in that vehicle. He seems oblivious.

I spend most of the afternoon with him, over the road in a cheap, tacky waffle house, drinking endless free refills of coffee and hearing of his days living in Germany. In those times, he was known as Roy Godenau and for

25 years was an active member of the NPD. His wife and kids still live there. The terrible heat sends dribbling rivulets of sweat down from his brows and trickling under his sunglasses. He doesn't remove them. Underneath are ice blue Aryan eyes. He often pauses, as though deep in thought. If the truth be told, I'm not really listening, despite the coup this should be. He offers to put me up in Duke's place. 'Yes, no problem,' he says in his deep rumbling voice. I'm not sure his boss would approve. Later, back in England, Armstrong will tell me he'll travel with me to Germany.

My mood of terror holds into the evening. I avoid Mark, worried he might be part of some plot to expose me. Instead I talk my way into the company of the intellectual elite – Sam Francis, Jared Taylor, Glayde Whitney and others, including a millionaire attorney named Sam Dickson. He's a friend of former BNP leader John Tyndall, has represented Klansmen, and brought David Irving to the States. We head to the other side of town and go for dinner in an amazing hotel. The place is huge, a stone edifice built into the side of a mountain, deep in the woods. It was a popular retreat during the 1920s and 1930s. Apparently, it also was the inspiration for Stephen King's horror novel, *The Shining*. I try not to reveal my identity, and simply talk. At least here I'm unlikely to be lynched.

The next morning, hungover again, I spend time with Don Black. Everyone speaks respectfully to him, yet he seems such a shy man. I have to ask him to speak up. I can hardly believe he attempted to lead a coup against the leaders of the island state of Dominica. Mark walks up to us, asking where I've been. In my panic, I call Nick Lowles. I can't get through. Shit. There's nothing he or anyone else can do. I'm going to have to tough it out, rely on my wits. It won't be the last time I'm threatened with exposure on this trip.

On the flight back to Washington, I'm mostly silent. Fisheye – Ed – seems to take pity on me, though, and we chat for hours about our mutual Irish ancestry. He grew up in the infamous Hell's Kitchen suburb of New York. In an airport bar, between planes, we share several quick beers and my mood improves.

TWELVE

AMONG THE DEAD MEN

2ND WEEK JUNE 2001

The world is a blur. I shift slowly, yawning, inside the sheets. White. The colour of the light soaking into the room. Something not quite as it should be. I reach over for the radio. It's not there. I click my eyes open, gummy deposits between the lashes. I rub, sitting up, looking about me.

Ah, yes. Mark Cotterill. How could I forget?

I pad over to my stuff, clad in my boxers, checking the laptop's still there. Groggy, I feel the gun metal beneath my fingers, then plug in the mobile and blast off a flurry of emails to my contacts back home. I also reply to the 'brothers' from the World Church of the Creator (and several 'sisters', too). And to William Pierce himself. My fingers ache; I must be typing like crazy. I sit with the laptop cradled on my knees, listening for Mark's voice next door. I carefully time my breaks between his movements and check the encryption software with each stroke of the key. I don't want to make any more mistakes.

Even amidst the gloom, I find a moment to chuckle silently. There's a message from members of the VJM back in Belgium, flashing curiously on my web mail. It contains an attachment, pictures showing them fighting with left-wing protesters. When am I coming to visit, asks 'Jo Vermuelen'? Almost like a holiday invitation. As one door closes, another opens.

Back in the main room, bedecked with pictures of his ageing mother, Mark hands me an email printout. He's unusually silent and serious. I look down and take the message from his outstretched hand. He raises one finger to his lips, pursing them and regarding me with a hooded expression. It's from someone called Billy Roper.

'Fat Billy is Pierce's number-three guy,' says Mark. 'Doesn't look like they want you up there.'

I read a few sentences.

Dear Mark,

Please inform Mr Ryan that upon further consideration and review of some of his past articles . . . Dr Pierce has reconsidered and is disinclined to grant an interview with him on Monday or for the forseeable future.

This will free him up so that you can let him wander around in DC on Monday and get to know some of the multicultural elements there up close and personal. It'll remind him of Leeds and Oldham, and keep him from getting homesick.

Sorry for any inconvenience this change of plans might cause you personally, but have you read the intentional lies and anti-White venom he puts out? It's beyond the pale, no pun intended. If he were to show up here, after reading what I've read by him, I might feel compelled to confront him with some of his blatant inaccuracies and misrepresentations, no diplomat I.

Once again, this is no reflection on our continuing feelings of comradeship for yourself and the AFBNP.

I hold my tongue, trying to breathe deeply and calm down. Fury and fear well up. Later I find a picture of Roper, chubby, bespectacled, in puritanical, sombre dress. Even Mark doesn't like him. Still, this is the world to which I've introduced myself. Conspiracy theorists, inadequates, misfits, loners, haters, the sexually repressed. Physics professors living on mountainsides. I laugh, bitterly. I'm so tired. I just want this to end. Why am I doing all this?

I move over to the tiny kitchen, opening the fridge – seeing the Ulster sticker, 'No Surrender' – then pour myself some lemonade. I don't want Mark to see my reaction. I don't know yet how much he knows, or cares, about my mission. I stand with my hand on the open door, looking at my fingers for a moment. Suddenly it occurs to me: Pierce and his people have missed another point. This is a direct reflection on Mark. After all, he's putting me up and introducing me to his network. If anything goes wrong, or if people say I'm an enemy – and I'm staying at Mark's – what does this say about him, and about the AFBNP?

Mark tells me not to worry about it. 'Pierce is like that sometimes,' he says, again. He thinks I may also have inadvertently offended the young acolytes with a mistake I made in an earlier article. I curse myself. There are so many twists and turns to follow in this tortured world. Then again, he'd told me that they viewed their heroes like Robin Hood. It was easy to upset them. Later, out with his pals, there are chuckles and shrugs of shoulders as I ask them about Pierce's penchant for Eastern European mail-order brides.

That first evening back, we take a call from Nick Griffin, breathless, desperate to tell us of his 'victory'. 'It's unbelievably hectic,' he tells me. 'There's been a real media frenzy.' Trust the media to do the extremists' work for them, whipping us into a frenzy of liberal panic.

Griffin says it's not just Oldham where they did well, but also Burnley.

They got just over 11 per cent. Golding and his pals in the south-east, however, reached only three and a half per cent. 'The change is coming,' Griffin says, with his usual self-satisfied arrogance. I wonder if the people voting for him have seen him speaking at meetings with National Alliance members. Or whether they'd even care.

Over the next few days, as I search for things to do, I hang out more with Mark and his friends. He tells me he's going to 'set something up', making a secretive series of calls to his contacts. I don't yet know what this will be. In the meantime, he follows his strange daily routine. He surfaces late, then checks his answering machine. Typically, there are dozens of messages on it each evening. Most he deletes, repeating 'nut' or 'no' as he presses the keypad. One is from the man I'm later to meet down in Arkansas, the Christian Identity minister. Then he leaves the apartment building, walking in his fast, flat-footed way through the brown-carpeted corridors, leaving the low-humming air con for the sultry humidity outside.

On the first day back from the conference, we have lunch with the anonymous benefactor. He's cursing about owing someone money. 'These people are fucking losers, lowlifes, low class,' he fumes, impeccable-looking as ever, ordering the waiter to bring us something not on the menu (and offering to pay him more for it). I just drink and listen, waiting for the end days to come, feeling drained beyond simple exhaustion. It's hard to describe my emotions at this point. Grateful for the chance to see yet another country. Yet fearful. My life twisted between mundane existence and mingling with puritans and zealots. Breathing the diseased air of these men's lives.

Most days, I meet Mark in the late afternoon. In the mornings I do a bit of sightseeing, wandering through the wide, planned streets of Washington, military helicopters occasionally clattering overhead. Often, Mark will come back with a stack of new AFBNP leaflets or magazines, stopping to ask my opinion – as a journalist – of their quality. Sometimes, we go back to the same printers as before. I'm amazed that I'm being allowed to see into this world.

Cliff also spends many evenings at Mark's place. He's continuing to build the new AFBNP website, adding new links, photos and audio reports. Mark seems to be using him a bit – 'Mark has this reputation,' admits Fisheye – in order to get this site up, and to get free rides into town. Mark, for his part, seems rather intolerant of Cliff and others, even though they're working for him for free.

In his strange transatlantic accent, Cliff tells me he used to be a member of the ultra-left Militant Tendency (a movement kicked out of the Labour Party in the 1980s) back in England. It's interesting how the extremes often meet. Cliff seems too soft, too nice for this movement. He maintains a bizarre affection for several cats and kittens. His younger, American girlfriend clearly doesn't like Mark very much. When we meet, the two are decidedly frosty. Then again, I never see Mark in close proximity with any women.

One evening, I overhear a conversation through the air vent. I stand quietly on the chair to get closer and press my ear to the grille. Mark's on the phone. For the past few days, he's been talking about his intention to bed one of Pierce's followers, a skin girl. He's trying to get her to come stay at the weekend – and therefore wants me out of the way. Cliff and the others think he's a bit mad. Snatches of the conversation come through, tinny and distant. He's talking about me now. I keep wondering if they've got the wrong guy. Maybe they think I'm Nick Lowles?

This girl is warning Mark that she knows all about me and my intentions. When he comes off the phone I hover around, trying to appear nonchalant. 'I was just speaking to [name] again,' he says. 'You really have got them riled, for some reason.'

'Don't know what I've done,' I counter.

'Don't worry,' says Mark, 'I don't care if you're working for the other side. I'd rather you told me, of course, but it doesn't bother me. [Name]'s a nut anyway.' With that, he turns and grabs the apartment keys, getting ready to go out. Bloody hell, he's candid. I've heard from Mark and his pals that this woman has some kind of reputation. What kind, I'm not sure. She's half his age, I know that.

'Is it wise to try and get her over, Mark?' I say. Despite our political differences, I do like him in a certain way. I wouldn't want him to be harmed because of me.

'I'll make sure not to leave my credit cards lying around when she's about,' he laughs, wryly. A sudden fit of dry coughing overtakes him.

Before the weekend arrives, a number of other events take place. I spend quite a bit of time socialising with Mark and the AFBNP network. The three of us Brits – me, Mark and Cliff – seem to 'click', although I feel secretly depressed about this. It's becoming too normal; I'm starting to wonder about my own sanity and opinions. I've stopped telling people I'm a liberal, because of the abuse it invites. I no longer flinch at the mention of Jews, One World government, or white power. In fact, I expect it. To help maintain my level, I speak secretly with Nick Lowles back in England and continue sending encrypted emails. I'm also in contact with members of the Center for New Community in Chicago, a church-based civil rights group who are going to help me penetrate the World Church of the Creator. With all these messages and calls flying about, I'm becoming incredibly nervous.

These days and nights together give me a chance to quiz Mark more about his background. He doesn't mind talking, but it's hard to drill beneath the surface. The family were raised in the West Country, first Worcester, then Torquay in Devon. Mark says he learned to hate his father and was barely on speaking terms with him when he died. 'He was a religious nut. We didn't use to see eye to eye, really. I ended up calling him Jesus, as an insult.' Clearly he dotes on his elderly mother, though. There are pictures of her around the bare walls of the apartment, and she's visited him several times. In fact, one of the first times I called Mark from the UK, he was sitting with her in a DC restaurant.

He became involved with the National Front at an early age, in contrast with other figures in the movement. The NF was his main group for many years. At the same time, he worked for a while in Worcester's world-famous porcelain factory. Despite lacking a formal education, he's clearly very intelligent. It would be foolish to underestimate him, I think. I've seen pictures of him enjoying a drink with Charlie Sargent, as they travelled together on the ferry to Diksmuide in Flanders. Two more links to my recent past.

Mark's a former Loyalist supporter, too (I spot a number of Loyalist flags in his cupboard) and once was a Conservative Party local candidate. All he will say about his reasons for leaving England is that he was subjected to a 'punishment beating' of some kind. He maintains it was from the far left. 'Why do you keep wanting to know?' he asks curiously, slightly aggressive. 'I've got nothing to hide. It's something I never want to go through again. Two blokes jumped me. They were definitely AFA.' I'm not so sure. Perhaps he upset some of his fellows on the Loyalist fringe? No, he says. It's a niggardly suspicion, though. I could be wrong. I ask him once more. He denies it, angrily.

At night, I continue to notice the various emails pouring into his computer, from his networks across the States and Europe. Clearly, Mark is on close terms with many far-right groups. And he's amazingly open in his opinions about them. 'You've got to understand, Pierce is a hardline cult leader in some ways,' he tells me. 'It'll all fall apart after he dies.' He dismisses the World Church of the Creator, based in Illinois and another organisation I'm soon to visit, as 'wacky'.

Our talk turns to the role the AFBNP played in the Reform Party's recent election campaign. Mark is still incredibly angry and bitter about being thrown off the campaign, and at Buchanan's poor showing at the polls.

Pat Buchanan was a presidential speechwriter for both Nixon and Reagan, a member of the Republican Party elite. He finally left the Republicans after twice failing to secure the party's presidential nomination. Almost everyone Mark introduces to me professes admiration for Buchanan. They admire – or, rather, admired – his controversial views on closing America's borders, withdrawing its troops from overseas and turning away from support for Israel. Until he proposed his black female running mate, of course. They see it as a clumsy sop to liberal opinion, which neither pleased them nor mollified the mainstream.

I think back on Peter Gemma. Short, respectable, keen to keep his name out of the limelight. As well he might. He was a longstanding Republican campaigner and is now a lobbyist for nonprofits. I wonder if there are many more like him out there. Unlike my anonymous friend, Gemma was actually quite careful with what he said. Yet he's a close associate of Mark's, it appears. Like many of his contemporaries, he also spoke in less than glowing terms about Pat's sister, Bay.

I found it odd, for the moment, that so many of those I would call white supremacists found Buchanan so alluring. It seemed they'd been seduced by his dance of words, of isolationism and anti-immigrant beliefs. Or perhaps they were attributing to him beliefs he never shared. Despite this seduction, many had dumped him at the last minute. Why would white supremacists and extremists have been drawn to him in the first place? I've been negotiating with Buchanan's staff for a while now. Today, an email arrives inviting me to his house.

* * *

'I'm going to do you a big favour,' he says. Mark's chin is unshaven this morning. Normally, he's neat and correct about his appearance. Bags have appeared under his eyes. Perhaps something is troubling him. Or it could be those beers we had last night, in a bizarre place called 'Hooters', where scantily clad waitresses on roller skates serve the mainly male clientele with expensive drinks and cheap, fried American food. Mark and his pals seemed to love it. 'We've got pictures of Nick Griffin with two girls here,' he joked with me. 'Don't tell his wife, though!' I laughed, but to me it just seemed sad. Sitting there, with these eager men, Mark thousands of miles away from his own homeland. They stared at the women, often silent but leering, as they dragged on cigarettes.

'Ssshush!' he cautions me, punching out a number on the phone. 'John, hi. How you doing, mate? Yeah, it is. I don't suppose you have a moment to talk?' I hear muffled comments. Mark's back straightens, as he turns to look at me. 'Really? Oh, shit, well, I'll call back later. Any particular time? Right, will do.'

He replaces the handset, carefully almost lovingly. 'Do you know who that was?' I shake my head. 'John Tiffany, editor of the *Barnes Review*. It's a revisionist magazine, part of Willis Carto's empire. I'm trying to get you a meeting with John. He's a good bloke, and one of the few still loyal to me. Maybe you can get something from this for the book. Y'know, now that we can't go up and visit Pierce. Anyway, Carto is another former heavyweight and once Pierce's friend.' He chuckles. 'They hate each other's guts now. I can't go in there any more.'

'Why not?'

'Oh, I don't want to go into it too much, but he owes me money.' He mentions he might put in a surprise appearance at a forthcoming *Barnes Review* conference. Then he huffs in a breath of air, and chuckles: 'Carto was actually in the office when I just called. I think Tiffany nearly shat his pants!'

Tiffany calls back about half an hour later, and the meeting is arranged.

The next day, I head over to Pennsylvania Avenue, where the offices of Carto's Liberty Lobby are based. Walking up the long steel escalator, the air's incredibly muggy. I manoeuvre past tourists and schoolkids. Much of this land was originally a swamp. The old joke goes that the Founding Fathers built this place so that the politicians would never become too comfortable. Tar melts by the side of the road. I keep my tie dragged to half-mast until the very last minute, when I enter the building.

The Liberty Lobby is on the site of an old German consulate, dwarfed by the striding steel and glass of Washington's new power across the street. Its peeling whitewashed walls and ramshackle, mouldering corridors speak of better days. Then again, the Lobby has been around since 1955 (*The Spotlight* since 1975). I announce myself to a young Asian woman. Then Carto's fearsome secretary, Anne, regards me suspiciously through the wire mesh entry area before allowing me in. I've heard about her from Mark. Strange figures and faces move up and down a central staircase off to my right. A crackling public address system announces various edicts to the staff, as I stand and wait.

I know from Mark that Carto is about to lose his struggle for control of this place. He's been stuck in litigation for years now with his former comrades at the Institute for Historical Review (the same people I'd been negotiating with to travel to Beirut), over millions they allege he misappropriated. In just a few days Carto will lose his battle and the network of offices will probably be shut down. Mark is gleeful, quizzing me each evening for further details, then calling California to pass on the news to Mark Weber.

'Third floor.' I turn away from the secretary, move past a drinks machine and start up the wide stairs.

Tiffany comes stumbling down, two steps at a time, to meet me. He's a shy, awkward, hippy-like figure, in his early 50s. His voice pitches oddly, deep at times, at others inflected with a nervous, staccato stumble. There are plenty of painful pauses. He speaks much like a scientist explaining some arcane theorem. He introduces me to an older man named Tony, holding a German shepherd dog. I inch nervously past.

In his office, Tiffany mumbles an invitation to sit down. I wrinkle my nose, but he fails to notice. He wears an incongruous baseball cap and his long hair disappears into a beard. Body odour hangs about him. Plants litter the floor.

I try asking about his background and how he ended up here. 'Uh, I like to see myself as something of a scholar,' he admits, licking nervously at his mouth. 'Someone fighting to air free academic opinions.' It's an increasingly familiar refrain from the revisionists I meet.

Constant PA announcements cut through our conversation. He

interrupts me a couple of times to field calls. I have to sit and listen to him shouting to his own answering machine, trying to get his wife to pick up the phone at home.

'I was a biologist by training. An establishment liberal, too. It's a fascinating thing, history.'

'Why?'

'That's partly what drove me forwards. And what keeps me involved. What's kept me involved, in fact.'

I scribble everything down, furiously, boiling in this stultifying heat. I notice an Ireland coffee mug on the table between us. Like Fisheye, Tiffany is a Celtic fanatic; the next time we meet, he's wearing a kilt.

'I became interested in the Constitution. I felt I needed to know more about the law, since I was an ignoramus,' he explains, detailing how he watched the government abuse its powers in Alaska, where he'd been working.

'I had it made there; you know how it is in the government. I was leaping into the unknown. By chance, I had a compulsion to correct things that I see are wrong. I always have my pencil out when I'm reading anything.' A German-sounding female voice crackles over the PA. Irritating. Tiffany's eyes switch back and forth, watery blue. He went to work on a Carto-owned publication called *The Mercury Magazine*, then on *The Spotlight* 'because of my position on income tax'.

'What position?'

'I thought it was unconstitutional and Marxist.'

Tiffany is obviously one of those people who is vehemently anti-federalist, but I still don't understand why he became so enslaved to right-wing opinions. Nothing he tells me explains how he came to this position. 'For a long time, I didn't know what I was,' he admits at one point. It's only when we get to the whole idea of revisionism that I gain an insight. He jokes that he and others refer to the Holocaust issue as 'Holocaustianity', snuffling an awkward laugh as he blurts out the word. I remember his words later when I visit the new Holocaust museum. According to Tiffany, revisionism usually holds that there were not six million deaths; no gassing; no evidence of a policy of genocide from the Germans; and no bones or ash to prove mainstream theories.

I ask if he can get me into this weekend's revisionist conference. It's being hosted by his magazine, after all. This will see one of the last East Coast gatherings of many major revisionist figures. I'm hoping he'll simply say yes, being the editor after all. Instead he says, 'Uh, perhaps we'd better go see Willis.' Oh damn.

We twist out of the room and up another flight of stairs. Tiffany raps on a partially open door. The fading light of late afternoon is bleaching the world into peach and sepia shapes, reflecting the colour of the ageing walls and yellowing blinds.

Carto is an old man. His silvering hair is slicked into a neat, old-fashioned 1950s cut, and a pair of braces cling to his skinny torso. Stick-like arms poke from his rolled-up shirtsleeves. A poster for Pat Buchanan sits on the wall. An ancient desk looms between us. He could be a figure from a B movie.

'Yes?' he snaps, unhelpful, irritated. His pinched, waspish face turns towards us. My mouth is suddenly incredibly dry and my knees weak. I'm afraid. Apart from William Pierce, this guy stands at the centre of it. His fearsome reputation, narrow features and dry, bird-like body only heighten my nervousness. An infamous figure within the right, with millions at his disposal. Where do I go from here?

I remember checking the files. He'd founded the national youth organisation for presidential candidate George Wallace, back in 1968, which became the National Youth Alliance then, after Pierce took it over, the National Alliance. The two men have been sworn foes ever since, and the list of people Carto's sued is impressive.

Tiffany backs out of the room, facing Carto all the time. I glance to my side, thinking what to say to the old man. I spot Tiffany collecting an aluminium scooter from the landing outside and heading off. What a bizarre-looking figure, I have one quick moment to think.

'What is it you want?' Carto's reedy voice makes me turn.

'Uh, I'm a journalist' – the words stumble, stuck in my throat – 'a journalist doing this project about . . .'

'What kind of journalist?'

'Well, more a writer, I guess. Someone trying to be neutral.'

'Liberal?' A curious little smile spreads from the corner of his mouth.

'Yeah, I guess so.'

'The liberal media are just whores!' he snaps, impaling me with a razor-sharp gaze. Perhaps it's all part of the game, a show of bravado – but it scares the hell out of me. Carto becomes very animated. My throat closes up. He launches into an attack on liberals, journalists and the powers of the Establishment. 'When's the last time the liberal media wrote about the power of the Bilderberg Group, eh?' He cranks up and squints one eyeball. 'Why don't you write about people like the Trilateral Commission and those really running things out there?'

'Er, what about an interview?'

'I never do interviews. Never.'

Mark has already told me not to mention to Carto that I'm staying with him. It sounds like Mark is thinking of gatecrashing this conference and confronting the old man. Mr Anonymous is also suing him, I'm told.

Croaking, I tell Carto that I've covered many territories and wars. I'm trying to be neutral. I offer to email him some of my articles. His tone suddenly changes. He huffs, grumpily, but says he'll take a look. 'It probably won't make any difference, though.'

A chubby, sweating figure enters the room, swaps a couple of words with Carto, then introduces himself. Unlike the old man he's instant smiles and friendliness. 'Hi, Mike Piper.' We shake hands. His palm is warm and wet, and large diamond-encrusted rings encase his fat fingers. A matt of blond hairs pokes from the open neck of an expensive-looking pink shirt. The folds of his skin do little to hide what seems a fake tan.

Piper enquires about my writing, then says he's written a book himself, revealing 'the truth' about JFK's assassination. Carto says he needs to work, so Piper and I walk out of the main building, over a creaking iron fire escape, and into a separate outbuilding. There's a Confederate feel to it; maybe it's the ancient wooden staircase, perhaps the old-fashioned fireplace in the boardroom. Or it could be the time-peeled painting of Willis on the wall. A fan turns, blowing cool air over me every few seconds. We sit at a mahogany table that's clearly seen better days, beneath a hanging US flag.

Piper starts talking about the difficulties the Lobby is facing, his voice sounding squashed, almost forced through his vocal chords. 'We've been under pressure from Jewish interests, and this is interesting, particularly the Israeli lobby and their connections in the CIA.' He begins detailing a long list of people who've sued them and claims that one of the latest lawsuits is led by a 'guy who has very definite ties to the CIA and Mossad'.

The difficulties have had their effects. 'We're a little shorthanded around here, as we have been for a while, because people are a little leery about coming to work for a company that's in bankruptcy.' It wasn't always like this. In 1981 they had nearly 70 staff, he says, and a subscriber base of 360,000 paying readers.

But there's a hard core to their support. 'Most of the people at the meetings tend to be older.'

'Older and male,' I point out.

'Yes, older and male at the big meetings. Partly because it costs more money to get to them, and young people don't have the same desire to travel. If you took a look at the ancestry of our membership lists, you'd find a lot of different types of people. Maybe people of Eastern European descent, for example.'

'Not Jews,' I quip, deadpan.

'Hah, presumably not!' But half of the readers are Catholics, he claims. Plenty of settled Hispanics and Asians, too. 'The reality of our subscriber base is not always the way we're painted in the press. You'd think we were only read by skinheads – most of them hate us! Well, some read us as well, but they mostly don't think we go far enough.'

Mark has told me about some ultra-right-wing rabbi who's on his subscriber list. I mention this to Piper. 'We have had friendly relationships with a lot of Jews who are anti-Zionist. Our attorney, for one, although he gets called a self-hating Jew and all that kind of thing.' He coughs occasionally. He regales me with stories of how they purchased a mailing list used by right-wing radio talk show host Rush Limbaugh, and when they removed all the ZIP codes associated with Jewish neighbourhoods, over half the list was gone. 'I guess that doesn't surprise me,' Piper confesses, speaking as though uncovering some major secret. 'Whaddya know about that?' he chortles, sounding self-satisfied, his cheeks rippling with each word.

We move on to Pat Buchanan, of whom Piper clearly is a fan. 'Pat would probably not want to acknowledge this publicly, but the demographics of his support, his mailing list, plus his philosophy in general, is probably about 90 per cent on par, for want of a better term, with that of Liberty Lobby.'

I start to talk, but he cuts me off. 'His philosophy is hardly different for what we equip for here at Liberty Lobby. His economic positions, his foreign policy positions, his position on immigration, could be taken word for word as the view of *The Spotlight* and Liberty Lobby. On the issue of trade, and the question of US support for Israel, we preceded Pat. He used to be a big free-trade supporter. Now he's a protectionist.'

'He's not a subscriber, is he?'

'Uh, he probably does subscribe, but he probably wouldn't admit to it!' He draws in a breath, leaning back and revealing the belly pushing against that expensive shirt. 'I met Pat one time. He knows who I am, and we know a lot of people mutually. But he's always made a strong attempt to separate himself from Liberty Lobby. But more than half the delegates at the recent Reform Party convention were *Spotlight* subscribers. He's walking a fine line,' he laughs.

'Who are these people, the subscribers?'

'They're basically grassroots American. Not your Tim McVeigh! Not someone with swastika tattoos. But that's your popular perception.' I mention the links to Pierce. 'Of course, McVeigh had advertised in *The Spotlight*.' He says he can give me some special info about 'very strange things' to do with the Oklahoma bomb.

We've both just seen an article in *Talk* magazine that discusses David Duke's relocation to Russia. 'Let me tell you about David,' Piper says. 'He's getting a raw deal. A very raw deal. The Feds have been looking for something on David Duke for years. When he ran for office, they threw everything at him – including the kitchen sink. That David was a womaniser, a gambler, an evil racist, a Holocaust denier. The only thing they didn't say about David was that he's an egomaniac, which everybody knows!'

I suddenly wonder why Duke and Buchanan never linked up forces. 'Number one, egos!' replies Piper. 'Number two, frankly,' he coughs, 'financial reasons. They have a very distinct overlap in their base of support. Buchanan has his own foundation, Duke has his organisation. The third reason is that Pat Buchanan doesn't want to be perceived as "extreme" as

David Duke. David always has that spectre of the Ku Klux Klan hood hanging over him.' Buchanan has even boasted about stopping Duke winning the Republican primary in 1992.

I find Piper's use of first names interesting: 'David' and 'Pat'. How he knows them both, especially Duke – who 'loves to be loved' – and how he has watched what he calls Buchanan's 'evolution'. I listen to this strange morass of opinion, simply nodding or noting points.

Suddenly Carto wanders through. He heads for a side office, but not before saying 'Hi, Nick,' in a friendly tone, as if the other meeting never happened. Have I missed something?

With Carto gone again, I decide to slip in my questions about Pierce. If I can't see the old guy, I might as well see what others in the movement think about him. 'He definitely is a major player out there,' Piper admits. 'Aside from *The Spotlight*. There are a lot of smaller groups, but most only overlap on the fringes.' He mentions the Christian Defence League and a paper called *The Truth At Last*. Some of the men behind these were, like Pierce, in the original American Nazi Party with assassinated leader George Lincoln Rockwell. 'These guys are all cogs in the movement, but Pierce – for better or worse – is probably the one that has the most influence overall. Aside from *The Spotlight*,' he adds, again. 'We're kinda maybe moving in the same direction.'

We talk about Pierce's mental health, and the possibilities of a split within his movement. 'We don't rely on Willis, personally. He's the boss, yeah, but there's an institution, too. With Pierce, it's so much a personal extension of his personality. That's the difference.'

He admits there's a personal rivalry (some say hatred) between Carto and Pierce, but not on a wider institutional level. 'The differences are in tone and in emphasis. But on the whole I would say we are moving in the same direction. I frankly am amazed at the following Pierce does have, because I personally find him a bit windy and boring. He runs transcriptions of his own speeches. After a while, you want it to be edited down. I just kinda get the idea no one edits him.'

When Piper and I are finished talking, we return to the main building. Carto himself lets me out a side entrance, smiling crookedly and saying, 'Bye, Nick.' Outside, back in the real world, I catch a glimpse of the old man turning, hunched, and disappearing again.

* * *

That night I join Mark, Sam Francis and Joe, the car park attendant, at a meeting of isolationists called the Tuesday Night Club. We gather in a Thai restaurant, in a suburb not far from Falls Church. We're the first to arrive. Mark tells me the group was set up during the Gulf War, to urge non-involvement in that conflict. A smart, tweed-jacketed figure approaches us and greets Mark in an East European or Teutonic accent. Turns out he's a

Hungarian of German origin. Cliff wanders in behind us, then Jeff from the other night. We sit down at a horseshoe-shaped table. Most of the others are older, male, balding.

I listen for a while to talk of the McVeigh execution. One of the people standing is a Dutch TV reporter who was present at the event. The last few official days, I've seen little else on television. Sam Francis then gets up to give the talk, which is on eugenics – the science of racial differences. 'The Mexicans are colonising America; the dominant white culture is being swamped,' he says. And everywhere he goes, 'I just hear liberal.'

'We are assimilating them, they are not assimilating us,' he stutters with repressed anger, his jowls quivering with each word. 'And today's capitalism is much of the problem.' A great deal of his argument seems to lie on the IQ differences between racial groups. Not everyone agrees with him. These are mavericks, but not all are racists.

Jeff and I chat. He's a staunch Buchanan supporter on Israel, the retreat from wars, the root of all economic problems, and opposition to abortion. To my right, Sam is tucking in with gusto.

Mark stands up, bangs his glass, and insists on introducing me. 'Everyone, quiet please!' he cries. 'I just wanted to say we had a guest tonight. This is Nick Ryan.' I grimace, waiting for the punchline. 'He's a left-wing reporter from London.' People shift, the table shakes and the gathering goes silent. Then someone shouts out, 'So he's a Commie?!' My face flushes. Mark looks back at me, innocently. Earlier, he'd said: 'I think I might introduce you about halfway through the meal. They'll probably all scatter after that.'

The rest of the evening passes without incident. We spend the late hours drinking whisky sour in some small, dingy cabin of a bar. Mark and I joke and chat, sealing the bond that's been developing between us. 'I may surprise you sometimes,' he says, mysteriously. 'For example, I'm in favour of abortion,' he adds, glancing at the rear end of a passing waitress, 'as long as it's for non-whites, of course.' Beneath that slightly odd-looking surface there's razor-sharp wit and humour for which I respect him.

By now, I'm a bit drunk, too. Mark, I ask, if you guys are the cream of the movement, where are your kids? Where are the families giving birth to the new master race? My tone is sardonic. He picks it up. 'Well, you have a point,' he sighs. 'We get a fair few nuts and losers. Then again, all movements do.' The joke, he agrees, is that under Hitler, most of them would have been executed. We both laugh.

* * *

Over the next three days, I have unprecedented access into the Liberty Lobby. It's odd, entering a place like that when you have a hangover. I've sent Carto some of my (carefully selected) cuttings. His tune changes and he asks me to write for his newspaper. Thinking quickly, I ask him for a signed copy of one of his conspiracy books. He looks genuinely surprised and eager to comply. From then on he's friendly, calling me 'Nick' and showing me around the building. I get permission to attend this weekend's *Barnes Review* conference.

I'm the only one who knows it's about to collapse. Mark is gleefully pumping me for information, spending his evenings talking and plotting with the IHR, which he knows has just won its final court case. He wants to hear what's happening inside Liberty Lobby, presumably so he can help bring it down.

That night, I learn that anti-capitalist riots have taken over the normally placid Swedish city of Gothenburg.

* * *

Pat Buchanan's Southern-style mansion is set deep in the woods in the upmarket suburb of McLean, Virginia, a short drive from Washington. Just behind it lies the headquarters of the CIA. I'm ushered in by a Chilean maid, who prepares traditional lemonade for me whilst I sit in Buchanan's reception room. Large oil paintings adorn the oak-panelled walls. Fading photographs show Buchanan with Nixon, greeting the Chinese premier. A grand piano sits in an adjoining lounge. To my left, a small alcove houses a bar area with little knick-knacks on shelves next to mirrored walls.

It's the sumptuous surroundings of an Establishment politician. I remind myself that Buchanan was Nixon's and Reagan's main speechwriter.

I hear footsteps and turn to see a stooped, frail figure emerge from steps under the stairs, walking with the aid of a stick. This is not the fiery character I've come to expect; certainly not the man I've seen many times on CNN. He greets me courteously and admits that he's been ill. 'I'm retired from mainstream politics now,' he says, walking over to one of the fine upholstered chairs. 'I'm writing a book on the decline of the West.' (I'm later told that Sam Francis – the guy I was drinking with last night – has helped edit it.)

He listens politely to my questions, and for two hours we discuss his views on America's past and future. It's a whistle-stop tour through what Buchanan calls 'paleo-conservatism'.

'I'm talking about the survival of Western civilisation into the twenty-first century. Various forces threaten that. Depopulation and mass immigration from different cultures, the Third World, different peoples, the decline of the nation state and the rise of the, er, of the World Government – of which the EU is well out in front.' He laughs at his own joke. I tell him about my experiences in Belgium. He sounds surprised. 'Oh, they do?' he enquires, after I tell him about the number of Vlaams Blok MPs in the Belgian parliament.

It's interesting to think that in the US, the radical right has so far spectacularly failed to cross over into the political sphere. Or when it's tried, as with Buchanan, it's achieved derisory results. 'We were trying to do it. But there's reasons why it doesn't work. One is that America's a huge country. Second is that it's very much a tradition as a melting-pot nation. This has always been a positive aspect of America, but we've simply never encountered the sudden volume rush that we've experienced since 1965.' His voice is husky and weak. He sips on his crushed lemonade. 'But I think you're getting an increasing apprehension about it.'

He complains that if you raise these issues you get marked down as a 'nativist' or xenophobe. 'There's another point,' he says. 'Your economic powers, the transnational corporations, are delighted with mass immigration, because it keeps a steady, constantly growing supply of labour and suppresses wage demands, and provides competition to union labour.' His voice lilts upwards, emphasising and punching certain words forward, despite his weakness.

Elites in politics and journalism are silent on the issue. 'Down the road, what you're probably going to get is balkanisation of the country.' It sounds remarkably similar to Sam. 'We're going to cease to exist as one nation, one people. Especially down in the south-west, where the Hispanic people will be tied to Mexico, as their mother country.

'Of course, another issue is the internal cultural war in the United States between traditional culture – basically rooted in Christianity – and what was the adversary culture, the Woodstock culture of the 1960s, which is now dominant.' I feel I've heard this refrain a thousand times, from the BNP to the Vlaams Blok. Blame the 1960s. 'Theirs is the dominant culture, ours is the dissident culture.' He laughs again, then blames the young and a 'Hollywood elite' for following this trend.

We've witnessed the 'de-Christianisation' of American schools and the launch of a war against the past. He keeps laughing at these references, as though fatalistic. 'I'm not pessimistic, but realistic,' he states. But he sounds bitter about established parties. 'The Democrats have a vested interest, in particular, in the naturalisation process [of new immigrants] because any foreign-born group is heavily Democratic to overwhelmingly Democratic.'

'Can't these just be assimilated, as earlier immigrant groups were?' I'm wondering if his arguments are based on race and ethnicity. America is changing. So what?

'Our ancestors came over, that's true, but they put them into these public schools which were very tough, and they learned about American heroes and American history. I grew up during World War II, and we all listened to the same radio shows, there was no television, and 90 per cent of kids were in public schools. We said the Pledge of Allegiance every day in the schoolyard and raised the flag for all the graduates who were killed in the War. And we had one language; because of the immigration law of 1924, immigration was virtually stopped for 20 years. People were virtually assimilated. I didn't know that the kids at this school were Italian, English,

Poles, or Scots-Irish like me, or German. We were all just Catholic schoolkids who were Americans.'

We talk about his views on Israel, America's foreign policy (how Europeans should not rely on the US for help), 'economic nationalism' and how 'Reagan was one of America's greatest Presidents'. We even talk a bit about his childhood, not far from where we're sitting. He looks and sounds like a spent force. He seems shocked – and irritated – when I mention the allegation that extremists are attracted to his cause. He claims they only ever discovered one, Mark Cotterill, and that this was the only time he had heard of the BNP. Which is odd, given that several of Mark's friends told me they volunteered for Buchanan's campaign, and that many more sympathised with him.

He also seems to have trouble remembering who Peter Gemma is. Again, surprising, given their friendship. It's clear to me there was a major push by the extremists to take power from within the Reform Party structure. Yet Buchanan asserts that he stood against David Duke when in the Republican Party and is not a racist. I mention my recent meetings with Liberty Lobby and the invitation to write for *The Spotlight*. 'Take my advice,' he says. 'Don't.'

As we part, he tells me he has to hop into town, to visit the University Club, the same gentlemen's club from which my anonymous friend has been banned. I think to myself how this man belongs to that groomed world of power. I find it hard to imagine him being comfortable with many of the people I've met so far.

'Oh, your friend says hi, by the way,' I call out, referring to the anonymous AFBNP member, as I watch Buchanan shuffle off down the steps again. Then he disappears from view.

* * *

On the way back in the taxi, I call Mark. 'How did it go?' he enquires, a little too lightly. Not too bad, I tell him. Got a few quotes. 'Good, good,' he says. There's a pause. 'By the way, I had a call from one of your friends this afternoon.'

Shit. Is he referring to Nick Lowles? I know he calls him from time to time. I don't like the sound of this.

'Larry O'Hara. He was a bit shocked to hear you were over here, I can tell you.' He sounds like he's smirking. I can't be sure. O'Hara is a self-styled investigator of the right, but himself politically from the hard-left or anarchist fringe. I've never met him or dealt with him, but he seems to be waging a personal war against *Searchlight*. I've also read plenty of pretty negative comments about him on the Net.

'He says he has proof that you know Nick Lowles.' Oh, bugger. 'That you took him to meet Steve Sargent, when you were writing an article for *The Independent*.' That much is true, but I don't know whether to reveal this to Mark. 'Well, did you? If you had, I wish you'd told me about it.'

I blurt out some stammering excuses. How I met Nick at the Sargent court case (I did) and how together we may have seen Steve (which we did). But that's it. 'No, don't worry,' Mark says, in his usual drawn-out tones, like an interrogator. 'I'm not bothered. Larry says he's faxing something over later. Proof of this. He told me I shouldn't be putting you up.' I could swear he's smiling. 'He sounded very shocked. Oh – if you are working for the other side,' he adds, 'as I said before, I don't mind. But I would rather know.'

Once the line goes dead, I put through calls to Nick. I get him on the third try, but there's not much he can do for me. I'll just have to tough and bluff it out.

* * *

Back at Falls Church, I join Mark for a swim in the condo's pool. He looks on, distastefully, as several Hispanic families start splashing around with their kids. Although polite, Mark speaks slowly and forcefully. He's bitter about his expulsion from the Reform Party. He seems to have a habit of joining or infiltrating groups, then being forced from them. The same thing seems to have happened with his membership of the Conservative Party, back in England. When he asks me more about my connections with Nick Lowles, I duck. He seems to enjoy watching me squirm.

I ask him why he associates with wackos. 'Believe you me,' he answers, pulling away down the pool, 'I know more nutters than you'll ever meet.'

'So why not do something else with your life? Why stay loyal to a cause that sees such infighting and futility?'

'I've been thinking the same thing myself. It's true, we all need money, and I certainly do.' He refers in disparaging terms to a leading member of Pierce's network who he says has 'never had a job'.

'So where do you see yourself in a few years' time?' I'm posing a standard interviewer's question.

'On a beach in Jamaica.'

'Presumably with a black girlfriend,' I joke.

'It's all meat on a hook to me, mate,' he says, deadpan, but obviously with humour.

The next evening, he introduces me to a friend named Martin Kerr, another veteran of the American Nazi Party. We tuck into bloody oozing steaks at an Australian dining chain called Outback. Kerr is a funny, nervous man, in black shirt and jeans, with thinning hair that he constantly smoothes with one hand, wide glasses and a greying beard.

'Martin was a member of the National Socialist White People's Party, too, but resigned when it became a cult,' says Mark. The sad face droops further, as Kerr tells me he lost his wife in a car accident, then 'the courts took away my daughter because they said I'm unfit to raise her'. I feel awful, but don't want to inflame things by asking if his political beliefs affected this.

It's nearly the weekend, and Mark's place is a hive of activity. Not only is he preparing to host one of his regular discussion evenings – taken, this time, by a visiting Canadian white nationalist and anti-immigration supremo, Paul Fromm – but Roy Armstrong, Duke's man and the NPD supporter, is turning up too. He appears late in the afternoon, in his battered old car with all the bumper stickers. He's just driven all the way from Louisiana.

'Wouldn't it have been easier to fly?'

'Oh, ah, I just like driving,' he says, this intimidating giant of a man, sounding embarrassed. He fiddles with the dark glasses. 'It doesn't bother me too much, going for a couple of days.'

The *Barnes Review* conference takes place at a luxury hotel in central Washington. A thunderstorm rages outside. Walking down into the basement, I spot numerous extremist figures. John Tiffany, clammy and nervous in a kilt, enters the hall with a pair of pipers. Outside, our conference mingles with guests from another event, making this seem even weirder to my eyes.

I bump into Peter Gemma and say hello; it's good to see a sane face I recognise around here. Roy Armstrong walks past, speaking fluent German to several elderly gentlemen. A slim, middle-aged man has a nametag saying 'Germar Rudolph' stuck to a tweed jacket. He looks very respectable. For some reason, the name rings a bell. Later, when I check up on the web, I see he's the same Germar Rudolph wanted in Germany, having been sentenced in absentia to 14 months for Holocaust denial. A chemistry graduate, he claims he scientifically 'proved' there were no gas chambers at Auschwitz. The web listing said he was in England, on the run. He'd also stayed at a former Nazi general's home in Spain.

I then hear numerous conspiracy theorists talk, suggesting for example that the government itself blew up the building in Oklahoma City and that the Bilderberg Group planned the removal of Maggie Thatcher. There are attacks on organisations such as the Anti-Defamation League (ADL). I watch the infamous Fred Leuchter – a greying figure with a black beret, nicknamed 'Dr Death' – take to the lectern. You can sense the crowd eager, shifting like an animal, to hear his words. He's also 'proved' there were no gas chambers in Nazi Germany (the quality of his research is vehemently disputed by many civil rights and Jewish groups). During the lunch break I get cornered by a Japanese woman who tells me she's a journalist. When I start learning she believes in UFOs and mind control, I rapidly make my excuses and leave.

The stress must be getting to me. Walking past Willis Carto, I just feel this whole thing, this gathering of ageing men, is faintly ridiculous. I wander off to the hotel bar and spend the rest of the afternoon drinking with Peter Gemma.

THIRTEEN

SMILING SOUTH

The Interstate flashes past, hypnotic. Behind me, Washington DC. Ahead, Richmond, the former capital of the confederacy. Civil war, slavery – and David Duke's territory.

I'm coming out to see one of Mark's closest contacts. Ron Doggett is the state leader of Duke's organisation, EURO (European American Rights Organization). He's often spoken at AFBNP meetings and has been instrumental in introducing Mark and Nick Griffin to Duke's network. I'm told he's also a member of the National Alliance.

The soft drumming of the Greyhound bus sends me drifting off. For the first time in a while I feel at peace, away from Mark and the paranoid world of the extremists. As I doze, thoughts from the past few days drift into my head.

Ed Cassidy, Fisheye, told me: 'I don't think the nazi groups are going anywhere. You know, the National Alliance, hardcore groups like the skinheads. If we're gonna have any success, it's gonna lie in different groups like the BNP, the C of CC, getting together, forming more of a united front, working together. I really can't see groups like the National Alliance or the extreme anti-Semites fitting in.' This appeared to be Duke's aim, too, at least until he fled the country.

So is the hardcore approach out now? Will America see the rise of that elusive 'third party', which is becoming so prevalent in modern Europe? It seemed the US two-party system, together with the great freedom of speech here – why tone down the rhetoric, if you won't get prosecuted? – might have been hindering such a birth. Where did that leave the National Alliance? I'd heard so much about them on my travels, painted as a kind of demonic force. Had they been over-hyped? 'Ah, I think most people view them kind of sceptically,' Fisheye chuckled. 'They attract skinheads, loonies. And you never know when one of 'em is going to go off and do something. We've heard stories at the National Alliance headquarters about rapes going on, and all kinds of assaults. When you're dealing with young hotheads, you're going to get that kind of thing. It doesn't do the movement any good.'

At that point, the anonymous guy wandered up, smartly dressed as ever, and I took the opportunity to ask both what they thought about those attracted to violence. This didn't affect only their movement, they said; just look at radical environmentalists. Weren't we really looking, behind all this, at confusion over the loss of traditional values and community? 'Yes,' they both chimed, forcefully, almost simultaneously. I was taken aback by how quickly they agreed. Gone were the ranting, the platitudes, the sly words about my being a liberal journalist. We were friends, discussing politics, society and the future. 'The America many people want is gone, and they can't get back to it,' said the nameless guy.

'A lot of people growing up now are probably having to see their mom and dad work harder, with less. They remember growing up 35 years ago, when their dad worked and their mom stayed at home. They had better vacations and all that.' But this was not racial. This was something else, I pointed out. Wider than race. But the guys still claimed it was, indeed, racial, that 'their people' were being used to reinforce buffoon images of the white man, that blacks and others were now shown in a favourable light. This harking back to times past was a familiar litany from my encounters with the right.

Mr Anonymous had gone on to tell me more about Pierce: about his intellect, how he was fundamentally shy, well-read, aloof. 'Lacking in common sense, though. To the extent that he's required to wear very thick glasses, because he once left his contact lenses in for three weeks when he's supposed to take 'em out the next day, and it ruined his eyes! He's just a man that marches to his own drummer. Remember, he came to this movement late in his life. It wasn't like Willis Carto, when he started right after World War II. So that's something to be considered.' Fisheye was silent.

Mr Anonymous said the National Alliance had not grown very much in the last 30 years, until Pierce – through him – had bought Resistance Records. So what kind of movement was it? 'It's political, social. It has skinheads in it. It also has professors in it. It has PhDs in it, and successful businessmen. It's mainly male, the average age is about 40; it's certainly a lot younger than the C of CC and Liberty Lobby. And they probably die a lot younger too, such as the guy who got killed in Chicago last week [Eric Hanson, an NA member and skinhead who died in a shootout with Illinois state police].'

We were sitting in a traditional, cabin-type diner, drinking whisky at midday. 'I don't think a lot of women like confrontational politics,' Mr Anonymous said. What people did Pierce surround himself with, up at Hillsboro? 'Uh, I'll be objective here . . . some of them are what you would honestly call misfits. Others are people that have had successful careers in other areas, but have decided they want to live down there. Some are hermits, and that's why they live on a mountain. And some are very presentable. But they all share his goals.'

* * *

As Grand Wizard of the Knights of the Ku Klux Klan in the 1970s, David Duke urged Klan members to 'get out of the cow pasture and into hotel meeting rooms'. For the past 25 years, he has increasingly followed his own advice, by using code words and disguising his ideas behind more mainstream-sounding conservative rhetoric.

Starting as a small-time leader of a campus white supremacist organisation at Louisiana State University in the early 1970s, Duke has had many incarnations. In an attempt to demystify Klan ritual, he renamed the position of Grand Wizard, 'National Director', and referred to cross burnings as 'illuminations'. In 1980, he resigned from the KKK and formed a 'political organisation' to promote the cause of 'White Rights', the National Association for the Advancement of White People (NAAWP). He also unsuccessfully attempted to host a racist radio talk show programme in Louisiana.

Another tactic in Duke's strategy of 'mainstreaming' racism has been his effort to run for political office. Although he was elected to the Louisiana State Legislature as a Republican in 1989, as a political candidate Duke has been largely unsuccessful. He lost bids for Governor and the US Senate in Louisiana, and for President of the United States in 1988 (via the Populist Party, backed by the Liberty Lobby) and 1992. Most recently, in May 1999, he lost a race for US Congress. Until moving to Russia, he served as Republican party chairman for the St Tammany Parish in Louisiana.

In November 1998 he self-published *My Awakening*, a 700-page autobiographical work with frequent references to Jewish power. Then, in January 2000, he announced the formation of a new organisation, NOFEAR (The National Organization for European American Rights), whose purpose was to 'defend the civil rights of European Americans'. He had to drop the name, because it was already owned by a clothing company. That was when EURO was born.

His talk of the dispossession of whites, the power of moneyed elites and rising immigration were to be honed and used by many other political extremists. When the BNP started sticking Nick Griffin at the top of its website, I continually thought of Duke's smiling, blond-haired, boyish image.

Until Buchanan, and perhaps even now, Duke was the closest thing the US had to a far-right politician. But he has relocated to Russia, and there are rumours of a sealed FBI indictment for his arrest and allegations that he spent hundreds of thousands of dollars of his supporters' money on gambling and women. Mark, though, still has extremely good contacts with Duke's network.

Many in the white supremacist (or, as they call themselves here, 'white nationalist') movement privately think he's finished in the US. But Peter Gemma had been telling me Duke was used as a protest vote against the 'party machine, which runs all the candidates and wins the elections, down in a place like Louisiana'. We were sitting in the hotel bar, at the *Barnes Review* conference. Roy Armstrong was hovering nearby, naming Germans he hadn't seen 'since they were in prison'. Gemma looked slightly uncomfortable in his company, but continued talking to me. 'In fact, I was stuck in a bar in Louisiana when Duke beat the incumbent Governor into third place. The place went crazy! "We got 'em, we stuck it to 'em! Nobody thought David Duke's going to be our Governor." They were sending a message.' He sighed. 'But America isn't built for third-party systems. Psychologically.'

Now it seemed the hardcore groups were gaining in influence because of this lack of a political way. Meanwhile, the search was on to build up a local leader in some backwater. 'A guy who can run for something more, someday,' said Gemma. To go for community politics. This is the model adopted years ago by the Front National in France, now being copied across Europe. Running people as independents, without a party ticket, but backed informally and behind the scenes by the different racial nationalist networks across the country. Campaigning on local issues, but part of a nationwide attempt to push forth a new figurehead. 'Political apathy will work for us, too,' Gemma had told me. Would some of Duke's people fill this gap?

* * *

I wake slowly. Most of the Greyhound passengers are black.

My thoughts drift to Roy Armstrong, in his hotel room and at the waffle restaurant at the C of CC convention in North Carolina. Another of Duke's men, dark suit, Ray Bans welded over intense blue eyes, classic Germanic features, and an odd, rumbling manner. Duke's caretaker, was what they called him. One of the first things he'd told me was how he'd known Hitler's butler: 'His first butler, who was replaced in 1939, not the second, who died.'

Armstrong had been a member of the NPD and a local representative for the Republikaner (REP) party. 'I also set up my own organisation, called the Citizens Action Committee, actually for repatriating asylum seekers and immigrants.' His political work had 'started irritating the government, so they started persecuting and harassing me. They wouldn't give me work for 18 years.' Another familiar refrain of the extremists: that their 'work' leads to their persecution. How had he survived? 'Unemployment.' His wife was unemployed too, because she was an active member of the REP. He'd lived like this for 25 years, occasionally taking odd jobs such as working as a night porter in a hotel, supporting a family of six children, from whom he was now separated. It seemed a frustrated, lonely existence.

But how did someone begin a life like this? Were the men (and a few women) I met simply social misfits? If so, how did that explain events back in Europe, where so-called ultra-nationalist and anti-immigrant parties were taking hold? Could it be, as many racists I met contended, that we had a natural, instinctive fear of the 'Stranger'? An evolutionary throwback, which had served us well and should not be abandoned? Yet I knew where that could lead. My own travels in many countries had shown me that.

For Roy it was his German ancestry, and a visit from David Duke when he was still living in the USA. 'Mr Duke visited me at one time,' he said. 'I had contact with radical groups in the USA [he mentions former colleagues of Willis Carto] and uh, I guess, Dr Fields [an extremist who publishes the *Truth at Last* newspaper] gave David Duke my address, and he visited me, because his sister used to live up in Washington. Yeah, Mr Duke stayed at my place in Germany several times, too.'

Roy believed the races were fundamentally different and should remain separate. 'It would be a catastrophe for mankind to mix up all the races. It reduces social cohesion and creates chaos. We need a certain group identity, but from people with a similar outlook on life.'

Interestingly, these separatists seemed as divided as they were united. Not for Roy the welcoming arms of religious fundamentalism. 'I'm not religious, as such. I believe that the Christian religion was injected into Western civilisation. I think it's a lot of times been very harmful. If you look at the Thirty Years War in Germany or the Northern Ireland conflict. I think it was used to undermine the Roman Empire, too.'

Roy had dismissed Pat Buchanan's attempts at political success, because of Buchanan's strong Catholic beliefs and choice of a black running mate, 'which probably cost him about 90 per cent of his support'. Would he have voted for him otherwise? 'I would have. I worked in his headquarters for a few days.'

After that minor bombshell – another extremist in the Buchanan campaign – we had moved over the road to the waffle house to talk about Germany, which Roy called 'a totalitarian state. There's no doubt about it. There's nothing even remotely resembling American freedoms.'

What had he done, then? He leaned forwards. 'I never participated in the Rudolf Hess march, although I did put up two large placards saying he was murdered. Also at one time, on the occasion of his 90th birthday, I went with some others to Berlin and we deposited 90,000 roses in front of the prison. We were arrested and detained for five hours.'

Had he ever been involved in violence? 'I was attacked on the streets by communists in 1997, I think it was. I fought back. I knocked the teeth out of the first person, then five of them hit me with clubs. I was hit under the scalp and covered with blood. The coverage went all over the world, got a lot of publicity.'

Roy liked to see himself as a racial nationalist, not a supremacist. He admired some other races and nations. 'I support Louis Farrakhan's ideas completely. I've sent him contributions. I was being investigated for this Iraqi involvement at the time,' he added, enigmatically. 'I sent them information to their Embassy regarding the undeniable possibility that the United States would attack them.' He was speaking in a low monologue, fast. 'It wasn't a bluff, I told them.'

Was that the first time he'd done this kind of thing? 'Well, when Libya was bombed in 1986, I sent some conciliatory notes, to which they did respond, which was nice of them.' When Gaddafi wanted to give Farrakhan a million dollars, he says he wrote to Gaddafi suggesting other ways of helping black people. The Libyans contacted him, apparently, and told him to come to Malta to talk about it. 'Which I did. I've tried to make arrangements to have this money transferred to individual blacks.'

I had no idea if this was fantasy or reality. In the background, I could hear orders being taken in the waffle house, and waitresses swapping gossip with young men. Roy continued to nail me with that Aryan gaze.

* * *

The bus jolts and my eyes open. A football stadium looms large on my left. An Indian brave, a mascot, parades above the concrete turnstiles. The vehicle swings smoothly to the right, up a little driveway, then I'm deposited inside a small whitewashed bus station. Grabbing my stuff, I move out unsurely, fishing for change, then call the pre-arranged telephone number. A deep voice answers.

'Hello Nick, good to hear from you at last! How was the journey?' Ron Doggett, I presume. The journey was fine, I tell him. 'I was just down there, but must have missed you. Wait a minute, and I'll start heading towards you.' He's on a mobile phone by the sound of his voice. The cent credits are disappearing fast from the little digital counter in front of me. I look towards the exit. A giant bearded man, wearing a baseball cap and casual clothes, is walking through the automatic doors. His powerful hands and forearms dwarf the phone wedged to his ear. A pearly grin splits through the undergrowth on his face as he strides towards me.

'Very nice to meet you,' he rumbles. His smile is warm and genuine. My fingers disappear in his bear-like grip. 'I guess the bus was a bit late, but Mark said what time you set out and I figured you'd arrive about now. Well, you're here now, so shall we head out?' There's no malice, awkwardness or intensity. In fact, after all the recent tension and subterfuge, I find myself relaxing almost instantly.

We walk out into a small car park. Light and heat reflect from the grit and tarmac crunching beneath our shoes. I jump into Doggett's car – 'Call me Ron, or Ronnie,' he says – as he quickly hits reverse. There's that baked seat smell, of plastic too long in the sun. He notices my gaze to the stadium opposite and tells me something of the local team. A moment later we're pulling away and cruising under bridges and flyovers, past rivers and old brown brick, shooting towards the cleaner, less choked suburbs.

He tells me he's traced his ancestors to the very first landings not far from here. 'In fact,' he says proudly, 'I've followed my family tree right back to England in the 1400s.'

This huge man's gentle manner belies his politics. He's one of Duke's leading supporters and a key figure on the right in Virginia. Everywhere we go people recognise him. 'Ronnie! Hey Ron!' they call out. His explanation is that for eight years he hosted his own white-rights TV show on a local cable network.

We fetch up at his house, in a quiet neighbourhood. Cool dark trees shadow our approach. The building seems almost shy, nestling down a side track, cottage style. Very English. A bit like Nick Griffin's place, in fact. 'Hi, very pleased to meet you,' his wife says. The kids just ignore me, but not in an unpleasant way. His twin girls, both blonde, play with a puppy. Ron kisses his wife affectionately, then cracks a joke with his son.

'Here, perhaps you'd like to take a look at this,' Ron says, searching in a small cupboard beneath the TV set and fishing out a videocassette. Hundreds of white faces crowd the screen. Ron is there, next to David Duke, protesting a boycott by African Americans in a local shopping mall. Fascinated, I sit down slowly in a rocking chair. Ron appears at my side again, handing out the family photo album, showing me pictures of his kids and of himself as a football coach for the local youth team ('I coach coloured kids, too'). He flashes a proud smile, and I notice that a few of his front teeth look as if they've been fixed.

We head into town. Ron is talkative and interested in my background. As we chat away, I gaze at the old Confederate statues and buildings. He asks me about my own life and my fiancée, and advises me to hurry up and get married. 'Best thing I ever did,' he quips. 'You can bring your new wife out here. You'd be very welcome.' It becomes clear to me he has a traditional view of women: he expects his wife to bear his sons and daughters and remain at home.

'What do you want to eat?' he growls, as we power down a long, straight freeway. First, we head into the town centre proper, past the scraping tower blocks and faded Confederate glory. It seems a little tired and dirty here. Ron takes me to a British pub, called The Penny Lane (run by a couple from Liverpool), but it's closed. I stand for a moment on the cracked sidewalk, flashing back to all the cities I've seen. 'C'mon, let's try somewhere else.' Out in one of the anonymous suburbs, we choose a nameless steak house. 'It's steak, and you can't go much wrong with that!' I joke with him that beef is a rare commodity for me, after all the BSE and foot-and-mouth scares in England. 'I bet!' he laughs. I choose something suitably bloody, with sweet potatoes, washed down with sugared iced tea. The cold air chills my exposed skin.

Ron says he works outside, as a tree surgeon. It's a job he loves, although he complains of some back twinges now and then. That explains the trunk-like arms and barrel chest. I ask him to tell me more about himself. 'Well, I'll give the biog. Thirty-nine years old. Married with four children. Born in Richmond, Virginia, and lived out here all my life. I'm certainly more politically active now than I've been in most of my life. But I've been active to preserve this race and our cause for, I guess, if you wanted to pinpoint it, since I was 14.'

We're interrupted by a waitress going through the usual half a page of instructions for side orders, and I lose my way with the questions.

'Okay, what is it you want to happen then, Ron?'

'Well, rather than asking our political leaders for change, we need to replace our political leaders.'

'Why?'

'They're promoting culturalism, diversity, internationalism, everything we oppose. For us just to go up and protest isn't enough. We have to replace them, and their ideology.' Something in Ron's persuasive manner has me thinking this sounds pretty normal. Clearly, he could be a dangerous force on the political scene.

He takes a few calls from his friends on the mobile. Later, they'll join us. I ask him about his main beliefs. He talks about preserving America as a 'white country'.

'Y'know, Europeans founded this country, created this country, and I believe the only way to maintain it is by our racial stock. If Americans are replaced by Mexicans, Haitians, or whatever Third World country we're talking about, then America will cease to exist as we know it and love it. I love my country, I love our culture, our heritage and our uniqueness, and I want that preserved.'

The building is large and cavernous around us. The constant hum of fans, kitchen clatter and drawl of passing waitresses make it hard to hear.

'America's more than an idea; it's a people.' Even though, as I suggest, America was formed by assimilation. 'But they assimilated a lot easier when it was all Europeans,' he suggests. Now people are 'vastly different'.

'If you have a place, a sense of community, a home, you want to keep that for the next generation, your children, your grandchildren. That may not be possible, because the demographics of the country might be changing. If I wanted my kids to grow up in Mexico, I'd move to Mexico. Instead, these places are coming here, and they're changing our country.'

Ron claims the Hispanics are 'balkanising' the US, overtaking blacks. He complains about Spanish language on cash machines and Spanish radio stations. 'Here in Richmond, until 15 years ago – when you had maybe a Mexican restaurant owned by one family – you didn't see Hispanics. And now where I work is majority Hispanic. So we're talking drastic changes in a very small amount of time.' He says he feels closer to a Bosnian Muslim refugee he knows – because he's 'white' – than to the Hispanics.

Eerily echoing my first fateful meeting with Charlie Sargent, Ron complains that his daughters are having to learn about other people's cultures at school. It's been a media invention, he contends, not to be proud of your race. 'You're attacked as a hater, prejudiced, racist, all sorts of negative terms. Everything in society is geared towards you not having these feelings. Yet people do have these feelings.'

I'm not sure what to make of this. I'm dealing with another guy who's been involved since his teens, when he picked up Duke's Klan newspaper. A guy who later joined the White Patriot Party, then the National Alliance, then Duke's organisation again. So I should be wary. My questions about his political origins lead him to the Klan: 'The problem with the Klan, and the reason it will never be successful, is that anyone can start one. You can get kicked out of one group, and simply start your own under a new name. So you have a lot of bad apples in there. That was something I learned.'

We tuck into our steaks. Blood and juice drip down the front of my shirt. Ron clearly holds Duke in high regard. 'He's an extremely intelligent man. Extremely intelligent. Very polite, very courageous. I've been in situations with him that were a cause for concern. He's very dedicated to his convictions; he lives these convictions. So I admire that about him. I'm kinda like that myself. Not to the rhetoric about "dying for the cause"; we wanna live for the cause. Because I've invested in the future, with four children.' Predictably, he doesn't believe the allegations levelled against Duke.

Ron looks up as a tall, ungainly guy wanders towards us. 'Hey Ron,' he calls out. Ron introduces me to Walter. He has a schoolboy face, with wide, surprised-looking eyes floating behind thick square specs. He seats himself next to Ron. 'Oh, hey,' he greets me, uncertainly, then falls silent. After a while, as Ron talks again about families (and my lack of one), Walter tells me: 'I have a little girl, she was prematurely born, that I'm looking after with my wife . . . I'm actually a house husband, I guess you could call it.'

We drive back into town, down the famous Monument Avenue with its statues of Confederate generals, back to The Penny Lane pub. I sink a pint or three of Guinness, as I hear about the 'perils' facing 'our people'. There's much talk of the balkanisation of the US and the potential for racial conflict. I tell Ron I've heard a great deal of talk of neo-Confederacy as a movement. He thinks this is misguided, foolish even: 'Ten years ago, maybe, I might have felt like that. About Yankees, like we call 'em down here. But they're all white at the end of the day, and we've got to unite against the blacks, Hispanics, and Asians.'

'Too right!' chimes Walter.

'Is there no political route out of this?' I ask.

'If Buchanan hadda been really serious,' he says, 'I would have voted for him. But that black woman he chose, she lost my vote, I'm afraid.'

We're soon joined by another of Ron's crowd, an intense guy called Travis, young and powerfully built, with tattoos encircling his upper arms, just concealed by shirt sleeves. It turns out he's an ex-skin, from the white-power scene. 'I've been friends with Ron for years,' he says. 'Yeah, we go way back, you and I, don't we?' Ron laughs. Travis's gaze makes me uncomfortable, as I speak to the other two. He makes a habit of locking his eyes onto mine. I feel he's judging me. There's a sense of déjà vu that takes me back to my days in The Princess Louise.

Travis says he's been a close friend of several white-power band members, and tells me about the scene in the States. To a man, they also claim to admire Mark Cotterill and the BNP's example in creating what they call a viable political party. Ron says he's going to use this as a template to create community, race-based politics in Virginia. 'We'll try and take seats on local school boards, then in county elections, and after that aim for the state legislatures.'

With the Guinness flowing and a Beatles cover band drifting in the background, I find myself slowly relaxing. They seem like pleasant, keen family men. I point out to Ron that this must make him feel different to most of the men I've met, half of whom can't even get a woman, let alone procreate. He smiles ruefully.

With his laid-back manner, Ron is exactly the sort of down-to-earth, working-class white man many conservative people would probably vote for. He doesn't sound extreme at all. But he can't understand national (as opposed to racial) dynamics, as easily as a European can. For example, why are whites fighting each other over religion in Northern Ireland? Race not nation, as Charlie Sargent had said.

In his calm, gentle manner, Ron says all he wants to do is make sure that 'white Americans and European Americans can celebrate their history and identity, just as the blacks and Hispanics can'. He recently set up a heritage day for Americans of European descent. It was very nearly adopted by the state governor, too, until he discovered who was behind it.

We polish off the afternoon looking at more pictures of their kids. Even Travis has a couple. I bid goodbye to them on friendly terms. Back in Ron's car, wondering whether I should go back to my hotel, I spot a flyer on the dashboard advertising a Klan barbecue – this evening! The Knights of the Fiery Cross. 'I'm not really bothered about going to this thing,' says Ron. 'But if you really want, I'll take you out there to see it.' I gulp nervously and answer yes. I'm going to stick out like a sore thumb, but I can't turn down this opportunity. I commit myself before I have time to pull out. Ron says he joined the KKK when he was 17, but left when it became apparent it was a joke, no longer a real force, a remnant movement for 'white trash' full of hate – those not wanting a real political solution. 'But some people still wanna follow that way,' he shrugs.

We drive down through Richmond's poorer black areas, the dilapidated houses reminiscent of movie scenes from the South. People sitting out on the steps. Cracking paint clinging to old boards. Few faces glance up at the passing of this cheap Japanese car. Once out of this area, the same faceless suburbs start creeping up, the homogenised malls and commercial outlets a signature of modern America.

We drive for ages. We stop at a convenience store, grabbing donuts and a drink, then hit the road again. It starts raining hard, fat drops cracking against the windscreen. Dusk approaches, then night falls. The beams of the headlights pick out hundreds of frogs leaping around the road, through the trees and undergrowth, dropping from the verdant boughs above us, squishing beneath our tyres. Finally, after many twists and turns, we find ourselves on a backwoods track. It's pitch black and silent. Eventually Ron finds the right turn-off and, after a minute's slow crawl, we pull into a small field.

A youth wearing a white Adolf Hitler T-shirt appears out of the inky background. He has some kind of walkie-talkie headset. He speaks briefly with Ron, then waves us through. We drive slowly over the wet grass, past a huge bonfire, then stop again. A drunk biker leans against Ron's door.

'Hey, how you doin' Ronnie, Mr Doggett?' he exclaims. His speech is slurred. Dozens of tattoos line his powerful arms and a bandana covers thinning hair. 'It's rilly good to see ya, did'n think you'd be comin' tonight.' He slips against the side of the car, belches and apologises. It's clear Ron is considered a celebrity guest. Ron gives me an embarrassed look, which I can just make out through the flickering gloom, and shrugs.

We leave the car and walk past a shack on low stilts. I nearly bump into a stack of tyres set against one wall. The thin beams of a spotlight pick out children and dogs running about in the gloom. Rifles lie next to corrugated iron. ZZ Top blares across the darkened fields.

Figures loom – people sitting on steps, wandering past, hollering – as we're ushered into the area where the barbecue is taking place. It's relatively empty; either people have left or they've failed to turn up. Many of those remaining are hardcore bikers, Hell's Angels types with beards, tattoos and guns, stripped to the waist and far gone on drugs. A wiry old fellow, clad only in shorts and wearing a Confederate bandana around his long hair, seems to be in charge. He and Ron greet each other like old friends. Backs are slapped, drunken platitudes are thrown around.

I busy myself with the food decked out on long trestle tables. Ron simply says: 'This is Nick, he's a friend from England.' I can't hide for long, though. A hippie-like woman in her 50s takes a shine to me and starts chatting away. She says she comes from California and is a nursing assistant. 'I look after this old lady.'

'Oh, really?' I answer politely.

I ask her how she finds life here, compared with California. 'You can't get good fruit out here in Virginia, not like back home,' she says. A dream-like grin is etched onto her wizened features, as she adds: 'I love your charming accent.' I squirm.

The drunken biker stumbles up, throws his arms around my shoulders and calls me 'bloke' in a mock Cockney accent. I stumble forwards. 'My mom said we came back from there, some fucking ancient time!' He's aggressive and laughs too hard, and his guttural words are peppered with 'fucking Jews' and 'fucking niggers'. 'Fuck 'em, we should wipe 'em out, they've got to go,' he says. Beer pours down his chin as he attempts to fill himself up from another can. I see Ron grimacing.

After nibbling some salad and hunks of beef, and stopping the main guy from electrocuting himself by connecting a power cord in the wet undergrowth, we make our excuses and leave. As we do so, the drunken biker stumbles up again and asks, 'When's old Duke comin' back, Ronnie? When? He's bin gone too long already.' Ron says probably in the autumn, although he later admits to me that he doesn't think he's coming back at all.

As we leave, Ron jokes, 'Maybe not all white folks should have kids!'

FOURTEEN

THE CHURCH

'Brother Ryan, so good to meet you after all this time!' The reedy, unctuous voice quivers as he struggles to pitch it lower. The grip on my hand remains surprisingly strong. Bony shoulders poke through the polyester suit jacket. His face is narrow and pockmarked, set in a regal pose. A rash sprouts from under the hairline. This is Matt Hale, Pontifex Maximus of the World Church of the Creator.

I've travelled from Washington to Illinois to track down the leadership of the Church, a bizarre neo-nazi network that claims 'your race is your religion'. In many ways, as I'm to discover, it's the poor man's National Alliance. Those who can't get into Pierce's outfit, which is relatively selective and charges hundreds of dollars a year for membership, often end up in secondary networks like the Church.

For months, Hale and I have been swapping emails about this meeting. I don't tell him that the real reason for my interest is the case of Ben Smith; Hale thinks I'm a sympathetic writer who simply wants to cover his meteoric rise. He's already sent out a circular email to his network about me, and my laptop has been deluged with messages from across the US and elsewhere.

There's one from Master Hardy. Another from 'Reverend Kenneth'. A Vietnam vet sends me long tracts about his life and beliefs. Several women contact me too, such as 'Sister Lisa' Turner, who leads the WCOTC Women's Frontier, based on the West Coast. Rumour has it that she is, or was, supposed to be coming to live with Hale at some point. I get one message from a lady with the monicker Babylon Liberation Front, with whom I remain in contact. Then there's Elite Eugenics, a woman who thinks I'm the documentary maker Nick Broomfield. A lady called Serpentis offers her husband – 'a VERY prominent National Socialist' – for interview.

Until 1999 the Church was simply another crazy-sounding sect. Then Benjamin Nathaniel Smith, a bright young criminology student, spent his Fourth of July weekend on a murderous killing spree, before turning his gun on himself. He killed a black man and an Asian man, and wounded nine others. He had deliberately visited ethnic and Jewish religious centres across Illinois and Indiana, choosing his target areas carefully before letting loose. Reading about Smith reminds me uncomfortably of David Copeland, the London nailbomber.

Smith was, or should have been, an all-American success story. He went to a top school and came from a privileged background. His parents were eminently respectable. Yet for more than a year he was a key leader of the WCOTC. He was also a close friend of Matt Hale. Since the killings, Hale's profile in the US has gone stratospheric.

* * *

In Chicago I'm staying with friends, part of the network. The intensity of spending so much time with Mark Cotterill & Co. has been getting to me.

Before I left DC, Fisheye invited me to his house. I met his wife (his fifth) – a nice, mousey-haired lady, who definitely didn't share his views and who called Mark 'a snake' – whilst being shown around the place. Fisheye's study was crammed with military memorabilia, Irish and Celtic images, and pieces of ancient and modern weaponry. They seemed a normal enough couple, except for all of Ed's extremist stuff. I saw fading pictures of him in his Nazi uniform. He told me about an English couple they'd met on a trip to Ireland, whom they'd visited back in the UK. 'A great couple,' Fisheye had said. 'Except the guy votes for Tony Blair, of course.' Like Ron, Fisheye had felt like another potential friend. I tried to see if I could talk him around to any kind of common sense. After all, he'd suggested, the politics hadn't gone down too well in his previous relationships. I felt sad, in a way, to be leaving.

Two figures greet me: one stocky, with dark stubble, glasses and an earnest expression; the other shorter, youthful, with flame tattoos around his ankles. Devin Burghart and Justin Massa, of the Center for New Community. We quickly swap welcomes and move out in Devin's car.

Perched on the wind-swept shores of Lake Michigan, Chicago seems to be a sea of striding spires. A myriad of modern blocks tower over the skyline. In the centre we pass fountains and the wonderfully Gothic main library, then drive under – and through – a huge, Soviet-like postal building. Along the freeway we travel down – following the famous El train, clattering high and rickety above us, towards the small building that houses the Center. Its Building Democracy Initiative monitors far-right groups in over ten states. Devin tells me he and Nick Lowles are good pals, brought together by someone who sounds like a one-man army, Leonard Zeskind. Lenny, as he's known, has been fighting extremism over here since before most of us can remember and is described in near-mythic terms by those I encounter. He's a former steel worker with a penchant for speaking his mind in the most forthright terms. Sadly, we never meet, but his influence is felt everywhere I travel.

The drive takes maybe half an hour. Hot, dry air blasts into the back of the car. I tilt my face forwards, tasting a new city again, my hair forced through the funnel of the open window. Vast, multi-laned highways stretch out on either side of us. The low roar of landing aircraft carves through the background, rumbling between the punk tracks thundering from Devin's MP3 stereo.

The Center is tucked away within the neat brick of suburban construction. Inside the low building, a small warren of rooms hides the work of half a dozen people led by Pastor Dave Ostendorf. We drink Cokes and chat about my recent experiences. My mouth is dry with excitement, recounting events. I must sound like a motorhead; thoughts running a thousand miles an hour, tongue struggling to catch up. I sway, dizzy with relief, then sit and let others talk.

'The problem's definitely growing,' admits Devin. 'Mainly in that they're using the theme of immigration to widen their appeal.'

'You basically have the subculturalists versus the mainstream white nationalists, who are political in their aims,' adds Justin. 'Aryan nationalists versus middle American white nationalists.'

They explain how the Cold War helped Americans to differentiate themselves, but that's gone now. Now America has begun turning inwards and the very idea of the American nation is up for grabs. 'Alienation is a huge problem, and white nationalists offer an easy answer,' explains Devin. 'These white nationalists, as they like to call themselves, offer a demographic slice of white male America.'

We joke about my experiences with Mark and the others, of how junk science permeates the lives of the Holocaust deniers and race eugenicists. 'If you want to kind of summarise their beliefs here,' says Devin, 'then the overall view among these white nationalists and radicals is that you have a Jewish elite at the top, and hordes of multicultural masses below. They claim the white man is trapped between these forces.'

Justin leaps up, over the thin carpet to the small office where his PC is located. 'Here, take a look at this,' he calls out. I watch over his shoulder as he clicks through a dozen or more sites, all linked to white-power bands. 'That's the kind of thing we have to tackle here, too.' He tells me he's been instrumental in creating a Turn It Down music and web-based initiative, to combat the spread of hate through music.

After tasting my first Chicago pizza, a huge wedge of dough stuffed with filling and smothered with a thick carpet of chopped tomatoes, we head back down the freeway to where Justin lives. I take a space on the couch, in a large apartment set within an even larger house on a quiet, sun-dappled road. Flaking strips of paint lift from the wooden window frames. Homages to the punk band the Dead Kennedys litter the place. I throw up dust as I slide over polished floorboards. Two other guys share with Justin; all seem to have tattoos and to form part of Chicago's burgeoning anti-capitalist punk scene. Justin and Devin are both involved, Justin as a radio DJ, running his station through the PC in a chaotic bedroom, Devin as a bass player. Both know quite a bit about the white-power music business.

In this area, the National Alliance has been able to grow – whilst other hardcore groups have declined – because of Pierce's financial muscle and sharp investments. 'Pierce is the mover and shaker in the youth scene now,' says Devin.

It's only a few days since state police shot and killed prominent local NA member Eric Hanson, following a near 14-hour stand-off in the town of Lindenhurst. The incident began when plain-clothes officers approached Hanson as he sat in his car outside his home. When they tried to arrest him for weapons violations, he fled to a fine foods store, where he opened fire. One policeman was hit in the neck and thigh, another in his bulletproof vest. From the store Hanson let forth a further volley, then ordered everyone out and hid in a meat locker. At seven the next morning, a police tactical weapons team broke in and, in the ensuing gun battle, Hanson was fatally wounded.

Hanson was a white-power skinhead, a former Marine, and an active member of the National Alliance. Recently he'd been leafleting at an anti-immigrant rally and a public meeting of my next quarry, the World Church of the Creator.

Like many ardent white nationalists, he didn't support just one group. He'd attended a Klan rally in Skokie, Illinois, in December 2000 but instead of standing behind the barricades with the National Alliance and American Knights, he walked through the throng of protesters wearing a Star of David T-shirt with a circle and a slash through it. After the rally, according to eyewitnesses, he attacked an African-American woman, then fled before police arrived.

In April 1999, Hanson was convicted of a hate crime and assault, stemming from an incident in which he harassed a mixed-race couple outside a supermarket. Testifying before the jury, he said: 'Whites and blacks should be separate. It made me upset to see them together.' He spent a year in prison, extended by 364 additional days when he was convicted on weapons charges.

National Alliance members memorialised Hanson in a barrage of emails, writing, 'Make no mistake about it, this is how they are waging their war and Eric was an intended casualty . . . He joins the growing number of brave warriors in the Record of Martyrs,' and, 'We are patriots, not terrorists, but rest assured. Eric will be avenged!'

'Yep, another of your hardcore warriors,' sighs Devin, as I flick through the reports.

Only a day or so later, we're reading of another worrying development. The Boston courts have just indicted an infamous neo-nazi and his girlfriend after they threatened a bombing campaign against Jewish targets. According to the reports, Leo Felton, 30, and Erica Chase, 21, wanted to incite a 'racial holy war' with their attacks. A search in their apartment (after they'd been arrested trying to use a counterfeit $20 bill) revealed notes on bomb-making and detailed pictures of the Leonard P. Zakim Bunker Hill Bridge, named after the former director of the Anti-Defamation League's Boston office. A calendar was circled on 20 April, Hitler's birthday, and a number of books on terrorism and subterfuge were recovered. Most worrying were newspaper clippings about a planned remembrance service at the New England Holocaust Memorial.

Also, Felton had written that he contemplated gunning down blacks in New York City. He'd recently purchased materials that could be used to construct bombs, including a 50-lb bag of ammonium nitrate and a coffee maker, from which he'd removed the heating and timing mechanisms.

The most surprising thing was that this 6 ft 7 in., heavily tattooed figure was of mixed race. He hadn't spoken to his estranged black father for years, and had already served over a decade for attempting to murder a black New York City taxi driver with a crowbar. While serving this sentence, he'd tried to slit the throats of two black inmates. His array of neo-nazi and white supremacist tattoos included references to the White Order of Thule and other groups.

Chase, whose body also bore various white supremacist tattoos, was a member of the WCOTC and of an Indiana chapter of the Outlaw Hammerskins. She'd been writing to Felton whilst he was in prison. Such outreach work, I discovered, is one of the roles carried out by The Sisterhood, the arm of the WCOTC headed by Lisa Turner.

Back at the Center, preparing now for my trip to the small town of East Peoria, where Matt Hale is based, we talked more on the influence of neo-nazi ideologues.

'The case of Hendrik Möbus was pretty interesting, if you want to look at how Pierce is reaching into the international music business, getting his claws into the young in various countries.' Devin's voice is low, certain, speaking with the authority of experience. Both guys have worked undercover or been on the receiving end of violence. They shrug, stoically, when I ask about it. 'Möbus shows that Pierce was making a play into the black metal scene. Music that he himself says that he can't stand – he's a classical music and polka lover – but which he knows is going to give him purchase with a certain amount of the youth out there.'

Möbus was arrested at the end of last August, in a town near Pierce's compound (where he'd been hiding), after US Marshals tracked him for nearly two months. But he'd been on the run well before that, beginning his tour of the American racist underground nine months earlier and more than 4,000 km from where he was finally cornered. Although there was an international arrest warrant out for him, Möbus flew into Seattle-Tacoma International Airport using his real name in December 1999. He then travelled to National Alliance headquarters via Ohio, Virginia and many points in between.

His travels included stays at the White Order of Thule, a small, esoteric neo-nazi group that draws inspiration from everyone from Savitri Devi to Nietzsche to George Lincoln Rockwell, based in Richmond, where I'd just been. After a short stay in the Seattle area in December 1999, Möbus went across the mountains to stay in Elk, Washington, north of Spokane, where he lived with Nathan Pett (a.k.a. Nate Zorn), head of the White Order of Thule and publisher of a photocopied fanzine called *Fenris Wolf*, described as 'the Revolutionary Voice of the Pagan Liberation League'. The publication is a crude attempt at melding arcane nazi ideas with the white-power skinhead scene. Pett had affiliated *Fenris Wolf* to the Pagan Front, an international coalition of organisations, record labels, bands, fanzines and individuals dedicated to promoting the neo-nazi black metal underground. Until he became a fugitive, the Pagan Front was led by Möbus.

Pierce described Möbus as 'a young German musician who has made a name for himself with resistance music in Europe' and used his time with him to secure entry into the black metal scene. 'I invited him to stay as my guest and help me establish new outlets in Europe for my records,' explained Pierce in one of his publications. 'And that's what he did for ten weeks. He stayed as my guest, and we talked about the role of music in our overall effort.' One of the developments to come out of the pairing has been the new role the National Alliance is playing in Cymophane Records – an American/Swedish black metal label with access to mainstream distribution channels in the US.

Möbus's nazi career had started early, while he was still at school in Erfurt, East Germany. At the age of 16 he and two classmates formed a death metal band, Absurd, which soon became famous for its actions rather than its music. On 29 April 1993, Möbus and two cohorts brutally killed Sandro Beyer, a classmate, whom they have since called a '*Volksschadling*', which roughly translates as 'race defiler'. In January 1994 the three were found guilty of murder and several other charges, and Möbus received an eight-year sentence. While the band members were serving their time, a member of the Polish neo-nazi black metal band Graveland released Absurd's demo tape, Thuringian Pagan Madness. It helped propel the group to fame within the scene. A flattering interview in the book *Lords of Chaos* also contributed to their notoriety, and Absurd has become a cornerstone of this turgid, twisted subculture.

Released on parole in August 1998, Möbus issued a public statement announcing that Beyer's murder had not been a crime. Apparently, he did not fit the 'picture' of the German race. Möbus ran foul of German law again in October that year, charged with displaying Nazi symbols.

* * *

East Peoria is a working-class town, a small blot on the map about three hours south of Chicago, famous for its Caterpillar construction plant. And that's about it. Devin's agreed to come with me, for which I'm grateful. Though I don't expect any major trouble – Hale wants to use me as a proselytising tool, a way of telling people, 'Hey look, someone important is writing about us' – I've learned that his motley network has been linked to several dangerous neo-nazis.

As the farmland rolls past, spreading all the way to the horizon, I ask Devin to tell me more about the Ben Smith case. Were there any clues to his behaviour? 'Talking with teachers and former classmates, they've said that aside from being somewhat emotionally distant, quiet, and slightly withdrawn, Smith was, to all intents and purposes, normal,' Devin replies.

Smith was an average student at a highly competitive private school. On the day of the shooting, his friend Matt Hale had lost a well-publicised appeal to gain a law licence in Illinois. 'It was the final straw for Smith,' says Devin. 'At least it appears that way. At that point, the 21-year-old criminology undergraduate decided that the "Jewish-run" system had gone too far, and that he needed to lash back.' He took time to gather up weapons and ammunition and got some things in order, such as removing items from a storage locker he shared with Hale. 'And then he began the shootings.'

They weren't random, but took place in areas he was familiar with, where he knew there would be Jews or people of colour. He picked his targets as they presented themselves, then simply shot at them. He started on Friday, 2 July, at dusk, choosing a location near a synagogue in Rogers Park, and shooting at a crowd of Orthodox Jews, injuring six. He then drove north to Skokie and came across Ricky Byrdsong, a black former basketball coach, walking with his young children. Smith shot and killed him, from the window of his blue Ford Taurus. 'He'd just drive up and shoot people,' Devin says.

Driving further north, he shot at – and missed – an Asian-American couple out for a walk. From there, he turned and journeyed downstate, through a string of small cities, ending up in the state capital of Springfield, shooting at (and also missing) two black men. In Decatur he injured a priest, and in another town he wounded a university student.

Heading across state now, to Bloomington, Indiana, Smith fatally wounded Won Joon Yoon, a Korean American graduate student, coming out of church. It was Sunday, 4 July, exactly one year since he'd first distributed WCOTC literature in the same place.

'After that, the law enforcement hunt was pretty intense,' says Devin, gazing out the lowered window at a series of water towers. They seem to march slowly, solemnly past, even though we're powering at top speed. 'They examined the pattern of the killings.'

'Did the Center help?'

'After the first day, we were able to speculate that it was Ben Smith, and that's who we notified to the law enforcement people.'

'How come?'

'Because of the locations, the events, because of the description of car, because of the cities chosen. It fitted the pattern perfectly.'

'But how did you hear about it?' I shout over the engine and the air blasting through the windows.

'We heard about the shootings on the radio. The first place, the synagogue, was not too far from where I was living. We went into an emergency mode, trying to figure out who it might be. Given that the targets were racially or religiously motivated, we suspected it was someone we were familiar with.'

By Saturday afternoon, they were sure it was Smith. It ended on the Sunday. He'd driven back into Illinois, where the police ran his car off the road, and taken his own life. 'It took him four shots to kill himself. Of course, Hale will tell you that it was the cops who actually killed him.' It was because he was such a poor shot that so few people were actually killed. It certainly struck fear into the Jewish community, as did the incident in LA (where ex-Aryan Nations security man, and mental patient, Buford Furrow shot up a Jewish day care centre). 'There was international attention brought to bear on these organisations; there was a media frenzy, both for Hale as well as us.'

Unlike the NSM in Britain after the Copeland attacks, when everyone had gone to ground, Hale seemed to revel in the attention. 'Absolutely,' agrees Devin, over the noise of a passing monster-sized rig. 'They were celebrating it. He made sure that he was on television – and anyone else he could convince – as much as possible. He was plugging his website and his organisation all the time.'

I ask Devin to tell me more about the WCOTC. He says they see it fairly regularly, and do a lot of community work to contain its influence. 'He's got probably around 300–350 members at the most, although he would claim thousands. It was around 200 at the time of the shooting.' He thinks the Church indirectly helps Pierce, by weeding out more of the losers from the scene. Even many of the 'brothers' in the Church itself joke about the Pontifex, apparently. 'They just don't take him seriously.'

In its heyday in the late 1980s/early 1990s, the Church was run by an infamous extremist named Ben Klassen, a Ukrainian immigrant who'd once been in the Florida state legislature. He'd founded the Church of the Creator, as it was known then, in the late 1970s. It was he who coined phrases like 'RAHOWA' (calling for racial holy war), as well as putting together books like *The White Man's Bible*. But it wasn't taken seriously until skinheads started latching on. It was easy to understand: your race is your religion. A black Gulf War veteran was shot by WCOTC members in Florida in 1991. Soon after, it was penetrated by FBI informants, and that – along with being sued by the Southern Poverty Law Center – led to Klassen killing himself in 1993.

There was no successor, and it fell into Hale's lap in 1995. No one else wanted it. 'He kinda latched onto it. It's still kind of a mystery,' says Devin.

'Does he have much on-the-ground presence in areas like Chicago?'

Hale is, to some extent, a virtual presence, remarks Devin. But Chicago does have four or five skinhead crews, like the White War Commission, or the Steel Front – all Polish and linked to WCOTC. There's been a strong skin scene since the early 1980s, often used as a proving ground for potential leaders of the wider white nationalist movement.

Eric Owens is a good example of this, Devin tells me. Owens started as a skin in California, then at some point picked up an acoustic guitar and started performing folk songs with a Nazi bent. He travelled worldwide with this music and formed his own organisation. Now he's an assistant editor at the IHR and became a California delegate for the Reform Party. He acts as a bridge between the skin scene and adults, and is another link to Pat Buchanan.

Others may go to the National Alliance, if they want 'vanguard' status, or the Hammerskins, if interested more in the 'cultural' scene of nazi music. 'Generally, if they don't filter off at a young age, they tend to stay and get deeply involved.' By this time, it's a self-fulfilling prophecy; your other friends and family have probably cut you off. 'And so you turn to where you're most comfortable.' It's never a full substitute, though. 'Many are still looking for something else. Even if it is a kind of a tribe, it's an incomplete one.'

* * *

As we near Peoria I listen to a tape of Matt Hale, recorded from one of his radio speeches, telling us how Ben Smith was a martyr.

There's little to see in the town itself. A small river, a bridge, one main street, a train track, a wooded hill. Then a tiny civic hall, a shopping mall, a couple of chain restaurants. Checking into our motel, we have to be careful. Hale is an avowed enemy of the Center, and he could have spotters out to look for us. He's insisted on knowing where I'm staying, and for me to contact him constantly when nearby.

Devin shuts himself in the room. I swallow hard and take a taxi the short way up the hill to Hale's house. The sky swirls grey above. We plough through a quiet neighbourhood, not rich but comfortable-looking. My taxi driver is a woman, chatting to me about the area and asking about England. Hale's house appears as a wooden, two-storey affair with grey shingles and a veranda. There's a black iron eagle bolted onto the front door. My leg trembles slightly as I leave the car. I set my city mask in place, walk up the drive and ring the bell.

I hear distant shuffling behind the plywood and the thin mesh outer screen. 'Brother Ryan, so good to meet you after all this time!' A gangly, thin man with a rash-eaten face appears at a side door. I have to double back towards the garage. He's formally dressed, in a faded shirt and cheap-looking slacks. He smiles and we shake hands. Someone else, whom I take to be a follower – a big plump chap, with a downy beard, presumably here for security – greets me quietly, with a mouse's whisper of a voice. 'Shane,' he pipes, just loud enough for me to hear. He shakes my hand, softly, then walks up the steps to the porch, clutching a clunky tape recorder. Them recording me, me recording them. Another bizarre experience to notch on the bedpost of life.

'Please, please,' Hale sweeps his arm imperially towards a seat perched at one end of the porch. I look down. The chair has been ripped out of a car, like all the seats on the veranda. Who is this guy? What makes him tick? He seems a strange, creepy fellow. A joker or nutter, perhaps. Except that his network includes a few people willing to kill. I sigh. Oh well, better get on with it.

'What should I call you? Matt?'

'The Reverend Hale, thank you,' he answers, formally.

'Oh, okay . . .'

'So, what do you want to know?' he smiles, eyes fixed unblinkingly on mine. One of them seems infected; there's a spot on the lid. The pupils, though, are what get me. There's something distant and cold there. Utterly, inconsequentially normal – a nerdy geek of a figure in some ways – and vaguely terrifying too.

'Well, what do people normally ask you about?' My accent sounds loud, English, out of place.

'Oh, they ask me about what motivates me, why I do what I do, uh, what do we seek to accomplish, how we go about it, that kind of thing.' He's attempting to be presidential, magisterial, speaking slowly. The language of the moderate, cloaking a barely fettered ego.

'We have a very deep belief system,' he bows his head, hands clasped together, to lend gravitas. 'This isn't politics. It's religion. That's very deep. A lot of people respect us, certainly in the white racist loyalist community. Some people feel we're a bit extreme,' he adds, almost as an afterthought. 'That's okay. As I like to say, today's extremist is, ah, tomorrow's moderate.' His face is set into a comically serious pose.

He claims they may field political candidates in the future, but are first trying 'to win the propaganda war'. He vilifies the media for its hostility. I can hear birds chattering away. Apart from them, and us, it's pretty quiet around here.

'We're unique, because we don't accept Jewish Christianity. Jesus Christ is a myth, for one thing. He never even existed.' This belief would chime well with William Pierce, but harshly with the next leg of my trip. Hale says they have their own scriptures. 'We have 13 or 14 books, and we're very public in what we want. We don't hide anything. We don't say we believe in equal rights for all, because we don't.' He chuckles quietly, looking at the other guy, who smiles back.

'What are the core beliefs, then?'

'It's a holy duty of all people to ensure the existence of the white race on this planet. That's our first command. And that really says it all. We have a duty,' he emphasises, 'to our own kind.' There doesn't seem much else apart from this, despite all the other rhetoric.

He starts on a roll. 'We're not meant to race mix. We're not meant to integrate.' The birds chatter away. I'm betting this is an all-white neighbourhood. Hale claims his 'observation of nature' has taught him this, that you don't get 'mixed' animals, just pure creatures, and that being territorial is simply a reflection of how many animals, even of the same species, are natural enemies. I'm hearing a speech, not an answer. 'And this earth is finite. Other races are irrelevant.'

How people would laugh, back in London, to hear this. I notice that I can lead Hale on, depending on what I mention. With the phrase 'the environment', he starts down another path, how 'actually, the environment is very important to us, and another thing that makes us unique . . .'

I observe that the Industrial Revolution has created tremendous problems, such as greenhouse gases, and we, the white race, are responsible. 'Certainly,' he begins, smoothly pushing aside my argument, 'the white race has been responsible for some problems. But it's still our people.'

'So why don't more people believe like you?'

'Oh, it's probably the media.' He answers quickly, with certainty. 'Television. A marvellous invention, but used against us. When's the last time a reporter talked about white consciousness or pride? When's the last time there was a report that white people were more intelligent than blacks, which I think most people know? If we had control of the media for one week, I tell my members, if we had control, then most people would be racists.'

At the moment, Hale says he's busy filing an appeal against the Illinois Bar for refusing his law licence (the state Supreme Court has refused to hear the case). It's a big part of the Church's struggle, for some reason. More like his struggle. I hear a kid call out, somewhere in the background. Such an innocent-looking spot, this.

'As a matter of morals, I know that there are people who should be punished for things they've done against the white race. But we've got to use the law.' He then witters on for several minutes about the importance of his law licence. I switch off. Something about supporters coming from across the board, 'sending money here so that we can accomplish our dream'.

'What's the end goal?'

'Oh, gosh,' he says, like a child. 'To have a whiter and brighter world.'

The Church was one of the first neo-nazi groups to make good use of the web. In fact, I would say Hale is a virtual, surreal presence. He talks of other races 'withering on the vine', if only we withheld aid from them. But where would that leave impoverished 'white' nations like Russia? When I also mention that the populations of Africa and Latin America are soaring, despite AIDS, he replies – as though talking patiently to someone who's mentally impaired – 'Oh yes, we look on AIDS as a natural remedy to the flaunting of nature's laws.'

Like Buchanan and others, Hale believes the armed forces should be on the borders, to prevent any immigration. 'Instead of the Coastguards helping Haitians off the boats, they should be shooting them, in our opinion.' All the while, I maintain my calm demeanour, not sure whether I should be laughing at all this or taking it seriously. Perhaps in some way, ludicrous as he is, Matt Hale reflects some of the baser fears of today's modern, white America. Those who are afraid to lose, maybe, their all-white, European family history. 'My great-grandfather built this house in 1910,' he says, slapping the wooden railing beside him. 'He came from Germany. His wife was German as well.'

'In terms of propagation of the white race, then,' I ask – trying to appear innocent – 'are you by any chance married?' A goods train toots in the background.

'No, no,' he replies sheepishly, voice dipping down.

'Children?'

'No.'

An awful lot of men are involved; I ask him why. He waffles for quite a while about being 'tunnel-visioned'. Sounds like an excuse to me. He claims it's more difficult to find mates because of their work. I'd counter that it's because of who they are in the first place.

Hale was very much a nobody until Ben Smith came along and shot up that Fourth of July weekend. A loner, who spent his time in school creating fictitious white-power groups whilst others were playing football or socialising. Pierce and others have dismissed him, but he contends he's more approachable, and not simply a dumping ground for those who don't make the NA's grade.

'I used to pass out memorandums in class, about my beliefs,' he says.

'Er, not exactly the average teenage thing to do, is it Matt – sorry, Reverend?'

'Oh yeah, ah, you see, I never really was a teenager. I've never been drunk, never smoked marijuana. I was a very serious kid.'

He describes his progress through various small extreme-right groups, before rekindling the Church whilst studying politics and music ('I still play the violin . . . I'd like to see *Resistance* magazine offering Mozart CDs') at university, then attending law school. He claims his whole life was preparation for his involvement in this movement. I still don't understand how he became interested in all this, though. He says he was enquiring and sceptical as a child, and that he started reading history books when he was 11. 'All the people I was reading about were white men. These individuals were white men. And this did not coincide with what I'd been taught. In fact, I can tell you that when I became 12, it was then that I dedicated myself to the Cause, to the white race.' It was when he was 12 that he read *Mein Kampf*.

All this seems to mirror Ben Smith's upbringing: talking of his 'Jew teacher' who manipulated his mind with her talk of the evils of slavery, the Holocaust and the destruction of Native Americans.

Why was this sort of stuff so important to them at these young ages? I put this to Hale: 'You weren't exactly surrounded by hordes of Third World immigrants around here, were you?'

'No, no, I wasn't. I guess it just supplied me with a reason for why white people have been so successful. How else do you explain that the First World is white and the Third World brown or black?'

He claims a shadowy group of Church figures called the Elders assented to his ascension, in 1996. Devin says the Church was simply dead, and Hale revived it. Again, whilst others studied or dated, Hale spent all his free hours handing out fliers. His subsequent attempts to join the Bar and practise law were thwarted due to these beliefs, in Illinois and several other states. At each step of the way, the Center has opposed him.

Hale is clearly uncomfortable that I know he was married for a while to a 16-year-old girl, who left him. 'It's better left in the past,' he says. Perhaps she found something strange in the fact that he still lives with his father, a retired police officer. On the pretence of needing to use the toilet, I get myself invited into the house. His front room is a darkened study with cheap wood-panelled walls, dominated by a PC glowing on a desk. This is the hub of Hale's mainly Net-based empire. In the living room I see his old man doddering about the kitchen, watching daytime TV shows. Bowls of raw fruit and vegetables hint at the odd diet Hale follows (he doesn't eat cooked food). The house is like a sepia shrine, frozen in time. Black and white photographs clutter the shelves. The curtains are drawn, and fading wallpaper creates a muted, dull impression on the senses.

Hale is furious when I suggest that the break-up of his parents' marriage may have led him to the neo-nazi extremes. 'They always say that,' he snaps, referring to his opponents. 'I still see my mom. There's nothing wrong in my past.'

Another follower joins us outside, a tough guy with tattoos, a moustache and a tan, who claims he was into paganism 'and all that kind of shit' before joining the Church. Now, he says – eyes shining, speaking prophetically – he doesn't need that any more. He knows the answer; it's your race. 'I'm a white man, and I'm proud!'

Hale seems to have an ability to speak as though outside of himself, looking in. Almost like a scientist, a cold fish, not an orator or rhetorician, even when he tries to quote Nietzsche. He waves to the kids playing baseball on the drive opposite. It's a world removed from the C18 gangs and race violence of my own country. No front-line, trench warfare this. Others are encouraged to go and do that.

But Hale has been the cause of mass protests, even to the very front door of his house, because of his incessant stirring of racial tensions. As he himself makes clear, he doesn't overtly condone violence or put himself in the firing line. Clearly, as in the case of Ben Smith, there are plenty of cranks and crazies who will do this, as I see from the emails that pour in from Church members.

Hale denies any prior knowledge of Smith's intentions. It's a claim heavily disputed by Devin and Justin. To my eyes, at least, Hale seems fairly unemotional about a man supposed to have been his closest buddy. 'Hey, y'know, some of our members go the ultimate mile,' he says, with a shrug. Most of the time, he claims, this is simply handing out leaflets (often in secret) and proselytising. One member in New York was even a prominent local member of the Democratic Party, he says.

'Am I going to see you on the front line one day? Physically?'

'Ah, that's a good question,' he laughs. 'I think my cause is a little broader, y'know, but certainly I wouldn't be averse as far as that goes.' He thinks for a moment. 'That's a tough one to answer. I know how to shoot.' Does he want to be a general? 'That's not my plan, really.'

He gives me a copy of the *White Man's Bible* – actually, I have to pay for it – then drives me around town, to his old schools, the playing field where he learned baseball, the house his German grandfather built. He tells me of his frustrations living with his dad, and how he wants to get his law licence so he can move out.

'RAHOWA!' he bids me goodbye. With that, I slip into the motel and recount the escapade to Devin.

* * *

Back in Chicago, I continue to receive emails from Hale's network. Several more women get in touch, which is intriguing. And worrying. Devin, Justin and I talk more, particularly about Christian Identity, in preparation for the final leg of my US journey. How these churches in rural areas of the Midwest are often linked to the militia movement, one part of the ideological glue that holds together a disparate network of malcontents.

On my final night, the guys take me out to Al Capone's old speakeasy, The Green Mill. We party into the small hours to the sounds of a big band. Devin tells me to enjoy the drink here. 'You won't get any down in north-west Arkansas,' he points out. 'You know that's where they shot the film *Deliverance*, don't you?'

FIFTEEN

CONQUER WE MUST

END OF JUNE, 2001

I long for home. The others around me seem oblivious, business folk considering their deals, tapping on laptops, thinking perhaps of the family they'll miss for a day or two, this small plane simply an elegant taxi.

I'm heading back south, into the sultry, humid Ozark Mountains in Arkansas, Bill Clinton's state and one of the poorest in the US. There, I'll encounter the heart of an isolationist fringe, including hardcore militia members, anti-federalists, and someone with links to the bombs I narrowly missed in London.

Gone now is my quest to find the political movements. It's become clear that the US arena doesn't allow for a viable third party (even if the extreme right had enough support). Not yet. God knows what it'd be like if they had proportional representation here. Even the Greens are still tiny, and they outshone the Reform Party. But there are other networks, shifting below the surface, crossing states and national boundaries. Issues like neo-Confederacy, gun control and the supposed erosion of liberties unite the extremists.

Immigration would also be a definite rallying cause, if ever a political movement developed. The music scene, into which William Pierce seems to have sunk himself, has proved a powerful tool in tapping youth rebellion and rage. And ideologies which cross boundaries, from the simplistic racial platitudes of the World Church of the Creator to religious fundamentalism.

Chicago, Detroit, Memphis – blurring cities, different transit areas. An exhausting day finally ends at a tiny airport in the north-west corner of Arkansas. When I'd booked this flight back in England, I'd had to tell the travel agent the code for this place. She'd never heard of it.

Twisting rolling hills and forest accompany me on the drive to the regional capital of Harrison, home to Kingdom Identity Ministries, one of the most visible Christian Identity sects in America. It has a powerful outreach ministry that's extremely popular with white-power prison gangs such as the Aryan Brotherhood. It's also the main theological organ of the Identity movement, offering advanced doctrinal courses to adherents worldwide. Its leader, Mike Hallimore, is not an orator or pulpit leader himself, but he's at the spiritual and intellectual heart of the heretical sect.

Pastor Dave, back at the Center for New Community in Chicago, invited me into his office and handed me a copy of Kingdom Identity's coursework folder, the words 'American Theological Association' emblazoned in gold letters on its cover. 'We see Christian Identity as the theological glue that holds together the whole white-supremacist movement in the US,' he told me. 'From that point, it's very important, a key phenomenon. It's highly influential within the movement, and beyond it.' Race was central to its ideology. 'And that's why I don't think there's any innocence in this movement. Jews are the offspring of Satan, and coloured races are referred to as "mud people".'

For several months I'd been emailing a chap called Pete Peters, one of the main Identity ideologues and speakers, based in LaPorte, Colorado. His Scriptures for America ministry, infamous among civil rights groups, proselytised in the depressed rural Midwest and had links to the militia movement. I imagined meeting Peters would be a coup. Right at the last minute, he simply – and aggressively – replied: 'No!' This forced me to change plans; hence the visit to Arkansas where, in the end, I found something far more revealing about the bedrock of white nationalism.

Other prominent Identity figures included Dan Gayman in Missouri – 'one of the key people, or pastors, a local who's built a presence and been a force in the movement for some years' – and the elderly Richard Butler, who until recently headed the infamous Aryan Nations, which acted as a kind of crossroads organisation. Robert Matthews, of The Order, was a member for a while. Butler lost his compound in Idaho after being sued by the Southern Poverty Law Center, following an attack by his security guards on a passing motorist.

The leadership is now ageing, 'and a lot of people think that with the demise of the Aryan Nations in Idaho, this movement's now dead. And nothing's further from the truth,' said Dave, his voice dropping to an ominous, quiet tone. 'It's a movement that's strong in its ideological roots and influence, and will continue with leaders who are coming up through the ranks. It's an ideology that has survived, as you well know, for actually going on for about 160 years.'

* * *

I nudge the car through the long, narrow strip of Harrison's main street, past the pale neon dripping from the chain restaurants and malls. Undulating, quilted hills surround the valley. Originally a centre for Scots-Irish immigration, Harrison is now a magnet for white-supremacist movements. Nearby are the headquarters of one of the USA's main Klan leaders, Thom Robb, as well as the men behind the American Front, a group with ties to English extremist Troy Southgate, once of the ITP.

The phone number I call at a pre-arranged time corresponds to a Harrison code. But the gruff male voice at the other end simply patches me through to another line. Where this is, I don't know. Hallimore's voice comes on, distant, deep, pensive, measured. I imagine a large man, perhaps a lantern-jawed cowboy.

'Ah. Hello, Mr Ryan. Yes, well, I, uh, I'll come over to your hotel and depending on how I view things, we'll talk from there. You'll be alone, right?' Yes, I answer. 'Good. I don't usually do this kind of thing, talking to journalists, so I'm relying on your trust here.'

We've already swapped more than a dozen lengthy emails, one of them asking if I could find a good Christian English lady who might be willing to work and live with him. I'd noticed a similar ad, 'For White Christian Ladies', on his website.

The night is sweltering, hanging close over the idyllic, sweeping woodlands and dotted farms. My motel is situated near the end of town, a collection of concrete buildings on the side of a steep hill. I sit near the doors, gazing up at a lazily turning fan and through the window at the infrequent passing vehicles. My eyes follow a cream-coloured jeep swinging in fast through the car park, crunching to a halt in a slew of gravel and dirt. A figure gets out, too far away for me to distinguish.

A tall, broad-shouldered frame gradually emerges from the dusk, then strides into the lobby where I sit. A slight paunch hangs over his shiny leather belt. His slicked, greying hair gives him a distinguished look, as do the navy trousers and carefully pressed short-sleeved shirt, whose front pocket holds a meticulously placed gold pen.

Mike Hallimore is nervous – more nervous, it seems, even than I am. He coughs and clears his throat. His hands fiddle with a pair of glasses. I notice he's holding a large envelope stuffed with papers. 'Can I, uh, trust you?' he asks, his searching eyes lingering over mine. 'I've dealt with a journalist before, and she really cheated me.' Yes, I tell him. You can trust me. Just understand that I'm not here to write a PR piece for you. 'Well, okay. I just need to make sure you're not an agent for the ADL or something. I've got 62 acres out there, and I don't want the wrong kind of person seeing it.' He coughs, then falls silent. I smile, reassuringly. 'Er, should we talk here, then?' I suggest finding somewhere like a bar. He doesn't drink. But there's a coffee shop down the hill and across the freeway.

Inside, drinking lemonade, Hallimore starts telling me about himself, and about Christian Identity. 'Call me Mike,' he says. Then, as the elevator music pumps into the air around us, 'Do you understand the Two Seeds theory?' Perhaps I should, but I shake my head, glancing at the pensioners and others sitting nearby. 'We're Seedline,' he says. My face is blank.

Mike explains that this is 'traditional' Identity belief; that the Jews were actually created as Satan's children. Through a very selective reading of the Bible, Identity adherents have convinced themselves that the Jews are the enemy, the agents of Satan. Seedline believers take that one step further, and make a literal argument that the Serpent seduced and lay with Eve, producing these 'anti-Christ' offspring. 'The Jews hear not because they are not of God,' Mike quotes, self-satisfied.

The other main area of Identity belief is that the 'white man' is a true descendant of the tribes of Israel, and not the Jews. Unlike other races, we, the sons of Adam, have true souls and bodies – plus a 'spirit' which can be 'quickened'. 'We're trichotomous beings,' is how Mike puts it. We're supposed to take dominion over these other peoples, which he frequently calls 'the nigger races', claiming 'colonialism is their natural state'. I cough and mumble something suitably neutral. 'By white Christian government, of course,' Mike adds, reasonably. 'Slaves can be well treated, you know.' Mike and hundreds of other preachers and pseudo-scholars like him have produced documentary and Biblical evidence to support their claim and await the day when the Kingdom of God comes down to earth.

As a movement, he says, Identity traces its development to a British Empire creed called British Israelism, which was used to explain and justify the domination of the British around the world as a sign of their 'Israelite' heritage. It sounds pretty tortured to my ears. To Mike, he's simply 'putting on the mind of Christ, becoming no longer part of the world'. His strangely unlined face doesn't blink once in irony, so I guess he believes what he's saying.

I recall something Lenny Zeskind wrote: that although it's tempting to write off Identity and laugh at its expense, it's a heresy based on Biblical scriptures. Thus it's fairly complex to understand, particularly for an unbeliever like myself. According to Lenny, Identity is one of the most widespread ideologies in the white supremacy movement. Aryan Nations chief Richard Butler preached it for 30 years. Leaderless resistance strategist Louis Beam found solace in it while hiding from the FBI. And each summer a couple of thousand believers flock to campground retreats for baptisms, sports contests and invocations against satanic conspiracies.

Identity doctrine holds that the patriarch Jacob, known later as Israel, had 12 sons, among whom his favourite was Joseph. Joseph had two sons, Mannaseh and Ephraim. Jacob blessed Mannaseh, saying he shall become a great people, and Ephraim, saying 'his seed shall become a multitude of nations' (Genesis 48:19). Thus were born respectively the United States of America and Great Britain. Other tribes migrated to north-western Europe. Supposedly the marks of Dan are found in Denmark, those of Judah in Germany (the Lion of Europe), and so forth. The 'Anglo-Saxon, Celtic and Teutonic peoples' are the racial descendants of the Twelve Tribes of Israel.

British Israelism flowered at the height of the Empire, when the sun never set on the Union Jack and the Admiralty held, as Genesis 22:17 says, 'the gates of its enemies'. Accordingly, it revered the blessings of white supremacy: world power, wealth and dominion over others.

Identity, on the other hand, developed after the Second World War in the age of decolonisation, desegregation and immigration. It explains the sins of the white race, its fall from grace and victimisation. In this era, it's the Devil who controls Israel's gates and commands world events.

Who is this all-powerful Satan? The answer is found in John 8:44. Referring to the Jews, the verse reads, 'Ye are of your father the devil, and the lusts of your father ye will do. He was a murderer from the beginning.' For Identity believers, the Satan of old is found in the Jews of today.

Two differing camps vie for adherents among the Identity faithful. Both rely on Scripture to describe a biological link between Jews and Satan, but they differ on its point of origin. One holds that the Jews descended from Jacob's brother Esau. In this scenario, they're a mongrelised race embodying satanic forces. The other contends that Jews are descended from Cain, who slew his brother Abel. This camp argues that two seeds were planted in Eve, one the result of a mating between Adam and Eve (Abel), the other planted by Satan (Cain). Genesis 3:15 is invoked as authority for this 'two seed' story. Addressing Satan as a snake, the Lord says, 'I will put enmity between thee and the woman, and between thy seed and her seed'.

If they disagree on the genesis of Satan, both camps agree that the Book of Genesis describes two creations of Man. At the pinnacle of creation stands the first white man, Adam, literally the father of the 'Adamic race', that is white people. Prior to Adam was a lower form of creation, 'man before man', to use the term of art in some Identity circles. This pre-Adamic creation is people of colour, who under God's Law are 'strangers' or 'aliens', outside the white Christian nation, 'mud people' doomed to slavery or death.

* * *

Mike was raised in Orange County in Southern California then studied engineering. This sounds normal to me. His claim that he is a direct descendant of Sir Francis Drake, the great English naval hero, is a little strange, but I let it pass. That he was a 'conservative rebel in my youth, not liberal' is moderately interesting. Even the fact that he deliberately chose to attend one of the most conservative Christian colleges in the US, to study theology, could be considered within the parameters of normality. Of his attempts to 'date a sweet woman' in the Christian bookshop – 'but she wasn't interested; women tend to hang up on me when I explain my views' – I think, fair enough. Until he talks about his first revelation from God – Yahweh – when he was eight.

He was given a bullet by his grandfather, which had been used to kill the first deer of the hunting season. Running out to play by a river on his grandfather's ranch, Mike lost the bullet. He couldn't find it, no matter where he looked. Distraught, he prayed to God as hard as he ever could. After 15 minutes, he looked down and saw the bullet in the grass, glinting by his foot. It was a miracle, he says. Tears spring into his eyes and run down his cheeks. I stare in disbelief and discomfort. I hope he hasn't got a gun nearby, is all I can think. I can't really pat him around the shoulders. Maybe these are tears of joy. All the same I remain frozen, my hands stretched out in front of me on the cheap plastic tablecloth, aware that the world is carrying on around us.

'Cherry cheesecake? Sure, darlin',' says the waitress to someone behind me. 'Do y'all want some pie with that?'

This is not the last time I see such behaviour from Mike in the days we spend together. He calms down for a while as we chat about his childhood, and I crack some banal joke about my journey today. Then he starts talking about his only companion all these years, a pet llama that went with him everywhere. He even used to kiss it, he says, but it died recently. His eyes turn red and the tears well up again. Oh, God, I think. I *really* hope that gun isn't nearby. This bloke's old enough to be my dad, yet here he is, calling for racial holy war and blubbing his eyes out in front of me in this shitty little café, in this hillbilly town, as the Southerners around us chow down on their fried chicken.

Later, we walk over to a restaurant called Western Sizzler, part of a ubiquitous American chain where you get all you can eat for a few dollars. Hot plates crammed with processed meat and bits of salad.

Mike piles his plate impossibly high several times with all kinds of stuff, mostly meat (all kosher; he follows a Biblical diet). He sits shovelling this food and spewing his beliefs, which in the context sound almost innocuous. No racist I've met has ever turned down a free meal. Then again, as he constantly wipes sauce from his mouth, Mike tells me he has to be very careful with his money. Not like others, he says, oh no. They'll talk to the Jewish media and take their money, no problem. I don't tell him I already know of another journalist, a British guy who's been out here to interview Thom Robb, Mike's former pastor, and whom he now can't stand.

Mike starts to trust me, debating with himself whether to let me visit his place. 'Hmm, I don't know . . .' Soon he's smiling tentatively, laughing and reminiscing about his days running a Radio Shack store and telling me how he was chosen for his role by Yahweh. Then we head back out into the cool, quiet night. He invites me over to the town nearest his house. I'd thought Harrison was it, but no, it's a small hamlet called Jasper, about an hour away along twisting roads, deep in the forested Ozarks. The town sign, set before a winding creek, says 'Jasper: Population 304.' I check into a small, crumbling motel – low cabins made of flimsy plywood, with ancient, rattling air con. Over the road is the only café. I drag myself across and sit at the bar, eating yesterday's pecan pie and ignoring stares from the locals. I think of civilisation and read one of the New York papers I've brought with me.

That night, Mike comes over to my room. My mobile phone doesn't work here, and I feel really cut off from everything and everyone I know. I sense that Mike doesn't have company very often, although he claims various members of the movement have stayed at his place, including some he suspects may have had trouble with the law.

He agrees to take me to his house – almost the first time this has happened with an outsider, he tells me. It's a wild, fast drive in his 4x4, through a pass and off onto a dirt track, down into one of the many mountain valleys. His long-nailed fingers barely grip the wheel. The world flashes by – fields and meadows where a few cows graze, dense woodland, a sandstone bluff. A tiny, whitewashed wooden church sidles up on our right. Is this his place? 'No, no, that's for the local Baptists. Judeo-Christians,' he nods, as though imparting some secret. Over the coming days I hear him speak disparagingly many times of 'Judeo-Christians' and, in a sneering voice, of 'mainstream churchianity'.

His home hides near the end of the road, over a creek, about 20 minutes from Jasper. It's a huge, two-storey building, painted blue and miles from anywhere. It's quiet here, beautiful, so different to my own life back in cramped old England. The surrounding woods and meadowland sit near a natural spring and towering cliffs, the only sounds rustling animals and the hoot of night birds. There's a river nearby in which he swims, that he shows me the next day. We step up the creaking back steps into a large kitchen, shrouded, for a second, in deep darkness. The light clicks on, and Mike turns to look at me and smiles.

He shows me through a warren of rooms, smelling of musty pine and cluttered with furniture that harks back to the '60s and '70s. Some house his printing presses, on sober brown carpets. Others have recording machines (he produces a weekly radio programme, broadcast nationally and internationally), and still others hold some of the thousands of items Kingdom Identity sells each week. It's clearly a flourishing business. Among all the books – he says he inherited the rights to publish works from several prominent Identity pastors – is a 'traditional correction stick', a long, thin piece of wood used to beat children. There are also kids' books, reprinted from decades ago. 'Traditional, wholesome works,' Mike calls them.

We walk outside. I chew on a slice of fresh watermelon he's just given me, spitting the pips into the darkness. A rich, heady scent drifts from the flowers and undergrowth. Mike takes me on a small tour of the land, starting to talk in greater detail about Christian Identity's development and doctrine, how he wants to bring about the government of Yahweh's anointed people and how he refuses to be bound by the laws of man. He has no social security number, for example. 'I'm called to teach the Truth!'

he suddenly thunders, pointing up towards heaven. It's past midnight now – Mike says he doesn't surface until the afternoon, and usually works until 5 a.m. – and trying to digest this stuff is difficult on the best of days. He reaches frequently for his electronic Bible, a calculator-type device he keeps in his pocket, to quote from Scripture. He furrows his brow, impatiently tapping at the keys. He also tells me snippets about his life, such as that he collects old movies, watching them alone into the pre-dawn hours.

According to Mike, Yahweh will provide for his needs, whatever he does. Events are pre-ordained. There's that strange light in his eyes again, as he speaks. He explains why, in the Bible, it's permitted to slay race mixers. An Israelite called Phineas slew a fellow Israelite who lay with a Midianite woman (ironic, as Moses himself had married a Midianite). Therefore, as long as a 'race warrior' is inspired directly by Yahweh, he's permitted to slay race mixers. There's even a term for this, as mentioned earlier, the 'Phineas Priesthood'. 'It's not my calling, though,' explains Mike. All the examples I mention, such as the London bomber or Ben Smith in Illinois, were deluded, he maintains, obviously not truly inspired by the Holy Spirit.

In an email he sends me later, he claims: 'Millions visit our website each year, but I am unaware of any visits made by David Copeland . . . As I told you before, the first prerequisite of being a warrior in a Holy War, is that you are holy! The individual must have a personal relationship with the Redeemer, which includes an active prayer life. They must follow His laws and the guidance of the Holy Spirit, not the whims of their own mind.' And, most tellingly: 'It is not really necessary that you or anybody else are able to "draw the distinction between being motivated by God/Yahweh, and motivated by illness or personal issues", the world certainly will not be able to understand.' What this comes down to, again, is belief. Belief allows you to remove yourself from the norms governing most human beings, and provides a comforting straitjacket for the difficulties of life. Mike's answer is: 'Do we neglect the truth because someone else may misuse it?'

There's another disturbing twist. Although there's no mention of it in the Bible passage he shows me, Mike insists that the spear used for the Phineas slaying was passed between the man and the woman – in fact, between and through their private parts – as they were making love. I have a strong feeling that Mike is a misogynist. He's not married. When talking about his elementary school teacher, he refers to her as 'that Jewish bitch'. Where does this vitriol, this hate and repression come from? Yet later, as we stand chatting in his kitchen, he takes a call from one of his flock seeking marriage guidance. 'Your wife is bound to honour and obey you,' he advises the parishioner.

He's at pains to point out to me the traditional role of women. She must obey, be a good Christian woman, and so on. He asks again if I can recommend 'a good Christian woman from England', who might act as his secretary. Not just the ordinary secretary, you understand, but the other one. The one who needs to live in with him. Not likely, I think. Mike, it seems, has lost quite a few secretaries in the past. I wonder why he doesn't just employ a man.

Then, in a piece of language reminiscent of William Pierce, he says: 'One day, some people will be hanging from the lamp posts in this country.'

'You can't mean that, Mike!'

'Oh yes,' he explains. 'The real danger in this country is our government, and its jackbooted thugs storming your house or church. We are exposing their New World Order.' He's already admitted believing in ethnic cleansing, and that 'racism has been planted on my heart since before birth'.

I know he'll be upset reading this, thinking I've betrayed his trust. And yet, to me, for all his innocence – yes, I would say he seemed innocent – his cause can bring about genuine human damage and unhappiness. What a sad waste of a life, I think to myself. The countryside is beautiful, of course. It's a real 'back to the land' existence, complete with a well, hundreds of acres and no disturbances from the outside world. Who wouldn't want this kind of existence? But without the hatred and loneliness.

I spend the next three days travelling to and from my motel to Mike's place, talking for hours on end, hearing of convoluted and weird groups in the surrounding hills – racist ministries that focus purely on songs, for example. I follow the same strange hours he does, pitching my body clock off-centre, which enhances the dreamlike state I find myself in.

He opens up and explains about his 'bitch' ex-wife. He also talks of the congregation he built up (he was the preacher, before running this outreach ministry), how they forced him to resign over allegations of sexual harassment, following complaints from some of his female parishioners. Unfounded, of course, says a bitter Mike. 'They accused me of everything: of celibacy, being gay, and having an affair! Now, how can I be all three?' He shows me a tract he's written on how Yahweh permits polygamy and concubines. Women are ready for marriage after puberty: 'Fifteen, sixteen, nineteen, whatever,' he tells me. Mike's also produced something on how oral and anal sex are not sins, for Scriptural reasons, and how common-law marriage is best, because he doesn't support the idea of a state marriage licence. 'You make a certificate with holy matrimony.' Why the resistance? 'Well, the Feds might try to put a woman agent to be my secretary, for example. But I'll spot a woman like that Hillary Clinton bitch.'

At one point, Mike hands me a list showing 'offences' which require the death penalty. These include idolatry, being a witch, blasphemy, abortion, adultery, 'unchastity of bride', homosexuality – and even 'stubborn and rebellious son'. Beside each is a Biblical reference. On another crudely printed list, I see a form of some kind. I pick it up off an old Formica table and read the heading: 'Accusation Form for Lawful Justice'. You fill this in if you see anyone transgressing 'God's Laws'. Bloody hell, I think, I'd be here all day if I had to do this. I read one of his little stickers: 'Only inferior White women date outside of their race. Be proud of your heritage, don't be a race-mixing slut!'

'Hah, that one goes down quite well with the movement,' he says. 'I'm quite proud of it, really.' A nervous smile plays on his lips. Well, I prefer seeing him smile, rather than misty-eyed as he starts referring to 'the hand of Yahweh' in everything and his 'calling'. Or being 'elect'.

In a way, I feel sorry for him. It might be laughable, except for the fact that thousands of white extremists believe in the tenets of Christian Identity and have used them time and again to justify acts of extreme violence. Identity has had links to the militia movement. The anti-abortion murderer Eric Rudolph – the same man who inspired David Copeland – believed in this stuff. Copeland himself visited Kingdom Identity's website several times, a charge Mike is quick to deny.

Other 'race warriors' have been in contact with Mike. David Lane, a founding member of The Order – the near mythical neo-nazi gang which slew opponents and robbed banks in the 1980s – has written to him from prison. Mike tells me this himself. Members of the Aryan Brotherhood prison gang are among his most ardent admirers. Another former member of The Order, Gary Yarborough, recommended a Swedish national socialist woman to come and stay with him.

Mike owes his position less to his personality than to his encyclopaedic knowledge of Identity doctrines. His ministry is also inheritor to the movement's two main historical figures and the only one that runs outreach courses by the American Institute of Theology, its most important doctrinal body. Many other figures have been to stay and work with him, he tells me. Several have ended up ripping him off, he says, but he doesn't mind. He only needs enough to live. Yahweh will provide the rest.

Yahweh's provision is a refrain repeated by one of Mike's close friends, Lang, on my final night in Jasper. Sitting in the diner once again, we eat what passes for Mexican food (I make a minor faux pas, forgetting to say grace) and talk over this man's beliefs and life. He's balding, wiry, with parchment-thin, tanned skin and veins popping from the side of his head. His icy blue eyes shine far too brightly. He's nothing to live on now, he says; his former wife has taken everything.

'What will you do? Do you mean you're going to starve?'

'I don't know,' he answers. The government have a land tax, which means they'll come soon to repossess his farm. He has armed himself for that day.

'In what way?'

But he just smiles knowingly and fails to answer, even when I ask again. He sighs, draws in a breath, and stares at me. 'Y'know, each day of mah life, mah fate is in Yahweh's hands. He will provide. And if he don't, that's his way, too.' Yahweh has also promised him five wives, even though the first of these women is already married. 'It don't matter, he won't be around for long,' Lang says, referring to her husband. His words have an ominous ring.

I part ways with Mike, the sad-boy-lost face flickering through the deep frame and voice of the frontiersman. As he walks out of the diner, he says, 'Don't forget to mention, I'm trying to set the standard, y'see, as the conscience for the movement.' I can tell he believes it. Then, with his large frame almost out the door, he calls out: 'Be careful in Little Rock. It's a nigger town now!'

I feel slightly melancholic. It'll be strange being back in an English city – tight, edgy, old – after this beautiful but dangerous mountain land. Yet even here, a bond is forged. I just want to tell him: Why do this? Why sacrifice your life to this crazy cause? Why not learn to love and understand yourself and those around you? Even have therapy, goddammit. But I can't. Perhaps I'd be pulling away the one fig leaf, the single piece of understanding, that separates someone like Mike from an awful realisation about life. Or maybe I'm just naive myself. My pleas would fall on deaf ears anyway, and would mark me as an enemy. Which is, sadly, what I'll probably be seen as now.

* * *

I fly to Alabama to spend a couple of days with the investigators from the Southern Poverty Law Center, one of the main anti-hate civil rights groups in the US. Mark Potok and Heidi Beirich of the *Intelligence Report* host me. Suddenly I can relax again and eat fresh fruit and vegetables, after all that fried food. This must be how war veterans felt, coming back for R&R into the 'normal' world, before being spat back into an unreal conflict. I tour around the civil rights sites, including the small red-brick church where Martin Luther King first preached.

We talk of our mutual beliefs and experiences, and what's happened to America, with a drop in real earnings for many people. How crime and race are often spuriously linked and blamed for a range of societal ills. Globalisation, it seems, is helping to foster tribalism, here in the heart of the West.

Back in Washington I spend my last days with a friend, drinking away the nights, visiting museums and cultural centres by day. I take time out to see the newly opened Holocaust Museum, a reminder of where hate leads.

Mark Cotterill and I share a final beer before I fly back to England. He seems happy. Soon, however, the SPLC will have smashed his ring of separatists and supremacists – action which could threaten Nick Griffin on the other side of the Atlantic.

Back home.

SIXTEEN

ENGLAND, MY ENGLAND

AUGUST 2001

It takes me a while to readjust to the relative normality of life again. To the crack addicts, street robbers, undercover police, beggars, ticket touts. Small flames of life, burning out fast, in the grimy streets of the former capital of the Empire.

After a brief recuperation, I'm travelling to meet the right again. In Italy, meanwhile, anarchy takes hold for several days at the end of July. The G8 summit in Genoa is turned into a battle zone. Anti-aircraft missiles and cruisers fail to deter a mass of anti-capitalist protesters descending onto these chic streets.

One anarchist is shot dead. The police raid a school hall being used as a centre by many members of the independent media and non-violent protesters. Hundreds are arrested in a pre-dawn assault, reportedly beaten up, and forced to sing fascist songs, as officers urinate on them. One British man suffers a collapsed lung, ruptured spleen and broken ribs. 'I thought I was going to die. I could hear my bones breaking inside,' says protester Mark Covell. There are allegations that many of the building's occupants are made to stand against a wall then savagely attacked. Around 20 people are taken to hospital. Scores more have minor injuries. Several protesters go on to sue the Italian police, in what turns into a national embarrassment for the new right-wing government. Is this the future, here in the developed world?

Back home, I take a colleague to London's East End, where we encounter Dave Hill, leader of the east London BNP. This is a former heartland of white power. It was these streets and white, working-class pubs that spawned so much 'Paki bashing'. Now the demographics of the area have changed. The newly constructed and renovated estates are mainly Asian. And a wave of yuppies has moved in, attracted to the relative proximity of the City and Canary Wharf.

We've already taken a tour, on a dull, rainy day, through the streets of Bermondsey (scene of an infamous BNP riot in 1991) and former C18 areas of the East End. I show my friend the McDonald's the crew used for their meetings. Then we wander near the infamous Millwall soccer club, which has a strong hooligan following. Eventually, I even retrace my steps to The Beast's house. We pause and stare at the net curtains and neatly trimmed lawn.

Back in Tower Hamlets, Dave Hill greets us at the Limehouse Docklands Light Railway station. A short, squat builder called Jim is with him. He has thick, blunt hands and unkempt grey hair, and peppers his sentences with obscenities. Dave is tall and stocky, going slightly to seed, with an earring and long hair tied into a ponytail. His skin is pale and doughy white, his manner friendly. In fact, as my colleague later remarks, he's amazingly open with his opinions.

Jim and Dave take us on a tour of the local estates, chatting about Dave's schooldays. How it all changed one day, 'when the Asians came'. The way Dave puts it, he was singled out for victimisation, as the newcomers tried to tear down any symbolic images – like the Virgin Mary – linked to the past. He could be right. Or simply covering his tracks.

At one point, Dave asks Jim to stop the van, just short of a Victorian railway siding. Dave is hiding in the back, worried that the local Asians may recognise him (he obviously has a reputation). He gets out, enters a children's playground, then proceeds to piss on the ground, in full view of others using the park. Asian families stare at us from outside their houses on the estate opposite. It seems a calculated insult, like a dog marking its territory.

Later, we drink in a dingy pub on Commercial Road, full of old white men and a few tattooed fellows by the bar. Dave drinks quickly, downing his pints of lager with little problem. He tells me how the area 'used to be' and how it has changed. The young Asians show no respect. They're all into drug dealing. It quickly transpires that Dave is what might be termed 'old BNP'. He's recently been involved in a knife fight in another pub. He took a knife in the leg, then pulled it out and slashed his assailant with it. He's been to Belfast 15 times, for as long as two months at a time. My colleague is uncomfortable hearing this, being Irish himself. It's clear Dave is a Loyalist supporter. Is this the new, moderate BNP? Links with paramilitaries? He offers to introduce me to members of Combat 18 – including Will Browning – as well as people from the British Ulster Alliance, the group linked to the Loyalist UDA. Hardly the 'new' electable image the BNP seeks.

Shortly afterwards, Dave is called over by a friend at the bar. This man has West Ham soccer club tattoos encasing his arm. Wearing a short-sleeved shirt, he has the depressingly familiar air of someone used to violence. Waiting, leering, watching – perhaps even hoping it's going to kick off. Probably from a football firm. He asks Dave who he's speaking to, and why. When he comes over to the table, Dave whispers to me that this guy is or was C18 and a major hooligan. Just before he tries to leave, I ask if I can interview him. It's a bit of a risk, but I don't want to miss a chance. He turns and locks hostile eyes, first on me, then on my pal. 'Nah, I don't think so.' I'm determined not to show my fear. It's difficult. 'Anyway, as far as I'm concerned, all the Paddies should pick up a Paki under each arm, and fuck off out of the country.' It's a clear threat. He's staring at my friend. We take the hint and leave.

A few days later, my friend and I meet up in Birmingham and take the train out to Nick Griffin's home town of Welshpool. Back to the Celtic fringe again. It's time for the BNP's annual Red, White and Blue festival, inspired by the Front National's similarly named event in France. It's only the second time the festival has been held, and I'm intrigued to hear that Gordon Baum – the C of CC leader I met in America – may be present.

From Welshpool, we have to drive our hire car through the narrow country roads that serve the Welsh hill farms. Security is tight; the town is swarming with police patrols, worried about the potential for a clash between the BNP and anti-nazi protesters. We pass through several roadblocks. Finally, we make it through the rain and mud to Griffin's smallholding, after getting lost (together with a convoy of BNP supporters) several times. High in the Welsh hills, this is the nearest thing in Britain, I suppose, to the Ozarks. Stewards usher us to a slush-filled spot outside Griffin's house. Back again, after all these months. I feel half-depressed, half-elated this time. My sensibilities are completely dulled by now; I've been too long in and around this damn movement. Some of these nuts are like my friends. Whereas my pal will choke, incredulous. 'What does that remind you of – 1933?' he says, handing me a copy of one of the BNP magazines. It shows a picture of Paul Golding's little blonde sister, looking out prophetically, plastered over the back.

As other cars turn into the field opposite, with its large marquee and scattered tents, we have to wait to be 'identified'. Flashing my press credentials, we're given large, distinctive yellow badges, which we're instructed to wear at all times.

I spot dozens of journalists, all keen to cover the BNP 'threat'. Half the time, in my opinion, they're just doing the party's job, helping to publicise its threat and create an image that's far greater than reality. A BBC radio journalist tries to pump me for information. I take the time instead to talk with the BNP's chief steward, a cold-faced, intimidating Scot with cropped hair and a bright-orange security vest. He says he's from Edinburgh. Under my (friendly) questions, he admits he's been on the Loyalist fringe. I chat pleasantly with him, not revealing my mission. Yet I later learn that this fellow, Warren Bennett, a 30-year-old former C18 supporter, has convictions for football hooligan-related offences and has attended Loyalist parades. When I mention I've recently been in America, he tells me he's met Sam Dickson, the same millionaire lawyer with whom I shared dinner at the C of CC convention. I also later hear that the BNP security is heavily staffed by other Loyalist Scots, as well as two ex-SAS men. This is serious stuff for the BNP. I wonder what's going on.

Griffin himself is preoccupied, standing at the top of the sloping field, seeming harassed. He greets me without much warmth. There's a rumour he's had a row with his former number-two guy, Tony Lecomber, about poor logistical arrangements. Down in the field there's mud, rain and chaos. Only one burger van serves the entire site. Most of the smaller tents have collapsed under the wind and rain. We wander down carefully into the valley, visiting some of the remaining regional stalls and tasting sticks of BNP rock. My pal tries a Cross of St George fairy cake.

We also meet several of the south-east London BNP crew. In particular, I chat with a worried-looking Paul Golding – he doesn't seem part of the event really, and I wonder if he still hero-worships Griffin as much as he used to – and Jay Lee, who's there with his young, submissive wife and amazingly passive baby. The marquee is incredibly noisy, traditional British hymns blaring through the PA system.

Sheltering inside, it's clear many hooligans and C18 members are in attendance. Dozens of young men quaff cans of lager, wearing baseball caps and casual designer gear. They seem at odds with the attempt to portray the BNP as the party of 'family'. The hooligans cheer and drum their feet in approval at the shocking tones of the speakers. Gone are the smooth, suave words of the past. After a somewhat bizarre rendition of the Welsh national anthem by two of his children, Griffin launches into a diatribe about living in a 'police state'. The police have been bused in from Manchester and Liverpool, and are 'just thugs' who are stopping BNP members from getting to the event, he claims. It's not the words you expect from a party seeking election, or supporting the traditional rule of law and order. Behind Griffin is a banner showing the ancient Saxon/British king Alfred the Great and the words: FREEDOM–SECURITY–DEMOCRACY–IDENTITY.

Speaker after speaker talks of 'taking back our land, street by street, town by town, house by house'. Ulster Loyalists urge reuniting Ireland with the British Empire. It's a chilling rendition, which receives thunderous applause from those seated around us. I notice a smart middle-class couple sitting behind me, oddly out of place.

The national student organiser, a small, close-cropped fellow in a smart new suit, pipes up in a reedy voice that they need 'White Power!' He thrusts his fist forward in a salute. There's a sickly nervous sheen to his skin, a hard thrusting edge of excitement quivering in his taut body. You can almost hear the BNP leaders groan. The BBC camera crew can't believe their luck, recording everything. When I later ask several BNP members what they understand about 'white power', they're clearly in difficulty explaining the meaning of the statement. It's obvious what it means, though: violence and hate. Indeed, there have just been new race clashes in Burnley and Bradford. A host of other English towns have reported minor incidents. The BNP has been propelled to a new high. Gone is the talk of farmers. Back, now, to the inner-city estates, the forgotten sink holes.

Something my colleague points out makes me think. The audience is like that of a religious cult: orgiastic, almost, in its unity of hate. There's no need to whip up the crowd, no pre-speaker, no comedian. The vitriol rises to the surface, unprompted. Something else he says strikes home. This is like a collection of loners. Apart from the various football hooligans (and I suddenly spot Del O'Connor, former deputy leader of C18), pumped up on steroids and drinking and laughing, there are many oddball characters who simply don't talk to one another. This is not like a business convention, where people meet and swap tales. Here, they huddle in their corners. It's an interesting observation, I think, as I watch Mrs Griffin storm past me.

We wander around the fields after the speeches have finished, ending up talking to Jay Lee once more. He's sitting eating sandwiches in his brown car. The rain pours down, drifting over the valleys, soaking through our coats as we stand and chat. Then a young, intense-looking bloke comes up to us. 'What are you doing?' he demands, rudely. We explain we're just chatting to a friend. Jay pipes up and agrees. But the guy tells us there've been complaints about us, that we're hiding our badges, and any 'further violations' will mean we're expelled. As he stomps off, his yellow oilskin retreating back towards the farmhouse, we're mystified. We look at each other, shrugging our shoulders. Jay's puzzled too. 'Dunno what that was about.' Neither do we, I respond. A moment later another figure wanders up, this time large-framed and fat-faced, with a faintly ridiculous nest of pudding bowl hair on a block head. He insists we have to leave. 'Now.' He ignores our protests, places a firm hand on our backs, and guides us away. Eventually he just shoves us, and we're left – a little confused and afraid – to clamber in the car and head back to civilisation.

This is really odd. It was Griffin himself who personally invited us here, keen to have a 'friendly' journalist on site. What's going on? Is there something to hide? I can't believe we've done anything wrong. Half the BNP people seem to know us already. No one has actually complained, as far as I can see.

My friend and I discuss events, sitting in a hotel bar back in Welshpool (avoiding the swarming police patrols and anti-fascist protesters). What actually seems to have happened is that the arrival of so many journalists caused paranoia. This is not some polished political movement. It still includes active hooligans and C18 members. And with guys like us around, the BNP people feel they can't say what they really want. And well they might. For later that evening, we learn that Stigger, Ian Stuart's former band member from Skrewdriver, has been playing a gig in the main marquee. One of the icons of the white-power music scene, playing at the main social event of what is supposed to be a mainstream political party. Earlier I'd seen German members of the Blood and Honour network wandering around. And an evening of racist comedy, some of which I've since heard on tape.

After all the suave words from Griffin, it's pretty clear now where the BNP's true sympathies lie. And events take another funny twist. It's revealed that Griffin's father, Edgar, who's answered phones for the BNP, is working on the campaign team of Iain Duncan Smith, the new leader of the Conservative Party.

SEVENTEEN

FREEDOM

OCTOBER 2001

In the weeks after 11 September, you're either with us or against us. I think back on my travels in the Muslim world and through the heartlands of Europe and the USA. How do we integrate, and preserve our identities too? Are the racists, fundamentalists and zealots right? Sometimes, I almost think so.

As this strange period of my life draws to a close, I sit in on a reading from a book called *09/11 8:48 a.m.*, a collection of stories about the immediate aftermath of the attack. Several American authors read their chapters. Some have produced poetry. Others speak of how the world stood still that day. Eloquent reportage, about the moment America felt herself wounded to the core. Yet behind me, a trio of Arab women angrily remonstrate with the writers. How dare they write such stuff! Don't the Americans know what the Arabs have had to suffer? And the Palestinians? If not for their arrogance and lopsided support for Israel, none of this would be happening. I see the gulf of understanding, and experience, open before me. And it's not long before extremist mailing lists are talking of a Jewish conspiracy behind the attacks.

* * *

The whisky gets a hammering after my return. The constant travel has taken its toll on my relationship, too. I have to retreat from the book for a while, ignoring Mike Hallimore's emails about his beliefs and his desire to read what I've written about him. I barely bat an eyelid when the AFBNP is shut down, after an SPLC investigation seems to reveal alleged illegal fundraising. Mark Cotterill disappears for a while, 'trying to get laid with some chick', suggests Fisheye in an email.

Slowly, my nerves settle back into a low throb, and I start again weaving in and out of the dark undersurface of London and the lost areas of Britain.

Sitting in numerous trains and buses, listening in to conversations, talking with victims of racial attacks, wondering about people's hopes and fears. What makes us who we are. Always sensing the spirit of Nick Griffin somewhere ahead of me. And, after it all, still feeling a stranger in much of my own land.

My eyes eventually turn abroad once more.

* * *

For months, I've been courting the leadership of the Freiheitliche Partei Österreichs – the Austrian Freedom Party, or FPÖ. Its ascendancy in an sleepy, conservative country of eight million has sent shockwaves worldwide.

Much of the West knows the smiling face of Jörg Haider, the FPÖ's charismatic leader. A multilingual sports fanatic, Haider has run the New York marathon and is a keen rock climber. Tanned, groomed, and a powerful orator with the common touch, Haider appeals to both young and old. Since he took the party helm in 1986, the FPÖ has slowly climbed in the polls. In October 1999, it took nearly 28 per cent of the national vote, enough to earn it a place in coalition government.

Calling for sharp curbs on immigration. Using coded language about Jews. Praising former SS men. In the country of Hitler's birth, where the army merged with the German *Wehrmacht* in under 48 hours, the FPÖ's success sends grave ripples of disquiet. Austrians are keen to portray themselves as among the first victims of fascism, taken over by Germany in the 1938 *Anschluss*. But I wonder if they're suffering from some form of collective amnesia. They welcomed Hitler with open arms.

Who is this man Haider? Is he simply a populist, playing the race card to garner votes? If so, why had nearly a third of the country voted for him and his party?

A grim-looking Austrian President, Thomas Klestil, swears in a new coalition of the conservative Austrian People's Party (ÖVP) and the FPÖ, in Vienna at noon on 4 February 2000. Even before the ceremony, political leaders across Europe are throwing a cordon sanitaire around Austria. Israel immediately withdraws its ambassador from Vienna, as does the United States. These events are unprecedented in recent history.

Within a few days Austria is being boycotted by everyone from Prince Charles to movie stars. Daily demonstrations against the new government in Vienna are accompanied by international protest actions and rallies in Berlin, Warsaw, Malmö, London, Oslo, Paris, Athens and the USA. Jewish organisations worldwide echo Israel's action. European rabbis immediately cancel a congress scheduled for March in Vienna. Auschwitz survivors lodge bitter objections to the new government, and the Israeli Sports Minister urges an international sporting boycott.

Haider seems completely unconcerned. He and the Conservative boss, Wolfgang Schüssel, sign a joint declaration pledging respect for human rights and democracy. As a condition of his party's entry into government, Haider accepts Austria's responsibility for the crimes of the National Socialist regime.

Then he flies to Berlin and appears on a TV talk show, presenting himself as the epitome of reason to millions of German viewers. As the international media speculate, and political reaction mounts, Israel slaps a ban on any visit by Haider. The French and Belgian governments demand complete isolation of Austria. Haider launches a charm offensive, comparing his politics with those of New Labour under Tony Blair.

Haider's performance on German television is seen as an unqualified success. He runs rings around the presenter and hostile studio guests and blandly threatens retaliatory action by exercising the Austrian right of veto on further expansion of the EU. Then the blandness evaporates, leaving only the offensive. Haider batters the EU for doing nothing about human rights violations in Chechnya and Turkey, and lashes out at what he calls 'the slander campaign against Austria'. Meanwhile, Haider's associates are awarded the key portfolios of finance, social security, defence and justice, as well as the vice chancellorship. At a tactical moment Haider steps down from the party leadership, handing the reins of ostensible power to his deputy, Susanne Riess-Passer.

What seems odd to me is that many other European countries have asylum policies not far removed from Haider's views. Is there something different or special about the FPÖ or Austria?

Certainly, there seems to have been a massive protest vote for the Freedom Party. After more than 50 years of political deep freeze, the old Social Democrat/Conservative consensus, where jobs often were handed out according to party quotas, is in tatters. The FPÖ has already been in coalition with the Social Democrats for three years in the 1980s, when nobody batted an eyelid. Haider's appearance on the scene in 1986 brought the arrangement to an end. It mattered little then that the FPÖ still included people who'd been genuine Nazis.

The party leader until 1978, Friedrich Peter, had been a member of the Waffen SS and acknowledged his past. But what I was reading seemed to suggest that Haider had surrounded himself with a collection of rabid anti-Semites, racists and pan-German nationalists. Was this true? I didn't yet know. His leadership election in 1986 certainly produced revulsion, as many party members quit. Others, though, were spellbound.

Out of power, Haider – a devoted son of equally devoted Nazi parents – reshaped the FPÖ in his own image. It benefited from the growing feeling among voters that Austria's government, as *Searchlight*'s Graeme Atkinson had once put it, 'was constipated and that some form of political laxative was needed'.

Haider and his party had certainly had become adept at exploiting every possible grievance. The eastward expansion of the European Union. Asylum and immigration. Corruption in public life. Government bureaucracy. The taxation system. Yet even amidst the panic, some on the left were calling for calm. They were convinced that the Freedom Party had no magic wand for all these problems. Soon enough its support would begin to fray and evaporate, as people saw it for what it was: a party of protest, a herald of change.

* * *

'How can they say that about us!'

'Hang on . . .'

'How can a party which got 28 per cent of the vote – *28 per cent* – be considered extremist?'

'Wait a momen–'

The line fizzles. The voice at the other end phases in and out. For a second or two I hear the sounds of a hotel lobby, then the click-clack of expensive shoes walking outside and a voice hailing a taxi.

'Look, some of my colleagues – even those near the top – are quite nervous about speaking with the press. I sometimes think that's a mistake, but there you go. They don't always have the same experience as me. At the end of the day, we don't want to be considered neo-nazi or something ridiculous like that. Or to be included in a work lining us up with extremists.'

'Well, I have interviewed some conservatives and nationalists of –'

'Listen, I've got to go. There's a vote due in the European Parliament, and I'm late. Send an email to my secretary, outlining what you want to do. I'll see how I can help.'

'Well, can we at least meet?'

'In principle, yes. Send that email, and we'll talk again.'

'Okay.'

I set the phone down. I hadn't realised it, but my pulse is racing. My shoulders had hunched forwards; I roll them back. Why do I bother? What reward will I get at the end of this?

* * *

I think back on that conversation with Peter Sichrovsky as I near Vienna. He's the FPÖ's general secretary, a Member of the European Parliament (MEP), and the party's only Jewish member. An interesting guy to meet, I surmise. The late October sun probes gently through the cloud cover, and I watch the city spread beneath me, glittering like a piece of jewellery, spread out on its imperial axes.

I'm billeted near the heart of the diplomatic quarter, Josefstadt, a collection of narrow, often cobbled streets, small bars, chic little restaurants and charming medieval churches. Buzzing cords of steel wire sail and hang over the roads, snapping with tension as trams pass beneath. Yet I don't want to be here. Not now. Not any place. Just home, wherever that is. I feel I'm losing my own identity.

I could sense the tension as I left. Watching the drooping, sad expression on her face, the void of depression behind her eyes. Feeling guilty, yet trapped, unable to stop myself. Just a quick peck on the cheek and I was gone. She used to come to the airport every time I left, and would often be there when I came back.

I haven't managed to get a reply yet from Haider's office. Unlike before, I have no other contacts to this party. I'm simply calling them blind. My emails and faxes meet with a blank. A slow courtship dance, trying to reel in a man famed for his love of the spotlight. Still, I hear nothing. The same goes for the official party leader (although everyone still whispers Haider is the main guy), Susanne Riess-Passer. Odd that a party portraying itself as so mainstream, so misunderstood, should shun the press.

I've made contact with a couple of other sources, though. A leader of the FPÖ's student movement. And *Searchlight*'s man in this former spy capital, a fiery, elderly Jew with a razor-sharp wit and intellect.

* * *

The air tastes fresh as I amble past a stately, whitewashed church on my way down towards Kärtner Ring/Ringstrasse, the wide avenue and tramway that encircles the old inner city. A leisurely ring road that speaks of the nineteenth century and empire, speckled with small food stalls serving a variety of traditional sausages. I survive on such fare for the next few days. Bratwurst with sweet mustard, delicious. Behind Ringstrasse lie the elegant, towering museums and palaces of the Innere Stadt. The fluted stone is majestic, despite a century or more of crusted grime.

The purr of Audis and Mercedes mingles with the bells of passing trams. An occasional horse-drawn cart trots past. I admire the melting brown of the autumn leaves, thinking back on my childhood, living in Paris, enjoying time playing with my dad on the infrequent times he had off work. Maybe that's why I don't know where I belong sometimes. Chasing extremists, them chasing me. All of us searching for identity.

I take a short cut through a grand, carefully tended park. The flower beds are bare now, dusted with a crop of crisp fallen leaves. Moving under a black iron gate, I glance at the time-worn statues ahead of me and to each side.

After the war – and the second of Austria's disastrous alliances with Germany – the country was occupied by the different Allied powers, including the USSR. Vienna itself was split into four sectors and became a

Cold War hub of intrigue. Only in 1955 did Austria regain its independence, after guaranteeing its neutrality.

Once the centre of the Austro-Hungarian empire, Vienna was the stopping point for the Ottoman Turkish forces as late as 1683. After the First World War, the city had a socialist government, but the rest of the country – federal, like Germany – was much more conservative. This was where Hitler grew up and spent several years as a struggling artist. I pass the same Opera House where he used to pay a few extra coins to stand in the male-only section.

In 1934, bloody street battles took place for several days between the left and the right. The right won. On 11 March 1938 the Anschluss – union – took place, when German troops marched into the country unopposed (in fact, cheered on). Ten per cent of Vienna's pre-war population had been Jews, and they'd suffered less than in Germany. But for them the Anschluss was a devastating turn of events, as they were forced out of jobs and made to wear the Star of David. During a night of violence on 9 November 1938, shops and synagogues were burned down. Many fled, but 60,000 Austrian Jews also ended up in German-run concentration camps.

Aside from that, Austria has cultivated much the same kind of sleepy, conservative image as Switzerland. Alpine, pleasant, cultured. A land of skiing, coffee shops and polite society. Perhaps the only hint of something different was when Kurt Waldheim, who had served in a German Wehrmacht unit implicated in war crimes, was elected president in 1986.

It was various remarks by Jörg Haider that were now causing disquiet again, particularly if you believed Austria had never quite had a complete reconciliation with its Nazi past. For example, in 1991 Haider said that 'In the Third Reich they had an "orderly" employment policy'. A year earlier, he had addressed an annual meeting of Second World War veterans at Ulrichsberg, known to attract former SS officers, saying: 'Our soldiers were not criminals, at most they were victims.' In a 1995 television interview he said, 'The Waffen SS was part of the Wehrmacht [German military] and hence it deserves all the honour and respect of the army in public life.' In a parliamentary debate, he referred to 'the punishment camps of National Socialism'. (Later that day, he declared he had meant to say 'concentration camps'.) At other times, he claimed 'all this apologising only stirs up emotions', referring to the war, and that compensation for Jews and for Germans expelled from the Sudetenland were 'equal cases'. Why, if he said these things and he was the party boss, did no one else in the FPÖ seem to want to talk about them?

* * *

I'm moving at a London pace. Too fast, too urgent. I step over a piece of dog shit, then pull out a crumpled slip of paper, an email printout containing instructions to my next contact. An old, tar-coloured façade spreads before me, an intricate crest of arms above the main doorway. This must be it.

I cross over a flagstone courtyard, under a cotton-cloud sky, and knock on a solid iron door.

A moment later, a concerned but friendly-looking middle-aged female face pokes through. '*Ja?*'

'*Grüss Gott,*' I greet her, using the polite form for 'good day'. I search for the next words. '*Er, bitte, ich bin Englisch . . . er . . . entschuldigung, sprechen sie Englisch?*' She stares at me, nonplussed, and blinks once. Guess my accent must be a bit off. I try again. 'Hello, this is the Dokumentationsarchiv Österreichischer Widerstand [Documentary Archive of the Austrian Resistance, or DÖW]?'

'Oh, Nick.' There's little surprise in the voice. I look over and see a short man, bald, with sallow skin. Stubble pokes over his shirt collar where he's missed shaving. He's standing next to a photocopier, down a narrow hallway. I recognise the features, dressed as he is in an old sports jacket and pressed trousers (this is a smartly dressed city, I've learned by now). It's Karl.

Karl Pfeifer is one of Vienna's most prominent campaigning journalists, and a member of its small Jewish community. A vociferous believer in freedom of speech, he's been highly visible in his condemnation of Haider and his party. Karl's also led an interesting life himself, having fought for the Hagana (Jewish resistance) during the formation of Israel, and living in various parts of the world. He's in his 70s now and can be an abrupt, no-nonsense man. But he knows what he's talking about and has the respect of the network. We've met once, at a conference back in England, and have been in email contact since.

'Hi Karl, didn't expect to see you so soon!' I exclaim. 'Come to think of it, why are you here now?' We're due to meet tomorrow. I didn't know he worked with the DÖW. This is one of the places that monitor the development of extremism in Austria, part of the *Searchlight* sister network.

'Ah, I just had this court case this morning. I lost.' His voice is abrupt. Then again, it usually is, so I can't tell if he's upset, or simply imparting a fact, or both.

'What happened?'

'Wait a minute, after I have finished this copying. I must do this now, then I will join you. Speak with Heribert first; he can start telling you something about the background to Haider and the right here.'

I'm pointed off down a corridor, as Karl turns back to the machine. I walk past display cases full of anti-Semitic material, then through a warren of corridors, rooms and stairs, before I find this 'Heribert'.

'Hi, hi, good to meet you.' Heribert is a close-cropped fellow, part academic, part left-looking guy. He shakes my hand warmly, his manner effusive, slightly nervous, but eager to help. Good. I need all the help I can get here.

'Just give me a moment.' He gathers a pile of papers, and we move out into a small, cold kitchen area, sprawling either side of a bench-like table. Karl follows moments later, sweeping in with a businesslike air.

'Look, if you want to understand democracy in Austria today, you need look no further than my case,' Karl tutors me. He throws a sheaf of papers onto the table. 'These tell you about something amazing happening in Austria today. The loss of democracy.'

The story begins in 1995, five years before Haider's party enters government. At the beginning of that year, the academic journal of the Freedom Party published an article titled 'Internationalism Versus Nationalism: Eternal Animosity'. The author, Dr Werner Pfeifenberger, an Austrian expert on political science who taught at Münster University in Germany, set out his version of 2,000 years of European history.

The Jews, or 'the internationals' as they're called in anti-Semitic jargon and in the article, were behind the decisive events in the continent's history. The Jews and their socialist values influenced the early Christians in Europe; the Jews fomented the French Revolution; the Jews played a key role in putting down the opposition in Russia; and also, no less, 'The Jews threatened war against Germany in 1933.'

In February 1995, Karl published an article in response. It appeared in the monthly paper of the Social Democratic Party, as well as the paper of the Austrian Jewish community. He edited this paper, in addition to his work as the Israel Radio correspondent in Vienna. In the Jewish paper, under the heading '(Neo-)Nazi Tones in the Freedom Party Yearbook', he quoted from Pfeifenberger's article and wrote that the author was reviving 'the old Nazi myth of the international Jewish conspiracy'.

Pfeifenberger filed a libel suit against him and against the institutions of the Jewish community, demanding $20,000 in damages. 'Before the judge, he tried to depict himself as a great friend of the Jews, like all the right-wing extremists do,' recalls Karl. 'He related that he even published an article in the Israeli lawyers' [association] organ.'

The defendants came armed with an opinion by a historian from the University of Linz, who confirmed what Karl had written. He and his co-respondents won against Pfeifenberger in two Viennese courts in 1997; a year later, these rulings were approved by the regional high court of Vienna, where Pfeifenberger had filed an appeal.

The failed libel suit now worked against Pfeifenberger. In Germany, where he taught, Social Democrat representatives expressed concern in the parliament about 'anti-Semitic tendencies' in his original article. The state government of North Rhine-Westphalia fired him from his post. In April 1998 he found work at another institution, but only as a researcher.

In Austria, members of the Social Democrat Party and the Greens also condemned Pfeifenberger's article and called for legal action against him and against the Freedom Party, publisher of the journal. Eleven days after the establishment of the Schüssel-Haider government, when Vienna was facing a boycott from 14 fellow EU members, the prosecutor general announced that he was opening criminal proceedings against Pfeifenberger. He accused the lecturer of a crime under a federal law that prohibits Nazi activity, a serious offence punishable by 20 years' imprisonment.

On 13 May 2000, two and a half months before he was due to appear before a jury, Pfeifenberger took his own life.

Three weeks after the suicide, *Zur Zeit*, a right-wing Austrian weekly closely associated with the coalition government (and part-funded by it), published an article headed 'Deadly Moral Terror'. It recounted Pfeifenberger's life history, described how a conspiracy had developed against him which led to his death, and cited portions of Karl's article, claiming: 'Karl Pfeifer embarked on a manhunt, which in the end caused the death of a hunted man.'

Karl's picture appeared alongside other figures who had criticised or acted against Pfeifenberger. It labelled him explicitly as the 'Jewish journalist' Pfeifer, under the headline 'Portraits of the Gang of Hunters'.

Now it was Karl's turn to file a libel suit. Together with the Austrian Journalists Association and with its financial support, he sued *Zur Zeit*. In March 2001, the court ruled that the paper had to pay him $4,000 in damages – but the paper appealed to the regional high court of Vienna.

'The moment I knew the identity of the court that would sit on the case, I had a bad feeling,' recalls Karl. And now the appeal judges have today said there was nothing libellous in the *Zur Zeit* piece. The writer had not directly accused Karl of causing Pfeifenberger's death. 'The facts described in the article,' ruled Judge Trieb, 'lead the reader . . . to reach a conclusion concerning moral responsibility only.'

So Karl was not criminally responsible for Pfeifenberger's death but, as *Zur Zeit* claimed, he was 'morally responsible'.

Karl slaps his hands on the table, making me start: 'The judge pointed her finger at me and said: "Herr Pfeifer, your article was the beginning of an avalanche that led the Greens and the Social Democrats to cause Pfeifenberger to lose his job." In my 20 years as a journalist, I have covered trials in Austria, and I have never seen a judge point at a defendant that way.'

He can hardly seem to believe it himself: 'When I criticised this article, Pfeifenberger's piece, my article was sent to the state attorney by two politicians. Not by me, but them.' His voice rises in emphasis and incredulity. 'The article – it did not change.' He laughs bitterly. The equally bitter smell of the coffee being brewed behind us reminds me that I haven't slept properly for a couple of days.

Karl says he personally confronted Haider in 2000, asking him at a press conference if he could 'cut the umbilical cord connecting you with Holocaust deniers and with extreme right-wing people. And then he started to teach me tolerance. So I interrupted him and said, now look, I was standing three years in Austrian courts because I said that in your yearbook there were Nazi tones.' This started a row between them. 'I'm just a small newspaperman,' says Karl. 'And this shows you cannot afford to write against Haider's party.'

Heribert points out that Haider's own lawyer, Dieter Böhmdorfer, the same man who sued several journalists for libel on Haider's behalf, has become the Minister of Justice. Karl is still incredulous over what's happened. 'In any civilised country, this whole case would have been condemned. You know, they have now published this *Zur Zeit* article on neo-nazi websites, together with my picture?' He gets up as suddenly as he arrived and storms out of the room.

So whom should I believe? Heribert says I should look at the report of the so-called 'Wise Men'. These three experts, led by the former Finnish president Martti Ahtissaari, were commissioned to produce a report on the new Austrian government for the EU. Their conclusion described the FPÖ as 'a right-wing populist party with radical elements' and 'extremist language'. They also stated that: 'The FPÖ has exploited and enforced xenophobic sentiments in campaigns. High-level officials of the FPÖ have over a long period of time used statements that can be interpreted to be xenophobic or even racist. The language used is seen by many observers to carry nationalist overtones, sometimes even undertones close to characteristic National Socialist expressions.'

It's a sobering quote. 'Yes, yes, now you see, right?' says Heribert. His eyes are gleaming, intense, behind his glasses. He points to another section of the document that highlights the frequent use of libel procedures 'against individuals who have criticised the FPÖ', leading to a worry by the wise men about the condition of Austrian democracy.

Haider's coded language seems quite clear. I'm shown many different examples. Before the Vienna elections in March 2001, for example, he referred to an American public relations advisor to the city's socialist mayor as from the 'East Coast'. The man's name was Greenberg. 'That of course is New York, where many Jews live,' sighs Heribert. 'They usually use this word as a code, not just today, but since the time of Waldheim.'

Open anti-Semitism has been banned by law since the Second World War, so you encounter only these careful, coded terms. Phrases like 'international capitalism' or 'international financiers' can have a clear double meaning. I'm shown several other examples of such wordings from FPÖ members.

Heribert explains how Haider and Böhmdorfer were in the same *Burschenschaft* in the 1970s. These are extreme Conservative student fraternities, venerable and popular in both Germany and Austria. Many encourage old rituals, one of which is the scarring of the face with a duelling sword. In some Burschenschaften, the wound is stitched without anaesthetic.

'There's a definite turn now to authoritarian politics,' laments Heribert, finishing the dregs of his coffee. 'We've got one of the highest levels of discrimination against foreigners in Europe. And it's becoming even more restrictive.'

Immigrants constitute only 8 per cent of the country, 'although the FPÖ is always telling us it's higher'. I see few obvious signs of them on my visit. Certainly, Vienna does not seem to have the same scale of different peoples as London, or the same crime level. Perhaps if I stayed longer, the situation would become clearer. The latest development is a new law, proposed by the Freedom Party, which will force all foreigners to learn German and naturalise, or be deported. Tony Blair's Britain soon follows suit.

Is there something in Austrian society that makes its people more racist? 'Yeah, yeah,' Heribert calls out, checking outside for someone in the corridor. His voice rattles off the old, high walls. 'They are very anti-Semitic. And used to authoritarian traditions.' He motions me to follow him down a series of corridors and into a crowded office. 'Democracy comes from the outside here, you know, not fought for from within.' This is a strong Catholic country, he points out, and people don't talk about or openly acknowledge the Holocaust.

For Heribert, though, the FPÖ election was not such a radical change. It's continuing many of the policies of the Social Democrats, who had become afraid of the FPÖ's power so started introducing similar platforms.

There've been no open neo-nazi demos here since 1991, although there are suggestions of some links between extremist groups and the RFJ (Ring Freiheitlicher Jugend) youth movement of the Freedom Party. Two neo-nazis who desecrated a Jewish cemetery were sympathisers of a German organisation called the Nationalistische Front, as well as of the RFJ. In another incident, neo-nazis made photocopies using FPÖ machines.

* * *

The towering, Aryan-blond figure hops slowly from one leg to the other, gently swaying against the cold. Behind him, the sweeping façades of the parliament buildings are pitched into stark relief. Spotlights pick out each magnificent column and the chariot sculptures against the expanse of night sky, as the temperature drops still further.

He glances first left, towards me but without seeing, then right, shuffling backwards and forwards. He clasps a leather folder. I approach carefully, from his blind side. Just in case.

'Markus?' I move towards him. His young, smooth face turns towards mine. Handsome, unworried.

'Nick?' A serious, earnest expression, through which a welcoming smile is starting to surface.

'Yes, hi, really good to see you at last!' I offer a gloved hand, which he shakes. This is the same Markus Tschank I've been emailing for a couple of months now, a leader of the RFJ.

'Shall we go and get a coffee at Landtmann?' A pair of clear, crystal blue eyes look down into my face – I'm over six foot myself – as he thumbs towards one side of the Ringstrasse. I raise an eyebrow. 'It's one of the best coffee houses, as I think you call it in English, in this part of the city. Where politicians and others often meet.'

'Yeah, okay,' I say after a moment – should be safe – 'lead the way.'

We pass a dark, looming baroque theatre and tread carefully over tram rails. Inside the café, a wall of heat, smoke and chatter hits me. I blink, my eyes suddenly liquid again in the warmth. We decamp to a table near the entrance, moving past smartly dressed waiters who glide with consummate ease between the patrons. Each carries a heavily laden silver tray, from which he pours tea and coffee in intricate displays of efficiency.

Vienna is still a city of such coffee houses, Markus tells me, a place to meet friends, swap gossip, or talk politics. 'Ah,' I murmur back, looking around me. I feel distinctly under-dressed, and I keep wondering if there's anyone famous in here.

Markus steeples his fingers together on the lace tablecloth. 'So, how can I help you?'

I haven't yet told him or any of the others about my past encounters. It would be impossible otherwise to get an interview. Still, this is a new kind of movement, and I'm intrigued to know if it fits the template of my previous experiences.

'You want to know what the Freedom Party is really about?' He smiles. His words are drawn out long, as he adapts his accent to English. 'How about family politics for a start? We need better family politics, and with this government it's possible.' Interesting, that race and immigration are nowhere near the front of his conversation. Maybe I've got the party wrong.

'It's necessary to get more children because of the old people, to help the system of pensioners.' Markus stumbles over the odd word or two, as he refers to the FPÖ's policy of paying mothers extra benefit to stay at home and raise their kids. They get 6,000 schillings each. 'We're also trying to make privatisation,' he says. 'With industry.'

'But why did so many people vote for your party? Was it just to give mothers more money?'

'No, no,' he admits, setting his spoon down beside his saucer. He's drinking fruit tea of some kind. His fingers absentmindedly play with the side of the cup. 'It was a vote against the old political system, too. For example, to obtain – how do you call it, high office? – you had to belong to one of the two main parties. Not just high office, in fact, but many jobs. Their influence was very strong.' In a year's time, the French and Dutch voters would deliver similar messages to their established political parties. About change, and about boredom with the old system's petty corruption and stifling, consensual ways.

'What about immigration, then?' I decide to test the point. No reason to delay. After all, this is the main reason I'm here.

'We had the problem in the early 1990s,' he answers, in a serious tone. 'A big wave of immigrants came to Austria and wanted to work here. And so the population recognised not too much [of them], we must regulate the level, because in comparison with other countries – like Switzerland – they only take immigrants they really need.' The coffee house clatters around us. I nearly drop my spoon, and curse at the interruption to his comments.

'So, do you have too many immigrants?'

'We took too many in the early 1990s,' he reiterates. Then he tries to make a distinction between refugees and immigrants. 'We are obligated to help the refugees. We must make a difference between economic migrants and the refugees. We don't have a problem to take them. It's only necessary to stop the immigration in the case of economic migrants.' The social security system is too generous here. 'Ten per cent of our population is now immigrants. And we have – do you say, a black number? – of 100,000 people.'

'Is there a threat of ghettos, then?'

'Yes, without this [new language] policy, we would have more social problems.'

Like his friends, he's concerned about rising levels of crime, and about the construction of a nuclear power plant over the Czech border. Some have said it's being manufactured to old-fashioned Soviet designs. Others feel Austria's reaction smacks of elitism and NIMBYism, or even racism. Markus is interested, too, in the plight of 'displaced' German communities, like those expelled from the Sudetenland area of Czechoslovakia at the end of the war. There have never been reparations made for this displacement. It seems a big issue for many of the FPÖ members I meet.

We chat like this for a while, then I ask him about himself. He's studying law and speaks several languages. He's also well-travelled. So when, and why, did he become interested in the Freedom Party? 'Oh, when I was about 15 years old. Because I was a very social person, I think.' His voice is loud, but I still struggle to hear him over the din. 'And I was a patriot, and I wanted always to solve the problems and make a better world.' It's quite young to be interested in serious politics, I point out. 'Yes, yes. My father also was a man very interested in politics, so it depends probably on the family. So I had an easier entry to the political system than other people.'

Markus claims he went to the meetings of the other political parties. 'But the Austrian Freedom Party was the strongest for reform and wanted a new politics in Austria.' Quite a lot of young people voted for it. 'It was very evident that Austria had a lot of problems.'

'Aren't you a party of extremists, though, as other members of the EU believe?'

'No,' he states, sounding aggrieved and somewhat angry. 'We used to be more extreme in the past, maybe, but that's because we were in opposition. We have radical elements but normal ones, too. We're not even left or right really. The party fits the Austrian example only.'

Markus is very proud of his country's history and empire. He talks of a 'freedom politics' and believes that 'the population in Austria is very helpful and open to other cultures. When there's problems in other cultures, we've always tried to help, and the immigrants, we always try to prepare money for helping these immigrants in Austria. We try to integrate them, and in history there are a lot of examples that show what we have done for the other countries near Austria.'

Markus clearly holds Haider in high esteem. 'Oh yes, he was the great leader, really inspirational.'

'Even though he's now in the mountains of Carinthia?'

'Even now, sure.'

'What about his past comments?'

'Well, maybe he said some things, but they were taken out of context, and I think he explained all of them now. He's changed his mind on some of these things.' He pauses, gazing earnestly into my face. 'The media are not objective. They wrote Haider is Hitler, for example. They want to create someone who's a danger for Europe. But Haider's not like that. He just has a very straight way to say things, and not more. He sees a problem and has a very direct argument to save them.' He drops some more sugar back into his drink and stirs it vigorously. His voice lowers, speaking as though stating the obvious: 'But he's not someone from the ideological far right.'

He says Haider was one of the reasons the party was so attractive to him and his friends. Perhaps there's even an element of hero worship. I'd love to meet the man myself, to try to understand this better.

* * *

'Herr Haider is very busy at the moment.' The voice sounds surprisingly close, but agitated.

'Can I call back?'

'Yes, ja, yes, you call back another time please!' The line goes dead. I curse and look out the hotel window, then drop the mobile phone onto the bed. I managed to reach his personal assistant – Markus gave me his number – but still couldn't break through the final barrier. Several other politicians have gone quiet, too. I'm getting the real feeling people here don't want to see me.

I scramble back down the stairs out into the smart streets, towards Café Landtmann. This time I'm going to meet another politician, a member of Haider's coalition partners, the ÖVP.

Bernard Goerg is an astute, sharp-faced man in his 50s or early 60s. His fit-looking frame is squeezed into a smart pinstripe suit. He sits at a small table at the far end of the restaurant, staring with cursory interest at the pedestrians passing outside. I feel a little nervous approaching him. He's one of the ÖVP's leading Viennese members.

'Ah, Mr Ryan!' I've managed to reach him through a personal contact. I'm wondering how others in Austria's political system really feel about Haider – whether all is as calm as it appears.

'How did you react when the EU imposed that diplomatic cut-off?' I ask, as I settle into my chair. I shift the tablecloth and napkins, nearly knocking over a glass in the process. For a second or two, as he speaks, I fidget with the cutlery and fixtures, busying my hands whilst my mind works.

'My reaction was a big surprise, because one of the arguments I used to my party was that it didn't make any sense to negotiate with Haider. Because he doesn't take it serious. He cannot win anything, joining a coalition government.'

He thinks Haider has sold himself to the 'little man' of Austria and has portrayed the ÖVP as the party of the distant, rich, globalised world. 'To our surprise, Haider meant it seriously,' he laughs.

His demeanour slips into seriousness again. 'There was a complete non-understanding of what the EU did, even from my side. Because I said that Haider is an outright populist, but he's not a threat to democratic structures.'

'Perhaps this is because of the sensitive war history?' I suggest.

'That is completely wrong. That he is the heir of Adolf Hitler. A new Führer. Completely wrong.'

'What about his comments? Such as "East Coast"? About the Jews, and that kind of stuff?' I keep my voice steady, neutral, innocuous.

'Well, he did that a bit to comfort that sector of voters. Because there are of course old soldiers or wives of old soldiers who want to hear that their husband has only lived up to their duty and is not a Nazi, et cetera, et cetera. Ja?' He draws out this last word. Again, like Markus, as though explaining the obvious. 'But of course, from his family background he has a little bit of that affiliation to that. But he's not a Nazi. It's right wing, and populistic, but not Nazi.'

A pool of protesters, modernisation losers, are his real core support. 'Of course, those people all have a certain tendency to autocratic structures, because they all think if there would be somebody strong, who takes decisions, then they would not have problems. In that form, he's an autocratic person.'

He agrees it's the downside of global economics that's helping feed Haider. 'The same sources are for all other right populistic parties.' The FPÖ has played the race card, by 'saying we have too many foreigners, taking apartments, jobs, things that deprive us from our identity'.

When I ask him about popular resentment towards immigrants, he seems a bit exasperated. 'Look, that went away after the last couple of years. We got used to that situation. But now with all the terrorist attacks, the notion of Islam being a clash of civilisations, that issue is coming up again.'

We discuss Austria's new integration laws. I thought it was just an FPÖ invention, but Goerg is quick to point out that his party had much the same ideas: 'We were always of the opinion that some people have to really integrate themselves. And the best means of integration is language.'

It all sounds very rational and persuasive. A similar thing happens soon enough in the UK. 'We spent a lot of money to help the immigrants with language courses, but the Freedom Party has always refused that. No, they always say they won't spend one single schilling on a foreigner. Now they have changed.'

I tell him I don't see many immigrants on these streets. Not like London. 'Look, there are certain districts where 50 to 60 per cent are foreigners.'

'Who?'

'Mainly Turks. We have schools where 80 per cent are immigrants, who don't speak the language.' He coughs, politely, into a handkerchief, then dabs his mouth. 'Excuse me,' he says. Then adds a caveat to his earlier sentence: 'Parents get nervous about their children.'

Perhaps there's deep-rooted insecurity in Austria about change and identity. Or maybe, as my friends on the left would suggest, they're just more racist than others. Like Germany, where there's a strong sense of *Volk* and blood identity. In Germany, it's not just the right that talks of *Volksgemeinschaft* – literally, 'community of the people'.

* * *

I place a couple more calls to Haider's office. No luck. Similarly, with all the different FPÖ parliamentarians I try. I enjoy another coffee session with Markus. Disappointingly, he fails to take me to a meeting of the RFJ. But he does hand me a brightly coloured, glossy invitation to an FPÖ social event.

About 10 the next night, in the east of the city, I make my way towards the sounds of revelry and music. Two beefy guys block the upper entrance to a club of some kind; it has an FPÖ sign above. I flash them my invitation, and they wave me gruffly through. A din of accordions, laughter and shouting spills across the bar in front of me. I shoulder my way through the mass of people. It all seems very jolly. Noisy, but friendly. Not like an English gathering.

There are two or three hundred people here, young and old. Elderly chaps in traditional, smart tweeds. Some wearing the long socks I associate with Bavaria. Young guys, too, with modern, Continental-style sports jackets and electronic organisers. I bump into Markus. 'Hey, Nick!' he calls out. He doesn't seem drunk. 'Let me introduce you to the father of my friend. He's a parliamentarian.'

He steers me through the gaggle of Freedom Party acolytes towards a tall, distinguished-looking guy, probably in his 60s, smartly dressed, with a lean, craggy face and red-rimmed eyes behind large spectacles.

'Oh, hello, you're English?!' He sounds at once surprised and amused.

'We like the English; you have a good attitude to these other Europeans!' I laugh. He glances at others passing by, as we shake hands. He seems much in demand for an audience.

'Who are you?' I shout.

'I'm what you call a member of the upper house. Like your House of Lords. We call it the Bundesrat.' He runs a hand through his crinkled, greying hair. Why's he in the party, I wonder?

'Oh, I've been in politics for 33 years now, 11 of those in Parliament. Always with the Freedom Party.'

'Why?'

'It was a very small party, and it was a kind of challenge to do it. At the moment Haider came, it made us flowing many flowers.'

Eh? The last sentence seems to trip out of his mouth. His spittle flecks me. I want to pull back, but that would be rude. I think the old chap must be a bit further gone than I'd thought. Still, it's easier to talk here than in an office. And I don't seem to be having much luck with the FPÖ otherwise.

I ask how things have changed since they joined the government. 'Hah, it was not the easiest way. Because to oppose something is much easier. Now we have to think about everything.' How true. That's a thought I take with me, a small glimmer of hope about the rise of the right. The FPÖ is already starting to lose some votes in local elections.

'So what kind of problems are you dealing with?' I ask, leaning in closer to make myself heard. I keep wondering if the tape machine will pick any of this up. I set it down on a beer barrel being used as a table.

'Yes, the problems of today for sure are the enlargement of the EU. Because it's our frontier for all the population of the neighbouring countries. We have to pay for them. The Czechs, Hungarians and Slovenians. We have many problems with immigration. It's these people from non-Europe countries that makes really a problem, because it's another culture, another religion.'

Seeing that he's pissed, I ask innocently: 'Do you have a lot of Islamic immigration?'

'Oh yeah, ja, ja. Unluckily we have.' He says the Geneva convention on refugees was not made for this situation. 'Not for other religions coming by airplane, cars, or by ships. It must be reformed.'

'What about these stories that you guys are a bunch of extremists? How do you react?'

'Ach, we are a right-wing party, but not extreme party!' he exclaims.

'So how's that different to the conservatives, the ÖVP?' I shout through cupped hands.

'In a way, we are a nationalist party. We are from the German cultural region. We are very patriotic. We want to pronounce our patriot history.'

I think back on Graeme's comments about many Germans and Austrians not fully coming to terms with what happened during their 'patriot history'.

Like who was the aggressor. How they feel unfairly blamed for the war and want to stop apologising for it. It's like some form of national amnesia.

I'm introduced to a journalist from *Zur Zeit* – the same paper that gave Karl so much trouble – then Markus drags me further down into the fray, towards one of the benches nestling near the back of the bar. I brush past numerous FPÖ flags hanging from the ceiling. Looks like this place is actually their own bar, not just rented for the occasion.

Markus seats me among a bunch of his friends. People stare. I feel exposed and vulnerable. I can hear them talking about me in German, not my best language. The city mask holds, though.

After the handshaking is through and a beer has been ordered – the stein of lager arriving with a huge, foaming head – I chat with a young student lawyer for a while. He mentions ghettos and, once more, the problems of immigration.

An intense, narrow-faced guy opposite soon butts in. 'You have to forgive me,' he says, in nearly flawless English. 'I'm just so drunk at the moment, but I want to talk.' I nod, taking in his angled, handsome features and slicked blond hair, half-finished beer slopping, unnoticed, in front of him.

'We have so much support from the youth now, you know,' he blurts out. 'For example, I went to a cadre meeting last month, and 90 per cent of the people there I'd never seen before. They were all new.'

'So what attracts you and your friends to the FPÖ, then?' My question can barely be heard over the background clatter, as I scrape my stool across the flagstones. I have to avoid a fat guy bouncing towards me with his beer.

'We stand for security in Austria. It's quite good for us, actually, after the terrorist attacks in New York. We're able to establish ourselves as a security party.' I duck to one side, as the portly guy goes 'ooop-la!' and careers sideways. A minor ruckus ensues as his drink spills on someone else's table.

'Maybe there's been a breakdown of traditional communities?' I suggest. This seems to be a common feeling amongst people I've met on this voyage.

'Oh yes, that's true,' he bubbles enthusiastically. 'Because of the '68 generation. I'm in the university now, studying economics. This place is more conservative than others, but I've got to admit that the situation even there is more critical for conservative persons like me.'

'So you guys are pretty right wing, then?'

'Well, we are conservative persons, not right wing.' He pronounces conservative with a 'w' for the first 'v', a typical German pronounciation. 'No one burns down asylum hostels here. We haven't got such a scene here. And I'm proud of that. I'm a conservative person, and that's all.'

It turns out he's from an aristocratic background, his parents from the Sudetenland, aggrieved that he's lost his homeland.

* * *

I spend much of the next two days wandering Vienna's streets, taking in the sights and sounds. I remember my mother talking of a month she spent here in the late 1950s, as a student. Try the cakes, she told me. They're really good. And see the famous horses.

I finally manage to get hold of Peter Sichrovsky again. It's my last day, and I spend much of it browsing through an English bookshop, then reading a paper in an Irish chain pub. Talk of immigration: I've found an Irish bar in just about every city I've visited.

I spot Sichrovsky's carefully groomed figure outside the Music House, a collection of music shops set into a cream-coloured, modern building. Tickets are on offer for various recitals. I follow Sichrovsky's back as he strides into the place. He's medium height, with a genial expression – mask – over his features. Greying hair and smart, Continental sports jacket and slacks give him the image of a relaxed businessman. Or a politician.

I find myself in an atrium. A waterfall gurgles quietly in the background, just audible over the piped classical music. A gleaming glass lift pumps up and down between the floors.

Sichrovsky is often used as the party's spokesman. Fluent in English – he spent some time in England, when his family fled during the war – he's travelled the world during his many years as a foreign correspondent. Much of the Jewish community here views him, rightly or wrongly, as a self-hating Jew.

Karl had told me much about him during a second, rushed meeting in a little pâtisserie. How Sichrovsky had written various books (his latest was about anti-fascists) and had had several marriages. Karl wasn't very complimentary.

'You must be a bit lonely then, I guess?' I suggest to Sichrovsky. 'I don't imagine there's too many other Jewish members in the FPÖ?'

He smiles – a little politician's smile – and stirs his cappuccino. 'I'm the only Jew in any Austrian party.'

'Why?'

'I don't really know.'

'But you're not too popular with the rest of your people, are you?'

'It's a very small minority,' he says, dismissing my comment. 'It became quite vociferous because the president of the community understands his role more as a political one, less as a religious position.'

And with that, he simply smiles. And falls silent again.

'Er . . . so if we move on to another point, why don't you tell me if you see similarities between your party and anywhere else in Europe?'

'With the Berlusconi parties [in Italy] on the conservative side. Not the Alleanza [National, Mussolini's old party],' he hastens to add, 'but what we call in German the *Volkspartei*, or people's party. You know, we had 28 per cent, and you can't reach this if you are a small right wing or left wing. And with our programme, I see a lot of similarities with the Labour Party on the left.'

There's that provocative statement again. 'Our ministers wouldn't like that too much,' I venture.

'When ideas come from us, it's called a typical racist approach,' he answers, raising his eyebrows quizzically. 'It's like a sandbox. Only five children are allowed inside this, and they decide who is allowed in, and who is allowed out.'

On immigration, I hit harder granite. 'How do you prove someone has the right to stay in your country?' he says, thrusting one neatly manicured hand towards me. 'The system has failed. Austria has the highest rate of foreigners, immigrants and asylum seekers in the whole EU. There's about one asylum seeker to 500 Austrians. In Great Britain, it's one to 17,000. We just can't handle it any more.

'You only invite people into your house if you have a guest room,' he continues. 'Er, you know who these people are. And if they stay longer, you have to find something to do with them. Otherwise, it is irresponsible to bring people into your own house who could become a danger to your own family. Politicians should protect their people like the head of a family. We have to be careful not to bring too many people into the country, because we don't have any jobs for them, or money for them.'

'So, you're appealing to people's fears, then?'

'You know, there are always some people motivated by fear. There's an anti-EU feeling, an anti-immigration feeling, the people always find something to be afraid of.' As we talk, anthrax attacks are being reported in the USA. He pauses for a moment, then suddenly snaps: 'Do former socialists who put crosses in the box suddenly become nazis? And then anti-fascists again if they vote for someone else later?'

I let the attack bounce off and make a show of checking my watch. I've got to catch the cab to the airport soon. 'What about Herr Haider? I don't seem able to see him, so can you tell me something about him?'

He smiles again, as though reliving some happy memory. 'Haider is still the star and has a very strong influence in the party and on the government.'

'Does he still want to be Chancellor?'

'You know, with Haider you never know what he wants next. I personally think it would be fascinating for Austria if he would become Chancellor. Besides the mistakes he made, which I thought were ridiculous and hurt him more than anyone else – he's one of the most fascinating, modern, extremely intelligent politicians in Europe.'

He likens this 'worship' of Haider to being with a beautiful, sexy, wonderful woman who has an affair once in a while – but you stay with her all the same. He laughs. I watch his skin crinkling inwards, towards his eyes. 'It's a very emotional decision to work with someone like Haider.'

EIGHTEEN

COMRADES

1 MAY 2002

This is it. Really it. Back to where it all began.

The car follows the U-Bahn tracks, dirty and grey above us, to Hohenschönhausen, a grim, windswept suburb on the north-eastern edge of Berlin. Towering Eastern Bloc apartments thrust crudely from the earth here. Small communal areas of land stretch untouched. A children's playground nestles, forlorn and empty, near a squat, corrugated iron bar.

There are few signs of life this time of morning. A jogger. A mother with two young children. An elderly couple. Trying to get through the barricades. I shrug the jacket from my shoulders; it's becoming warmer. I shield my eyes from the sun and look upwards.

A burst of hardcore punk screams from a stack of loudspeakers, sitting on a car roof. 'It's against the fascists,' she tells me. 'Look, here they start to come.' She points. I follow the slim fingers, staring past her spiked orange hair, towards the station. 'The nazis,' she whispers.

* * *

My year had ended with a visit to John Tyndall, the man who used to lead the National Front, then the British National Party. Israel and the Palestinians were slugging it out again in their protracted war. India and Pakistan very nearly launched a nuclear conflict. Belfast was hotting up, too. It was not a promising time.

Maybe the world had ever been so, I thought, stepping out from the station at Hove. I set off down a wide, sloping avenue, into a land of Georgian town houses and civility. Tyndall's house was a several-storeyed affair near the sea front. The salty air was steadily stripping the paint from the building. It seemed to lean forwards as I approached; impressive and old. Cancerous blotches had sunk into the flaking pigment, revealing a dark undercoat, like the mottled vellum of an old man's skin.

COMRADES

The man who answered the door seemed the epitome of respectability. A small grey-haired fellow, clasping the wispy remnants of his locks to a balding pate. Someone's lost granddad in an old sweater and slippers.

'Ah, Mr Ryan,' he answered formally, in a deep, educated voice. Only last week, I'd seen him featured in a documentary programme about black Britain. He'd led the NF in the infamous 1970s period, when it was at its height and riots were taking place.

He shook my hand, stiffly. 'Do come in.' I stared up at a large entry hall, as he guided me quickly and efficiently into the front room. 'Thanks,' I muttered, as he took my coat. I brushed past a clump of dried rushes in an antique vase. A huge mirror dominated one end of the high-ceilinged room, above the fireplace. I noticed there were no radiators. 'Please,' he gestured, pointing me towards an antique-looking Victorian-style couch.

'Am I right in believing that you know, or knew, William Pierce?' I asked, trying to sound innocent.

'Oh yes,' he exclaimed. 'We've talked several times, and he was over here once.' A small smile surfaced. 'He sat in that very same chair, in this same room, where you are now, in fact.'

He seated himself opposite me, comfortable, legs crossed. I watched him push forward the slippers, first from one foot, letting it slide down, then the other. He twiddled his thumbs, too. It was only a couple of months since 11 September, and even the old guard could sense the mileage in a new enemy.

'We've got to be careful about the Muslims in this country,' said Tyndall, adopting a reasonable tone. 'They could be potential helpers for terrorists, after all.'

'Why?'

'Well, it's mainly Asian Muslims that are the problem,' he outlined, as though beginning a university seminar.

'But most of them are British, now,' I pointed out.

'Yes, well, Mr Ryan,' he said formally, 'even if half of one per cent of them are disposed to terrorism – there's millions of them.'

Then the conversation took off, on globalisation and how the 'Israeli lobby' controlled much of US policy. I felt uncomfortable, finding myself agreeing that there were downsides to globalisation. It was too easy for the right to jump onto this bandwagon.

'The US should retreat back to its splendid isolation of the past,' Tyndall asserted. I described hearing similar sentiments from Pat Buchanan. He was politely interested, and impressed. He was similarly impressed with my encounters with Willis Carto, 'who is, you know, vehemently anti-British'.

In turn, I listened politely as he told me how politicians were all motivated by ego and manipulated by government agencies. 'Isn't that just a bit paranoid?' I asked, innocently.

'Mr Ryan, you'll find out when you've been in this game as long as I have, it's a fact of life.' He fixed me with a stern look.

'So perhaps we need to circumvent these powers?'

'Our methods must always be law abiding.' He coughed, a long 'hrumpf', into his hands. 'Anyone else who says it should be different is thinking pie in the sky.'

'Don't you ever get frustrated by this, though? You, for example. You've had years of this, and a prison sentence.'

'Yes, well, we have faced ridiculous measures in the past,' he seemed gratified to admit. I'd allowed him to say what he wanted. 'Although we suffer from our conspiracy nuts like anyone else. I even count one of them amongst my good friends.'

Tyndall's chinless figure had become a regular spectacle on the extreme right. He'd been in various movements for over 40 years, as he himself admitted to me. Brought up in an affluent family in Kent. Half-Irish, which was something of a surprise in this nationalist and Loyalist-influenced world. Obsessed with sports as a teenager, he'd started out on the left, then drifted right, reading and writing proto-fascist stuff during his National Service days, 'like the works of Mosley [the 1930s British fascist politician], whom I found very interesting'. He moved into different fringe groups, tiny organisations such as the National Labour Party, which even I hadn't heard of. 'I began to see the importance of the race issue.'

A fiery speaker, inspired by Oswald Mosley's style, he became a leading member of groups such as the White Defence League, the National Socialist Movement (an earlier incarnation than David Myatt's organisation) and the Greater Britain Movement. His convictions included possession of a gun and organising a paramilitary movement. Old as he was, he was still a zealot. He'd joined the fledging National Front in 1967 and within a short time became its chairman. As the party grew, Tyndall was attacked for his authoritarian leadership style. When he left in 1980, the party was already in decline, falling into the hands of Nick Griffin and his allies, as Tyndall complained it had been taken over by skinheads and gays. He formed the New National Front and, two years later, the BNP.

Like many of his contemporaries, this veteran of the nazi scene was interested in the Holocaust issue. Or rather, as he put it, that it 'couldn't' be questioned. 'These laws are an example of a police state,' he told me, likening it to a siege mentality, as we talked about Israel and 11 September. His conversation meandered into talk of Russia's Tsarist police, who tried to split groups opposed to the regime. Presumably, he meant similar things were happening here.

'We're in a war,' he said, impassively.

'So, is it time to revive National Socialism?' I asked, probing for a weakness.

'I'm not a National Socialist.'

'So why not be a Conservative, then? What's wrong with that route?'

'The Tories represent the easier, more comfortable route for most people,' he almost spat. 'If only we had proportional representation, it might be different. Still, politics teaches one to be patient.'

'You're not by any chance the same man who was filmed with the leader of the American Nazi Party, George Lincoln Rockwell?'

He looked ruffled momentarily, then recovered his composure. 'Many of us had our wild, youthful flings,' he said.

'What about David Copeland?'

'One isn't responsible for the oddballs. Anything on the fringe is likely to attract them.'

This reminded me that he'd also mentioned the 'brash little boys' surfacing out of the NF. When I mentioned Griffin, he smiled ruefully. 'You encounter rattlesnakes in this business,' he said. 'Very unpleasant, dishonest people. You don't get emotional about it.'

I went upstairs to use the toilet. There were no heaters there, either, and it was ramshackle. Lots of old flowers strewn about; chandelier-style lights hanging from the ceiling. I could hear his wife shuffling about in the kitchen. 'I rely a lot on her opinions,' he said, when I came back down. 'But she won't want to come out and see you, because she's feeling a bit scruffy.'

As he drove me back to the station, talking about his only daughter and her plans for life, I asked if he was looking forward to spending more time with his family, retired as he now was.

'No, I'm not retired. Oh no, definitely not.'

Just when do these guys give up? I wondered.

* * *

BERLIN, 29 APRIL 2002

The French have just voted Jean-Marie le Pen, leader of the infamous Front National, into their national presidential run-offs, defeating the incumbent Socialist prime minister, Lionel Jospin. No one can quite believe it. There's a national crisis. The international media can talk about little else.

Le Pen had been written off. Yet he trounced his former deputy, Bruno Le Megret, and his Mouvement National Republicain, leaving Jospin looking shell-shocked. Nearly six million people have voted for the former paratrooper, who once referred to the Holocaust as 'a detail of history'. He wants to pull France out of the EU and repatriate immigrants, and once punched a female Socialist party candidate. Are the French, like the Austrians, just fed up with the old order, or are they really supporting a fascist revival?

Meanwhile, as I take the S-Bahn from Schönefeld airport into Berlin, the BNP are gearing up for local elections in Britain. I imagined the *Searchlight* team working full-tilt, firefighting, trying to stop any far-right gains. Privately, they were already conceding a certain defeat. 'They'll almost certainly get a few seats,' Nick Lowles told me. 'It's just a question of how many.' The northern city of Burnley seemed their most likely target area. Perhaps Oldham too. The media launched into 'nazi' overdrive. How they would respond to Le Pen's success in France led to a wry smile on my part. If the BNP were nazis – shock, horror! – what hyperbole would be left to describe the FN? Pandering to prejudice did little to curb the rise in xenophobia.

I look out the window, etched with the names of young graffiti artists. Gazing through the scribble, Berlin seems much as I remember. Bohemian, yet ordered. Dirty, but not like English cities. Civic. A place where everything functions. Trams linking with trains. Trains with buses. Buses with the metro. A network of cycle lanes looping past grand old apartment blocks and brasher Soviet-style construction. A city of good beer too.

* * *

Rolf is waiting for me at the station nearest his place. He smiles from atop the concrete steps.

'All right mate, good to see you again!' I cry.

'Ja, ja, umm hmm,' he replies in characteristic, understated fashion. 'Um, how was your journey?'

'Fine, fine,' I grin.

I shake his hand enthusiastically. It is, indeed, good to see a friend. I hadn't really been looking forward to this trip. Germany's been one of the most difficult places for me, struggling to make some form of contact with the extremists. The scene is massive here. And more dangerous, paranoid, closed. Extremely dangerous, in fact, dwarfing the situation in Britain. Particularly in the former East Germany, where many of the 'liberated zones' are supposed to be, the heartlands of the Kameradschaften.

I've been emailing and faxing the Nationaldemokratische Partei Deutschlands (NPD), the country's main neo-nazi political group, for over a year, and still haven't managed to arrange an interview. Perhaps they're having a bad time with the press. They've certainly taken centre stage, trying to fight a government banning order, accused of being a National Socialist organisation, fomenting racist violence and promoting Holocaust denial.

In a common far-right refrain, the party has talked of 'jobs for Germans first' and of 'returning' people. It bracketed anti-Semitism with anti-capitalism, using phrases such as 'grabbing capitalism' to suggest Jewish control (as opposed to 'productive capitalism', which did not). Much has been made of a connection between crime and foreigners, and Germans as somehow victims of outside events. And, of course, there was the omnipresent importance of German 'blood'.

From humble beginnings in 1964, the NPD's fortunes waxed and waned.

At one point it gained enough votes to win representation to several West German state assemblies. Led since 1996 by a man named Udo Voigt, the NPD was now primarily a grassroots network of neo-nazis. Its closest US ally was, once again, William Pierce. NPD men had just left Mark Cotterill's apartment to visit Pierce's compound when I arrived in Washington last year. The head of the party's youth wing had visited Pierce in 1999 and, in 1998, Pierce himself had attended the NPD's national convention in Germany, three years after he visited the BNP's rally in England. It was at this NPD convention that veteran neo-nazi Manfred Roeder called for the violent overthrow of the German government. Roeder, now in his 70s, had already spent eight years behind bars for a 1982 firebomb attack that killed two Vietnamese immigrants. A roving neo-nazi ambassador to the US, he was a longtime associate of Roy Armstrong/Godenau, David Duke's main liaison, to whom Mark Cotterill of the AFBNP had introduced me. The closer I looked, the more involved this extremist network became.

Ironically, the German government itself was now in hot water. A court had just revealed that several senior NPD members were actually informers for the Verfassungsschutz, the German internal security service. If the information being used to ban the party was coming from paid informers, it could compromise the whole process.

'What a mess, ja?' says Rolf, with an affable smile, as I follow his stooped frame up over a bridge. He pushes down on each knee, puffing slighty. Rusting rails and sprouting tufts of grass spread to either side of us. Numerous bikes plough past on the wide pavement. We cross tram tracks, heading towards his apartment.

Funny, I think, how we're so close to this place, back home in England. Only an hour and a half flight, quicker than most train journeys I make. Yet it might as well be a world away. Eurosceptic Britain knows little, at street level, about its continental neighbours.

Setting up my laptop at Rolf's place, I check my webmail and efaxes. Paul's emailed. He's an old Aussie, living in Hamburg. I'd first heard from him via Matt Hale's network, a few months ago. What was an Australian, in his 60s and living part of the year here and part in Sydney, doing with the World Church of the Creator? He's suggesting I contact someone he knows called Werner, who can introduce me to others. 'These guys are adults not stupid skinheads and they have a good grip on the situation,' he writes.

'Coffee?' Rolf calls over my shoulder. I'm sitting in his kids' bedroom, feeling guilty about taking up space. 'Don't worry,' he's said. 'Until five years ago, Hannah and me were living in communes.' They've been part of the left scene here for decades, trade unionists and into communal living experiments. Hannah told me later that she still missed it, even though she was now well into her 40s.

I phone Werner's number and leave a message, hoping whoever hears it can understand English, then open an efax. It's from Christian Worch. I'm momentarily taken aback, seeing his name emblazoned in boldface. Worch is one of Germany's top neo-nazi leaders, a former legal clerk who's served several prison sentences. A truly infamous figure.

He's based in Hamburg, and is the national organiser of a network known as the *Freie Kameradschaften* (Free Comradeships). This is the real underground, the real power of the neo-nazi movement here. The Kameradschaften are social and community-based extreme-right networks. They've often tried, successfully, to infiltrate other networks, such as the NPD, to resist the bans that have destroyed other National Socialist organisations. At some local levels, in nearby Brandenberg province, for example, the NPD organisation is simply the same people as the local Kameradschaften.

So, Worch has finally replied to my faxes. I've been trying to raise him for about a year. He's inviting me to their May Day demonstration in Frankfurt. What an opportunity. These guys want a Fourth Reich, and thousands of them are going to be out on the street.

* * *

30 APRIL 2002

'The Kameradschaften are the most dynamic part of the movement,' my guide says, pointing towards a sheaf of papers. A long, narrow nose sprouts from angular cheekbones, and he holds a cigarette between bony fingers. He crosses his wrists frequently when speaking. 'You should be careful, dealing with them.'

Jimmy is one of the main guys at the anti-fascist press archives (APABIZ) here in Berlin. We've met before. Like Rolf, he's using a pseudonym; the people working at APABIZ are in constant danger from neo-nazi attacks.

'They're the modern form that most neo-nazi movements here take,' says Jimmy, rolling the cigarette between his fingers, before pausing for another drag. 'They can really mobilise the young people, and they have a strong influence in Germany's youth culture.'

I've heard a lot more about the culture and character of Germans since arriving yesterday, some of it familiar from my Austrian trip. How there'd been a refusal in some parts of the national community to acknowledge the horrors of the war unleashed by Hitler. Aggrieved youth in the East and in rural areas, hearing tales of how the Wehrmacht was really the best army in Europe, and how it was defeated by treachery. Doubting the scale of the Holocaust. Some were fed up with apologising for the past and didn't really think the country had done anything *that* wrong. And they wanted the order and certainty they attributed to Hitler's regime.

It struck me that there might be a peculiar kind of conservative mindset here, at its most extreme among alienated youth and 'globalisation losers'.

Not just about the war and the Holocaust, but reflected in the fact that the State itself had existed only since 1870, and exacerbated by the fall of Communism and the rapid change of the 1990s. A historical insecurity over identity, which expressed itself in these more conservative forms, like the student Burschenschaft. There'd been a German nation, and peoples, long before this, but scattered over hundreds of principalities and kingdoms. Had an aggressive sense of nationhood coalesced into the German character, early in the twentieth century?

Jimmy leans back in the hard plastic chair, his long legs wrapped in drainpipe leather trousers. An arc light flickers overhead. The archive is part of Berlin's alternative anti-fascist ('Antifa') network, a few stops from Rolf's place on the U-Bahn, past Turkish grocery stalls and community centres.

Tomorrow is one of the year's main neo-nazi shows of strength, a time of high tension and controversy when the extremists try to march in half a dozen cities. On this traditional day of the left, the right likes to thrust its cocky head high. I need some help and advice before deciding where I'm going to end up: in Berlin for the NPD's demonstration, or in Frankfurt, with Christian Worch and the Kameradschaften. I've already received an email from another part of the network, advising me not to go; there's often violence among the extreme right, the hard left, and the police.

There was another message, too, from a most unlikely source. Horst Mahler had been a lawyer and a founding member of the Red Army Faction – or Baader-Meinhof Gang, as many knew it – a left-wing terrorist group. Up to 100 Germans joined this network between the early 1970s and its dissolution some 20 years later. They'd been responsible for more than a dozen deaths. After ten years in jail for armed robbery and taking part in an attempt to spring the gang's leader, Mahler had converted to the extreme right. Regarded with hostility by former comrades, he was now the NPD's lawyer. His email invited me over to his place. He even told me where he was going to be at a regional NPD demonstration tomorrow.

'When I say modern, I don't mean that these things are really new. It all started back in the 1970s, when there was a split in the NPD,' continues Jimmy. The archive is busy, people drifting past the top floor of the old building. Computers glimmer softly on desks. The place buzzes with quiet urgency.

Jimmy says the NPD has been around since the 1960s. Its electoral highlight occurred towards the end of that decade, when several members won seats in regional parliaments. A split in the 1970s pushed out those seeking a more ideological organisation. They looked towards the left and its tactics, calling themselves the 'New Right'. Particularly those from the Jungen Nationaldemokraten (JN), the NPD's youth group, containing many radicals interested in National Socialism. (In Germany, it's illegal to declare yourself an NS supporter or to question the Holocaust.)

'There were more splits over the years,' explains Jimmy. 'The common theme for many of those leaving was that they wanted to re-establish the NSDAP [the old Nazi party]. Michel Kühnen was the main leader of this group, trying to recreate a 'brownshirt' movement like Ernst Röhm's stormtroopers, the SA, of the 1920s. They were street activists, with a paramilitary belief, intent on recreating a National Socialist political system. And Christian Worch was Kühnen's key lieutenant throughout these years.'

Kühnen is a legend on the neo-nazi fringe here in Germany and abroad: a former army officer who spent his short lifetime on the extreme right, credited with building the foundations of many of today's neo-nazi movements, particularly the Kameradschaften.

Kühnen's faction started up something called the NSDAP/AO – literally translating as the foreign group of the Nazi party (but also suggesting a new Nazi party was 'in construction') – under the tutelage of a US Nazi figure, Gary Lauck. I'd already visited Lauck's website during my attempts to link up with Swedish extremists. He was, or had been, a key player in an attempt to foster a National Socialist revival in northern Europe. Through Lauck, the NSDAP/AO had many links to other foreign extremists, as well as to genuine old Nazis hiding in different corners of the globe.

'Kühnen and Worch were also quite good at using the media,' adds Jimmy. 'They knew the power of mass media and information. Kühnen once said that he wanted to distribute as many swastikas as possible, so that people would one day get used to them.' Swastikas are illegal in Germany.

These hardliners kept creating different front organisations. At the core was a dedicated set of cadres, who eventually coalesced into something called the GdNF (Gesinnungs-gemeinschaft der Neuen Front). The front organisations – prisoner solidarity groups, trade union friendship movements, local election parties, single-issue campaign outlets – sat around this secretive core. The neo-nazis even took over existing organisations, like FAP (Freiheitliche Deutsche Arbeiterpartei), the Freedom German Workers Party, which they subjugated from within. As each group was eventually banned by the government, another would take its place, with the same core. It was a cat-and-mouse game with the authorities. Occasionally the real leadership – people like Kühnen and Worch – would get sent to jail, but the cycle continued.

Another series of splits occurred in the 1980s, when rumours began to circulate about Kühnen's alleged homosexuality. But after German reunification, Kühnen and his cohorts took advantage of the situation, finding fertile recruiting ground in the depressed east. 'They even had a strategy, called Working Plan East,' says Jimmy. New groups, such as Deutsche Alternative, were created solely to recruit and build in these areas, linked back to the same secret core.

'It never showed up as an organisation,' explains Jimmy, leaning close, 'but it existed. It was the place where all the leaders decided what to do next.'

In 1991 Kühnen died of AIDS, and Worch took over. By now, though, the

German government was wise to the neo-nazis' tricks and banned nearly all the front organisations between 1992 and 1994. This was also a time of increased racial tension and violence, putting the authorities under pressure to act. People were being kicked to death, stoned and petrol-bombed, and migrant hostels were being attacked. Amazingly, some of the groups which were banned at this time had existed since the 1950s, for example Wiking Jugend (Viking Youth), which organised camps and weapons training.

After Christian Worch emerged from his latest jail sentence, and numerous raids had jailed several of his comrades, the GdNF core began bickering about the future. 'The fascists had the problem how to organise. Some of them said it was bullshit. Some said they had to arm. Others said they had to build a "united right" movement like the Republikaners or the DVU [another right-wing party].'

Such struggles led to the strategy of organising the Kameradschaften. 'This meant you gathered people on your side in such a way that the State cannot ban them,' says Jimmy, drawing on a piece of paper how all the gangs and groups relate to each other. 'It was Worch, mainly, that did this.' I watch, fascinated. The image is intricate, like a flow chart. These new groups had no official membership. They could simply be a few people in a small town, or in a whole region, gathering at social, rather than political, events. The aim was the same, though: to draw out a hard core of cadres and leaders to create a National Socialist movement.

Guys like Worch and his deputies, such as Thomas Wulff (nicknamed 'Steiner' after a famous Waffen-SS general), act as the national organisers for the decentralised Kameradschaften. 'It's Worch holding all the pieces and the ideas on strategy,' says Jimmy. Worch and Steiner both belonged to several earlier NS groups, such as Hamburger Sturm (Hamburg Storm), which was later banned.

'How many Kameradschaften are there?' I ask.

'No one really knows. Maybe up to 120. Right now, they call themselves *Freie Nationalisten* – or Free Nationalists. Sometimes also *Nationaler Widerstand*, or National Resistance. It's an NS network which gathers inside, and through, the Kameradschaften.'

Worch and other organisers, such as Steffen Hupka, had been trying to use the NPD as a legal front for their activities. During the 1970s and 1980s, Hupka rose in a neo-nazi group which was a rival to Kühnen's GdNF. The Nationalistische Front (NF) saw itself more as an elitist SS organisation, with higher levels of physical training (including weapons training) and membership fees, than the street/mass movement – or – SA approach of Worch and Kühnen. It also took longer to join; you had to serve a six-month apprenticeship period. But in the end, the new Kameradschaften had brought them together: men now well into their 30s and 40s, experienced, hardcore neo-nazis. They'd very nearly succeeded in taking over the NPD, too. Until this year, Hupka was a leading member of one of its factions. The NPD had only 6,000 listed members, but many more sympathisers through the Kameradschaften. Hupka had been thrown out after the NPD leadership came to see him as a direct threat.

The NPD was legally allowed to march and received state funding as a political party. It made sense to try to use it. And after 1996 the new NPD leader, Udo Voigt, wanted to use these groups in turn as a source of potential recruits. 'Before this,' Jimmy explains, 'the NPD didn't want to associate with National Socialist groups. Voigt changed that.' Each, it seemed, was trying to use the other. The JN was particularly attractive to the former GdNF guys, filled as it was with eager neo-nazi youth. Worch himself never joined the NPD, however, even though he said on several occasions that they needed to use it.

It was around this time that the first mention was made of the *National befreite Zonen*, or NBZs (liberated zones), in an article in an NPD student magazine. After that, there was lots of discussion in the nazi movements about what this might mean. 'It was already a reality in the East, of course!' jokes Jimmy, somewhat sadly.

'Doing what?'

'Well, many Kameradschaften were already forcing out non-right groups. Influencing youth clubs in their area, taking over the youth social scene. They arrange their own meeting points and want to dictate what's happening in "their" area.' A coughing fit overtakes him for a moment. He lights another cigarette, brushing aside the ash from the old one. 'They talk of cleaning up the streets. And they often create or sell merchandising, CDs, propaganda material like books and newsletters. Even kids' gear.' The music scene can form an important interface here with Blood and Honour and similar networks.

The goal, it seems, is to force out everything that is 'un-German', to encourage people to be *Völkisch*. There's a bloodline, and a racist connotation to this word. And a cultural essence too: defining yourself by what you are not. You are not 'un-German'. This can even extend to listening only to traditional German music, or avoiding kebabs and hamburgers. There's hatred for MTV and 'nigger music'. That's why there's such attention paid to the music scene, through forms such as Oi!, dark wave, folk, thrash, black metal, even techno (as long as it has the appropriate lyrics).

I thank Jimmy for his time and mull over my thoughts. Worch's fax referred to this Hupka guy, I remember. He said I could call him, and listed his mobile number.

Another thing's becoming clear to me now. This is not William Pierce and The Order at work, nor leaderless resistance. Nor Haider's or Le Pen's xenophobic populism. This is a genuine attempt to lay the foundation stones for a new Reich.

* * *

1 MAY 2002, HOHENSCHÖNHAUSEN, BERLIN

'Frei! Sozial! Und Nation-aal! Frei, Sozial und Nation-aal!'

Each word explodes in a guttural burst. The noise around me is deafening. Music, klaxons, whistles, screaming abuse, threats, spitting. The tramp of thousands of feet. A mêlée of skinheads, anarchists, riot police, bystanders. Banners and boots. I weave in and out of the procession.

'Does that mean what I think it does?'

'Yes!' she shouts, cupping her hands close to my ears. I can see the nicotine stains sunk, like tumeric, into her fingers. 'Free social and national. Or, in other words, a code for national socialism, which they can't say together, because it's illegal.'

Tammy is walking beside me. She has that enigmatic look on her face again. *'Nazis Raus!'* ('Nazis Out!') a group of protesters screams to our left. They're wearing bright colours, ripped jeans, studs, rings. Young and idealistic anarchists, Greens and anti-fascists locked in a ritual of combat with their traditional enemy.

'Antifa, ha ha ha!' about 30 boneheads chant in response, pointing as one towards the anti-fascists marching either side of their column. They look incredibly young to me, and diminutive. I had imagined this a land of Teutonic giants. Many seem to be wearing dark glasses over flushed faces. Still, there are some serious nutcases amongst these lost youth. Fanatics a bit like The Beast, as well as veteran neo-nazis. The green-clad riot police look on nervously, marching in time with the NPD, toying with their batons and shoving people back when tempers fray. I watch one skin stare past me towards two young women, anti-fascists, catcalling at his mates. A slim, pale young man with an earring, white sweater and gold chain, he's probably no more than 20. He's drawing his finger across his throat.

I'm in Berlin, in faceless, usually quiet Hohenschönhausen, part suburb, with ugly tower blocks, part village with ramshackle barns, wildlife and an ancient, meandering river. Now witnessing scenes not seen for 60 years or more.

I spoke last night to Steffen Hupka. The Kameradschaften leader answered his mobile, 'Hup-ka?' his voice rising, high and innocuous-sounding. He told me the courts had insisted that the Kameradschaften march start at 9 a.m., too early for me to get to Frankfurt, over four hours away by train. I'd opted instead for the NPD event here in Berlin. Hupka said we could meet another time.

I've counted about a thousand nazis already. My adrenaline is surging as Tammy points out the different leadership figures. We're just behind one of the NPD vans, crawling slowly along the route, surrounded by skins. In other circumstances they'd probably be tearing me apart, but the cops are keeping a close watch on things. Curious residents observe us from apartment balconies. The sun begins to shine. Another blast of surreal German folk music starts up from the van's speakers.

We pull off to the side of the road. Rolf joins us, sweating, beads of moisture matting his beard. My other companion, a young student with orange hair, scrunches up her face and laughs. 'You see, they don't have such good taste in music!' Her laugh is still innocent. I chuckle, in agreement. 'I don't know how they can stand this shit. It always drives me mad.' She giggles.

'It's like this at every demonstration,' Tammy concludes, in a resigned, war-weary tone. As she speaks the van stops, and so do we. An uneasy stand-off ensues between the marchers and the protesters. The van begins to turn sideways, setting its speakers towards the faithful. The police look nervous, stepping between the two groups. Rolf points out a small, tubby man who mounts a podium inside the vehicle. He begins thundering out a speech in a direct Hitlerian style. I can't understand the words, but Rolf is swearing under his breath: 'This is such shit! Nick, you should see this guy. He's really short and comical, speaking just like Hitler!' I'm reminded of Mark Cotterill's comment about who would be first up against the wall, come the NS revolution.

* * *

We spent an hour or two by the station, watching the skins arrive in dribs and drabs. The cocky smiles became warped as the cops forced them to stand to one side, against the railings, and submit to a search. I could see more cops below us, too, beside the track and on the platform. I spotted several undercover units, fitting stab-proof vests under their casual gear.

Individually, the KKK lapels, Valhalla T-shirts and Hail Victory jackets of the skins looked faintly ridiculous. Together, though, they painted a more ominous picture. Across the road, the anti-fascists had gathered in similar numbers, chanting, blowing shrill metal whistles – painful to the ears at close range – and raving to the hardcore blasting from mobile sound systems. I spotted several variations on the old Soviet flag. I felt like an envoy before a battle, shuttling back and forth between warring tribes. Tammy and Rolf both told me there were anti-globalisation riots last night in the part-bohemian, part-Turkish Kreuzberg district. More trouble is predicted tonight.

Early in the day, I asked Rolf to help me translate as I spoke to some of the young skins. I approached a couple of guys holding a banner with the word *Antikapitalismus* written on it. A red-haired bloke with sideburns regarded me with open hostility. He had a sort of Mod look, in a starched white shirt buttoned to the top and a blue-piped cardigan. Where he lived in the East, he said, there was no work. 'They closed down my factory. I lost my job about two months ago.'

'So why join the NPD? Why not the REP or DVU, the other right-wing parties?' And slightly less controversial, I added, in the back of my head. He and his friend looked at each other, laughed, and sneered back at me.

'Internal immigration's our worst problem,' he said. 'We have people fleeing from the East to the West [of Germany] all the time.' He coughed, then spat a wodge of phlegm towards the ground, near my feet. 'We don't even speak English where we come from. We had to learn Russian.'

'What about the Kameradschaften, then?' I ventured. 'Why bother with the NPD at all?' I didn't realise, truly, that these groups were really one and the same at ground level. It was reflected in his answer.

'The cooperation between the NPD and the Kameradschaften is wonderful. We don't work together politically, but we come together when necessary.'

* * *

'C'mon, Rolf, let's move on,' I say, as a fat guy waddles past us. Rolf taps me on the shoulder. 'He was in prison for attempted murder and torture, that one,' he says. 'He's a local *Kameradschaftsführer*.' The roly-poly figure is shouting into a megaphone. Bloody hell, he looks in his early 20s. And a bit of a geek, too. But a hardened psycho, all the same. As if to punctuate the point, Rolf points out a Kameradschaften banner being held by NPD supporters.

We negotiate our way towards the front of the march again, weaving between the protesters, who remonstrate frequently with the neo-nazis. One ape-faced guy with lank, greasy hair and a Ché Guevara T-shirt runs forward and tries to snatch a megaphone from one of the organisers. A bunch of heavies descend on him, but the police intervene quickly and drag him out. He just sneers, a stocky, tough-looking street fighter, and spits on the pavement. Then he runs on, to attack another part of the march.

There seems a lot of activity around an elderly gentleman. 'That's Friedhelm Busse,' says Tammy. He must be in his 70s, at least. He wears a smart, brown tweed jacket, pressed slacks, shirt, tie and some sort of red NPD kerchief. An old schoolteacher or professor perhaps? 'No,' replies Tammy. 'He's not allowed to speak openly at the moment, because the court just handed down a sentence against him, for Holocaust denial. I think he's even waiting to go to jail.'

'What, this old bloke?!'

'Yeah, he's been in this for years. In armed, paramilitary groups. Part of the original stay-behind network, after the war. He was a leader of the FAP too, a rival to Kühnen. He's a really important guy here. All these skins will look up to him. He's got respect. He's served prison time and is a real veteran.'

I try to push forward to speak with him – I don't even know if he understands English – but an NPD steward shoves me back. I glare at the guy's dark glasses, framing the cockily tilted head. He says something in German, but his attention is diverted by a camera crew wandering past. He runs over to them instead, coolly chewing his gum and puffing himself up inside his bomber jacket. A couple of eggs are thrown in his direction, splattering across the side of his face.

As we walk on, Rolf points out one particular guy, stocky, medium height, dark, trimmed beard, sunglasses, baseball cap. 'Oliver Schweigert. He's a real psycho.'

'How do you mean?'

'He's got convictions for various things. Violence. He attacked some friends of mine once. He's been around since the 1980s. He's got a real reputation.' My eyes follow the guy, drawn to the muscular back disappearing amongst the other skins. He's older, confident, full of bravado. Glancing around, looking for confrontation.

And here it comes: a tall fellow – a Green party lawyer, I'm later told – has been leaning over the barriers, as several anti-fascists try to snatch an NPD banner. Schweigert's body angles in fast, as he leaps towards the guy. They disappear into a psychotic mêlée. An animal shift takes place in the skins in front of me. They leer and surge forward. Panicked-looking police rush up, shouting, pointing, drawing huge, nasty wooden batons. They start laying into the two groups, yanking them apart. Schweigert has the Green guy and a woman pushed right back into a railing near a bridge. The cops shove the nazis back into the centre of the road. Then Schweigert smiles, an enigmatic little twist of his face, before sauntering off, leaving the shaken Green guy to remonstrate with the police in shock and rage.

'I'm going to try and speak with him,' I tell Rolf, further up the march. 'Do you want to try and translate?'

'No, not really.' He looks at me with disbelief.

I walk past a shop entrance, duck beneath a railing, swallow hard, and slip into the band of skins surrounding the bearded fellow.

'*Bitte, sprechen Sie Englisch?*' I try to make myself seem friendly. Half a dozen heads turn silently towards me. '*Ich bin Englisch. Sprechen Sie Englisch?*' I put the question direct to Schweigert's face. His thick arms are thrust into his pockets. The enigmatic smile surfaces. He shrugs his shoulders. 'You don't speak English?' I thrust my notebook forward. The skins lean in closer. I'm afraid, but I want a comment.

'Y-y-y-yeah!' an aggressive young guy starts jabbering in my face. His mates laugh. I'm guessing this is some sort of joke. He laughs again, repeating the phrase over and over. I sigh inwardly but try to keep my composure.

'Look, I'm – me – a writer.' I point towards my notebook and my pen. 'Writing a book?' It's no use. Schweigert isn't even looking towards me. He just smiles, an angelic choirboy expression.

'Hey, I'm crazy about my country!' another skin calls out to me. Then they move off again, leaving me by the side of the road, my heart pounding.

About 20 metres up, I see them lock horns with another group of protesters. Schweigert and a black guy, pounding away at each other. A ritual frozen in time. Hate unchecked.

* * *

1 MAY 2002, KREUZBERG, BERLIN

Fires, bricks, paving stones. The police charge up and down the streets as I sit in a small Indian restaurant, watching events like a football spectator. Kreuzberg is edgy. The cops I saw earlier in the evening looked nervous, clumped in little groups at traffic junctions, surrounded by skulking youth. The whole thing was ready to explode. And it has.

The smell of burning cars permeates the cooling night around us. Sound systems scream from windows high above. It feels odd to walk down the centre of a road, moving among scores of people. It's part street party, part uprising. The Palestinian flag hangs from a window. A Muslim mother gazes down in bewilderment at the anarchists and young Turks wandering these narrow, dark streets.

Safely ensconced in the restaurant, I meet up with Mark Potok of the Southern Poverty Law Center, in town for a conference. We sit drinking beer and reminiscing. Occasionally we walk to the front door, when a water cannon opens up or the police line charges. In the evening we follow the police lines and snatch squads as they charge into the bars. Hundreds of glasses and bottles hurl out of each place towards them. Broken and cracked cobblestones litter the streets. It's strange, being a riot tourist. Spending the morning surrounded by neo-nazis, and the evening with hardcore anarchists. Disenchanted youth, divided from each other, yet members of the same tribe.

* * *

When we get back – after being subjected to numerous police searches – Rolf recounts a sad story. He knew a family of Turks who'd saved up money from Berlin and moved to Pirna, a town close to Dresden, near the Czech border. The area was a declared NBZ – 'liberated zone' – patrolled by a banned organisation called SSS (Sachsen Schweiz Skinheads). It was one of the worst NBZs in Germany. The family's kebab house was attacked; windows were smashed; youths would often Sieg Heil outside the premises. The attacks started only in 2000, after the family moved their restaurant closer to the town centre. So they decided to fight back. During an anti-nazi demo, young neo-nazis had insulted, then harassed them. So the father put a Turkish flag in the window. Then the mum ran out with a stick. Seeing this, a policewoman beat her, so the daughter pushed the officer away. A ruckus ensued, leading to all sorts of trouble and a prosecution for assault. Even worse, this evening Rolf had just had a call on his mobile. There'd been more trouble. The whole family had confronted taunting youths, and in the ensuing fracas the dad had stabbed one of the neo-nazis.

'It's really sad,' he says. 'How it comes to this. He was already looking at a possible jail sentence. Now he'll go down for sure.'

I also chat with Hannah, Rolf's partner, about her frustration with East Germans. I find it strange at first, but then I begin to understand. 'They're more used to authoritarian ways of thinking, always complaining, and to a man they're against foreigners,' Hannah explains. 'If you try to argue with them about changing their position, they won't listen. They just change the topic.'

How ignorant I've been. Many former nazis never disappeared. They simply joined the West German government, or melted into the postwar spy networks.

In the morning, Rolf says right-wing extremists are beginning to march with Arabs here in Germany. I could see the same thing on the email lists I monitored. 'Let's hook up with any Palestinians we can find in our local area,' wrote one American KKK member.

* * *

3 MAY 2001

A child's bike leans outside the whitewashed house. Wooden shutters grip the windows. As I approach, finger hovering near the buzzer, I hear the yapping of a dog inside. I turn and look behind me. An affluent, shaded surburb, probably full of lawyers, doctors and other professionals. A leaf flutters down from one of the tall trees that parade either side of me. Kleinmachnow, on the far southern outskirts of Berlin.

Rolf says Horst Mahler has been responsible for pushing the NPD to an even more radical stance. Mahler has said he hasn't changed views at all: 'The labels "left" and "right" don't apply anymore today.' This born-again nationalist claims he's fighting for the identity of German people and the survival of German culture. But Rolf maintains: 'Mahler's main topic is anti-Semitism – and that is what fascists at grassroots level can pick up.' I'm about to find out. I push the buzzer.

There's a second of silence, then the dog starts up again. The solid wood cracks open. A balding, grey-haired, somewhat fat man stands there in black jeans, denim shirt and glasses.

'Ah!' he says, pointing down at his watch and holding back the hound with his other hand. I'm late. I know. I didn't realise how far off the beaten track this place was.

I apologise profusely as we move over a tiled floor – it's cool in here – through a spreading, open lounge, then out into a small, tidy conservatory. Mahler is silent. He growls something to the dog. It runs before me, leaping into a chair.

'Coffee?' He indicates a tall, modern-looking flask. I can make out my reflection in the gleaming metal.

'Please.'

Thick, chunky hands grip the handle and neatly pour out two cups. As I fiddle with the tape recorder's controls, I suggest he tell me something about himself. He tuts, muffling his words into his beard, and tucks his chin downwards: 'I don't want to talk about myself. I make that a rule.'

'Oh.'

He sits and stares, hands clasped together, belly wobbling above his jeans. 'I'm just an ordinary party member, not a leader,' he explains.

'What about this banning, then? How are you involved with that?'

'The reason for banning the NPD is because of its connections to the youth,' says Mahler. He says that until this point he had no interest in the party, that it's only because he's a lawyer that he felt compelled to help. In fact, several times during our interview, he takes calls from Udo Voigt, the NPD chairman, as they discuss the latest developments in the court case. They're hopeful it will be dropped, because of the revelation about the use of government informers.

Then he starts talking about immigration, with the gravitas of someone discussing philosophy or political theory.

'The youth growing up in this country think that there are too many foreigners. And the NPD is the only party which has a very clear standpoint on this. The NPD is very clear that they must go back to their own countries.'

'How many immigrants are there, then?'

'Officially, seven million. But there's at least eleven million. In our great cities, Germans will be a minority within ten years. It's an awful situation.'

I look outside. A lovely old tree is dropping blossoms onto a neat lawn. Tweeting birds sit in the branches.

'These people want to change Germany into an Islamic country. They think like they're in Turkey. They believe in Allah, one God.' The irony, as Rolf told me, is that these Turks are usually more settled than Mahler thinks, and often view more recent immigrants as potential rivals.

'We don't want to lose our Heimat . . .' He searches for the word. I supply it: 'Homeland.'

'Ja, that's it,' he agrees, with a curt smile.

For Mahler, much of this seems to go back to the war. 'We lost our identity after then.' When I ask about the German character – about

285

being inflexible, having this racist notion of the 'community of the people' and so on – his face sets stony hard. 'We can discuss if Communism is good or bad – millions of people died under Stalin – but not National Socialism,' he says. 'Neither will be the solution, however. There will be something else.' This eventual outcome will be a 'third element', that elusive sense of Volksgemeinschaft, the community of the people. In National Socialist ideology, this idea of community means you exclude 'non-folkish' people.

'So you believe in the power of community?' I suggest.

'Yes,' he agrees. 'It's important to preserve community. People feel uncertain and aggressive. When I speak to them, they tell me they are so full of anger.' He laughs harshly. 'Because of this process of individualisation you mention, and the pursuit of private profit.'

He doesn't feel he's moved his position. Rather, the world has changed and placed him on the right. It simply confirms my own suspicions about extremism, although I keep my opinions private. 'I'm convinced this order can only be realised on a national scale. If this is National Socialism, it's a good thing.'

'Really?'

'I don't want historical National Socialism [which he calls a tragic mistake] but we have to get back with our thinking and see the essence of National Socialism. It's an answer to a problem that no one until now has been able to answer.' Then, in an echo of my Austrian experiences, he says: 'The American structure on the East Coast think that they and not any power dominate the free world.'

'Through organisations like the Bilderberg Group, perhaps?' I tentatively venture.

'Oh yes. Jewish influence on financial institutions is overwhelming.' He talks of Cromwell bringing Jews to England and even quotes from the Bible to show how Jews are supposed to lend money, to gain credit for themselves. 'They are the enemy of mankind.' Through them, presumably, the USA is trying to divide and rule the world. And it 'wants to keep Germany unpure and weak. It's their role to destroy, and that's why they're hated. This is the historical role of Judaism.'

He ties these comments in with the question of modern Israel. The whole Jewish/Israel question is 'the centre of our problems'. He perks up considerably when I tell him of my own experiences in the Middle East and tells me of his time in Syria and Jordan. In Mahler's view, Jews 'destroy communities, and therefore they feel hated'. They are 'an element of alienation and unrest'.

So I ask about revisionism. I know he's into this. We were both due to travel to Beirut last year, for the Institute for Historical Review conference. Mahler says it's a sign of oppression that you can't question the Holocaust. 'The Third World War has started already,' he states, mysteriously.

'So in this war there'll be cooperation between those people you see as enemies? Such as the Arabs?'

'The enemy of my enemy is my friend,' is all he'll say. He thinks that 'in two to five years, a popular uprising will take place'. He's waiting, like many, for the economic system to tumble. 'The dollar is the biggest fraud in history.'

I change tack, asking him about his background. He seems happier to talk now, warmed up as he is. He was born in 1936, one of four children. His mother got a medal from the Nazi regime for having so many kids. 'I know what a happy family is. My father was a dentist. We had two women servants. My parents were happy and good natured.' From this period, he learned that women should be the centre of the family.

After studying law in the mid-1950s, he went into practice, then slowly gathered an interest in politics and the burgeoning protest movements over the Cuban missile crisis and Vietnam. He was ten years older than most of the other students who became involved.

At this point he starts quoting Hegel (one of his favourite topics), and relates how during his prison years he came to a realisation that Marx and Lenin had failed fully to understand Hegel's thoughts. Then he elaborates on his view that Germans were somehow victims of the war. 'We had thoughts about the USA bombing German cities in the war. I always had an uncomfortable feeling about the war when I met foreign students.'

He spends much time explaining the role of the Jews and their influence on Franklin Roosevelt in launching the Second World War. How the Versailles Treaty was manipulated, then the Japanese tempted into attacking the US, in order to bring their German allies into the conflict. 'He [Roosevelt] wanted to destroy the German Reich, so that US power could rise.' I become more and more bored as he rambles on about Hegel and the spirit of man. 'The German people are very friendly to strangers,' he says. 'Right now they're stressed.' Yet when talking of Hegel, he also mentions the notion of repulsion – you attract communities together, then they repel each other apart. It's natural. In this scenario, 'the process of people throwing stones and burning hostels is quite natural. I hate it, but it's normal'.

The phone rings again, and he takes the call. When he gets back, he checks his watch – I can hear his wife moving somewhere else in the house – then continues. 'We need to take our lessons from history, if we want to preserve peace in Europe.'

'How so?'

'We want to be as we were. I don't ask if it's legitmate. It's our being.' He coughs. As I prepare to leave, he says: 'Everyone thinks the Nazis were the devil. And this will change very soon.'

* * *

Christopher Nsoh's face is wide and expressive. We'd shared a beer and talked in a small kebab house near Berlin's main Zoo station, straight after my meeting with Mahler.

Christopher is an international public law graduate. He shares many of my interests and wants to travel. He's also suffered persecution and torture.

'This is it,' he says, his English accented from his homeland, Cameroon. He points to a large apartment building. 'The hostel.'

Mud squelches through my shoes. The station's a couple of minutes behind us. It's only an hour to the relative comfort of Berlin, away from here, the town of Rathenow in Brandenburg province, in the rural East.

A liberated zone.

'C'mon, you'll need your passport ready for the security guard,' Christopher says, pulling on my arm, as we approach the dilapidated block. An old factory, brown and crumbling, lies off in the distance. Tiny allotments sit across the road, near a small bar. Old men and women bend over and toil at each plot, pausing to stare as we walk past. One white man, one black.

The burly blond guard is sprawled inside a cabin-like office. He takes my passport, staring furiously at the picture, appearing puzzled, then scratches his stubble and eases the belt holding back a bulging stomach.

'Okay,' he mutters, and waves me through. An enigmatic look plays on Christopher's face. We head up the central staircase.

'Hey, Christopher, my man!' another African salutes us from inside a bedroom, as Christopher beams and walks in. 'Andy John, how you doing!' he laughs, in return. Andy's from Chad, another asylum seeker. A quiet man with a slow, patient smile and prominent gold chain around his neck. Christopher tells me Andy was busted up by some locals recently when he tried to order a glass of beer across the road.

'You know, people get very bored here. Four people to a room, nowhere to go, not even being able to talk to your lawyer – who's usually in another city anyway. Andy and another guy went to get a beer in the bar, and they were quoted a price of 20 Deutschmarks. Well, usually it's just five Deutschmarks.' When he and his friend queried the price, several guys turned on them. The friend got out, but Andy had his face busted first, before escaping. He lost several teeth.

'Is this kind of thing pretty unusual?'

'No! No, that sort of thing happens all the time.'

When we climb another set of stairs, negotiating the warren of corridors and rooms – the Africans are all very communal, leaving their doors open – I hear similar talk from a bunch of guys from Togo. The room is heavy with the scent of sweat and exotic cooking smells. They prepare some spicy chicken stew, and griese – a sort of maize meal you eat with your hands – specially for us. I listen to their stories of persecution back home, and of violence from the locals here. Being attacked on their bikes. Spat at. Refused service in shops. Called 'nigger'. Waiting, in vain, for the police to arrive.

'If I had known what Germany was like, I would never have come here. Never.' Christopher is adamant. He spits the words. They sound especially harsh, coming as they do from one so intelligent, once a student leader in Cameroon. These are people who have seen friends beaten to death, who've been arrested and tortured. ('I was pissing blood for three days,' says one young guy, recalling his interrogation.) Highly educated members of society, who could contribute, if allowed, now fighting the system here.

'They can't do anything else to me. I don't care. I spent four years in this place, and I'm not going back,' says Christopher. The others nod their heads.

Christopher is treated as some kind of returning hero by most of the asylum seekers. He married a German woman and is finally sorting out his residency. We take a walk outside, through the nearby woods.

'Did you know this is the most racist area of Germany, by statistics?' He says the asylum seekers can purchase goods only with a voucher system (Britain adopted a similar system, disastrously), using some sort of smart card. 'And we're not even allowed to travel out of a certain distance from the city. You know, man, the way the asylum seekers are kept here is traumatising. Really traumatising.' You can see it in the sad smiles of men who know they won't see their families again.

Christopher reels off a list of racial attacks that makes my stomach churn. 'Things are happening almost every day. It's a social problem,' he laughs, bitterly. 'You know, you can't go outside here in Rathenow, on your own, after 8 p.m. You'll be attacked; it's that simple. You even need permission to go and see your own lawyer.'

He talks of Germany being 'a racist state', as he explains that in Brandenburg, asylum seekers and migrants make up only 3 per cent of the population. Yet with an unemployment rate of about 18 per cent, people are quick to blame them for their troubles.

'Is there a racist German mindset, then?' I ask. We're walking past a local soccer ground. The rain is beginning to drizzle, softly, in a fine mist. It's quiet. Almost idyllic, in a weird kind of way.

'Sure! Sure. They are not doing anything to destroy the past. Even the Minister of the Interior said, only a few years ago, that the boat is full.' It echoes something Rolf said: that Germans, like many others, are beginning to vote through fear.

Back in the hostel we move between the rooms, meeting guys from across Africa: Nigeria, Togo, Kenya, Cameroon, Sierra Leone, all speaking a patois. Locked into this unwilling world, waiting for news of their case. Or deportation.

One is lucky enough to have his own room. He's been here two and a half years. A passionate man, with high intellect. He comes from Kenya and is frustrated at his situation and disgusted at his treatment by the local authorities. Once a leading member of an opposition party, he's now reduced to sitting in a cramped room, smoking, watching CNN, constantly eating – through depression – drinking, lying on dishevelled sheets. A proud father, who worked his way up from the shop floor to become a top engineer. Then this.

'Why come here, then?' I know my question is incendiary, but I must ask.

'When you're fleeing your country, the people putting you on a plane don't tell you where you're going to end up,' he says, gesticulating. 'I used to fly to Tanzania, Mozambique and other countries for my job. I'd never been outside Africa. So when they started killing members of my party – including the general secretary – I had to go into hiding. You pay people to help you get out. They smuggle you onto the plane. I only worked out it wasn't going to Africa, when I started counting the hours I'd been on board.'

'You know, we are allowed to do some community work,' says Andy John. He comes into the room followed by a young Nigerian. Both are holding cans of beer. Much of our day revolves around talking politics and drinking. 'I was digging graves – you know, for dead bodies – for one euro an hour. One euro. Do you call that fair?' The Kenyan speaks disparagingly of many Germans, claiming many expect the State to provide for their every need: 'I have never been brought up to work for nothing or given anything for free,' he declares.

'Listen, Nick,' Christopher rumbles in his deep voice. 'I had these guys – you know, I went up to them here in Rathenow, I talked to them direct. They said, "I hate you." I asked why. This was a young man. He told me, "You are a foreigner." I said that there were foreigners in my country too. Refugees, migrants, workers. So he just looked at me, and told me, "Go back to your own country, then, and fight all the foreigners there." Can you believe it?' He snorts, with a mixture of contempt and incredulity.

He gestures, twisting his hand open and pointing upwards. 'We have women here prostituting themselves now.'

'Really?'

'Oh, yes. This whole place, it's an unnatural way of living. Andy here, he wakes up at 4 a.m. and starts drinking, because he knows his girlfriend is now sleeping with his roommate. These are the kind of pressures you suffer, forced into this building, this way of life.'

'Do you see hope?'

He laughs bitterly. 'Very far from it.'

As I leave, his friend is near tears. Despondent, sorry to see me – the outside world, someone interested – go. I feel terrible. 'Yes, you are welcome any time,' he mumbles, looking down towards the floor. CNN babbles on in the background.

NINETEEN

NEW REICH

MAY 2002

Piped classical music haunts the soaring spaces above me. Even on a Sunday Hamburg station is busy. The reverberating call of a tannoy signals the arrival and departure of intercity and international trains. The cafés and burger joints hum like an ancient bazaar.

I look over each shoulder. My quarry is late.

According to Rolf, Christian Worch is one of the most important figures on the militant neo-nazi scene, the main organiser and coordinator for all the demonstrations and marches of Kameradschaften and skinheads.

'Where are you?' I curse, pacing in front of the Mövenpick restaurant, our rendezvous point. It's impossible to relax. I look down at my mobile, nervous, wondering whether I should call the number.

There was something about Worch. The fact I'd been chasing him for a year, and that he was talked about as a leader of these neo-nazi social movements. The harder it was to find him, the more anxious I became.

'I think he's probably boring to talk to, so don't worry,' advised Rolf, shortly before I left.

I tried to brush up further on the man's background. With Michel Kühnen, Worch had founded the violent ANS (Action Front of National Socialists) in the mid-1970s. He left school with few qualifications and worked as a legal clerk for a firm that defended right-wing individuals. He received his first conviction after honouring the Nazis executed during the Nuremberg trials. In 1978, Worch and Kühnen demonstrated here in Hamburg, wearing donkey masks and placards with the sentence: 'Me donkey. I still believe that Jews were gassed in concentration camps.'

Worch was also part of the NSDAP/AO network – the so-called foreign branch of the nazi party – later becoming one of the main forces behind the Anti-Antifa campaign, a kind of intelligence initiative to keep tabs on left-wingers and liberals. His career has weaved in and out of National Socialist groups, such as the GdNF, for decades now, organising marches, including the first Rudolph Hess event, pushing the limits of the ban against National Socialism. 'He's not a person who can be easily characterised by party politics, like the NPD, but will play an important role in the "free" National Socialist scene, like the Kameradschaften today,' Rolf told me.

Many of today's Kameradschaften leaders seem to be ex-GdNF members. 'They have access to the racist youth,' explained Rolf. 'The whole youth and racist subculture. They have an input in ideology and training. They can mobilise several thousands.'

I start thumbing the keys on the phone. I wonder if he got my last message.

'Violence against left-wing groups and refugees already happens in the East without fascist cadres,' Rolf's voice echoes in my memory. 'But Worch helps bind and organise the infrastructure, and ideology, of this neo-nazi trend.'

'So what's the eventual aim?'

'Oh, the creation of a legal National Socialist party.'

* * *

'It's a problem with all western European countries; it's a kind of degeneration.' He laughs at his own pronunciation – he can't quite get the 'g' right. The laugh is too loud, drawing attention to us in this 1970s-looking restaurant. My pock-faced companion doesn't notice.

'It's a problem of becoming rich. Perhaps it's the same situation as in the Roman Empire. Because of living in the status of being rich, having people from other countries doing the dirty works.' He flicks ash from a cigarette, then lifts it to his lips. 'In the future, perhaps the whole German population cannot make any normal work.'

There's an abrupt sucking, smacking sound as he pulls the cigarette from his mouth. Christian Worch is in full flow. He's already apologised for being late and told me of his one and only time in England, and about how he came across Charlie Sargent during a march in Roskilde in 1995. 'I had to find someone to control him, to stop him from fighting!' he laughs, rather loudly.

An innocuous figure in jeans and a work shirt, Worch rests a hand casually on the tablecloth between us. He's arrived only moments before, looking flustered and carrying a small Filofax. He recovered his composure quickly and smiled through yellowed teeth.

'Why does this degeneration exist?' he continues, mispronouncing the 'g' again. 'First, we have lost the war. Then you get this de-Nazification and re-education,' he laments, 'and we were demilitarised. The military in Germany has always had a strong role and of which the people are proud. It was a part of the sense of their life. Sometimes I wish we were an isle like England,' he laughs, through a smoker's cough. A waiter appears with our food. Worch bemoans 'special German laws' that 'ban some parts of the opinions, so things cannot be discussed so free, like England or the United States'.

Looking at him as he speaks, he certainly doesn't fit the stereotype. Too respectable. Brown hair swept back, medium build, somewhere in his early 40s, I'd guess. The only leather he wears is a faded brown jacket slung over one shoulder. Another person who melts into the crowds. He's polite, too, his manner correct and precise, his English somewhat formal and stilted.

Of course he's had problems. 'Oh yes! I spent five and a half years in prison because of freedom of speech, no other reason. That shows you how the situation of Germany is.'

'Why were you sent to prison?'

'If you make the salute of the Third Reich, the Hitler salute, you know, you could be condemned to prison, up to three or five years. And also some opinions about historical facts, like the concentration camps or gassing of persons, and so on, if you say this in the public, you can be sent to prison or fined.'

'Are you interested in those, what you call historical questions?'

'Not really,' he says, which I find strange. 'It's only for me a political interest, of course,' as he cuts into his schnitzel.

'So who are you, what do you do?'

'Me?' he grins. 'Normally, I don't use a description for myself, because the mass media call me a neo-nazi.' I nod politely. 'For me, it's very good that they called me so, because it's not necessary that I say I'm a neo-nazi, because they named me as one. It's good, because people are thinking I'm the radicalest of the radicalists. I'm not really so. But politically it's better for me that people say so.'

'How do you consider yourself, then?'

'Um, German nationalist, I think.' We discuss his opinion of the NPD, how they're 'dreaming' when it comes to electoral success. He admits to surviving off an inheritance (a large one, according to Rolf) and how I'm 'a little bit right' when I tell him people say he's trying to recreate the SA movement of the past, and from that a new party.

I seem to have touched a raw nerve. 'Yesterday it took me four hours to get to this place of the demonstration. I was 500 metres from the station where it should begin, and it took me four hours to get there, because there was the police, and around them and all the streets were left-wing counter demonstrators. And before them, nothing. So if you want to come into the area, you have to go through the counter demonstrators, who are militant. You cannot handle the problem yourself.'

'So why bother with all this?'

'I'm sorry?' he shouts, his voice clipped, startling me. I think I've offended him, but he apologises and explains he's deaf in one ear.

I repeat the question. 'How can you ever build a movement?'

'Because of the strongness of our idea,' he exclaims, raising his eyebrows as if to add 'of course'. 'We are getting a United States of Europe, a bit like the USA.'

The talk moves onto globalisation, then immigration. I breathe in a jet of smoke he blows over the table. Pieces of ash land on my arm.

'It's hard for an Englishman to understand this, because you have had colonies for hundreds of years. These countries are trained to live together with foreign cultures.'

'Germany has had some colonies, too,' I point out.

'Yes, but not since 1918, so there is no living German who has had contact with colonies.'

'Well, how bad is the immigrant situation?' Since meeting Christopher and his friends yesterday, I'm finding it hard to restrain my feelings. I succeed – just.

'It's no problem to have one million foreigners. A little more than 100 years ago, we got one million Poles. So I have comrades with Polish names, from their grandparents or great-grandparents. But more than one million people, in just two or three generations, I think it's too much. Especially from countries where the Islam is strong. They don't want to integrate in your country.'

I probe deeper. 'Is Islam a greater threat than international Judaism – especially since 11 September?' I'd be surprised if Worch wasn't connected with the Holocaust denial movement.

'The enemy is changing,' he says, lecturing me calmly. 'You must learn that the right-wing movement in Germany is a little anti-Semitic. Not every member, but a lot of them. That has historical reasons. I as myself did not see me in this way.'

There are other surprises. At one point, he admits that Turks could be integrated into German society. They are near-Caucasian, after all. Nor does he seem to believe in a One World conspiracy. This seems a little at odds with the label 'neo-nazi'.

'We have lost the last war. We have had the best soldiers, the best weapons, but we lost the war. That is a kind of traumatisation. The population needs an idea that we did not make a mistake, that if anything we went wrong, we did not have an influence, for example, God Almighty or whatever you want.' His voice is now very loud. We're starting to draw stares. I wonder if anyone else understands what we're discussing. A train rumbles beneath us. Worch looks uncomfortably out the window. He later admits he's afraid of heights.

I mention the US nazi Gary Lauck, the comic Hitler lookalike who operates an international neo-nazi website.

'Yes, I have had contact with him,' Worch says, struggling to tear open a sugar packet, then sprinkling it into his coffee. 'We have met each other perhaps three or four times.'

'Do you still talk with him?'

'Yes. One time I met him in prison, in Germany, from 1995 to 1999. He's a great strong man, a nice guy, a lot of laughing. He speaks German.' He then starts recounting, jokingly, how people tell him he speaks German with an English or American accent. 'I also heard this accent from Mr Zundel.'

I mask my surprise. He clearly knows at least two leading, internationally infamous Holocaust deniers. I roll other names in front of him, fishing for a reaction. He just goes 'hmm' as we speak, then rambles on for a while about religion and history. He's not a particularly inspiring orator. Then again, few men of the right seem to be.

With a curt snap of his fingers, he summons the waiter and pays my bill, saying I've had to wait for him and travel from Berlin, so it's only fair. I find his sense of honour intriguing.

We decamp to a modern-looking bar across the road. He runs straight into the place and gets a beer for me, a coffee for himself, almost shouting the order at the barman.

'I'm living in a ghetto, you know,' he says matter-of-factly as he sits down. For some reason, he wants to talk about himself. 'In a house with 16 families. Half of them are German and half of them are foreign. I am living in my flat alone, and the other German parties are living one man or two people, alone. If you have time, I can show it to you. But the number of the foreigners are much greater than the Germans, and they are families too, not single people like me or elder couples.'

'You mean there aren't enough Germans – in general?' He nods. 'What's the answer, then?'

'Getting more children!' he chuckles. 'But it's easy to say, I also have none.'

'Are you married?'

'I was married some years ago, for seven years. We did not have children and then we were divorced. It was not my idea, it was her idea. She wanted children, and I did not. You know, I have spent five and half years in the prison. It could be that somebody hurts me in a street battle, or I am killed, something like this.'

He tells me he was adopted, then his adoptive parents divorced. His father, a doctor for the Waffen-SS, was imprisoned by the British after the war for helping Klaus Barbie, 'the Butcher of Lyons'.

'I grew up only with my mother. Like other young men, I didn't like it, you understand? I did not want to have the situation that I have any child or any children who could come in the same situation. If your father is in the prison and you are a small child, it is a really bad situation. Neurotic problems, psychotic problems, perhaps become a mass murderer in later years, you don't know. Also the situation where children's father is killed, not naturally, it is a great shock for the child. That is the reason I don't want any children and the reason we were divorced.'

'Do you still have the same opinion?'

'Yes.'

'Really?'

'Yes, and I'm now 46.'

He laughs when I say he doesn't look his age, then again when I observe that so many right-wingers have no kids, yet talk about the destruction of the white race.

'I did not miss children for myself. At the moment, my girlfriend has a child from another man who is one and a half years old. I am together with her about a year. It's a nice boy, but sometimes he's testing. I'm not trained to live together with children,' he says, voice rising, 'and I'm really not willed to live together with them. We are together, but we will not marry. We don't have the same flat. Sometimes we spend a weekend together, or two or three days in my flat with the little one, but after that I need some days to relax from that. It means going to any place. I, for myself, I leave the flat, close the door, get in my car, drive away. Together with her.'

He admits that his adoptive parents' divorce probably hurt him. 'I was probably a very sensitive child, Mr Ryan. It was not possible for me to wake up in the morning without any ache.' I find his candour a little startling. He adds that this gave him 'a special strength' to handle problems on his own. 'If you are in a fight, all that counts is the will to win.'

I lean back, waiting a moment to launch my question. 'So, did you find a new family with the Kameradschaften?'

He raises his eyebrows. 'I don't think so. To some of them I have a personal contact, but it is a very small number. Because I prefer to live for myself. I think the word is loneliness, but that does not mean I feel sad for the situation,' he booms, oblivious. 'I like to be alone for myself. I like sometimes to be in contact with people, but not for a long time. I'm not a real member of the pack.'

'So you're quite different to many of the younger Kameradschaften?'

'I think, I think.' He tries to suggest this is normal.

'Isn't it ironic that Kameradschaften means comradeship, though?'

'Hmm, yesss,' he admits, drawing the word out. 'For me, it's only the question of political work. It's not a greater family for me or something like this. That means fighting together, but not living together.'

'What made you interested in this movement, then?'

'It was a historical view of this last century, and the idea that some of the ideas that are today banned are not so terrible as they say they are. To find the ideas that I find right and bring them out in today's world.'

'Would you call that National Socialism?'

He says that this is difficult to answer, given that the German phrase for National Socialism can be spelt in two different ways, with slightly different meanings (*Nationalsozialismus*, or *nationaler Sozialismus*). 'You can say it's a kind of national socialism.'

When I ask him to define his beliefs, he just laughs and says even his comrades sometimes doubt he's on the right. Why? Because he doesn't support anti-Semitism, he claims, then recounts how he became friendly with a black man whilst in prison. Then, how Germany needs to be carved into different zones, some of which would be 'multicultural zones'.

I have a reverse question. 'Are Germans more racist than other Europeans?'

'I think yes, because of the following reasons. We Germans are a mixed race, from about 3,000 years ago, when two peoples met together. Other European countries have had mixing and immigration not so far away as we in Germany. The Romans came to England, then the Saxons. After that, the Normans. So you have had a lot of different peoples.'

In the background, I can hear Freddie Mercury sing 'I Want To Break Free'. For some reason, it reminds me of Worch's old boss, Michel Kühnen. Worch has already said Kühnen was a great man, then denied – laughing as he said it – that they had enjoyed a 'relationship' together.

I still don't quite believe his comments on Jews, though. He admits he has a problem with the question of whether six million died or not, 'but even if they were gassed, I say it's very shocking, but that, this fact, don't make other parts of the national socialism bad'.

'You mentioned Zundel earlier. Are you interested in the Holocaust issue in an academic or revisionist sense?'

'No, no less. A few years ago it was opener to discuss this question.'

'But what about that picture of you in Hamburg in 1978, with Michel Kühnen and the donkey placard?'

'Yes,' he replies somewhat starkly, uncomfortable. 'Yes, yes, yes, yes, YES!' I sit, silently, watching the aggression build. Then, as suddenly, he relaxes again. 'It was not far from here. We made this action together with an old man, a soldier from the war, an early revisionist. We are not real interested in this historical or political question. It was a political action to shock. Because the dogma of Kühnen was that before anyone can love you, they must know you. The first step to get political influence is to say here we are, as a radical opposition. Because we can't use the mass media.' He says that if I spent a week and drank beer with them, they would reveal their real thoughts to me. 'In a situation of oppression, they will not tell you anything they are thinking because of getting a penalty.'

I tell him it's interesting he spent most of his adult life in the right wing, that he didn't do anything else.

'Two reasons,' he offers, bluntly. 'First, I have the opinion that I am right. So I see the duty to fight for it. Second, the struggle – particularly the legal struggle – is exciting.'

'But can you win your overall struggle?'

'I don't know. I don't know,' he almost whispers. He gazes out the window. 'I just fight. I don't know. You can lose, but if you don't fight, you have lost.'

'What do your friends say?'

'What my friends say is not so much interesting, I think, because I have not so much friends.' He laughs again.

'But I still don't really know how to describe you,' I protest. Who is the real man beneath this shell, I'm thinking, and why did you set out on this path?

He looks oddly at me for a moment, as if pondering some hidden thought, then steeples his fingers and asks casually: 'Do you know the story of Jesus, when he tried to exorcise the demon from a man?' I'm not sure, but I nod. 'He asked it its name. It said its name was Legion, because we are a lot.' He pauses and grins. 'My name is Legion too,' he says. The table goes silent. We remain like this for several uncomfortable seconds.

'Er . . .' I start to say.

But with a swift movement he stands up, drags the jacket around his shoulders, and locks his eyes onto mine. 'As Dr Goebbels, you know, once said, it doesn't matter that they say good or bad about you, it's just important they talk about you.'

I blink, twice, in rapid succession.

'You know,' he adds, perhaps wistfully, 'if we had won the war, National Socialism would not be the same as it was in the 1930s.'

And with that, he disappears into the traffic. It's as if the last three hours never were.

* * *

The journey is drawing near an end now. I can sense it. These years of wandering, this search for identity, belonging, belief. A reconfirmed notion that humanity lives on a diet of fear and suspicion, huddling into its twenty-first-century tribes. That the world is moving too fast for most of us.

I too am changed. Tired. More careless. Older. Withdrawn from those once close to me. Estranged from friends, living on the bright surface of life. I've given up trying to tell them, or my family, much of what I do.

Back at Rolf's apartment, I muse over my meeting with Worch. Rolf is fascinated. I'm not so sure. 'Is that it?' I think. These bland zealots, are they really at the heart of white supremacy? Preaching the road to separatism and the promise of the Balkans, to an all too eager audience? Apparently so.

The next morning I rise early and speak on the phone to Sascha Rossmüller, a leading member of the Jungen Nationaldemokraten. He's another I've been trying to reach for months. His English is excellent. I discover, though, that he lives in Bavaria, too far away for the limited time I have available.

So I swap emails instead with Paul, the Australian member of the World

Church of the Creator. Like Worch, he lives in Hamburg. We weren't able to meet, but I learned that his family had migrated to Australia from Germany in the late 1920s. There, his father was interned during the war, and Paul remembers being nicknamed 'Adolf' by other kids.

'I grew up with a hefty guilty conscience about the Holocxxcx [sic],' he writes. 'But living with my grandparents instilled in me the wish to return to Germany. Whenever she got the chance my mother would tell me stories of the "Sagas" [the old stories of the Germanic gods, etc].'

Following a career in photography and film production, he travelled to Germany and settled there in the 1970s. He describes a period of studying, to find that there was a 'German version' of history, as well as a 'British Empire' version. It's a familiar litany of victimhood and lost identity; how the Germans were never the aggressors and suffered greatly at the hands of others. His sentences are peppered with mention of 'Communists', 'Bolsheviks' and 'Internationalists'. The 'New World Order', too, and 'International Bankers or International Money Lenders as I call them . . . we will all be paupers living in THE BANKERS land.'

Then he confirms, probably without realising it, something I've come to expect: 'These fears keep me involved.'

'The only thing we have to fear is fear itself,' Franklin D. Roosevelt said in his inauguration speech in 1933. One of my favourite phrases. I laugh grimly to myself, realising that even this is not sacrosanct. According to extremists such as Horst Mahler, Roosevelt was orchestrating a world war on behalf of Jewish interests.

* * *

The Irish tricolour is planted over one side of the flat cap, pulled tight onto a solid-looking head. The eyes flash a challenge, twin beads of suspicion disappearing into thick brows. The words 'Murphy's Stout' are emblazoned across the shamrock-coloured polo shirt.

It's early, a quiet Sunday. Weak sunlight plays over the traffic outside. An attractive waitress hovers around our table. The thump of acid chillout drums through our conversation.

'I didn't have a love deficit. My mother was just a mother. We had a factory, a good life. I'd love a big family myself. I wasn't socially isolated. I was a normal small-town boy.'

The words drip out then pick up speed. 'You could say I was from a very conservative background, though,' he adds, scratching a pug-like nose. 'It sounded like the good old days when people talked about the Third Reich.'

Matthias Adrian is an intriguing figure. A thickset grafting of bone and muscle, he signs his emails 'Slan' (Irish shorthand for 'cheers') and is a counsellor for the EXIT programme, a project that tries to encourage neo-nazis to quit the scene. I've taken a blind chance to meet this former rodeo rider and state leader of the Jungen Nationaldemokraten. Until two years ago Matthias was a rising star within the NPD. Now, he's foregone it all and left the movement. I wanted to speak to someone who was or had been a footsoldier, to know why he became involved – and, in Matthias's case, why he'd left. Perhaps by speaking to him, I can come to a better understanding of this New Reich fundamentalism. So far, my encounters with Worch and Mahler have left me more puzzled than enlightened.

Matthias describes a small-town upbringing in a rural area in the west of the country. His grandparents were apologists for the Nazi regime, who declared they didn't see anything wrong during the Hitler period, didn't know any Nazis, and chose therefore to ignore it. People who remained convinced that concentration camps were simply 'punishment camps' for political prisoners, that there were no gas chambers, and that the war was where real (German) men were produced.

'You know, the attitude was like, "We didn't think it was right to kill all those Jews. That was wrong. Then again,"' he smiles cynically, '"they did nail Jesus Christ to the cross, so what can they expect?"' He rubs one large ear, then carefully sips his Earl Grey tea.

I avoid that intense gaze, shifting my eyes to the huge silver claddah ring encasing one of his blunt fingers. There's certainly an affinity for things Irish here. A new form of family or identity? We talk a lot about his grandparents, with whom he seemed to identify – more than with his parents, it seems. How they didn't trust teachers, telling him they were left-wing extremists, and how his whole family voted for the Christian Democrats, because of their Catholic beliefs. 'They never really thought about politics, except that they were anti-Communist.'

It was in this highly conservative environment that he was raised. 'In one way, I thought like a child: We're the Germans, I'm a German, so we must be good.'

He tells me he began reading an extreme-right newspaper called the *Deutsche National Zeitung*, produced by the leader of the right-wing DVU party. 'Once I started reading this paper, which blamed the Allies for many problems and was calling for a national re-education, I thought my teachers were trying to re-educate me. That's how I became a right-wing extremist.'

From then on it was a slow, steady spiral into extremism. Arguing with teachers and family members, pressing for answers – for identity, he agrees now, speaking in excellent English. 'I became something like a missionary,' forming his own Kameradschaften, joining the DVU, and daubing swastikas on the sides of buildings (illegal under German law).

'Perhaps your dad was spending too much time running his business, and not enough with you?' I tentatively suggest. I'm slightly paranoid he might flash up in anger. But he nods, sadly.

'You might be right. I was revolting to provoke them. I ended up becoming a neo-nazi,' he states, deadpan. 'A real neo-nazi.'

He was kicked out of his local school, and says that 'until this point, I hadn't listened to rock music, because my granddad said I should listen to German music. Rock music was nigger jazz, he told me.' He crumbles another piece of sugar crystal into his tea. 'I hung out with a rocker billy gang – is that how you say it in English? – then I worked as a stunt man, a rodeo rider, and roadie for a country band.'

'Had you stopped the right-wing stuff then, at that point?'

'No, no. I was still reading right-wing books all the time.' These included David Irving, he says. 'I was very influenced by SS thoughts.'

During a slide show in college, he remembers engaging in a blazing row with his teacher, who'd just returned from Israel. How his anti-Zionist rants (picked up from the DVU paper) earned him respect from young Muslims in the class. 'I never had to pay at the doner stalls again!' he smiles. His voice is melancholic. This is, after all, a life he has left behind.

Following an accident on the rodeo circuit, he found himself with more time on his hands, 'a time for change in my life, which is when I joined the real neo-nazi scene'.

Fed up with the DVU, Matthias signed up to the NPD. 'I wrote a letter to Frank Rennicke, a singer-songwriter for Viking Youth, asking his advice. Three or four days later he wrote back, sending all this stuff, and so I joined the JN.'

I mention my conversations with current JN leader Sascha Rossmüller. Matthias sneers. He clearly doesn't hold Rossmüller in much regard.

Rennicke's package mentioned a coming NPD march. 'It all sounded so secretive,' Matthias laughs. However, when he went to buy his ticket from a nearby neo-nazi-run shop, he was shocked to see 'this huge skinhead with a tattoo on his head' running the place. He was even more shocked when he got on the coach to the event and saw dozens of boneheads sitting around him. He sounded dreadfully naive. At this point, he explains, he was wearing traditional 1930s German clothing (including a haircut and moustache from that era: the picture on his passport is somewhat amusing) and believed in reviving a historical version of National Socialism, 'a very old style of NS, and I dressed like one'.

Despite his misgivings, Matthias describes a rapid rise through the JN ranks, as he read further and developed ever deeper and more twisted National Socialist beliefs. He would build runic stone circles in his garden during parties, and regularly entertained regional NPD leaders. Eventually he became head of security for the JN and its 'secret service' within his local region, then was appointed a spokesman for the group. 'I became more and more radical,' he explains, popping another sugar crystal into his mouth, 'seeing the Jewish conspiracy that was controlling America and Wall Street.'

Then his mouth curls, as if tasting something bitter. 'I became a pathetic anti-Semist.' There's self-loathing in the words. 'I didn't have a hatred to foreigners, though, unlike the skinheads, because I thought they were just victims who had been uprooted themselves. But I linked everything to a conspiracy.' He agrees that you can find 'proof' for any conspiracy, if you're looking for it. Then he stops, seems to gulp, lets out a long sigh. 'It's hard for me to say this, because I have a lot of Jewish friends now.'

As he describes his deepening involvement, he admits that he became manic, then often depressed, during what he calls his 'fight'. 'I was angry that normal Germans didn't see what was going on, but when you're in the scene, you only hang around and speak with people in the scene. It's like a vicious trap, a locked-up circle.'

But Matthias clearly went deeper than most. He developed the kind of extreme mystical beliefs that key Nazis once shared, becoming part of a secret, neo-nazi elite dotted around Germany. 'We call this *Artgemeinschaft*. Steffen Hupka is a member. So is Manfred Roeder. Even the daughter of Heinrich Himmler.' Blending an obscure mix of National Socialist ideology and German mysticism – including a belief in the old Germanic gods – adherents viewed Christians as simply 'reformed Jews'.

'You find people from the REP, DVU, NPD and others, all connected through this movement,' he maintains.

Yet his role as NPD steward brought him into contact with the despised skinheads, forever drinking and brawling. A far cry from the disciplined Aryan heroes of myth, the image that fanatics such as David Myatt would wish to portray. 'It was unbelievable!' Matthias cries, startling me for a moment. 'Could these be the master race, a bunch of drunk weirdos?!'

He was thrice beaten by Blood and Honour skins when he tried to remonstrate with them. 'I hated them, and I hated the skinhead music and the whole subculture. Who would vote for us with these people at our sides?' Despite this, one part of his job was to record tapes of skinhead bands and hand them out at school gates. 'The skinhead scene was just a subculture to recruit the cadres,' he says.

'How did you feel at this point? Like giving it up?'

'No, not yet. I would say I was a right-wing member of the NPD party – that is, more right-wing than most other people there.' He reflects for a moment, looking over my shoulder, then his gaze sharpens. 'I wanted a Fourth Reich.'

Perhaps something had to change. 'I don't feel like a resistance fighter any more,' he says. 'I feel like a criminal. I realised I had become a criminal.'

He goes on to describe the NPD's three-pronged strategy. There's a fight for parliament, which few really believe they can win (although it affords them state funding). There's the struggle for the mind, such as getting people used to criticism of Israel and Zionism, rather than simply parroting hatred of the Jews. Then there's the battle for the street.

By this point, Matthias explains that he was expelled from his national service in the army because of his neo-nazi beliefs. However, he'd found love, with an older woman who was working for the HNG neo-nazi prisoner support group. 'She was brainwashed, but I really loved her.' A wan smile opens for a moment, then quickly flees. 'She always wanted to do more. We had trouble with the police. One day, she and her daughter – she was 37 and her daughter about 14 – went to desecrate Jewish graves. After that, she seemed to change. After one or two months, she started to think about it.' Someone in her own family had died. Within four months, she'd decided she was leaving the scene. Matthias couldn't cope.

'I was shocked! It was impossible for me to be with someone else not in the scene. I was so confused about her, how she could change so quickly.' He moved out, and his life fell into crisis. He began to see, for the first time, the intentional lies the NPD put out, how people would twist history to support a nationalistic view of events.

He left the NPD and considered joining the slightly less rabid Republikaners. His comrades didn't believe him. 'I became more and more critical against extremist ideology. It was a chain reaction, as I uncovered more and more things. I realised I was being fed war propaganda.'

The breakdown came after the police did a house search of his flat, looking for evidence of the graveyard desecration. Both he and his girlfriend, with whom he was living again, were arrested. The cops were surprised that most of their neo-nazi paraphernalia had already gone; that the swastikas on the wall were painted over; and that Matthias was compliant.

'They were there, all these special forces types. The dogs, pistols, explosives guys. Usually, I would say nothing and call my lawyer. This time I told them everything.'

'Why?'

'I realised I was simply a criminal.'

He takes a sip from his mineral water. I can see the mixture of defiance and sorrow struggling on his features, even now. 'That was a very hard time for me,' he continues, almost in a whisper. 'I had a complete mental breakdown.'

For six months he was depressed and suicidal, afraid of the light, hardly leaving his room. But he spent the time searching the Net, and remembered his dad once describing the Irish band The Dubliners and their song 'Dirty Old Town'. He bought one of their CDs, and from there his fascination with all things Irish began. 'There were parallels between my life and the Irish struggles,' he maintains. 'It helped me set things clear.'

Matthias wipes his long eyelashes, then tells me about his discovery of a website engineered for people just like him. It had been created by another ex-nazi, who wanted to debate extremist issues with former comrades (and thus help persuade them to leave their movements). For six months, they chatted over the Net for three or four hours a night.

'I was confronted with my own words. I felt used by ideology. By myself. It was a very hard point in my life.' To make matters worse, his girlfriend died suddenly in a train accident. 'My life really fell apart.' Matthias had reached a nadir, but with help from the ex-nazi website and the EXIT programme, he gradually pulled himself clear.

From that point, he began talking again with at least some of his estranged family members. He found himself attending debates held by other political parties, and has now joined the Social Democrats.

He finishes the last forkful of his breakfast and, wiping his mouth with a napkin, jokes: 'I learned that the world was not all black and white. Now I try to make others think, too.'

I feel strangely uplifted, as I walk out of the café and on to the last – and most revealing – meeting of my trip.

* * *

This is it. Really it. Back to where it all began.

We're three hours south-west of Berlin, in the heartland of the East. Trebnitz village is a remote hamlet sunk in a wilderness of fields. The drive here has been tense, pregnant with expectation.

'Look, I think that's it,' whispers my journalist colleague, even though there's no one else in the car with us. I follow his finger. Over the farm courtyard, past what seems to be a church, looms a large, stately presence. Looms is the right word. The grey stone and brick lurks, massive and half-seen, behind a spread of trees.

It's silent. A calm breeze stirs the back of my neck as I step out of the car and move over to the wall surrounding the property. Broken windows stare back from the crumbling mansion. My translator calls it a 'castle'. We both glance around, then take out our cameras, snapping a few pictures before anyone arrives.

After a few moments, an old guy with a pot belly pulls up on a bike. We pretend we're shooting the surrounding vista. He asks what we're doing, scratching his sideburns, glaring suspiciously.

My colleague does some fast talking, explaining our mission. The caretaker grunts, then clicks open the huge, rusting gate. We're in.

Would we like a tour? he asks, as we walk into a tradesmen's entrance. Not believing our luck, we agree, stepping past building materials, rows of discarded radiators, moving through thick motes of dust drifting in the air. The rooms sweep up, eerily quiet. I'm left wondering what once went on here, my imagination supplying dire scenarios.

We wait for Steffen Hupka to arrive.

Hupka is a regional leader of the Kameradschaften and an important figure on the national scene, who's clashed frequently with the authorities. He's recently been expelled from the NPD, following a failed putsch. A close associate of Christian Worch, his expulsion seems to represent the end of the Kameradschaften's dreams of dominance within the NPD. My colleague mentioned that Horst Mahler had been one of Hupka's main opponents.

The caretaker ushers us into a room bare except for a table, a few chairs and a newly connected fax. I sneak out and look around upstairs, as my colleague makes small talk with the old man.

Arriving a few minutes later, Steffen Hupka dabs a sweating brow and apologises for his delay. 'I had a meeting with some other journalists, from *Stern*. They wanted to know all about this place,' he smiles.

'Oh, why's that?' I ask. My colleague has already told me the press are desperate to get pictures of the building and find out its purpose.

'There's 2,000 square metres of living space,' he gestures, seating himself at the table. 'It will make a training centre for us, one which is unique in Germany. We've been looking for something like this for three or four years.' He leans back and smiles through prominent teeth.

I smile in return. This is not someone you would pick out in a crowd: smart shirt, rolled sleeves, expensive watch, slacks, loafers. A bland, elongated face with blue eyes and a large nose, dusted with blackheads and topped with dark, greying hair drawn towards a receding hairline.

Shifting, and seeming still a little nervous, he links his fingers together and coughs self-consciously. 'I was in the NPD until a month ago,' he says, 'and then I and my colleagues left the party because we think it's not enough a, er, national party, yes?' He makes a reference to recent reports of government informers within the party's ruling body. 'So I think the NPD is an organisation for the enemy.'

Hupka curls his lip and rolls his eyes up when I ask about his current relations with Horst Mahler. 'I don't make work with him, I think he's not a nationalist, not honest.' We've obviously hit a sore spot, as he spends the next five minutes detailing his battles with the man.

I raise my eyebrows. 'So who will you work with?'

'In Sachsen-Anhalt [this region] we have many free comradeships from about five to twenty [people]. We do demonstrations, renovate this house,' he points, making me laugh, thinking how this place could ever be described as just a house, 'but there's no party, no association or institutions.'

'Why?'

He listens as my colleague translates, nods, then smiles again. I can sense him relaxing, even as he turns to stare without blinking into my eyes.

'Because the danger is very big that the State will ban an organisation and then the State will confiscate the property.' In a rather telling comment, he adds: 'And the owner will be a private person in the future, so nothing can be confiscated.'

He draws in a breath. 'Next month, you know, we'll found an association for German culture in this house.' My colleague's body language, a subtle shift and slight cough, tell me this is something significant. 'Why?' he asks Hupka, in English, then in German.

Hupka tells us he's spent five years in the NPD and is sorry to leave. He's remarkably candid, as though chatting with old friends. He describes the circumstances surrounding a failed attempt by his supporters to oust the old leaders.

'Does that mean you've given up on building a party?' I ask, innocently.

'In the last 12 years, the State has banned 13 organisations from national opposition, so many people think they can't found a party or big organisation and so decide to make little groups.' My gaze is continually drawn to his thin arms, cocooned in a dark mat of hairs. 'We will make a new central organisation, but I think we must prepare this organisation very well, and we must have one.' This seems a significant point. It appears he's suggesting the development of a new party and movement, beyond what's gone before. Something to take over from the NPD.

With a sneer and a little laugh, he dismisses the DVU and REP. Then he claims that all the best NPD people will come over to their new organisation. 'But we don't want to fight against the NPD.'

'Well, what is it that will unite you and your new comrades?'

'The most important thing, I think, for us is to be a German nation in a white Europe, together with the other people of the other nations. The EU destroys these nations, cultures that have stood up in the last 10,000 years.' His voice is gradually picking up speed. 'It is God's will that these nations stand.'

I draw breath to interrupt, but he carries on. 'International capitalism will destroy this, and Wall Street, because they want a world with people who have no identity and no culture.'

I already know the kind of people behind all this. The Bilderbergers, the Freemasons, the Jews, he replies, asking if I know Bill Clinton's administration had 53 Jews. 'We want a New World Order, and these people want a new One World government, and I think this nearly exists already. You can see the powers of the USA in all areas, such as political, military, and economic.' His brows draw together, and he hunches his thin shoulders forward, a transformed figure full of passion. 'We need a strong organisation with cadres, and in the future I think in Germany, and in other lands too, we will have a situation which we had in the GDR [East Germany] in 1989.'

'What situation?'

'When the Wall came down. And this will happen in the next ten years in Germany. It's then that we must have our strong organisation, and I hope there is the same development in other European nations.'

His face has shifted into an expression of earnestness. A new Reich movement. He talks of developing ties and appreciation with other groups around Europe – 'What happened in France is important' – although he doesn't mention anything specific. One reason is that the Kameradschaften are seen as neo-nazi in their beliefs, and these other groups are not.

National Socialism is illegal under German law. I decide to press the point: 'Are you a National Socialist?'

He laughs. 'Ahem, ahem, yes, yes, yes. But you write this in the English magazine?'

It's only later that I realise the significance of this comment.

We move on to his background, how he read a book as a child that told the story of the Native Americans – 'their tradition, nation, courage and culture' – which proved inspirational for his interest in the extreme right and desire to save Germany. David Irving was another one he enjoyed: 'He has a standing for his opinion.'

Now 39, Hupka started his career in the JN in 1980, then moved through a variety of groups such as the HNG prisoner solidarity movement, and working with individuals such as Friedhelm Busse, the same neo-nazi I'd seen on May Day. In 1985 he helped establish the NF, which was banned in 1993. He denies it was a militant, violent organisation, but *Searchlight*'s German sister magazine, *Antifaschistisches Infoblatt*, has photos from the party's internal archive showing people training with guns and military clothing. One of the reasons for its ban was the idea to build up hit squads (*Einsatzkommandos*) for street battles. From 1996 until last month, Hupka was in the NPD.

'So why have you stuck with these groups?'

'Good question!' he replies, chortling. 'I think it's in the genes.'

'What, you mean you're born with it?'

'Yes, nationalist views are in the genes.' My colleague raises one eyebrow at me. I can see he wants to say something, but he holds his tongue. 'We live in a war against our German people and against the white race in Europe, and against all culture in the world. It's a war without weapons. We must work so hard because we have a war. We need people to fight for ideas.'

'A physical struggle?'

'No. Well, perhaps in the future. I don't know.'

Strong stuff, I think to myself, glancing at the grounds outside. Here we are in a mansion confiscated by the Soviets – were its former owners Nazis, I wonder? – soon to be a training centre for a new political movement of the extreme right, in a country with high social tensions in the east, and which gave birth to Nazism. It's a heady, disturbing mix.

He ruefully admits that this battle means he has little time to spend with his two young children and partner, 'but I make the fight for my children to have a good future, for our culture, for Germany'.

'Does this mean others have to get out?'

'Yes, all!' he exclaims, later claiming some attacks on foreigners have been by agents of the State. Young whites assault foreigners because they don't come to the Kameradschaften's meetings, apparently, not the other way around. 'But this is the fault of the State, of society,' he maintains. 'In this fight, the enemy has the same aims as 60 or 70 years ago.'

'Which is?'

His face twists into a sneer: 'International capitalism.'

His own family were involved in the last war, which he describes as 'a fight by good people against bad'. His father signed up in 1945 at age 16, and his uncle was a lieutenant in a bomber – a leader of the Hitler Youth, shot down and killed over England. Hupka remembers reading his diaries. His eyes take on a wistful look. 'He was a model for me.'

His words trail off. I wait for him to continue.

'There were some bad things in the Third Reich, but generally it was right, and I think Hitler and his government want to make good things for the people and Europeans. And this was the cause for the war against our nation.'

I can hardly believe I'm hearing this. But that's not all.

'What they say in the paper about us and the Holocaust was not true. We think there were concentration camps, but the people must work, and they died by the work. That is right, I think. But there was no mass annihilation.'

'Do you think the issue of the Holocaust is used by Israel and the international Jewish community in some way for punishing German people?'

'There were many reasons for these lies,' he continues, lecturing me. 'To put Germany down, they got millions from us in the past, and they will have money in the future and the next thousand years.' Bitterness drenches his words. 'They destroy our self-consciousness because of what they say we've done. But I don't think it's so.'

I realise how quiet it's become. Dusk is drawing down. The lazy drift of sunlight is dipping below the horizon. Suddenly, the ghostly presence of the past seems to linger around us. I have a flashback to the children's mental hospital I saw in eastern Croatia, a huge old building just like this one, but full of bloodstains and bullet holes where the kids had been dragged out in the snow and shot by Serbs.

The shrill call of Hupka's mobile phone disturbs the reverie. He moves to the window, voice booming in the high room and, without realising I'm taping, starts speaking with one of the Kameradschaften's street generals, 'Steiner'.

'I've got to go, sorry,' he smiles professionally, cold and formal, as he re-pockets the phone.

'Okay.' I've got more than enough. Enough this last six years to last me a lifetime.

Outside, Hupka poses for one last photo, a stark figure against the old Nazi stone. Then we're off.

EPILOGUE

SUMMER 2002, AMSTERDAM

The coffee shop is lazily busy this time of afternoon. The world drifts by through a haze of smoke. I sip peppermint tea and take another drag, thinking.

The end of the journey. Perhaps. But even as I slow down, events around me gather pace. Just a couple of weeks ago, the Dutch anti-immigrant politician Pim Fortuyn was shot outside a TV studio in the nearby city of Rotterdam. An animal-rights fanatic has been arrested for his murder. One extremist gunning down another.

Fortuyn was the leader of his own political party, the Pim Fortuyn List, anti-immigrant but pro-homosexual (he was gay). Since his death his ratings have gone stratospheric, and his party has just taken over 30 per cent of the vote in Rotterdam, becoming the second-largest bloc in parliament and moving into coalition government.

A striking bald-headed man, Fortuyn said he objected to Islam because it militated against Dutch liberal traditions; he himself supported gay rights and legalised drugs and prostitution, the very hallmarks of Holland's permissive society. The other paradox was that his many mourners included hundreds who objected strongly to his views. They wanted to register disgust at Holland's sudden descent from a land of consensus and tranquillity into a brutish shadow of America.

The young receptionist at my hotel told me this morning that Fortuyn wasn't an extremist like Haider, that 'it was okay' that he was able to raise the issue of immigration. I looked at her: no sombre dress or sense of the right. She was attractive, blonde, modern.

'He made it okay to talk about this,' chimed in an older lady, polishing glasses behind the counter. 'He created a debate, you know, threw open the doors of discussion.'

'I didn't like him,' added the younger woman, with a shrug of her pretty shoulders. 'But many did.'

'There are some Moroccan women who've been here 20 years and still need their husbands to come with them to the doctors, to speak English,' said the older lady. 'It's ridiculous. We've been too open for too many years. We even pay them to go home!'

I blow a wreath of smoke, studying the faces around me, a patchwork of colours representing former Dutch colonies and international travellers. Both hotel women claimed they were multiculturalists, liberals, and that Fortuyn was 'very Dutch, gay, not a typical right-winger'.

Strange to think, too, that Jean-Marie le Pen's challenge for the French presidency also reached dizzying heights, then crumbled. The Front National leader took nearly 20 per cent of the vote in the first round, helped partly by a fractious left wing and widespread voter apathy. But the country has swallowed the bitter pill and decided to rally around Jacques Chirac – who himself faces many allegations of corruption – giving him a massive vote of confidence. Or a desperate attempt to keep out something even worse, depending on your point of view. Le Pen is smashed, settling once more below the surface of French political life. By comparison, the BNP's sudden gain of three council seats in Burnley seems almost trivial, even though the news rocks England. Nick Griffin, the man who introduced me to so many zealots, was slowly achieving his political makeover. Sad to see how ready people were to believe. Soon he'd be meeting the NPD, David Duke, and other nationalist groups in Germany, plotting a new Euro alliance.

As this chapter of my life draws to a close, other events seem to pour in towards its epilogue.

The leader of the National Front gets in touch, talking about a meeting with the now-secretive group. Several synagogues are defiled in France. Suspicions fall on Muslim extremists. Another synagogue is attacked, this time in Wales. With George W. Bush's War on Terror promoting a wave of patriotic fervour and a crackdown on immigrants, the Israeli Defence Force pushes into the West Bank, as Palestinian suicide bombers make ever more desperate attempts to strike at the heart of Israel.

In Australia, wave after wave of asylum seekers attempt to break out of distant detention camps, aided by hundreds of protesters pulling down the fences. Not everyone shares John Howard's or Tony Blair's vision, it seems.

Sitting in a canal-side bar towards evening, watching the football, we hear that thousands of Russian soccer hooligans have gone on the rampage in Red Square, after their team lost in the World Cup. One man is killed, dozens of others seriously injured. Later, Croatian skins attack their country's first-ever gay parade, hospitalising several people.

In Germany, veteran neo-nazi Manfred Roeder is arrested. Mike Hallimore tells me he's getting good responses from his ad in the *Final Conflict* magazine in England. I've been signed on to an email list full of Identity believers, and watch from my laptop in silent mirth as they rage against a fellow white supremacist who admits she's a committed Satanist.

EPILOGUE

A supporter posts a tract on paganism; it's from Steve Sargent's alter ego, Albion Wolf.

On Bastille Day, 14 July, a known neo-nazi tries to assassinate Jacques Chirac during a parade along the Champs-Elysées. Maxime Brunerie, 25, pulls out a hunting rifle and squeezes off a shot at the President, before being wrestled to the ground by spectators. It could have been a chilling rendition of Frederick Forsyth's famous novel, *The Day of the Jackal*. Continental Europe is already reeling from the rise of nationalism; my Dutch friends only seem more confused by this turn of events. Brunerie is carted off to a mental hospital, and the French media soon dub him a 'psychiatric case'. Chirac shrugs off the event with a characteristic 'Oh really?' Like David Copeland, though, more details begin drifting out.

A part-time chauffeur and accountancy student, Brunerie was a member of a number of underground groups such as Unité Radicale, a federation of France's disparate ultra-right clans, which had provided protection for Le Pen's May Day demonstration in Paris. The guest speaker at UR's latest meeting, in April, turns out to have been NPD lawyer, and former terrorist, Horst Mahler. Brunerie stood as a local candidate for the FN breakaway party, the Mouvement National Républicain. In fact, *Searchlight* also reveals that he joined the fascist Groupe Union Défense, which had a reputation for bloody attacks on its opponents. Acting as a liaison with skinhead bands, he became a supporter of the hardline Parti Nationaliste Français et Européen, whose leaders have for many years had close links with the BNP, circles around Christian Worch in Germany and activists from the Vlaams Blok in Belgium. I have to read the sentence several times, as the words sink in.

There's one final twist. Combat 18's website carries a short message from Maxime Brunerie himself, posted the day before the assassination attempt, 13 July: 'Watch the TV this Sunday. I will be the star. Death to ZOG, 88!' The Princess Louise, Charlie, Steve: the story comes full circle.

And then, as I ready myself for home and the next chapter of my life, William Pierce dies. After a short, private battle with cancer, he's gone. Just like that.

GLOSSARY

ADL: Anti-Defamation League (USA)
AFA: Anti-Fascist Action (UK)
AFBNP: American Friends of the British National Party (USA)
ANS: Action Front of National Socialists (Germany)
APABIZ: Anti-fascist press archives, Berlin (Germany)
ARA: Anti-Racist Action (USA)
BILDERBERG GROUP (THE BILDERBERGERS): network of industrialists and politicians, often believed to be "secret rulers of the world"
BM: British Movement (UK)
BNP: British National Party (UK)
BUA: British Ulster Alliance (UK)
CARE: Christian Action, Research and Education (UK)
C18: Combat 18 (UK)
C of CC: Council of Conservative Christians (USA)
DNSB: Danish National Socialist Movement (Denmark)
DÖW: Dokumentationsarchiv Österreichischer Widerstand (Documentary Archive of the Austrian Resistance) (Austria)
DVU: Deutsche Volksunion (Germany)
EURO: European American Rights Organization (USA)
FAP: Freiheitliche Deutsche Arbeiterspartei (Freedom German Workers Party) (Germany)
FN: Front National (France)
FPÖ: Austrian Freedom Party (Austria)
GdNF: Gesinnungs-gemeinschaft der Neuen Front (Germany)
GDR: German Democratic Republic (former East Germany)
HNG: German neo-nazi prisoner support group (Germany)
IHR: Institute for Historical Review (USA)
IRA: Irish Republican Army (Northern Ireland)
ITP: International Third Position (Europe)
JN: Junge Nationaldemokraten (NPD's youth group) (Germany)
KKK: Ku Klux Klan (USA)

GLOSSARY

LVF: Loyalist Volunteer Force (Northern Ireland)
MEP: Member of the European Parliament
MHP: National Action Party (Turkey)
MNR: Mouvement National Républicain (France)
NAAWP: National Association for the Advancement of White People (USA)
NAR: Armed Revolutionary Nuclei (Italy)
NBZ: National befreite Zonen (liberated zones, Germany)
NF: National Front (UK)
NF: Nationalistische Front (Germany)
NFU: National Farmers' Union (UK)
NOFEAR: National Organization for European American Rights (USA)
NPD: Nationaldemokratische Partei Deutschlands (Germany)
NSA: National Socialist Alliance (UK)
NSDAP/AO: foreign group of the Nazi Party (Germany, USA, Europe)
NSDAP: original Nazi party (National Socialist German Workers' Party)
NSF: National Socialistik Front (Sweden)
NSM: National Socialist Movement (UK)
ONA: Order of the Nine Angles (international)
ÖVP: Austrian People's Party (Austria)
PLO: Palestine Liberation Organisation
RAF: Red Army Faction (Germany)
REP: Republikaner Party (Germany)
RFJ: Ring Freiheitlicher Jugend (Austria)
RTS: Reclaim the Streets (UK)
SA: Sturm Abteilung (Storm Section, Nazi Storm troopers) (Germany)
SPLC: Southern Poverty Law Center (USA)
SSS: Sachsen Schweiz Skinheads (Germany)
UDA: Ulster Defence Association (Northern Ireland)
VAM: White Aryan Resistance (Sweden)
VB: Vlaams Blok (Belgium/Flanders)
VJM: Vlaamse Jongeren Mechelen (Belgium/Flanders)
WCOTC: World Church of the Creator (USA)
ZOG: Zionist Occupation Government

INDEX